PRINTED
EPHEMERA

The changing uses of type and letterforms
in English and American printing

JOHN LEWIS

W.S. COWELL IPSWICH, SUFFOLK

First published in 1962
by W. S. Cowell Ltd
8 Butter Market, Ipswich, England

Distributed by
Faber & Faber Limited
24 Russell Square, London W.C.1

PRINTED IN GREAT BRITAIN BY W. S. COWELL LTD
AT THEIR PRESS IN THE BUTTER MARKET, IPSWICH

Contents

Acknowledgements and Author's Note

The illustrations from Public Collections have acknowledgements printed under their captions. I would like to express my appreciation to the Controller of Her Majesty's Stationery Office, the Director of the Public Records Office and the Trustees of the British Museum for waiving their reproduction fees. The illustrations without acknowledgements are from my own collection, or from the collections of friends in Canada, the United States of America and in Great Britain, including Miss Margaret Leischner and Messrs George Arnott, Edward Bawden, John Brinkley, Milner Gray, Alan Fletcher, Allan Fleming, Harold Hutchison, Ruari McLean and Martin Simmons, whose kindness I would like to acknowledge here. I would also like to thank the numerous officials in Libraries, Museums and Collections on both sides of the Atlantic; particularly Mr A. F. Johnson at the British Museum; Mr Philip Hofer and Mr William A. Jackson at the Houghton Library, Harvard; Mr Vivian Ridler, the Printer to the University Press, Oxford; the late Dr John Johnson's assistant, Mrs Thrussell at the Sanctuary of Printing at the University Press, Oxford. Mr Karl Kup and Mr Lewis Stock at the New York Public Library; Dr James J. Heslin and his assistants, particularly Mr Paul Bride, at the New-York Historical Society; Mrs Mildred Constantine at the Museum of Modern Art, New York; Dr R. W. Ladborough at the Pepysian Library at Cambridge; Mr S. Rawlings-Smith, Principal of the Pilotage Department of Trinity House, London; Mr Gilbert J. Wiles, the Press and Information Branch, Metropolitan Police Office, New Scotland Yard; Mr Brian Yates and Mr A. S. Durward at W. D. & H. O. Wills of Bristol; Mr F. D. Shew at Carreras Ltd, London; Messrs Lea and Perrins Ltd of Worcester; Messrs Tanqueray Gordon and Co. Ltd of London, the Curator of Historical Records, British Transport Commission; Mr Andrew Block, most famous of all dealers in printed ephemera in Holborn, London; Mr James Mosley of St Brides Printing Library for his unstinting help both in identifying certain typefaces and for reading the proofs of this book, and lastly my wife for her patience and help in many different ways, during the production of *Printed Ephemera*.

Author's Note

In the captions, the measurements refer to the printed (i.e. type and illustration) area of the original and not to the overall size of the paper. In these dimensions, the height is always given first. The copy following these measurements refers to the printer (if known) and place of origin. If the name of the typographer is known, this comes before the name of the printer, e.g.

317. 1957 DINNER INVITATION

$2\frac{3}{4}'' \times 5\frac{1}{2}''$ Allan Fleming typ. Cooper and Beatty, Toronto.

In the case of an engraving, or lithograph or drawn design it would read 'Sturt sc' or 'Peter Maverick lith' or 'Milner Gray des.'

The idea of a history of jobbing printing is an attractive one, at least to think about. Its execution is another matter. John Bagford, notorious Bagford, is said to have made his collection in order to write a history, but nothing came of it. The late John Johnson, whose 'Sanctuary of Printing' as he called it in his lifetime, has provided a number of specimens in this work, also intended to write a history of jobbing or ephemeral printing. But even his unusual firmness of purpose was overcome by the sheer torrent of material which his enthusiasm and the thrill of the chase brought upon him, and he found time to write nothing more on the subject than a short paper.

Now comes John Lewis. Undismayed at the size of the task, he has spent the last five years compiling, not indeed a history, but something perhaps more rewarding and certainly more manageable, an illustrated survey of English and American jobbing printing, with the purpose of showing the changes in type design and in the use of type since the beginning of the art.

The change in the appearance of books over the last five hundred years has been gradual rather than violent, because the demands made upon the book printer are essentially conservative. But the needs and whims of an expanding society created the jobbing printer, whose existence came more and more to depend upon responding to fashion. Once he had forsaken or was forced to forsake his one or two simple book types for an ever-increasing variety of display types, he was lost in the confusion. An eighteenth century playbill has the unsophisticated assurance of someone working safely within a simple tradition. You had your type; you chose your sizes, started at the top, and worked your way steadily through the copy. A similar approach less than a hundred years later produced something very different. Although distance now lends a certain enchantment to the robustness of the mid-nineteenth century playbill, the effect, viewed objectively, is chaotic: it is as though stocktaking in the composing room was a daily occupation. It has taken the twentieth century typographers' rediscovery of space and of type as pattern to restore Humpty Dumpty to anything like his true shape.

All this of course, is to oversimplify, but designers, students and typophiles now have the opportunity of drawing their own conclusions from the remarkable collection of illustrations (most of them reproduced for the first time) which Mr Lewis has assembled in the pages which follow. He is himself a designer and teacher, and his examples have been selected with a designer's eye and with the student designer prominent in his mind. We are indebted to Mr Lewis and to his publisher-printers (whose history began in 1818 with the enviable combination of job printing and the importing of wines and spirits) for providing so much in so concise a form.

VIVIAN RIDLER

May 1962   Printer to the University, Oxford

A dozen years or so ago, I bought from a bookseller in Ipswich, Suffolk, an album compiled about the year 1820 by a Dr Lodge, sometime librarian to the University Library at Cambridge. Dr Lodge's album contained a wide variety of printed matter including over a hundred engraved title pages, a large and comprehensive collection of early printers' devices, a rare Baskerville specimen sheet and an Indulgence printed by Thierry Martens.

As librarian to a great library, Dr Lodge's opportunities for collecting pages from damaged books and packings from broken bindings were extensive. It would seem that this particular Indulgence may well have lurked for three hundred years or more inside some vellum or calf-bound volume, doing duty for the paste-boards which in those days did not exist.

This Indulgence, issued for the repair of the Hospital of the Cathedral of St James at Compostella, was the starting point of my collection, which soon developed in a rather haphazard manner into a kind of designer's scrap-book.

A suggestion by Mr A. F. Johnson led me to some of the collections in the British Museum. The most rewarding of these was the series of albums made by an un-educated shoemaker and bookseller called John Bagford, who, in addition to assembling a great number of book pages, collected quite a few pieces of printed ephemera, including some lovely engraved trade cards.

Bagford made a formidable collection of print, ranging from the title pages of books to the most humble pieces of ephemera. (For generations he has laboured under the reputation of being a despoiler and mutilator of books, in order to enrich his collection. It is, however, more than likely that the books came to him by way of his trade as damaged and broken volumes.) All this collecting was to provide him with the material for a history of printing. The book was never written. The collection remains and in it are the exquisite trade cards shown here on pages 173–6 and the engraved tobacco labels on pages 220–2.

Dr Lodge's album started my collection. A first look at the Bagford collection gave me the idea for this book. From Bagford's collection I worked my way through others in the British Museum, such as the Fillenham and Ames collections, and collections elsewhere such as in the Victoria and Albert Museum, where there are several scrap-books, mainly of nineteenth century material. At the Pepysian Library at Magdalene College, Cambridge, I found a volume called *Vulgaria* which had some fine early Trinity House licences and certificates. At the British Transport Commission's Museum of Historical Relics I found a wealth of railway tickets and bills. And then somewhat belatedly I went to Oxford to see the late Dr John Johnson's 'Sanctuary of Printing' at the Oxford University Press. It is a unique collection of print, still being sorted, mounted and documented. The printed ephemera ranges from fine early proclamations to penny tickets for lavatory and cloakroom. As the Doctor said, 'Nothing is too humble!' This part of the collection was appropriately called 'Jobbing in the

Service of the Community'. Dr Johnson started his collection in 1925, when he became Printer to the University. He bought several collections made by Oxford men and methodically began to put in order these squirrel-like hoardings. Then through the years, to this basis he added an enormous collection of printed ephemera.

My next move was to start a correspondence with Mrs Bella C. Landauer, whose collection is housed at the New-York Historical Society in a fascinating room crowded with nineteenth century playbills, decorative lettered mirrors and facia boards, posters and travel notices etc. She was a lady of tremendous vitality, who had begun collecting ephemera in 1923, by purchasing out of charity a portfolio of book plates and odds and ends of graphic art from a young man in sore need of a hundred dollars. It later turned out that he had stolen the portfolio! She soon added to her collection of book plates, then turned to collecting as wide a range as possible of American printed ephemera. The Bella C. Landauer collection contains, apart from book plates and trade cards, fans printed with advertising matter, menus, Valentines, invitations and announcements of social events, lottery tickets, railroad passes, tobacco, beer and other labels, posters and various other kinds of ephemera which give a vivid picture of the professional and business history of America.

Much more attention has been paid to this subject in America than we have given it here. I don't know how many historical societies there are in the U.S.A. but there are certainly collections of printed ephemera in the American Antiquarian Society at Worcester, Massachusetts, at the Historical Society of Pennsylvania in Philadelphia, at the University of Michigan at Ann Arbor, at the Houghton Library at Harvard and a superb collection in the New York Public Library, with material ranging from Benjamin Franklin's *Poor Richard's Almanack* to late-nineteenth century political, travel and theatrical bills.

Some results of my searches in these various libraries and collections, and through the kindness of many friends, can be seen in this book. However, the greatest excitements of the chase, for I can describe it in no other way, were in finding things for myself from many sources, such as in antiquarian bookshops and in printing works, factories, businesses and shops, in waste-paper baskets and even garbage bins. One beautiful hardware label I found in a muddy Ipswich gutter.

At what stage I decided to 'do' a book (I won't say write) on 'Printed Ephemera', I am not sure; it is the kind of folly that Bagford might have undertaken. A certain Reverend John Lewis (author of *A Life of Caxton*) wrote in 1737, some years after Bagford's death, 'He lacked judgement, even common sense.' My reverend namesake may have been right, but what he missed was the tremendous fun Bagford must have had in making such a collection. I know I have enjoyed every moment (and there have been plenty of them) that I have spent in collecting material for this book.

Printing was a Germanic invention that occurred during the last years of the Middle Ages. The first purpose of early printers was to serve the needs of the Church in duplicating Bibles and Psalters. However, the oldest dated example of printing is neither Bible nor Psalter, but a piece of printed ephemera. This was one of the Mainz Indulgences, printed by Gutenberg in 1454 two years before he printed his first Bible. Probably long before this, jobbing printers were producing playing cards and other pieces of ephemera.

This fifteenth century printing was influenced by the Gothic culture of the German cities where it originated. This style of printing, using various versions of Gothic letters, spread through the Low Countries to England, where Caxton and his followers used it, not only for Bills and Indulgences but also for proclamations, petitions and almanacks.

Early Indulgences have a vitality and a richness of colour that after the introduction of the roman typeface, was not to be seen in ephemeral printing until the bold black display faces of the nineteenth century came into use. Their style and length of line is comparable to the work of some modern printers, working in a post-Bauhaus typographic idiom.

The constant factor in Indulgence, Almanack, Trade Card, Ticket or Label was the letter forms, whether they were roman or black letter, engraved or typeset. The development, change and use of the engraved letters and typefaces is the underlying theme of this book, though this is no history of printing, for the development of printed ephemera does not altogether parallel the printing of books. The book printer tended to be a sophisticated tradesman, if not a scholar; the jobbing printer and the trade engraver were as often as not barely literate. In producing their tobacco wrappers, broadsheets and chapbooks, they were practising what amounted to a peasant art.

The roman typeface, originating in Italy within fifteen years of the Mainz Indulgences, completely altered the appearance of books and all kinds of printing, and not always for the better.

In England, the limitations imposed on printers by the Court of the Star Chamber had the indirect effect of lowering the standards of their work. Letterpress printing in the United Kingdom in the late-sixteenth and seventeenth centuries reached a lamentable state. In reaction to this miserable letterpress work, the copper-plate engravers provided a happy alternative for the production of pieces of business printing, such as trade cards, tobacco wrappers and billheads.

The work of these engravers, who had long been occupied in engraving title pages and illustrations to books, provided some of the most pleasant pieces of ephemeral printing. One of the earliest shown here is a sailing notice (from the Pepysian Library) engraved by John Sturt about 1680. Many of these trade engravers were of Huguenot origin who had settled in London after the Edict of Nantes.

These copper and steel engravers had their hey-day in the eighteenth century when, for letterhead and trade card, they could indulge in all the happy frivolities of baroque and rococo decoration; but for the letterpress printer, apart from printing crude wood cuts, his work offered little scope for design from the time the roman letter was adopted in England in the early fifteen hundreds until Robert Thorne, of the Fann Street Typefoundry in London, produced his Fat Face, the first real display typeface, in 1803.

From then on, and for the next three-quarters of a century in both England and the United States, the jobbing printer or his compositor had the time of their lives, making artless but often brilliant use of an ever-increasing range of display letters. Thorne was the great innovator and produced, long before anyone else, fat faces and fat Egyptians which were, to quote Talbot Baines Reed, 'Unique for their boldness and deformity'.

Not every printer approved of Robert Thorne's innovations. Or of the success of William Thorowgood, his successor at Fann Street. Vincent Figgins, another English typefounder, said in 1823 in a specimen sheet of his 'Two-line Great Primer Antique': *'The increased fatness in job letters is an improvement but is it not in many instances carried to an extreme?'* And in 1828, Dr Edmund Fry, a letter founder, who had a considerable custom with the Americas, said that after forty-six years he had decided to dispose of his foundry. After describing how he had started with improved versions of Baskerville's typefaces, he had found that there was more favour given to the Caslon style of letter, so he had set about copying all Caslon's types. He had no sooner completed these copies of the productions of the Chiswell Street Foundry, when, as he goes on to say ' . . . *a rude pernicious and most unclassical innovating system was commenced, which in a short time was followed by the most injurious and desolating ravages on the property of every Letter Founder and Printer in the Kingdom, by the introduction of Fancy letters, of various anomalous forms, with names as appropriate. Disgraceful is a profession once held so sacred as to have its operations confined to sacred buildings of the highest class* . . . '

It must have been galling for him. Thorne and Thorowgood did not share his regret, nor on the other side of the Atlantic did the Wells family at the Cincinnati Type Foundry. The productions of the jobbing printer in both the U.S.A. and in Britain between 1810 and 1880 showed a splendid appreciation of this new typographic material, whether for starkly simple notices or for highly complicated playbills or for little tea and tobacco labels. This vitality, the product of somewhat naïve craftsmen, was not to be recaptured again in jobbing printing until today. In the 1880's, with a great increase of mechanization in printing, two movements sprang up, both largely fostered by *The Printers' International Specimen Exchange*, published by Messrs Field and Tuer, from the Leadenhall Press in London.

In the introduction to the 1885 volume the editor has some pertinent things to say. After praising the American printers to the sky, he gains some comfort for the inadequacy of British printers by quoting the *Chicago Printer & Stationer*. '*In the matter of taste, job printers seem to be lagging behind the average of the community that keeps them in bread and butter. Complaints are met with everywhere from businessmen that they have to search long whenever they want anything printed in the latest styles of type . . . printers should remember that this is a progressive age, and that those who do not keep up with the procession are trampled down to bankruptcy and death.'* Strong words!

The two movements I have referred to above were called 'Artistic Printing' and 'Antique Printing'. In the former, the compositor attempted the task of producing a formula for jobbing printing that owed nothing either to book-work or to the vigorous displays of the earlier years of the century. This formula consisted of an asymmetrical arrangement, possibly influenced by *l'Art Nouveau*, of panels of colour, patterns of printers' ornament and brass rules bent and twisted in all kinds of unlikely ways. To produce these contorted and twisted rules an American, John Earhart, had invented an abominable little machine called a 'Wrinkler', as he said, 'to satisfy the prevalent taste for anything oriental.' *The ingenuity and skill, both of composition and press-work, that was expended on 'artistic printing' was worthy of a better cause.

'Antique Printing' was the particular pride of the Leadenhall Press's printer, Andrew Tuer, who styled himself 'Olde style or antique printer'. For this sort of work he used seventeenth century chapbook cuts or pastiche seventeenth century cuts by Joseph Crawhall (by no means a bad artist), early nineteenth century borders and late nineteenth century typefaces, which were battered about to give them a feeling of antiquity. Some of his work was not without charm, but 'Antique Printing' was in keeping with the worst aspects of the Arts and Crafts Movement, which was a movement that had much to its credit, but must also be held responsible for that cosy cult of Olde Worldiness that has taken such a firm hold of the Englishman's home and is displayed for the tourists' delight as 'Ye olde lobster Potte Inne' or 'Ye olde Tudor Tea shoppe'. These movements in printing soon exhausted themselves and gave way to the spaciousness and the weakness of *l'Art Nouveau*, with its Oriental overtones, and later to the good manners and the monotonous severity of the revival of Renaissance printing.

This revival of an interest in good printing owed much to the private presses. It set the book and job printers on both sides of the Atlantic on to half a century of well-mannered derivative printing. At least it was better than Mr Tuer's 'Antique Printing', for though derivative, it was based on scholarship. It was not until the New Movement in Typography got under way in the 1920's, when through the work and experiment of such men as Moholy-Nagy and Herbert Bayer at the Bauhaus, a new light was shed on the problems of job printing.

Yet the impact of this new thinking was slow, painfully slow, to have much effect on the appearance of ephemera. By the 1930's, a few letterheads in this new style began to make their appearance. New sans serif typefaces were cut. Those in Germany were based on the antics of the compass and set-square; those in England on classical Renaissance letterforms. (Eric Gill, on being congratulated on his sans, said 'Yes, but

* Vivian Ridler: 'Artistic printing; a search for principles'. *Alphabet and Image 6.*

13

how much nicer if it had had serifs!") It was not until mid-twentieth century printers and typographers rediscovered the nineteenth century grotesque letter that they had a typeform that really matched their needs. For, like architects, they had turned their backs on Renaissance culture and also on traditional typography. The simplicity of medieval typography and medieval letterforms was more to their taste. Of all the private press printers, William Morris, and only he, had an inkling of this; his feeling for the Middle Ages produced only mock medievalism, yet his rejection of Renaissance culture provided Gropius and his fellow teachers at the Bauhaus with a new starting-point, thus enabling them to formulate certain principles for modern design. All this is reflected in the humble sphere of ephemeral printing.

Ephemeral printing, as I have said, has a longer history than book printing and by its unselfconsciousness often provides a truer picture of the time. The scope of the subject is, of course, endless, for a lot of ephemera has been printed since Caxton set up his press in the precincts of Westminster Abbey, or even since Benjamin Franklin printed and published his *Poor Richard's Almanack*; my choice of subjects and pictures had to be arbitrary, otherwise this book would never have been completed. My reasons for ranging as widely as I have is by sheer weight of material to reveal the richness of invention of the typographer, the compositor and the engraver, and also to show the extraordinary continuity of certain themes, designs and arrangements. This aspect can well be seen in the licences and other pieces from Trinity House, London.

Samuel Pepys, Secretary to the Admiralty, managed by judicious manoeuvring to get himself appointed Master of Trinity House under its new charter. It was from Pepys's own scrapbook that these early Trinity House pieces come. The 'Orders to Attend' of 1680 and 1960 are remarkably similar. This similarity of arrangement is largely based on the similarity of the wording. The words dictated the form in 1680, they still do so today.

The most striking comparison can be seen on page 42 where two certificates for 'Admission as a Freeman of Newcastle-upon-Tyne' are shown. The layouts are almost identical, but the first of 1818 has a vigorous semi-fat face letter used for the type; the 1956 certificate follows the same formal arrangement but makes use of a wretched Egyptian typeface. A comparison of a different order is in the two little auction bills (pages 78–9) both printed by the same Dorsetshire printer, one in 1815 and set in a bookish style with roman typefaces, the other in 1827 making a full use of display fat faces and shadow letters. In those twelve years the whole appearance of ephemeral printing in England had changed. And this was due mainly to Robert Thorne and his successor, Thorowgood, at the Fann Street Foundry. The change came about a little more slowly in the U.S.A., but once the American typefounders really got into production with these new display faces, they soon caught up their English rivals and by the last quarter of the nineteenth century they had surpassed them in the variety of their display letters and had made considerable inroads into their markets.

Most of the illustrations in this book that date from before 1900 are the products of unsophisticated printers; the bulk of the twentieth century work *shown here* comes from the drawing boards and layout pads of designers, printers and typographers who are anything but unsophisticated.

It is sad that even today it is not always easy to find jobbing printers who can lay out even a tobacco label, let alone a playbill or a police notice with the same verve as his predecessors, but they are to be found, as a glance at the eminently satisfying auction bill on page 84 will show. This was produced in a very small print shop in the country town of Woodbridge in Suffolk.

As a direct result of the work of private presses, such as the Kelmscott, the Doves and the Eragny, a growing number of typophiles in England and America turned their attention during the 1920's to jobbing printing. Beautiful ephemera, cast in the mould of fine bookwork, came from a number of printers such as the Riverside Press in Cambridge, Massachusetts, or the Curwen Press in London. The New Movement in typography had little effect on these printers, who had too much respect for tradition to feel the need for any liberation from the formality of a symetrical axis and classic typefaces.

Today, on both sides of the Atlantic, there is a new generation of print-designers who, as graphic design students, typographers, and (like so many innovators in printing) amateur printers, have started playing about with type, ink and press. Discarded Columbian and Albion presses saved from the rubbish dump or the scrap dealer have been turned to good use. With these presses, and a wealth of display letter in wood and metal, experiments in colour and overprinting can be carried out producing results which could not possibly be achieved on the drawing board or by the jobbing printer wishing to stay in business. These young print-designers have learned to solve their typographic problems in the way those problems ought to be solved – by a proper use of the printers' materials.

Their influence can have nothing but a beneficial effect on the printing trade. In such hands, printing, even of billheads, labels and the simplest pieces of ephemera, once again becomes an art.

Black letter THE GOTHIC OR BLACK LETTER typefaces were the first types to be cut, because the gothic script was the contemporary formal writing in Germany at that time (*c.* 1440). There were various forms of gothic letter, including the batarde, used by William Caxton in his 1487 Indulgence. This typeface is distinguished by its dagger-shaped downstrokes. The most common form of black letter in use in England between 1500 and 1800 is that shown in John Edwards' trade card (Fig. 352). A completely new life was given to black letter with the introduction in 1808 of a fat face version. This was a sparkling little letter, one of the many happy products of Regency England.

17th century 𝔍𝔬𝔥𝔫 𝔈𝔡𝔴𝔞𝔯𝔡𝔰

Fat Face 𝕷𝖔𝖓𝖉𝖔𝖓 𝕺𝖗𝖕𝖍𝖆𝖓 𝕬𝖘𝖞𝖑𝖚𝖒.

Open 𝕴𝖓𝖉𝖊𝖕𝖊𝖓𝖉𝖊𝖓𝖈𝖊 𝕭𝖆𝖑𝖑.

Roman and Italic THE OLD STYLE ROMAN typeface is based on the obliquely stressed pen letter of the humanistic script used in Italy in the fifteenth century. It was first cut in Venice for the great Italian printer-publisher, Aldus Manutius, in 1497. William Caslon, the first important English typefounder, cut his own agreeable version of this letter in the 1720's.

Old Style – *Caslon Old Face* Oxford, Bath *and Bristol*

TRANSITIONAL is the name given to the typefaces produced by John Baskerville in the 1750's. They are more vertical in stress than Caslon's and owe something to the engravers and the work of contemporary English writing masters.

Transitional – *Baskerville* Town and Port *of Liverpool*

THE MODERN typefaces of G. B. Bodoni in Italy and Firmin Didot in France were true engravers' letters, based no longer on the pen but on the characters that the burin could most easily cut. They were vertical in stress, with unbracketed hair line serifs.

Modern – *Bodoni* The *Officina* Bodoni

OPEN TITLING. Roman and italic capitals were often opened up to produce a lighter form of titling. Richard Austin added a lozenge halfway up the stems of his capitals in 1789, to produce the typeface known as Fry's Ornamented.

Inline – *Imprint Shadow*   A THOROUGH GOOD COOK

Ornamented – *Fry's Ornamented*   TO BE SOLD

Fat Face   FAT FACE LETTERS were based on the Bodoni style of typeface, beginning with semi-fat faces such as those used in the Boston Mail notice (Fig. 113) and ending up in that splendid full-faced letter (Fig. 548) invented by the London typefounder Robert Thorne, and first shown by him in 1803. After this the first real display typeface, a number of variations were made. Amongst these were the shadow letters shown by Blake Garnett in 1815. These soon became widely popular and were produced by practically every English and American typefounder. Later on, fat faces became elongated, then no longer fat. These were first shown by Thorowgood in 1838. Another variation was to retain the fat face form but to decorate the surface in various ways.

Modern Number 20   Boston *and Sandwich*

Ultra Bodoni   **Martin van Buren**

Italic – *Thorne's Fat Face Italic*   *Railway Coach*

Shadow – *Figgins Shaded*   W. HOLLOWAY

Condensed – *Elongated Roman*   SPACIOUS MARQUEE

Ornamented – *Macdonald*

Egyptian EGYPTIAN. In 1815 Vincent Figgins showed a slab seriffed fat face which he named Egyptian. This was a brilliant typographic innovation and even more suitable for rough presswork and massive display than the fat face, whose hair lines were liable to damage. Egyptians appeared in all weights, and in elongated, expanded and shadow forms.

Expanded – *Egyptian Expanded*

OUR GAL

Extra Heavy

WARES

Condensed

UNCLE TOM'S

French Antique FRENCH ANTIQUE is a happy development of the Elongated Egyptian. It has club-like serifs and first appeared in 1860.

Playbill

ALDEBURGH

Italian ITALIAN, shown by Caslon in 1821, is a curious and not very successful variation on the Egyptian theme.

Unidentified, *c.* 1840 GARDEN GROUNDS ⅝ FLORA AND POMONA

Sans serifs SANS SERIFS (also called Doric, Gothic, Grotesque and Sans Surruyphs) were shown in a light form by Caslon in 1816 and in a heavy version by Figgins in 1832. By the 1850's they were very popular, and shadow and ornamented forms appeared. Sans serifs were revived in the 1920's; Futura in Germany in 1928 (compare American Type-founders' Spartan, a very similar face, in Fig. 348). This was a precise and mechanical type. Gill Sans appeared in England in the same year, but was based on a classic roman, shorn of its serifs and made relatively even in weight. The modern grotesques (Figs. 346–7) are revivals or redrawings of nineteenth century types, which were produced under the influence of the Gothic Revival, and were often called gothic. In their bolder forms these typefaces were much nearer to black letter than to the roman faces. There were endless variations, including semi-sans serifs such as Albertus, which is based on a metal-cut letter, or Klang which is almost a script.

19th Century (wood letter)   **CAUTION**

20th Century Mechanical – *Spartan*

20th Century Classical – *Gill*   Modern Masters

20th Century Grotesque – *Series 215*   Graphic Design Diploma Exhibition

20th Century – Grotesque – *Grotesque No 9*   **Spencer**

Shadow – *Sans serif shaded*   STRONG ALE

Ten-line Sans serif Ornamented   

Semi-sans serif – *Albertus*   Double Crown Club

Klang   JANUARY

Clarendon CLARENDON (sometimes called Ionic) was introduced by Robert Besley and Benjamin Fox, from the Fann Street foundry in 1845. It was copied in the 1850's in America, by the Cincinnati and Bruce typefoundries. Clarendon is the first of the so-called related bold faces; that is, faces that could be set in company with an ordinary roman text face and would align. It is architectural in quality and probably in origin, for the capitals are very similar to mid-nineteenth century street name plates.

Consort **Solid leather portmanteaux**

Decorated **HOWARD,**

Latin LATIN is a Clarendon with sharp triangular serifs. It was first shown by Miller and Richard in 1870.

Latin Antique **Festival of Music and the Arts**

Tuscan TUSCAN is a fat face capital letter with bifurcated serifs. Figgins showed one in 1815 and Thorowgood in 1825. It is a gay little letter and later took many forms, both shadow and ornamented. It is curious that there have been no modern revivals of Tuscans.

Heavy Italic **STEED MEG!**

Shadow **BY CALEB LEWIS,**

Shadow Ornamented **J. POLITO**

Ornamented **COTTAGE ORNEE,**

Rounded ROUNDED is the name given to certain sans serif capitals for very obvious reasons. Caslon showed a plain rounded letter in 1844 and also an ornamented version in the same year (Figs. 127 and 680).

Ornamented **BLENHEIM,**

Stencil   STENCIL letters are typefaces based on the kind of letters stencilled on packing cases. There are, as far as I know, no nineteenth century stencil letters. Tea-chest was the first typeface of this form and was produced by Stephenson Blake in 1936.

Tea-chest   # VAT 69

Ornamented   ORNAMENTED letters are legion. In addition to ornamented romans such as Fry's Ornamented and the little Union Pearl (the first English display letter which was produced by the Grover typefoundry in 1690), and ornamented fat faces etc, there are other ornamented types of quite original shapes such as the curious lozenge letter used for 'STADIUM FETE' in Fig. 181 and the 'artistic' letters for 'Tobacconist' (Fig. 549). I have called this 'artistic' for no better reason than that it belongs to the 'Artistic Movement' of the 1880's, where a Gothic culture was applied to the design of roman letters, sometimes with very curious results. There were also perspective letters and even letters in the form of twigs and branches, appropriately called Rustic. In 1887, Miller and Richard showed over ninety ornamented typefaces in their specimen book, mostly superbly cut. After that the fashions changed and ornamented letters fell out of favour.

First English Display Type – *Union Pearl*   The Mermaid Theatre

Lozenge   STADIUM FETE

Artistic   TOBACCONIST,

Perspective   PAPER-HANGER,

Rustic   STEAM NAVIGATION

Scripts   SCRIPTS. The script typeface might include all italics, based as they were originally on a Chancery script. The modern Bembo Narrow Italic is the nearest to such a hand. The copperplate English hand was first cut as a type face in 1777 and is still used today. Modern scripts have taken many free forms. Of these, Mistral, used here for 'Type and Illustration', is a brilliant typographic invention, the letters knitting closely together in any combination.

Chancery Script – *Bembo Narrow Italic*   Chapel of the Cross, Coventry Cathedral

Copperplate – *Marina*   The Compliments of the Manager

Free Drawn – *Mistral*   Type and Illustration

The Concise Oxford Dictionary gives a particularly concise definition of the word 'ephemera.' After some brief observations about certain insects such as the May fly, it says: 'A short-lived thing', based on the Greek word *ephemeros*, 'lasting only a day'. My short-lived things are the products of letterpress printers, lithographers, etchers and engravers.

LETTERPRESS. Printing from raised surfaces, type, wood or metal blocks. The bulk of ephemeral printing is the work of the letterpress printer. From the time of Caxton up to the first few decades of the nineteenth century, the methods of the job printer were very similar. Even today such things as auctioneers' posters and handbills are sometimes printed on a hand press.

How many copies of Indulgences, Proclamations etc. the early printers ran off I can't say. There was no limit except time. To show what kind of runs could be produced on hand presses one only has to consult Charles Hindley's *The History of the Catnach Press*, where he shows that the 'Last Dying Speech' of the Suffolk murderer William Corder, who buried the unfortunate Maria Martin in Polstead's red barn, sold 1,166,000 copies in two weeks. Two hundred sheets per hour would be pretty good going, and by printing them four-up, even if this improbable figure is true, Catnach must have had at least half a dozen presses working twelve hours a day to reach this figure.

LITHOGRAPHY is a process of printing from the flat surface of a porous stone or grained plate. It is dependent on the antipathy of grease for water. The process dates from the beginning of the nineteenth century. Chromo-lithography is the term given to hand-drawn colour separation work. Today practically all lithographic work is photographically reproduced and printed by offset, where the image is inked on the plate, printed onto a rubber roller and immediately re-transmitted to paper.

ETCHING AND ENGRAVING are intaglio processes of printing from a recessed surface. These processes are nearly as old as letterpress. In times of indifferent letterpress printing, publishers turned to the engraver and the etcher to provide illustrations for their books; the tradesmen in such times likewise made use of intaglio processes for their trade cards, wrappers and labels.

A short glossary of terms

ALBION PRESS An iron hand printing press, invented by R. W. Cope of London about 1822.

'ANTIQUE PRINTING' A style of printing originated in 1844 by the Chiswick Press, with the use of Caslon Old Face; supported to excess by the Leadenhall Press in the 1880's.

ARABESQUE A shape made up of an assembly of printer's flowers and based on Near-Eastern decoration

'ARTISTIC PRINTING' A typographic style, fostered by *The Printers' International Exchange* in the 1880's, notable for the complexity of border and rule work.

L'ART NOUVEAU The name given to a style of decoration that began in Europe in the 1880's, identifiable by an endlessly repeated motif of the long sensitive slack curve of a lily's stem.

BAROQUE The architectural style that followed the Renaissance, and lasted approximately from 1630 to 1780. Baroque buildings are notable for their feeling (particularly in their interiors) of movement. The detail, though enormously rich, is always subordinated to the whole design. Portuguese *barrocco*: an irregular, misshapen pearl.

BROADSHEET Large sheet of paper, generally printed on one side only.

CHAP-BOOK Popular literature in pamphlet or book form, at one time hawked by chapmen (pedlars).

CHINOISERIE A mid-eighteenth century development of the rococo with a Chinese flavour. Chippendale made many pieces of furniture in this style.

COLUMBIAN PRESS An iron hand printing press invented by George Clymer of Philadelphia and introduced into England in 1817. *The Ceremonial of the Coronation of George IV* was printed in gold on one of these presses.

CUT A term used in the printing trade to describe illustrations (originally wood cut) printed with the text.

ENGLISH HAND The name given by scribes of other countries in Europe to the copperplate style of writing that came into use in the early years of the eighteenth century.

FLEURON OR PRINTERS' FLOWER Decorative matter, both abstract and floral, cast in typemetal to type sizes.

GREEK KEY BORDER A typefounder's border based on the pattern of the Greek key.

IMPRINT The name and address of a printer.

JOBBING WORK Single sheet printing; most printed ephemera is jobbing work.

KERN The head or tail, or any other part of a letter, usually italic, that overlaps the type body and has to rest on the shoulder of the next letter.

LIGATURE Tied letters, such as ff, fl, etc, cast on one body to save space and to avoid damage to kerning letters.

MATRIX	The copper mould, struck by a steel punch, used for casting type.
MINUSCULE	A small or lower-case letter, as opposed to a capital letter.
'NEW TYPOGRAPHY'	The typographic movement that started in Germany in the 1920's, based on certain principles of functionalism. Recognizable in its original form by a wide use of heavy sans serifs, black rules and asymmetric layout.
PRE-RAPHAELITE	The name given to the romantically inspired movement in painting, founded in 1848 by Dante Gabriel Rosetti, associated with John Millais, William Holman Hunt, Arthur Hughes and Ford Madox Brown.
PRESSWORK	The actual machining of type or blocks. The man who prints used to be known as a pressman. Today, in England he is called a machine minder; the older term remains in use in the U.S.A.
ROCOCO	The decorative style that started in France *c.* 1730 as a development of the baroque; distinguished by its asymmetry and use of half abstract, half vegetable shell-like forms. French *rocaille:* shellwork. Widely used by engravers of trade cards, etc.
STEREOTYPE	A duplicate of type or block cast in typemetal from a *papier mâché* mould.
STOCK BLOCKS	Stereos of woodcuts held by printers to decorate customers' work; e.g. coats of arms, sailing ships, race horses.
SWASH LETTERS	Italic typefaces with decorative flourishes.
SWELLED RULE	A rule, fat in the centre and tapering outwards, sometimes decorated.
TITLING	Capital letters that occupy the whole body of the type.
TRADE CARD	Cards used from the seventeenth century onwards as a form of self-advertisement, often richly decorated and usually engraved.
TYPE SIZES AND NAMES	In America and England until the point system for type sizes was introduced towards the end of the last century, sizes were identified with special names. There are several references to these in the book. A list of the names and equivalent sizes are given below.

4½ pt	Diamond	10 pt	Long Primer	22 pt	Double Pica
5 pt	Pearl	11 pt	Small Pica	24 pt	2-line Pica
6 pt	Nonpareil	12 pt	Pica	28 pt	2-line English
7 pt	Minion	14 pt	English*	36 pt	2-line Great Primer
8 pt	Brevier	18 pt	Great Primer	44 pt	2-line Double Pica
9 pt	Bourgeois	20 pt	Paragon	48 pt	Canon

There are approximately 72 points in an inch.

* English was not only used to describe the 14 pt body, but also was the name applied to all sizes of black letter type. For derivations of these names, which lingered on after the introduction of the point system, see T. B. Reed's *Old English Letter Foundries.*

Part I MISCELLANEOUS EPHEMERA

Indulgences, Proclamations and Official Printing

The earliest pieces of ephemeral printing were indulgences. They were issued by the Roman Catholic Church from the time of the First Crusade and were described by the Catholic Church as for 'the remission of the temporal punishment which often remains due to sin after its guilt has been forgiven'. In the Middle Ages, such a remission was called a *Pardon*. The first printed indulgence, which was, as far as we know, the first dated piece of printing, was issued by Pope Nicholas V to all Christians who had helped in the war against the Turks. This indulgence was set in a neat round gothic type, and was printed either by Gutenberg or Fust and Schoeffer in 1454. William Caxton, first English printer, on the instructions of John Sant, Abbot of the Benedictine Monastery at Preston, printed an indulgence at Westminster in 1476. Caxton printed another in 1480 (Fig. 1) which he set in a batarde, a free letter with dagger-shaped descenders, based on the style of hand writing used in Bruges, where he lived for many years. The Thierry Martens indulgence (Fig. 2) is superbly set in a very small size of a *lettre de forme* (pointed gothic) typeface, with about twenty-five words to the line. A very similar typeface was used by Wynkyn de Worde, Caxton's successor at Westminster. The two indulgences illustrated opposite date from the end of the fifteenth century. There is no modern counterpart, for printed indulgences are no longer granted by the Catholic Church.

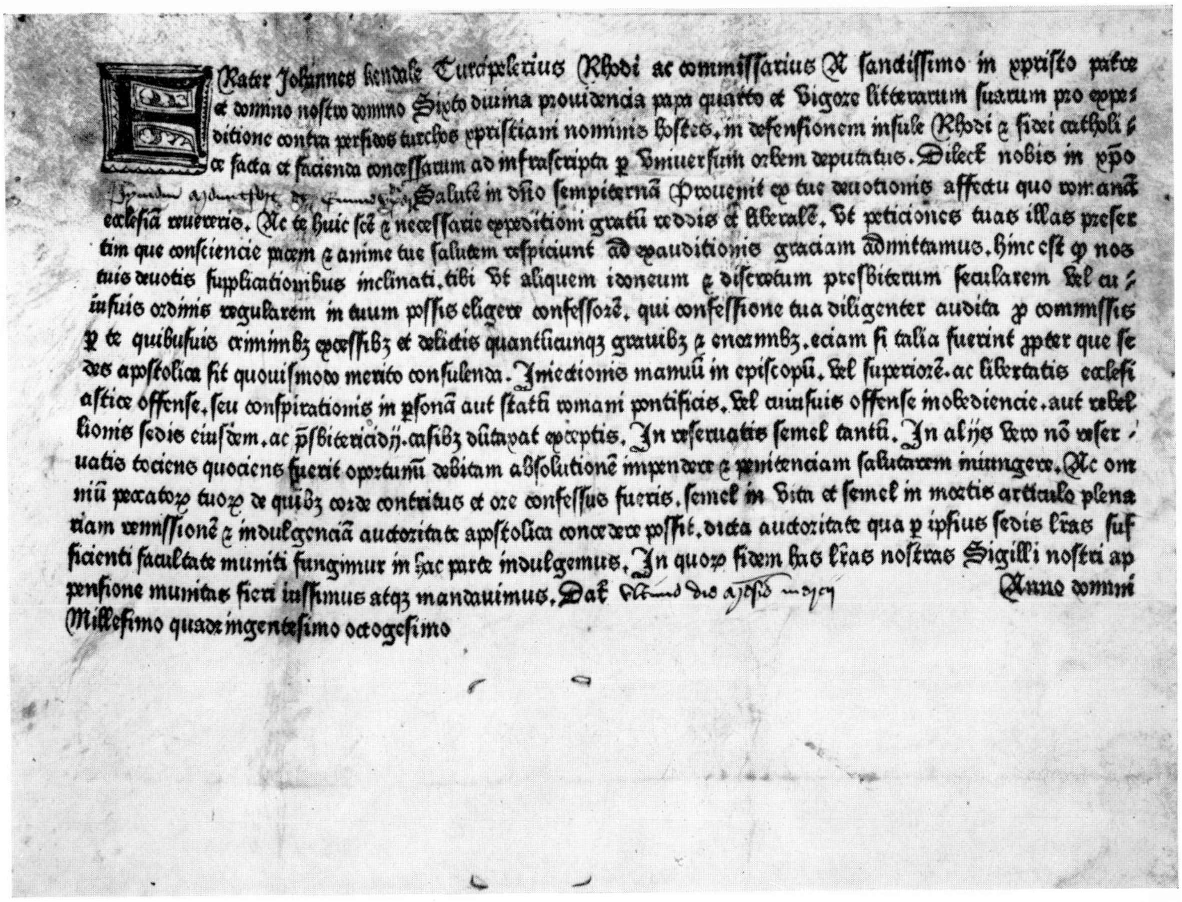

I. 1480 INDULGENCE

$4\frac{3}{4}'' \times 8\frac{1}{2}''$ approx. William Caxton, Westminster. This Indulgence of nineteen lines was granted to those who contributed to the defence of Rhodes against the Turks. The blanks are filled in with names 'Symoni Momet forti et Emme uxori ei' and the date 'ultimo die mēsis marcij'.

The Trustees of the British Museum

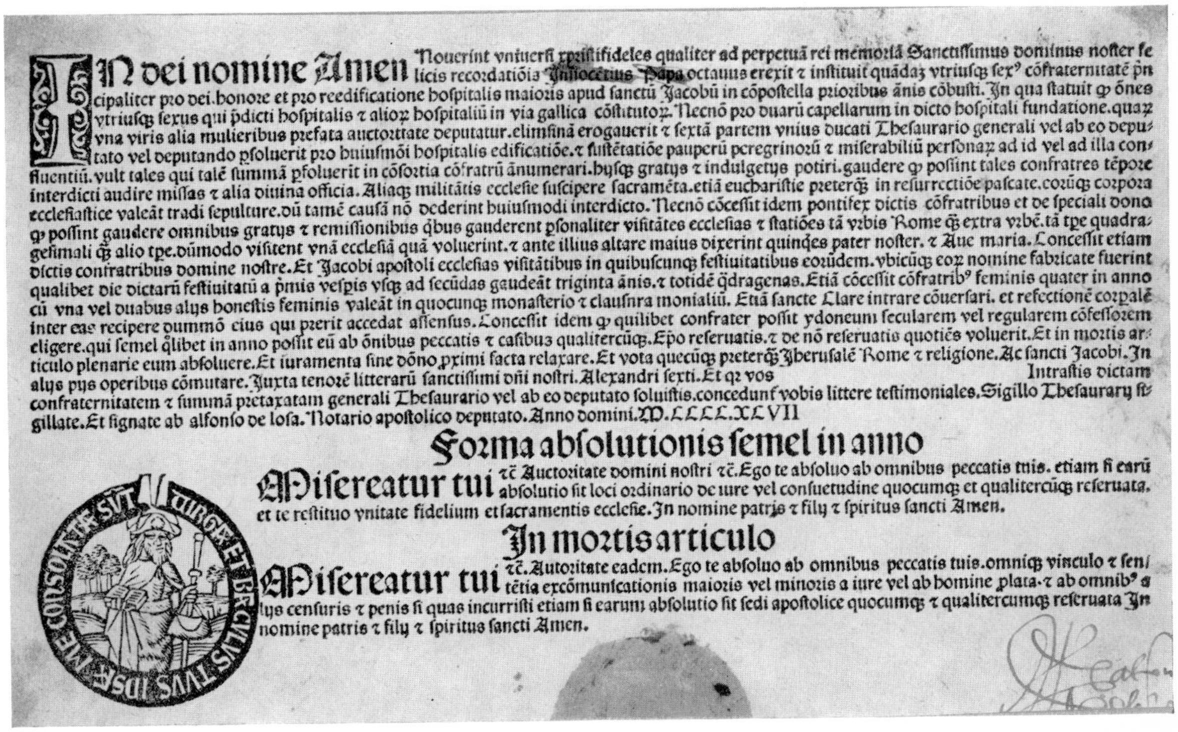

2. 1497 INDULGENCE

$4\frac{3}{4}'' \times 8\frac{1}{2}''$. Printed by Thierry Martens, Antwerp. This Indulgence was for the repair of the Hospital at the Cathedral of St James at Compostella. Martens printed at least five separate impressions from five different settings of gothic type. It was reprinted in the next year by Wynkyn de Worde at Westminster.

By the King.

A Proclamation for restraint of killing, dressing,
and eating of Flesh in Lent, or on Fish dayes, appointed by
the Law, to be hereafter strictly observed by all sorts of people.

Whereas, for the benefit and commoditie of this Our Realme of England, as well in the maintenance of Our Nauie and Shipping (a principall strength of this Iland) as for the sparing and increase of Flesh victuall, diuers good Lawes and Statutes haue beene prouided, for the due obseruation of Lent, and other dayes appointed for Fish dates, which from time to time haue beene seconded and quickned by sundry Our Proclamations, and other Actes and Ordinances of State; And whereas, notwithstanding the many good prouisions heretofore had and made in that kind, wee yet find the inordinate libertie now usually taken by all sorts of people to kill, dresse, and eate Flesh in the Lent season, and on other dayes and times prohibited by Law, is become an euill of such inueterate growth, as it requireth more then ordinary care to suppresse the same:

Wee therefore much affecting the Reformation of this so great an euill (and enemy to the plentie of Our Kingdomes) haue thought fit eftsoones (and that thus timely, the better to take away the extense, and to preuent the prouisions of Flesh that usually men make against the Lent season) To expresse Our selfe and Our Royall Commandement in this behalfe : wherein without any future declaration of Our pleasure in this kind, we shall expect and require from all Our Subiects, that due Notice be taken, and that a strict and continued obedience and conformitie be yeelded thereunto in all succeeding times.

And therefore wee doe straitly Charge and Command all and euery person and persons whatsoeuer to whom it may appertaine; Carefully to prouide and see that these Orders following may be duely obserued and put in execution, vpon paine of Our high displeasure, and such penalties as by the Lawes of this Our Realme may be inflicted vpon the offenders for their contempt or neglect of Us and Our Lawes, whereof wee shall shew Our selues most sensible.

And first, whereas wee finde that the chiefest cause of these disorders hath growen from the Licences that haue bin granted to Butchers to kill and vtter Flesh contrary to Law, And that by Our Lawes no such Iustice of Peace, or other person of what degree or qualitie soeuer, can grant any Licence in this kinde, And that the Lords and others of Our Priuie Councell, doe by Our direction forbeare to grant the same, or to giue way thereunto; Our will and pleasure is vpon the penalties prouided by Law, and such further punishment to be inflicted vpon the offenders, as shall be thought meete, that no such Licence shall be granted for the killing or vttering of Flesh, And that no Butcher or other person whatsoeuer, doe by colour thereof, kill, vtter, or put to sale any Flesh contrary to the Lawes established and prouided in that behalfe.

And for the auoiding of such inconueniences hereafter, Our will and pleasure is, That the Lord Maior of Our City of London, and euery other Officer & Iustice of Peace, shall call before them, and send for any of the seruants of any Inholders, Victuallers, Cookes, Alehousekeepers, Tauerners, and keepers of Ordinarie tables, and such others that vtter victuals, and to examine them vpon their corporall Oathes, what Flesh is, or hath beene during the Lent season, or other dayes prohibited by the Law, dressed, killed vttered, or eaten in their houses, which if they shall refuse to doe, then to commit to prison the said seruants so refusing vpon their Oathes to declare the trueth.

3. 1570 PROCLAMATION
$13\frac{1}{2}'' \times 9''$. Anon. Possibly printed by John Day of London.
This proclamation 'for restraint of killing, dressing and eating of Flesh in Lent' was intended to provide support for the fishing industry.

Proclamations, Decrees and Petitions

Whatever their intended purpose, the appearance of these is still much the same, though in the past black letter seems commonly to have been used for the text of proclamations and the roman type for petitions. The royal coat of arms was invariably used at the head and a decorative initial letter, often larger than the coat of arms, launched the proclamations. The king (or his government) proclaimed on a variety of subjects. The most potent and limiting, from the English printer's point of view, was the Star Chamber Decree. This was the final move in limiting the freedom of the press. Restrictions on printing in England had started in the middle of the sixteenth century and continued to the end of the seventeenth.

4. 1642 PETITION TO THE HOUSE OF COMMONS
12″ × 9″. Anon. Printed for R. Lownes, Ludgate,
London.
An anti-papist petition set in a roman typeface.

The layout of proclamations and petitions remained constant, but the slow replacement of gothic by roman letters produced a subtle change in their character. A less subtle change was towards display types and fat face letters, as in the 'Congrès de Paris' and the 'Queen's Proclamation'. The 'Jonathan Trumbull' proclamation is, on the other hand, an impeccable if bookish piece of job work. The George Washington Proclamation of 1795 was issued for the 19th February, to be set aside as a Thanksgiving Day. It is as bookish as the Trumbull Proclamation and still retains the long 's', which had been generally superseded in England since John Bell had introduced the full use of the short 's' in 1788. (See Figs. 5, 6, 9 and 10.)

Proclamations

BY THE HONORABLE

JONATHAN TRUMBULL, ESQUIRE,

Captain-General, and Commander in Chief of the State of Connecticut,
in America.

A PROCLAMATION.

WHEREAS the Honorable Continental Congress have resolved that Eight Battalions of Troops be raised within this State as soon as possible, to serve during the present War, unless sooner discharged by Congress; offering to each non-commissioned Officer and Soldier, over and above the Wages which have heretofore been allowed by Congress to them respectively, Twenty Dollars to be given as a Bounty, One Hundred Acres of Land, and the following Articles of Cloathing annually, viz. For the present Year, two linen hunting Shirts, two Pair of Overalls, a Leathern or Woollen Waistcoat, with Sleeves, one Pair of Breeches, a Hat, or Leathern Cap, two Shirts, two Pair of Hose, and two Pair of Shoes, amounting in the Whole, to the Value of Twenty Dollars, or that Sum to be paid to each Soldier who shall procure those Articles for himself, and produce a Certificate thereof from the Captain of the Company to which he belongs, to the Paymaster of the Regiment; and that each Soldier receive Pay, and Subsistance from the Time of their Inlistment.

And whereas the General Assembly of this State, have resolved to raise Eight Battalions of Troops within this State, to serve upon the Continental Establishment, during the Term aforesaid, in Pursuance of the Resolutions of Congress, and as a further Encouragement, have resolved, That every non-commissioned Officer and Soldier, Inhabitants of this State, who shall inlist into either of the Eight Battalions, now ordered to be raised in this State, as aforesaid, shall have and receive from this State, so much over and above the Wages that are, or shall be allowed and offered by Congress, as to make up the Pay of a Soldier to be TEN DOLLARS, per Month, during said Service, and the Pay of the non-commissioned Officers in Proportion thereto. And have further resolved, That each non-commissioned Officer and Soldier, that shall inlist into either of said Eight Battalions, as aforesaid, shall annually have and receive from this State, a good Blanket, in addition to the Cloathing offered, and to be provided by Congress during the Term of their Service as aforesaid.

And whereas said General Assembly have further resolved to make suitable Provision for furnishing said Troops with Cloathing, and other Necessaries not provided by Congress, on the best Terms that they can be procured, which are to be delivered to them at prime Cost and Charges; and also to take Care that the Sick and Wounded be well accommodated and provided with Necessaries for their Comfort and Relief.

I HAVE therefore thought fit, with the Advice of the General Assembly, to issue this Proclamation, promising that each non-commissioned Officer and Soldier, Inhabitants of this State, who shall inlist himself into the Eight Battalions now to be raised for Continental Service during the Term aforesaid, shall be entitled to have and receive, not only the Bounty, Wages and Allowances, offered by Congress, agreeable to their Resolves, but also all such further Encouragements as are offered and granted by the General Assembly of this State, agreeable to the forementioned Resolves.

Upon the generous Encouragement here given, the good People of this State, are once more desired to step forth voluntarily in their Country's Service.

The Justice of our Cause, and Reliance on the favourable Presence of the God of Armies, it is hoped will inspire you with that Fortitude and Magnanimity necessary to expel our Enemies from our Coasts, and to restore Tranquility to our Land.

Given under my Hand in New-Haven, the Sixth Day of November,
Anno Domini, 1776.

JON^{TH.} TRUMBULL.

5. 1776 PROCLAMATION
$11\frac{3}{4}'' \times 6''$. Anon. Issued by the Hon. Jonathan Trumbull, C.-in-C., State of Connecticut.
This elegant proclamation is set in two sizes of Caslon's types and shows evidence of the hand of the printer who must have been experienced in book work. The proclamation refers to the raising of troops to strengthen the 'Continental Line' and ultimately to drive the British troops from their shores.
Bella C. Landauer Collection, New-York Historical Society

BY THE PRESIDENT

Of the United States of America,

A Proclamation.

WHEN we review the calamities which afflict fo many other nations, the prefent condition of the United States affords much matter of confolation and fatisfaction. Our exemption hitherto from foreign war—an increafing profpect of the continuance of that exemption—the great degree of internal tranquillity we have enjoyed—the recent confirmation of that tranquillity, by the fuppreffion of an infurrection which fo wantonly threatened it—the happy courfe of our public affairs in general—the unexampled profperity of all claffes of our citizens, are circumftances which peculiarly mark our fituation with indications of the Divine Benificence towards us. In fuch a ftate of things it is in an efpecial manner, our duty as a people, with devout reverence and affectionate gratitude, to acknowledge our many and great obligations to ALMIGHTY GOD, and to implore him to continue and confirm the bleffings we experience.

Deeply penetrated with this fentiment, I GEORGE WASHINGTON, Prefident of the United States, do recommend to all religious focieties and denominations, and to all perfons whomfoever within the United States, to fet apart and obferve Thurfday the nineteenth day of February next, as a Day of Public Thankfgiving and Prayer; and on that day to meet together, and render their fincere and hearty thanks to the Great Ruler of Nations, for the manifold and fignal mercies, which diftinguifh our lot as a nation; particularly for the poffeffion of conftitutions of government which unite, and by their union eftablifh liberty with order—for the prefervation of our peace foreign and domeftic—for the feafonable controul which has been given to a fpirit of diforder, in the fuppreffion of the late infurrection—and generally, for the profperous courfe of our affairs public and private; and at the fame time, humbly and fervently to befeeeh the Kind Author of thefe bleffings, gracioufly to prolong them to us—to imprint on our hearts a deep and folemn fenfe of our obligations to him for them—to teach us rightly to eftimate their immenfe value—to preferve us from the arrogance of profperity, and from hazarding the advantages we enjoy by delufive purfuits—to difpofe us to merit the continuance of his favours, by not abufing them, by our gratitude for them, and by a correfpondent conduct as citizens and as men—to render this country more and more a fafe and propitious afylum for the unfortunate of other countries—to extend among us true and ufeful knowledge—to diffufe and eftablifh habits of fobriety, order, morality and piety; and finally, to impart all the bleffings we poffefs, or afk for ourfelves, to the whole family of mankind.

In teftimony whereof, I have caufed the SEAL *of the* UNITED STATES *of* AMERICA, *to be affixed to thefe prefents, and figned the fame with my Hand. Done at the city of* PHILADELPHIA, *the firft day of January, one thoufand feven hundred and ninety-five, and of the Independence of the United States of America the nineteenth.*

L.S.

Go: Wafhington.

By the Prefident,
EDM: RANDOLPH.

6. 1795 PROCLAMATION
9¾″ × 5″. Anon. Philadelphia.
George Washington's proclamation refers to the putting aside of a 'Thanksgiving day'. Still retaining the long 's', the text is set in one of Fry's typefaces, 'A Proclamation' in Alexander Wilson's 5-line pica.

New-York Historical Society

A DECREE

OF
Starre-Chamber,
CONCERNING
PRINTING,

*Made the eleuenth day of July
laft paft.* 1637.

¶ Imprinted at London by *Robert Barker*,
Printer to the Kings moſt Excellent
Maieſtie: And by the Aſſignes
of *Iohn Bill.* 1637.

7. 1637. A DECREE OF STARRE–CHAMBER
9″ × 5½″ approx. Printed by Robert Barker in London.
This decree limited the number of letter-founders in
England to four and no printing was done outside
London, Oxford and Cambridge until the repeal of
the Licensing Act in 1697.

Second Letter.

Fellow Weavers!

Since I last wrote to you, I have been considering within myself what class of persons amongst you is injured by Machinery? I shall therefore ask each of them separately, and desire them to put the question to their own breast.

Who is injured by Machinery? As I understand that the *Colliers* were particularly active in the late wicked outrages, I shall address myself first to them :---

Colliers! Are ye injured by the demand for Coals to work the Steam-Engines, that set in motion the Machinery? Do the Steam-Engines or Machinery consume food?

No,---but they save that which must otherwise be consumed by *Horses*. They are even named from this, as the *ten-horse power* saves the food of ten horses, for the use of man.

Canal-Diggers! Are ye injured? Have not the canals been dug to carry our goods and our coals to other markets, and to bring us food?---At those markets we could not undersel other persons, unless the goods were made cheap by machinery; and both the goods and the coals cheaper by canals. If we could not sell our goods, how are we to pay for our food?

Spinners and *Weavers*, are ye injured? Least of all persons are ye entitled to complain. For four times your number are employed since the invention of machinery :---and why? because your little children, by the help of machinery, can earn their own livelihood, and it is easy to rear a family.

Smiths, Carpenters, Engine-makers, in short tradesmen of all kinds, which of you is injured by having clothes made cheap, and employment more plentiful?

But if here and there one man has less employment because another makes goods cheaper by improvements in machinery, must it not be so in all trades?

Which of us will not go to the cheap baker, the cheap carpenter, and why not to the cheap manufacturer?---When all but a few receive benefit, what right have those few to complain?

What right has any man to prevent thousands from buying their goods cheap?

Besides in our great concerns cheapness in any *one* branch gives employment to *all*. If the thread is spun cheap, the whole piece, when woven, may be sold cheaper, and thus there will be a greater demand both for spinning and weaving.---So if the weaving is cheaper, there will be a greater demand for thread, and more work for spinners. What right then has any man, because his branch of work is made cheaper, to riot and put others out of employ?

I will tell you an instance, to shew you how unreasonable this is, and have done.

A New Bridge was built over the river Thames, above a quarter of a mile wide.

Before it was built, every body was forced either to go round some miles by the Old Bridge, or to go over himself, his horses, and carts by the Old Ferry; and sometimes they were stopped by the wind;---sometimes by the tide;---sometimes the horses were unwilling to go on board the ferry boat, and frequently a horse was lamed in getting on board.

And besides this, they had to pay a *considerable Toll*. All this trouble, loss of time, and expence, were saved to thousands, and thousands, by the New Bridge.---Yet the ferry-men had the impudence to make a riot!

They were not more unreasonable than those who now provoke a riot, because some weavers have contrived to make goods cheaper by improvements in machinery, and have thus found a *New Bridge* for sending our GOODS OVER THE WORLD.

I am, as before,

Your Well-Wisher,

An Old Weaver.

W. Cowdroy, Printer, Hunters'-lane, Manchester.

8. 1812 LUDDITE PROCLAMATION
13⅞″ × 9¼″. W. Cowdroy, Manchester.
This proclamation was issued as a counterblast to the Luddite Rioters. The fat face italic used for 'Fellow Weavers!' and the decorative swelled rule below probably come from Caslon's foundry.

The open letter used for the initial letter 'S' is 2-line English Ornamented probably cut by Richard Austin. First shown by S. & C. Stephenson in 1789 and later issued by Fry. (It is known today as Fry's Ornamented No. 2.)

Public Record Office

By the QUEEN.
A PROCLAMATION.

VICTORIA R.

WHEREAS Our Parliament stands prorogued to the Twenty-second day of *October* one thousand eight hundred and seventy-three: We, by and with the Advice of Our Privy Council, hereby issue our Royal Proclamation, and publish and declare that the said Parliament be further prorogued to *Tuesday* the Sixteenth Day of *December* One thousand eight hundred and seventy-three.

Given at Our Court at *Balmoral*, this Thirtieth day of *September*, in the Year of our Lord One thousand eight hundred and seventy-three, and in the Thirty-seventh Year of Our Reign.

God save the Queen.

LONDON: Printed by GEORGE EDWARD EYRE and WILLIAM SPOTTISWOODE, Printers to the Queen's most Excellent Majesty. 1873.

9. 1873 PROCLAMATION
22″ × 15¾″. Eyre & Spottiswoode, London.
Set in Thorne's Fat Face throughout.

Oxford University Press

Proclamations were not only issued by the Crown. The 'Second letter to Fellow Weavers' of 1812 was presumably issued by the government of the day to try to suppress the smashing of machinery in the Luddite Riots. This was a movement that had started in the previous year in the Nottingham district and was so named after a weak-willed lad called Ned Ludd, who in a rage had destroyed a couple of frames used in stocking manufacture. The 2-line English Ornamented initial and the text with over twenty words to the line, combined with semi-fat faces displayed at the top and bottom gives this proclamation a transitional look. A mixture – not altogether happy – of two quite different typographic cultures.

The Royal Proclamation of 1873 is set in a fat face throughout and very effective it is. The text is set to a measure of reasonable length and is heavily leaded. It is far closer in character to the black letter proclamations (Fig. 3) than to the roman letter proclamations of Trumbull and Washington (Figs. 5 and 6).

CONGRÈS DE PARIS.

30 MARS 1856.

La Paix a été signée aujourd'hui, à une heure, à l'Hôtel des Affaires Étrangères.

Les Plénipotentiaires de la France, de l'Autriche, de la Grande-Bretagne, de la Prusse, de la Russie, de la Sardaigne et de la Turquie ont apposé leur signature au Traité qui met fin à la guerre actuelle et qui, en réglant la question d'Orient, asseoit le repos de l'Europe sur des bases solides et durables.

10. 1856 PROCLAMATION
16″ × 15¾″. Bouquin, Paris.
Set in a heavy condensed Egyptian and a Didot style of letter for the text.

Oxford University Press

AT THE COUNCIL CHAMBER, WHITEHALL,

The 23rd day of January, 1901.

ON Tuesday the 22nd day of January at half past six o'clock p.m. our late Most Gracious Sovereign Queen Victoria expired at Osborne House, Isle of Wight, in the eighty-second year of her age and the sixty-fourth year of Her Reign.

Upon the intimation of this distressing event the Lords of the Privy Council assembled this day at St. James's Palace in order to wait on His present Majesty King Edward the Seventh.

Printed by EYRE and SPOTTISWOODE, Printers to the King's most Excellent Majesty. 1901.

11. 1901 PROCLAMATION
8⅛″ × 6½″. Eyre and Spottiswoode, London.
Proclamation announcing the death of Queen Victoria. In the original there is almost as much space above the top line as there is below the body of the text.

Public Record Office

5¾″ wide. H.M. Stationery Office, London.
The black letter has been dropped and two columns
are a concession to legibility. *The London Gazette*
deals with State Intelligence, petitions, public and
legal notices. The heading is set in Joseph Moxon's
Canon Roman, shown in his specimen of 1669.
William Caslon adopted this type and added his own
capitals in his specimen book of 1764.

By permission of the Controller, Her Majesty's Stationery Office

No. 41986   2025

The London Gazette

Published by Authority

Registered as a Newspaper	⁂	For Contents see last page

FRIDAY, 18TH MARCH 1960

STATE INTELLIGENCE

PRIVY COUNCIL OFFICE

At the Court at Buckingham Palace, the 16th day
of March, 1960.

PRESENT,

The QUEEN'S Most Excellent Majesty

Lord Chancellor
Lord President
Mr. Secretary Butler
Sir Michael Adeane
Chancellor of the Duchy of Lancaster

Her Majesty was this day pleased, in pursuance of
the Royal Marriages Act, 1772, to declare Her
Consent to a Contract of Matrimony between Her
Sister Her Royal Highness The Princess Margaret
Rose and Antony Charles Robert Armstrong-Jones,
Esquire, which Consent Her Majesty has caused to
be signified under the Great Seal and to be entered
in the Books of the Privy Council.

W. G. Agnew.

At the Court at Buckingham Palace, the 16th day of
March 1960.

Present,

The QUEEN'S Most Excellent Majesty in Council.
Sheriffs appointed by Her Majesty in Council for
the year 1960—

ENGLAND

(except Cornwall and Lancashire)

Bedfordshire—Harold George Brightman, Esq., of 51
Whitehill Avenue, Luton.

Berkshire—Lieut.-Colonel (Brevet Colonel) Hugh
Alfred Gorton Vanderfelt, T.D., of Penhallow,
Cookham Dean.

Buckinghamshire—Major John Darling Young, of
Thornton Hall, Bletchley.

*Cambridgeshire and Huntingdonshire (Cambridge-
shire name)*—Miles Crawford Burkitt, Esq., of
Merton House, Grantchester.

Cheshire—Lieut.-Colonel Ronald Henry Antrobus,
M.C., of Eaton Hall, Congleton.

Cumberland—Archibald Henry d'Engayne Wybergh,
Esq., of Borrans Hill, Dalston, Carlisle.

Derbyshire—Robin Henry Rowland Buckston, Esq.,
of Sutton-on-the-Hill, near Derby.

Devonshire—Lieut.-Commander Richard John
Bramble Mildmay-White, R.N.R., of Mothecombe,
Holbeton.

Dorset—Sir Thomas Edward Lees, Bt., of Post Green,
Lytchett Minster, Poole.

Durham—Lieut.-Colonel Robert Macgowan Chapman,
T.D., of Cherry Tree House, Cleadon, near Sunderland.

Essex—Charles Hubert Archibald Butler, Esq., of
Shortgrove, Newport, Saffron Walden.

Gloucestershire—Major Anthony Biddulph, T.D., of
Rodmarton Manor, Cirencester.

Hampshire—Commander Richard Augustus Bagot
Phillimore, R.N., of Shedfield Grange, Shedfield,
near Southampton.

Herefordshire—Thomas John Hawkins, Esq., O.B.E.,
of Wilton Oaks, Tarrington.

Hertfordshire—Brigadier Richard Nigel Hanbury,
C.B.E., T.D., of Hay Lodge, Braughing.

Kent—Peter Victor Ferdinand Cazalet, Esq., of Fair-
lawne, Tonbridge.

Leicestershire—Willoughby Rollo Norman, Esq., of
Pickwell Manor, Melton Mowbray.

Lincolnshire—John Richard Bergne-Coupland, Esq.,
of Skellingthorpe Hall, near Lincoln.

County of London—John Nicholson Hogg, Esq., T.D.,
of 22 Pelham Crescent, London S.W.7.

Middlesex—Sir Christopher George Armstrong
Cowan, Kt., of Kiln Farm, Rickmansworth Road,
Northwood.

Monmouthshire—Brigadier Gerald Birdwood
Vaughan-Hughes, M.C., of Wyelands, Chepstow.

Norfolk—Desmond Gurney Buxton, Esq., of Hoveton
Hall, Wroxham, Norwich.

Northamptonshire—Major-General Evelyn Dalrymple
Fanshawe, C.B., C.B.E., of Guilsborough House,
Guilsborough, Northampton.

Northumberland—Lieut.-Colonel William Edward
Hedley-Dent, of Shortflatt Tower, Belsay, Newcastle-upon-Tyne.

Nottinghamshire—Lieut.-Colonel Thomas Eben
Forman Hardy, M.C., T.D., of Car Colston Hall,
Car Colston.

Oxfordshire—Colonel Herbert William James Morrell,
O.B.E., M.C., of Caphill, Sandford St. Martin.

Rutland—John Ernest Michael Conant, Esq., of The
Old Hall, Nether Hambleton, Oakham.

Shropshire—Arthur Nicholas Fielden, Esq., O.B.E., of
Cruckton Cottage, Shrewsbury.

Somersetshire—Lieut.-Colonel Geoffrey Walter
Fownes Luttrell, M.C., of Court House, East Quan-
toxhead, Bridgwater.

Staffordshire—Martin Alfred Butts Bolton, Esq., of
Croxden Abbey, near Uttoxeter.

Suffolk—David Stanley Pierson, Esq., of Abbey Oaks,
Sproughton, Ipswich.

Proclamations

The proclamation, shown on the opposite page,
from the 'Congrès de Paris' announcing the
signing of the Crimean War Peace Treaty,
makes good use of heavy Egyptian and bold
Didot style letters.

In contrast to this, the Proclamation of 1901
announcing the death of Queen Victoria, is a
departure from any of the earlier bills, set in (for
the heading) an attenuated Miller and Richard
typeface and a weak 'modern' face for the text.

The layout of this is interesting, with very deep
margins at the top (not shown here) and bottom
of the sheet (Fig. 11).

The continued use of gothic letters for formal
utterances lasts even to today, where 'Published by Authority', the subheading of the
London Gazette, is still set in black letter. This
is rather an austere little publication, lacking
either the bookish dignity or the vitality of
earlier proclamations.

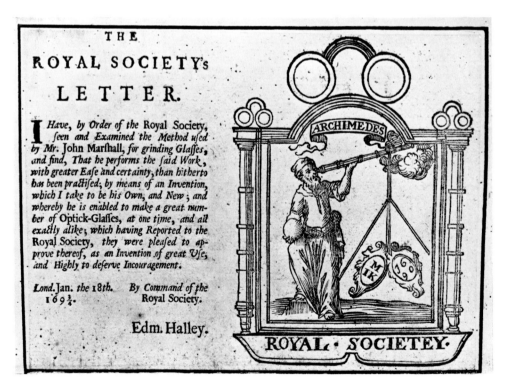

Licences and Certificates

The Form of a Licence from y Trinity-House to Watermen to row on y Thames.

WE the Master, Wardens, and Assistants, of the Trinity House of Deptford Strond, do License

                                                    of   Marriner
to Row in a Wherry with Oars or Skulls, up and down the River of
Thames, between Graves End and Windsor, and to ply his Fare between
Voyages as other Watermen commonly called Wherry-men use to do
upon the same River to his most and best advantage, for the better
Relief of himself, his Wife, and Family; As also for keeping him from
Idleness, lewd Company, and folly, so long time, as we shall see cause
for him to use the same, Sealed with the usual and Common Seal of
the Corporation; Given the   day of
1 6 7 , and in the   year of the
Reign of our Soveraign Lord King Charles the Second of England, &c

Memorand. That this Lycense is Granted to the above-named
                  with this Proviso, That he is not to sell fruit or strong-Waters in
or upon the River of Thames, Nor to Row in any Bum-boats to have any
dealings with Ship-keepers, upon any occasion whatsoever.

13. 1670 LICENCE
$3\frac{3}{4}'' \times 5\frac{1}{4}''$. Anon. London.
This form of a licence was issued by Trinity House
for watermen to row upon the Thames. The drop
initial letter is made up of two V's.

Pepysian Library, Cambridge

THE
ROYAL SOCIETY's
LETTER.

I Have, by Order of the Royal Society,
seen and Examined the Method used
by Mr. John Marshall, for grinding Glasses,
and find, That he performs the said Work,
with greater Ease and certainty, than hitherto
has been practised; by means of an Invention,
which I take to be his Own, and New; and
whereby he is enabled to make a great number of Optick-Glasses, at one time, and all
exactly alike; which having Reported to the
Royal Society, they were pleased to ap-
prove thereof, as an Invention of great Use,
and Highly to deserve Incouragement.

Lond. Jan. the 18th.   By Command of the
    1 6 9¾.   Royal Society.

                Edm. Halley.

ROYAL · SOCIETEY.

14. 1694 CERTIFICATE
$5\frac{1}{2}'' \times 7\frac{3}{4}''$. Anon. London.
Letter issued by the Royal Society of London giving
their approval to an inventor. Set in roman and italic
typefaces with a woodcut device. The liberal use of
italic was to give the letter something of the appearance of the formal engraved letter.

Oxford University Press

Scilly.

KNOW all Men by thefe prefents, That We the Mafter, Wardens and Affiftants of the Trinity-houfe of Deptford-ftrond, by Virtue of an Act of Parliament, made in the Eighth Year of Queen Eliz. are impowered from time to time at our wills and pleafures, to Erect and Maintain fuch, and fo many Sea-marks, as to us fhall feem moft meet and requifite, for the avoiding all fuch dangers as Ships are incident to upon the Coaft of England. As alfo by Virtue of certain Letters Patents from the Kings Majefty, bearing Date the Four and twentieth Day of June, in the Two and thirtieth year of his Reign, Licenfing and Impowring us to Erect a Light-houfe, or Light-houfes upon the Iflands of Scilly, as we fhall fee caufe for the purpofe aforefaid; and to Receive fuch Allowances for the Maintenance of the fame, as fhall be reafonable, Thereby requiring all Mayors, Sheriffs, Juftices of the Peace, Bayliffs, and other Officers or Minifters to whom it doth, or fhall appertain, That they upon Requeft made to them, be favouring, aiding, and affifting to Us, our Succeffors and Affigns, in and concerning the Premifes. WE therefore have, and do hereby Depute, Authorize and Affign you   of   to be our Deputy Collector in the Port of   and the Members, Roads and Creeks thereunto belonging, to Receive and Collect all fuch Duties or Sums of Mony, as fhall from the Thirtieth day of October, One thoufand fix hundred and eighty; arife and grow due to Us, for the maintenance of a Fire-light then kindled on a Light-houfe by us Built upon Agnes, one of the Iflands of Scilly, that is, One Half-penny for every Tun of the Burden of every Englifh Ship outward bound, and One Half-penny for every Tun of the Burden of every Englifh Ship inward bound, which have or fhall pafs by within or without the faid Iflands of Scilly, and of every ftrangers Ship paffing by, within or without the faid Iflands, double the faid Duties, or Sums of Mony.   GIVEN under the Common Seal of this Corpora-tion, this   day of   In the   of the Reign of our Soveraign Lord King Charles the Second, &c.

15. *c.* 1670 CERTIFICATE
5″ × 7″ approx. Anon. London.
Issued during the reign of King Charles II, to authorize the collection of Light Dues.

Trinity House

16. 1959 CERTIFICATE
H. K. Wolfenden del et sculpt. London.
Letter addressed by the Royal Society of London to an elected Fellow. Hand-written and reproduced by photo-offset lithography.

The Royal Society
of
London
March 19

Sir
We have the honour of acquainting you that you were to-day elected a Fellow of the Royal Society in consequence of which the Statute requires your attendance for admission on or before the fourth Meeting from the day of your election, or within such further time as shall be granted by the Society or Council, upon cause shewn to either of them. otherwise your election will be void.
You will therefore be pleased to attend at half past four of the clock in the afternoon on one of the following days. viz:-
Thursday   Thursday
Thursday   Thursday

We are.
Sir.
Your obedient Servants

Secretaries

Licences

The Pilot and Waterman Licences shown here are a fair commentary on the typographic development of such pieces of printing. The first issued by Trinity House in the 1670's, dates from a barren period of typography and shows no more invention in design or display than would a news-sheet of the day.

The Royal Society's letter is quite pleasantly balanced and is of some typographic interest in that the body of the text is set in italic, and roman letters are only used for emphasis for such words as 'Optick-Glasses.'

The Royal Society today reverts to an older tradition, and spurning the use of type, turns to a modern scribe, who, in a fair humanistic script, pens out a certificate for an Elected Fellow of the Royal Society.

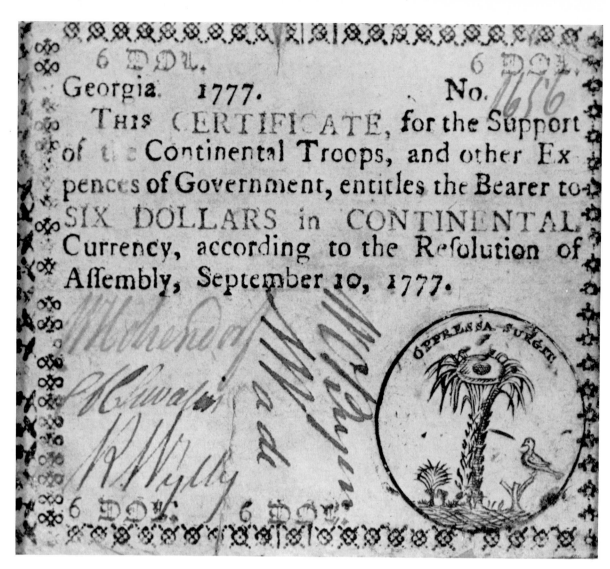

17. 1777 CERTIFICATE OF SUPPORT
5¼″×6″ approx. Georgia, U.S.A.
This certificate was for the support of the continental troops and entitled the bearer to six dollars in continental currency.

Lucius Battle

PATENT HAY-SCALES.

NO.

Load of _____ drove by

Mr. _____ of _____

to Mr. _____ of _____

Weight,

Tare,

Fees, Nett,

Windsor, _____ 184_

Weigher.

18. 1842 CERTIFICATE
2¾″ × 3¾″. Anon. Windsor, Ontario.
A small certificate set closely within a border which is very similar to one Caslon showed in 1844.

Bella C. Landauer Collection, New-York Historical Society

Certificates

19. 1836 STOCK CERTIFICATE
$6\frac{7}{8}'' \times 7\frac{1}{4}''$. Anon. New Orleans.
Share certificate set in a script typeface with 'Carrollton Bank' set in a shadow and decorated Tuscan.
A beautifully composed certificate printed by letterpress. The influence of the engraver is obvious. What is remarkable is the skill with which this engraved appearance has been carried out. Borders and typefaces both help to foster this illusion.

The 'Continental Troops' certificate, though a hurried piece of printing, does make an effective use of capital letters and with some skill fills the space within the borders. The use of printers' flowers and borders is skilfully applied to the little 'Patent Hay Scales' certificate. A combination of fleuron and decorated, shadow and script letters is used in the American Share Certificates; that for the Carrollton Bank is a deliberate attempt to produce a piece of printing that would pass for an engraving. The Pawtuxet Turnpike Company's Certificate is avowedly letterpress, but is many stages removed from the 1777 'Certificate of Support'. The 'modern' vertically stressed typeface and heavy leading, give it a displayed formality that close-set old style types could never achieve. Added to this, the subtle use of small bold Egyptian capitals and the shadow gothic produce something quite new to letterpress printing. The introduction of heavy fat faced letters completely altered the appearance of bills and posters. The more restrained use of 'modern' typefaces and small display letters had just as much, and as beneficial, an effect on smaller pieces of ephemeral printing.

20. 1825 CERTIFICATE
$7'' \times 6\frac{1}{2}''$. Anon. Providence, R.I.
Share certificate set in a condensed 'modern' face, Binney and Ronaldson's Double Pica, with 'Pawtuxet Turnpike Corporation' set in an unidentified but handsome little shadow black letter.

Bella C. Landauer Collection, New-York Historical Society

Licences

No 85 Branch Pilot Boat No 2

TO ALL WHOM IT MAY CONCERN BE IT KNOWN.

That the bearer James Martin Journeyman in the Pilot Boat Kitty No 2 Joseph Pattison Master aged Twenty seven years Five feet six Inches high Fair Complexion Grey Eyes & wears his own hair - has been examined for a Pilot by the Pilot Committee, and found qualified to Conduct a Vessel into or out of the Ports of Liverpool, Beaumaris, Chester water, Pile of Foudre & the Isle of Man.

We therefore grant him this Licence or Branch to take charge of a Pilot any Vessel into or out of the said Ports for — One Year — provided the said James Martin — doth comply with all the Pilot Laws and every order made by the Committee, and behaves with Conduct and Prudence. given under our hands this Second day of May in the year of our Lord one Thousand eight Hundred and one.

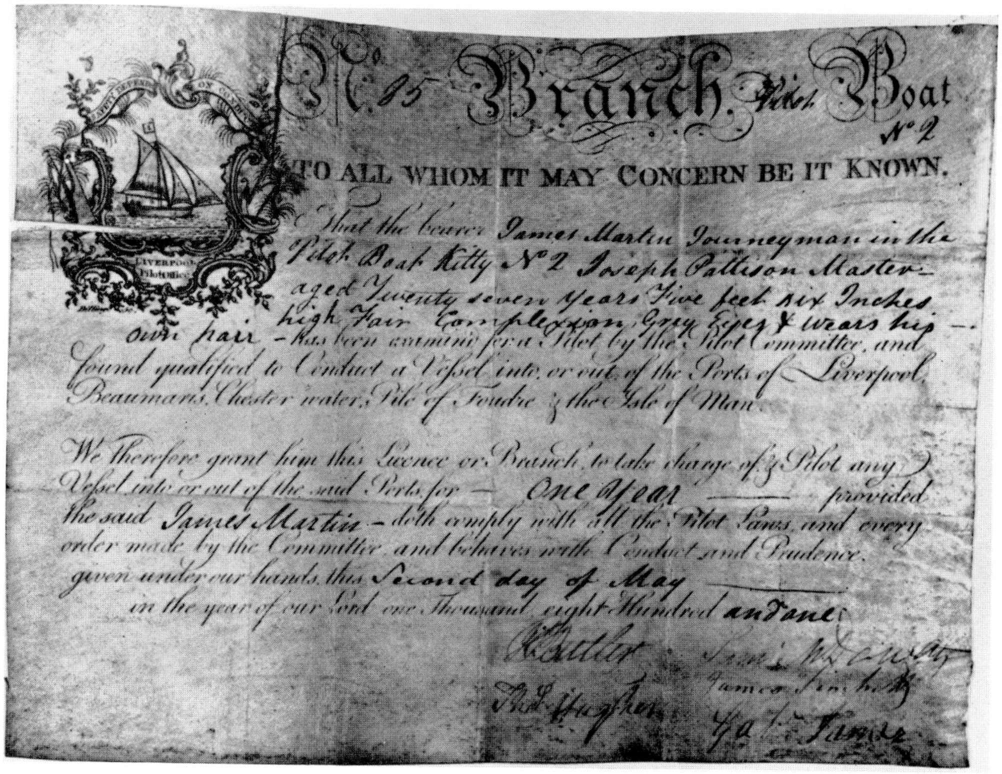

21. 1801 LICENCE
$5\frac{3}{4}'' \times 9''$ Anon. London.
Engraved licence issued by the Liverpool Pilot Office, using the English hand, open roman capitals, and the ubiquitous gothic.

Trinity House, London

Cinque Ports. ARTHUR DUKE OF WELLINGTON, LORD WARDEN of the CINQUE PORTS, CONSTABLE of DOVOR CASTLE, KNIGHT OF THE MOST NOBLE ORDER OF THE GARTER, and FIELD MARSHAL OF HIS MAJESTY'S FORCES, &c. &c. &c. and ROBERT HENRY JENKINSON, Esquire, LIEUTENANT of the said CASTLE, and DEPUTY WARDEN of the said CINQUE PORTS,

To All *Mayors, Sheriffs, Justices of the Peace, Bailiffs, Constables, Head-Boroughs, and all other His Majesty's Officers whom it doth or may concern, greeting.*

Whereas, there hath been time out of mind, and now is, a SOCIETY or FELLOWSHIP of PILOTS of the TRINITY HOUSE, of *Dovor, Deal*, and the *Isle of Thanet*, who have had the Pilotage and Loadmanage of all Ships from the said Places up the *Rivers Thames* and *Medway*, which said Society or Fellowship have been confirmed by various Acts of Parliament for regulating the Pilots of *Dovor, Deal*, and the *Isle* of *Thanet*, commonly called CINQUE PORTS PILOTS. And Whereas the said LORD WARDEN and CONSTABLE, or his LIEUTENANT, have always heretofore been empowered to appoint the Pilots or Loadsmen of such Society, and to make Bye Laws and Regulations for their better government. And Whereas the powers of the said LORD WARDEN and CONSTABLE and his LIEUTENANT, have lately been confirmed and enlarged by an Act of Parliament, made and passed in the Sixth Year of the Reign of His present Majesty KING GEORGE THE FOURTH, intituled, "An Act for the amendment of the Law respecting Pilots and Pilotage; and also for the better preservation of Floating Lights, Buoys, and Beacons." And Whereas Trevanion Austen of the Town and port of Dover in the County of Kent Mariner having been first duly examined, and found fit and competent and duly skilled to act as a Pilot, for the purpose of conducting Ships and Vessels sailing, navigating, and passing within the limits hereinafter mentioned, was, on the Fifteenth day of October One Thousand Eight Hundred and Twenty first admitted, licenced, and sworn a Pilot or Loadsman of the said Society or Fellowship of Pilots. Now Know ye that by virtue of these Presents the said Pilot is confirmed anew in his said Office, and is hereby re-appointed and re-licenced to act as a Pilot, for the purpose of conducting Ships and Vessels sailing, navigating, and passing from or by DUNGENESS, up the RIVER THAMES, as far as the Public Landing-place at GRAVESEND, commonly called the TOWN QUAY, and up the RIVER MEDWAY, as far as the West Point of STANDGATE CREEK, and all and every the several Channels, Creeks, and Docks of the said Rivers; and from the South Buoy of the BRAKE, to the Westward as far as the West End of the OWERS, and into and out of RAMSGATE, DOVOR, SANDWICH, and MARGATE HARBOURS, and also upon the Coasts of FLANDERS and HOLLAND; and so to continue so long as he shall be found capable of well executing the same, and shall duly conform himself to all the Bye Laws, Rules, and Orders of the COURT of LOADMANAGE of the said CINQUE PORTS, or until this Licence shall be annulled, suspended or adjudged to be forfeited, by the LORD WARDEN and CONSTABLE of DOVOR CASTLE, or his LIEUTENANT for the time being.

These *are therefore to will and require you not to interrupt, or in any wise molest or hinder the said Pilot in the execution and discharge of his said Service and Duty.*

Given at DOVOR CASTLE, under my Hand and Seal of Office there, the First day of July, One Thousand Eight Hundred and Twenty-nine.

Registered No 127 Custom House Dover 29 July 1829

DESCRIPTION OF THE SAID PILOT.
Age, Thirty seven *Years.*
Height, Five *Feet,* — *Inches.*
Complexion, Fair
Hair, Light
Marks, None

Registrar.

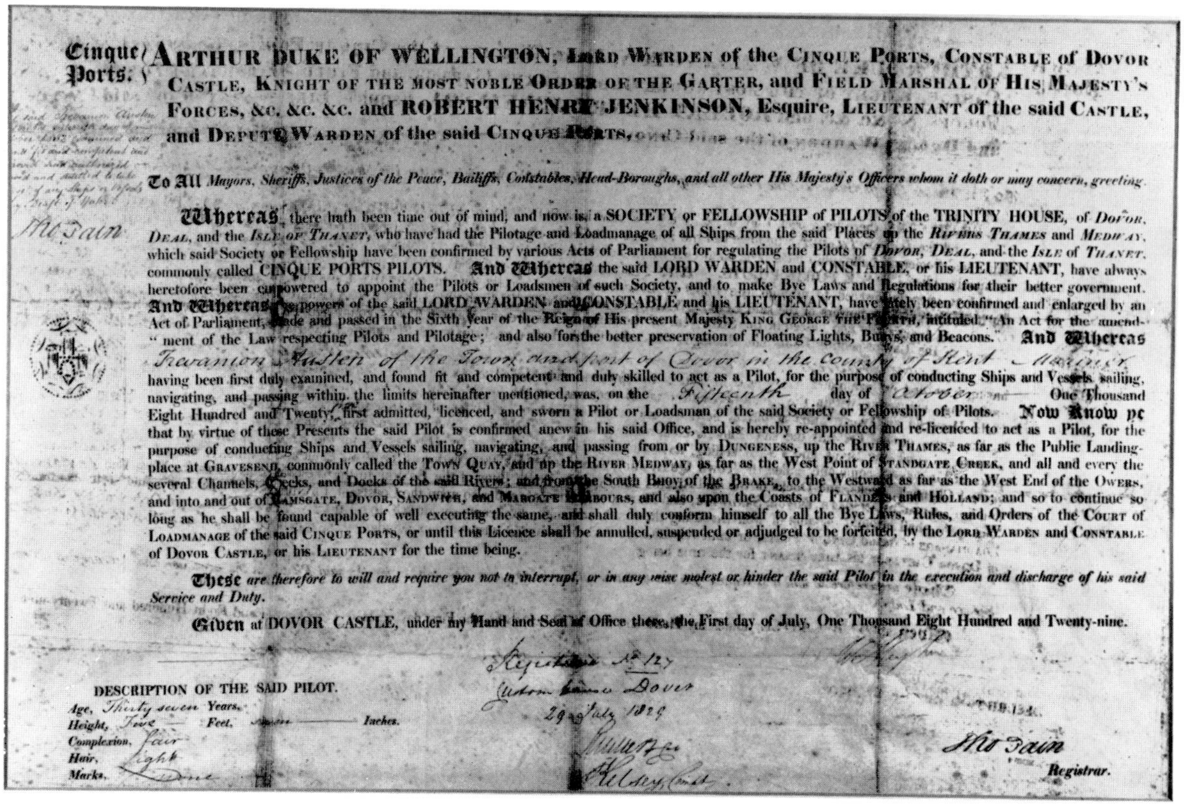

22. 1829 LICENCE
$12\frac{1}{4}'' \times 19\frac{1}{4}''$. Anon. London.
Issued by the Lord Warden of the Cinque Ports for Pilots bringing vessels between Dungeness and Gravesend. Fat faced types are used for both roman and gothic in this handsome letterpress licence.

Trinity House, London

No._____

To all to whom these Presents shall come, The Corporation of Trinity House of

Deptford Strond, send Greeting, **know ye** that in pursuance and by virtue of the powers given them for that purpose in

and by The Pilotage Act 1913, and of all other powers them enabling, the said Corporation, having first duly examined

of _____ **Mariner,**

(the Bearer hereof, whose description is endorsed on these Presents) and having, upon such examination, found the said

_____to be a fit and competent Person, duly skilled to act as a Pilot

for the purpose of conducting Ships, sailing, navigating, and passing within the limits hereinafter mentioned, **Do** hereby

appoint and license the said_____to act as a

Pilot, for the purpose of conducting Ships from **London Bridge down the River of Thames to Gravesend and back again to**

London Bridge.

And this Licence (if the same shall not be revoked or suspended in the meantime, as in the said Act provided), is to continue

in force up to and until the 31st day of January next ensuing the date of these Presents, but no longer, unless renewed from

time to time by Indorsement hereon.   Provided always that the said Pilot shall so long comply with all the Bye-laws and

Regulations made or to be made by the said Corporation.

*This Licence shall not authorise or empower the said*_____

_____*to take charge as a Pilot of any Ship or Vessel drawing*

more than Sixteen Feet Water *(except when an upper draught Pilot is not available to offer his services), in the*

River Thames or any of the Channels leading thereto or therefrom, until it shall be certified hereon that the said

_____*has acted as a Licensed Pilot*

for three Years, and has been on re-examination approved of in that behalf by the said Corporation.

Given under the Common Seal of the Corporation of Trinity House of

Deptford Strond, this_____day of_____19

Deputy Master.

Secretary.

23. 1960 LICENCE
12″×9″. Anon. London.
Licence issued by the Corporation of Trinity House
to Pilots on the River Thames. The first words are
set in Tudor Black; the text in Modern No. 1,
Modern Italic and Times Bold.
Trinity House, London

The licences that are shown in Figs. 21 and 22 offer an interesting comparison of the ways of reaching the same end by radically different means. Engraving on metal as a method of reproductive printing probably deserves the cachet it still has, for even in the dreariest periods of typography, the engraver managed, within strict conventions, to produce agreeable works. However, here the typographic solution of the Cinque Ports licence has just as much assurance as the Liverpool engraving. The asymmetric arrangement and use of bold 'modern' typefaces carry the typography of Fig. 22 into a different world to that conceived by the printer of Figs. 13 and 15.

The modern Trinity House licence, above, shows its antecedents; it has the coat of arms of Fig. 15 but not the dignity; it makes the same use of the black letter as in Fig. 22, but lacks the virility of the 1829 one, and its phraseology has many similarities to those of the 1680's.

Orders to attend

Trinity - House.

SIR,

Y OU are hereby Required to make your perſonal appearance before the Maſter and Wardens of this Corporation, at their ſaid Houſe in Water-lane, near the Cuſtome houſe, on

the   of   between Ten and Eleven in the Forenoon, hereof you are not to fail.

By Order

24. *c.* 1680 ORDER TO ATTEND
5″×6″. Anon. London.
Order issued by the Master and Wardens of Trinity House to one of their pilots and watermen to appear before them. The typeface is probably of Dutch origin.

Pepysian Library, Cambridge

P425

Trinity House,
London, E.C.3

Y OU are hereby instructed to attend before the London

Pilotage Committee at Trinity House, Tower Hill, London,

E.C.3, on Friday, the

at 1100, in connection with

You are to bring your Licence with you.

By Order of the Committee.

To Mr.

Pilot.

Clerk to the London Pilotage Committee.

P.T.O.

25. 1960 ORDER TO ATTEND
8″×6½″. Anon. London.
The modern counterpart of Fig. 24. Set in a 'modern' typeface except for the gothic used for the address. The splendid coat of arms has become a trifling thing. The drop initial Y is still there.

Trinity House, London

This Indenture Witnesseth, That

with him after the manner of an Apprentice to dwell and serve from the

unto

the full end and term of   years from thence next en-
suing, fully to be compleat and ended; during all which said term, he, the said
Apprentice, his said Master well and faithfully shall serve, his Secrets keep, his Commandments lawful and
honest, every where gladly do and perform; hurt to his said Master he shall not do, nor of others see or know
to be done, but that he to his power shall let, or forthwith give warning to his said Master of the same; the
Goods of his said Master he shall not waste, nor to any unlawfully lend; Fornication he shall not commit; Matrimony he shall not contract; at Cards, Dice, Tables, or any other unlawful Games he shall not Play; Taverns
or Alehouses he shall not frequent; from his said Masters service by day or night unlawfully he shall not absent
himself, but in all things as a faithful Servant and Apprentice he shall bear and behave himself towards his said
Master and all his, during the said term: And the said Master his said Apprentice in the Art he now useth, after
the best manner he knows or can, shall Teach, Instruct, and Inform, or cause to be taught and informed with
due correction, finding his said Apprentice meat, and drink,

In testimony whereof the said Parties to these presents Interchangably have set their hands and seals the
day of   168

26. 1680 INDENTURE
5½″ × 7½″. Anon. London.
Indenture issued by Trinity House, to apprentices,
watermen, pilots and lighthouse keepers. Set in a
roman face with the first line set in a gothic letter.

Pepysian Library, Cambridge

This Indenture made on the

day of   19

BETWEEN

of

(hereinafter called "The Apprentice") of the first part;

of

(hereinafter called "The Guardian") of the second part;

of

(hereinafter called "The Master") of the third part Whereas the said Master exercises the

art, trade, or business of a

Now this Indenture witnesseth that the said Apprentice of his own free will and

accord, and with the consent of the said Guardian (testified by their executing these

presents), Doth bind himself to the said Master to learn the art, trade, or business of

a   , and with him, after the manner of an

Apprentice, to serve from the   day of   19

until the full end and term of   years thence next following, this period of

27. 1960 INDENTURE
10½″ × 6¾″. Anon. Ipswich.
Part of a modern Indenture set in a roman type but
still retaining the black letter for the opening and for
points of emphasis.

NEWCASTLE ff.
UPON TYNE.

...OU swear, That you shall from henceforth hold with our Sovereign *Lord* ———— the *King's* ———— Majesty that now is, and with *His* Heirs and Successors, Kings and Queens of Great Britain, against all Persons, to live and to die, and maintain the Peace and all the Franchises of this Town of Newcastle upon Tyne, and be obedient to the MAYOR, ALDER-MEN, SHERIFF, and all other the Officers of the same, and their Counsel keep; and no Man's Goods avow for yours, unless he be as free as yourself, and of the same Franchise: And you shall observe and keep, to the best of your Power, all lawful Ordinances made by common Consent, on High Court-days; and all other Things you shall do that belong to a FREEMAN of the said Town.

So help you GOD.

George Hutton, Son of Thomas Wilkinson, Ropemaker ———— *was* this *Sixth* —— Day of *April* —— in the Year of our Lord God 1818 admitted a Free Burgess of this Corporation, before the *Right Worshipful Robert Clayton Esquire, Mayor* ———— and stands charged *with* a Musket for the Defence thereof.

NEWCASTLE
UPON TYNE

YOU declare that you shall from henceforth hold with our Sovereign Lady the Queen's Majesty that now is, and with Her Heirs and Successors, Kings and Queens of *Great Britain,* against all persons to live and to die; and maintain the Peace, and all the Franchises of this City of *Newcastle upon Tyne,* and be obedient to the LORD MAYOR, ALDERMEN, SHERIFF, and all other the Officers of the same, and their Counsel keep; and no Man's goods avow for yours unless he be as free as yourself, and of the same Franchise: And you shall observe and keep to the best of your Power, all lawful Ordinances made by Common Consent, on High Court days; and all other Things you shall do that belong to a FREEMAN of the said City.

	was
this Day of	in
the Year of our Lord, 19	admitted a Freeman
of this City before the Right Honourable	
	Lord Mayor,
and stands charged with a musket for the defence thereof,	

Lord Mayor.

28. 1818 CERTIFICATE
10½″ × 6″. George Angus, Newcastle-upon-Tyne.
This admission to a Freeman to Newcastle-upon-Tyne is laid out in an asymmetrical fashion and set in a bold 'modern' typeface. The printer's imprint runs vertically down the fore-edge and the coat of arms is used most ingeniously as a decorative initial.

29. 1958 CERTIFICATE
11½″ × 7″. Anon. Newcastle-upon-Tyne.
The same document 140 years later still has the same asymmetric arrangement though the crest sits foolishly in the position of an initial without serving as such. Set in Rockwell, a modern Egyptian typeface.

Orders, Certificates and Bills of Lading

Comparisons are shown by Figs. 24 and 25, the 'Orders to attend' issued by the same authority, the two Indentures Figs. 26 and 27 and, above, the two certificates issued to the Freemen of Newcastle-upon-Tyne. The 1818 certificate is a fine piece of free, asymmetric layout with the coat of arms doing duty as an initial. No doubt the printer felt the three towers, arranged as they were, looked like enough to the letter 'Y', but perhaps on the instruction of a higher authority he dropped a little capital 'Y' into the middle of the shield. The modern version follows the arrangement blindly, but no longer does the crest do duty as an initial, and the very fine semi-fat face used in the 1818 version of the text is replaced by Rockwell, a despicable modern Egyptian.

Ship's Manifests have been wonderfully consistent through the years. They still follow the formal style of the engraver even though for the last hundred years they have been printed by letterpress or lithography. The Bewick bill for Newcastle-upon-Tyne is a superbly elegant piece of engraving and depicts the stern of a Jarrow collier.

The 1870 Le Havre 'Bulletin de Chargement' is typeset, though it apes in every particular the engraver; the ship is engraved on wood and printed with the type. The modern bill of lading is actually engraved on copper, and transferred to the lithographic plate and printed by offset. This is where tradition becomes pastiche and the full-rigged ship serves only as pleasant decoration.

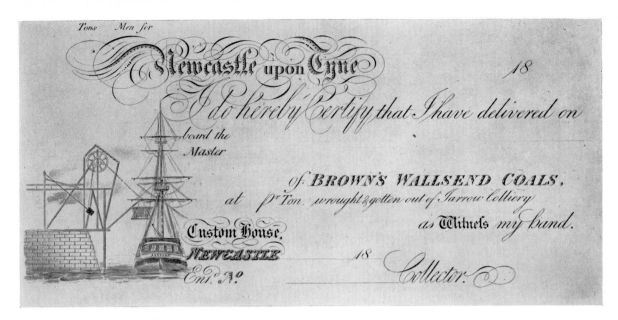

30. *c.* 1800 BILL OF LADING
4¾″ × 9¾″. T. Bewick, Newcastle-upon-Tyne.
This lading bill comes from the Bewick Sale of 1884
and was probably engraved by one of Bewick's
associates.

Bills of Lading

31. 1870 BILL OF LADING
6¾″ × 9″. Anon. Bordeaux.
This French 'Bulletin de Chargement' though
damaged at the right-hand bottom corner, is suffi-
ciently typical to be worth showing. It is printed by
letterpress from type which apes 'copperplate'. The
wood engraving of the barque adds to the illusion.

32. 1950 BILL OF LADING
4⅝″ × 8¾″. W. S. Cowell Ltd, Ipswich.
This modern lading bill is engraved on copper but
printed by offset.

Legacy Duty forms

To be used from and after the 31st Day of August, 1815.

Directions.

STAMP OFFICE.

LEGACY DUTY ON RESIDUES OF PERSONAL ESTATE, &c.

FORM of Account to be delivered by Executors and Administrators, retaining the Residue, or any part or share of the Residue, of Personal Estate, either to their own use as residuary Legatees, or next of Kin, or as Trustees for the use and benefit of others; and by Executors and Trustees retaining the Residue, or Part of Residue of Monies arising from Real Estate, ordered to be sold, &c. for the purpose of having the Duties imposed by the Act of 55 Geo. III. c. 184, on Legacies, Annuities, and Residues of Personal Estate, and of Monies arising out of Real Estate, passing to Children or their Descendants, or the Father or Mother, or any lineal Ancestor, or Collateral Relations, or Strangers in Blood, to the deceased, charged and assessed pursuant to the Acts of 36 Geo. III. c. 52, and 45 Geo. III. c. 28.

REGISTER *S J* No. 2   18*34* Fol. *277*

State these Particulars accurately, and strike out such parts as are not applicable to the Case.

An Account of the Personal Estate, and of Monies ~~arising out~~ of the Real Estate, of *Mary Taylor late of Orford Street in the parish of Saint George Hanover Square in the county of Middlesex Widow* — who died on the *3rd* day of *May* — One Thousand Eight Hundred and *33* **exhibited by** *Sarah Ann Morse the universal Legatee* ~~the Executor, or Administrator~~ of the Deceased, ~~or Trustee of the Real Estate, directed by the Will to be sold, &c.~~ acting under the Will, ~~or Letters of Administration of the Effects,~~ of the deceased, proved in, ~~or granted by~~ the *Prerogative* _____ Court of *Canterbury* on the *fifth* — Day of *June* — One Thousand Eight Hundred and *thirty four*

State when sold.

State the Times when Stocks sold.

Here specify any other Stocks or Funds which have been sold.

1. Money Received.

Cash in the House..

Cash at the Bankers ....

Cash arising from the SALE of the following Articles, viz.

   Household Goods and Furniture............................

   Plate, Linen, and China ....

   Books, Prints, and Pictures ....

   Wearing Apparel ....

   Jewels, Trinkets, and Ornaments of the Person ....

   Wine and other Liquors..................................

   Horses and Carriages ....

   Farming Stock and Implements of Husbandry...............

   Stock in Trade ....

   Leasehold Estates ....

£   Bank Stock ....sold at   per Cent.

£   3 per Cent. Reduced Annuities ....sold at   per Cent.

£   3 per Cent. Consols Annuities ....sold at   per Cent.

£   3½ per Cent. Annuities 1818 ....sold at   per Cent.

£   3½ per Cent. Reduced Annuities ....sold at   per Cent.

   New 3½ per Cent Annuities................sold at   per Cent.

£   4 per Cent Annuities 1826 ....sold at   per Cent.

   Long Annuities, Expire 5 January, 1860....sold at   years purchase

£   India Stock ....sold at   per Cent.

£   South Sea Stock, div. 3½ per Cent ... .sold at   per Cent.

£   Ditto   3 per Cent ....sold at   per Cent.

Carried over....

(For General Directions see the last side)

33. 1834 LEGACY DUTY FORM
14″ × 9″. Anon. London.
The use of fat face types gives a lot of vitality to pieces of printing of this kind. The fat faced gothic used for 'An Account' is particularly effective.

Form No. 3—1　　　　　　**INLAND REVENUE**　　　　　**LEGACY** *or* **SUCCESSION** } **DUTY**

Name and address of the person }
who forwards this account.

This form is to be used in accounting for duty on funds retained in trust, and chargeable with **Legacy or Succession Duty** upon the capital value thereof **upon the determination of a life or a limited interest** under a will or intestacy. Where necessary, explanatory schedules, with a short history of the trust funds, should be annexed.

The **form when filled up in duplicate** should be transmitted to the Controller, Estate Duty Office, Inland Revenue, St. George's Hotel, Llandudno.

E.D./File.................................../19　.　　　　　　　D.C../194　.

(1) Real or personal (or the investments thereof).
(2) The testator or intestate.

An Account of the (¹)　　　　　　　　　estate of (²)

late of

(3) Death, marriage, alienation, etc., of life tenant or annuitant, etc.

who died on the　　　day of　　　　1　　which estate became divisible
on the (³)　　　　　　　of
　　　　　　　on the　　day of　　　　　　19　.

Names and addresses of the accounting parties, and the capacity in which they act. }

Acting under Probate of Will, or Letters of Administration [with Will annexed] dated the

(4) State which registry. }
day of　　　　　　1　　issued by the (⁴)
Registry of the Probate Division of the High Court of Justice.

Names of the beneficiaries, giving dates of death of, and dates of representation to, any who are dead.	Relationship (*See back*)	Short description of bequest : if residue, state what part or share.

Description of Property	Price of stocks, shares, &c.	£	s.	d.
N.B.— *If any sums have been advanced for maintenance or otherwise, or any capital divided during the continuance of the trust, full particulars, including amounts, dates and names of beneficiaries, should be furnished.*				
Total c/f				

34. 1959 LEGACY DUTY FORM
12½″ × 7½″. H.M. Stationery Office, London.
The modern version follows much the same form;
typographically it is hardly as well balanced as the
earlier one, where more importance is given to the
opening paragraph. 'An Account' still survives in
black letter.

By permission of the Controller, Her Majesty's Stationary Office

It is certainly hard to imagine much romance in the layout of the forms used by the Inland Revenue Department, yet there is still a dim, faint echo in the use and the arrangement of the black letter for 'An Account'. And here, of course, lies much of the reason for the continuity of design from one century to another, of such forms. Where the words remain the same, the layout – except in times of extreme mannerism – tends to follow the sense of the words. Modern legal documents, like decrees and proclamations, still hang grimly on to the use of gothic typefaces, for emphasis and possibly even for the air of legal respectability that black letter seems to possess. This is clearly shown in the two indentures (Figs. 26 and 27) and in the 1834 'Stamp Office Legacy Duty Form', which is a handsome and well-balanced piece of official printing. The restraint in the use of fat face and bold black letter gives an agreeable richness that its modern counterpart, clear though it is, certainly lacks.

NOMINATION.

At a respectable Meeting of *REPUBLICAN CITIZENS*, from different Parts of the State of New-York, convened at the Tontine Coffee-House in the City of Albany, on Saturday, the 18th day of February, 1804 :

William Tabor, Esquire,

of the Assembly, was chosen Chairman, and *JOSEPH ANNIN*, Esq. of the Senate, Sec'ry.

Resolved unanimously, that

Aaron Burr,

be and he is hereby nominated a Candidate to be supported at the ensuing Election for the office of GOVERNOR of this State.

Resolved, That the above Nomination be published in all the Newspapers printed in this State; and that the Secretary transmit a Copy thereof to the Corresponding Committees in the City of New-York and elsewhere.

William Tabor, Chairman.

JOSEPH ANNIN, Secretary.

36. *Above right.* 1804 ELECTION NOTICE
10¾″ × 6¾″. Anon. Albany N.Y.
Set in a mixture of Alexander Wilson's types of 1789.
and for 'William Tabor, Esquire' in Joseph Moxon's
Canon, *c.* 1670, cast by Caslon in the eighteenth
century.

New York Public Library

Town and Port of Liverpool.

THOMAS LEYLAND, Esq. MAYOR.

THE MAYOR and MAGISTRATES, impressed with serious Concern at the many UNFORTUNATE ACCIDENTS which have lately happened, and may still occur, by the CARELESS-NESS and INATTENTION of the Persons employed to LOAD and FIRE the GUNS on BOARD the MERCHANT SHIPS in the RIVER, THINK IT THEIR DUTY to apprize all MASTERS and COMMANDERS, and other OFFICERS, belonging to the MERCHANT SHIPS, and their SHIPS' COMPANIES, that they are determined to put the LAWS in force against all Persons who shall WILFULLY or NEGLI-GENTLY FIRE any GUN LOADED with BALL or SHOT, or other HARD or DANGEROUS SUBSTANCE, *within the LIMITS of the PORT of LIVERPOOL*, and do therefore earnestly recommend and insist in the strongest Terms, that in future all possible Care be taken by the COMMANDERS and other OFFICERS of MERCHANT SHIPS to have their GUNS SCALED, *at all Events*, before they TURN the ROCK upon coming in, and and that they do not FIRE in the RIVER, *or even within the LIMITS of the PORT*, on any Account whatever, upon the Penalties that will ensue.

By Order of the Mayor and Magistrates,

COLQUITT, TOWN CLERK.

BRUNSWICK-STREET, 2d FEBRUARY, 1799.

35. 1799 PORT ORDER
10″ × 5¾″. Anon. Liverpool.
An order by the Mayor and Magistrates of Liverpool
concerning the use of firearms within the port of
Liverpool. Set in a transitional typeface with a ready
use of capitals for emphasis and owing much to the
Baskerville style of typography.

---

37. 1805 ELECTION NOTICE
10½″ × 6½″. Anon. Westchester County N.Y.
'Electors' is set in Fry's Open and the body of the
text is in a typeface from Fry's Foundry. The small-
sized capitals in the first line are Bell's Paragon
capitals of 1788. The word 'Westchester' and the
signatures are from Robert Thorne *c.* 1803.

New York Public Library

TO THE INDEPENDENT

ELECTORS

OF THE COUNTY OF

WESTCHESTER.

Several meetings having been held in various parts of the County, to nominate fit persons to be supported as Members of Assembly, at the approaching election, and no satisfactory nomination having been made at any of them; a number of respectable inhabitants of the county, uninfluenced by the Party zeal which a few violent men have endeavoured to excite; and truly desirous to promote the true interests of the county, take the liberty to recommend, to the support of all good citizens, the following persons as Members of Assembly, viz.

SAMUEL MARVIN, of Rye.
EZRA LOCKWOOD, Poundridge.
ELI CROSBY, of Stephen-town.
JOEL FROST, of Cortlandt-town.
APRIL 20, 1805.

KIDDERMINSTER
NEW
Toll-free Fairs.

THE Public are respectfully informed, that at the Request of several FARMERS and DEALERS in the Neighbourhood, TWO NEW FAIRS will be held for the Sale of CATTLE, SHEEP, and HORSES *(Toll-free)*; one the *last Monday in November*, and the other the *last Monday in January*, to be continued annually.

THOMAS JONES,

HIGH BAILIFF OF KIDDERMINSTER,

Lessee of the Tolls.

WE, whose Names are hereunder written, being fully convinced of the utility and convenience of the above Fairs, are determined to give them our support :—

E. Grove *(Kinlett)*	T. Crane *(Habberley)*
H. Downes, *ditto*	J. Crane
J. Baker, *ditto*	E. Crane
B. Poutney, *ditto*	T. Baker
P. Whitcomb *(Eastham)*	G. Styles
E. Strafferd, *ditto*	J. Winnall
W. Weaver, *ditto*	J. Walker *(Rock)*
J. Bishop, *ditto*	T. Cooke
W. Price, *ditto*	F. Moule
J. Adams *(Lindridge)*	J. Watkins
J. Walker *(Stanford)*	I. Godfrey
T. Lowe	A. Godfrey
R. Bagnall	S. Chellingworth
H. Turner	J. Chellingworth
J. Lamb	J. Nott

SEPT. 1st, 1823.

T. PENNELL, PRINTER.

38. 1823 TOLL FREE FAIRS
8½″ × 5½″. T. Pennell, Kidderminster.
Well arranged with the judicious use of fat faced letters. One word 'NEW' in Thorne's Shaded and one decorated rule gives this little sheet richness.

AT A MEETING OF THE
INHABITANTS
OF
WOODBRIDGE,
HELD AT THE
TOWN HALL,
On the 14th. June, 1832,
For the purpose of deciding in what way to celebrate the passing of the
Reform Bill,
MR. THOMAS GRIMWOOD IN THE CHAIR.

Resolved unanimously,—That this Meeting feels anxious to celebrate the passing of the Reform Bill, in such a manner as may evince a high approval of the Measure, be of a public benefit, and at the same time not hurt the feelings of those who may differ in opinion. And that this Meeting conceives a Dinner given to the Poor, will be the best mode of celebrating so beneficial an event, and be far preferable to an Illumination, or other measure liable to abuse.

That a Dinner be accordingly given, and that a Committee be appointed to arrange all details.

That the Committee be open, and that any Inhabitant be at liberty to attend the Meetings of the Committee, and that five members be empowered to act.

That the thanks of this Meeting be given to the Magistrates for the use of the Hall, and to the Churchwardens for their kind and prompt compliance with the Requisitions of this Meeting.

That these Resolutions be printed.

THOMAS GRIMWOOD, Chairman.

The Chairman having left the Chair, the thanks of this Meeting was unanimously voted to the Chairman for his able and impartial conduct in the Chair.

At the close of the Meeting it was resolved to have a Public Dinner of the Inhabitants of the Town and Neighbourhood, on the Town Hall.

Tickets, 5s.—Dinner and a Pint of Wine included.

39. 1832 NOTICE OF A POLITICAL MEETING
11″ × 8¾″. Anon. Woodbridge.
Fat face and Egyptian typefaces give notice of a meeting to celebrate the passing of the Reform Bill.

Close of the Poll,
FIRST DAY.

	Henniker.	Vere.	Shawe.
Woodbridge - -	255	264	226
Ipswich - - -	513	529	348
Needham-Market	165	168	94
Saxmundham - -	200	188	131
Framlingham - -	306	261	307
Halesworth -	340	319	293
Beccles - - -	365	348	395

MAJORITY
In Favor of the Blues, - 285 !

WOODBRIDGE, *January 14, 1835.*

J. LODER, Printer and Bookseller, Woodbridge.

40. 1835 CLOSE OF THE POLL NOTICE
9″ × 11¼″. J. Loder, Woodbridge.
The printer has run out of sorts, and has to make do with a variety of founts for his numbers.

Official notices and election printing

Notices continued until the early years of the nineteenth century to follow the style of book work, as does the one issued by the Mayor of Liverpool concerning the misuse of the firing and loading of guns within the limits of the port. The Notice for Aaron Burr's Nomination as Governor of the State of New York, apart from its typographic qualities, has a rather melancholy interest. Mainly through the efforts of Alexander Hamilton, Burr was defeated in this election. Smarting under both his defeat and Hamilton's jibes, Burr issued the challenge for the famous duel, which resulted in the death of Alexander Hamilton on 12 July 1804.

The moment bold types were available, their usefulness for such notices was at once apparent and they were used for every purpose. They appeared, first as in Fig. 38, with the little semi-fat face and shadow, three-dimensional letters, to be followed by the splendid blast of Fig. 42.

Official notices

DORSET.

DIVISION OF

STURMINSTER.

SPECIAL SESSIONS

AND OTHER PUBLIC MEETINGS,

Appointed to be held by Her Majesty's Justices of the Peace, acting in and for the said Division,

At the Police Court, Sturminster Newton Castle,

FOR THE YEAR 1866.

ACTING MAGISTRATES.

JOHN HUSSEY, Esq., *Nash Court.*
MARWOOD S. YEATMAN, Esq., *Stock House.*
THOMAS B. HANHAM, Esq., *Manston House.*
Rev. H. T. BOWER, *Fontmell Parva.*

The Rev. H. BOUCHER, *Thornhill.*
MONTAGUE WILLIAMS, Esq., *Woolland House.*
H. S. BOWER, Esq., *Fontmell Parva.*
Lieut. Col. GLOSSOP, *Inwood.*

	1866.		
Monday,	January	15th	Special Sessions for the Highways.—Transferring Ale-house Licenses.
,,	February	12th	Hearing Appeals against Poor Rates.—Special Sessions for the Highways.—And for granting Licenses required by the Gunpowder Acts.
,,	March	12th	Special Sessions for the Highways.
,,	April	9th	Appointment of Overseers.—Appointment of Parochial Constables.—Transferring Ale-house Licenses.
,,	,,	30th	Special Sessions for the Highways.—Swearing in Parochial Constables.—And for granting Licenses required by the Gunpowder Acts.
,,	May	28th	Special Sessions for the Highways.—Hearing Appeals against Poor Rates.
,,	June	18th	Special Sessions for the Highways.—And for granting Licenses required by the Gunpowder Acts.
,,	July	16th	Transferring Ale-house Licenses.—Granting Licenses to deal in Game.
,,	August	13th	Special Sessions for the Highways.
,,	September	3rd	Hearing Appeals against Poor Rates.—Granting Ale-house Licenses.—And for granting Licenses required by the Gunpowder Acts.
Thursday,	,,	27th	Returning and verifying Jury Lists —Special Sessions for the Highways.
Monday,	October	22nd	Special Sessions for the Highways.—And for granting Licenses required by the Gunpowder Acts.
,,	November	19th	Transferring Ale-house Licenses.—Special Sessions for the Highways.
,,	December	17th	Hearing Appeals against Poor Rates.—Special Sessions for the Highways.—And for granting Licenses required by the Gunpowder Acts.

☞ NOTICE IS HEREBY GIVEN,—That Her Majesty's Justices of the Peace, acting in and for this Division, will hold a PETTY SESSIONS, at the POLICE COURT, in STURMINSTER NEWTON aforesaid, on EVERY MONDAY in the Year, at Eleven o'clock in the Morning, for proceedings under the Criminal Justice Act, (18 and 19 Victoria, c. 126,) and the Juvenile Offenders' Acts.

All Constables must be in attendance by Ten o'clock in the Forenoon, to make a due return of every Warrant and Summons delivered to them to execute, and on failure the penalties for neglect of duty will be strictly enforced.

No appeal against Poor Rates will be heard unless entered with the Clerk on the Saturday preceeding the Special Sessions for hearing the same, nor unless twenty-one day's previous notice shall have been given to the Assessment Committee, in pursuance of the 27 and 28 Victoria, c. 39.

R. R. HARVEY, Clerk.

QUARTER SESSIONS, DORCHESTER,	JANUARY	2nd,	1866.
Ditto - - - -	Ditto - - - APRIL - -	3rd,	,,
Ditto - - - -	Ditto - - - JUNE - -	3rd,	,,
Ditto - - - -	Ditto - - - OCTOBER	16th,	,,

W. TRITE, PRINTER, STURMINSTER NEWTON.

41. 1866 SPECIAL SESSIONS NOTICE
16″ × 8¾″. W. Trite, Sturminster Newton.
The juxtaposition of fat face letters, shadow letters and ordinary letters gives this otherwise legible notice a rather pepper-and-salt appearance. The word 'Sturminster' is set in 4-line Antique Ornamented, produced by H. W. Caslon in 1854.

The 'Special Sessions' notice (Fig. 41 above) is rather more sophisticated and far more effective than any comparable notice today.

In the election for President of the United States in 1836, Martin van Buren, a Democratic Republican, received 170 electoral votes, a clear-cut victory over his opponents, the Whigs. The vigorous vehemence of this broadsheet, of course, owes everything to the fat faced display types, which are in such violent contrast to the bookish types on the Aaron Burr bill.

DEMOCRATIC REPUBLICAN

TEMPLE of LIBERTY

REGULAR NOMINATION.

FOR PRESIDENT,
Martin Van Buren

FOR VICE PRESIDENT,
RICHARD M. JOHNSON.

FOR GOVERNOR,
William C. Bouck.

FOR LIEUTENANT GOVERNOR,
DANIEL S. DICKINSON.

FOR SENATOR,
JOHN B. SCOTT.

FOR CONGRESS,

| JOHN McKEON. | JAMES J. ROOSEVELT. |
| FERNANDO WOOD, | CHARLES G. FERRIS. |

FOR ASSEMBLY,

WILLIAM B. MACLAY,	SOLOMON TOWNSEND,	ABSALOM A. MILLER,
PAUL GROUT,	CORNELIUS H. BRYSON,	CONRAD SWACKHAMER,
NORMAN HICKOK,	GEORGE WEIR,	WILLIAM McMURRAY,
EDMUND J. PORTER,	DAVID R. FLOYD JONES,	ABRAHAM B. DAVIS,
	JOHN L. O'SULLIVAN.	

FOR SHERIFF,
MONMOUTH B. HART.

| For County Clerk, | For Coroner, |
| NATHANIEL JARVIS. | CORNELIUS B. ARCHER. |

SAMUEL L. JONES, | Secretaries.
JOHN TIMPSON, |

WILLIAM CHAMBERLAIN, *Chairman*

C. C. & E. CHILDS, Jr., PRINTERS, 50 VESEY STREET.

42. 1836 ELECTION NOTICE
36″ × 23″. C. C. & E. Childs Jr, Washington D.C.
This enormous bill is relieved of some of its black-
faced severity by the assembly of engravings at the
head. The 'Temple of Liberty' has a plaque at the
foot of the central figure, a Redskin, with 'Preserved
by Concord' inscribed on it.
New York Public Library

49

IPSWICH THEATRE,

Beg most respectfully to inform their Patrons and the public in general, that they have, at a very considerable outlay, completed their arrangements, and having also engaged some of the best Vocal Performers, in addition to their Establishment, intend opening their Theatre on the 31st inst., with the popular Comedy of

WHIG GRATITUDE :

OR,

A NEW WAY TO PAY OLD DEBTS.

In which the celebrated Performers will introduce the following New Songs, written entirely for the occasion, and of which the Managers have the entire Copyright.

BILLY BLOATER,

ALIAS,

THE MITY MAN.

"Did I not Soap the knowing ones."
"Could I refuse, when he *married my sisters.*"
"I'm badly off, for *Tin,* my friend."

SHUFFLING JOHNNY.

"Oh Give me, Give me, *Burton* Ale."
"I've Butter, Cheese, and Lard in Store."

Allen Broadbrim

"The Renegade."
"Can I not tell a *dirty tale.*"

JERRY SMOOTHFACE.

"I'd golden Hopes in Railway Shares, Alas! they now are gone."

HOOKEY GEORGE.

"We are all in the Hadleigh Line."

TOMMY DYE.

"My Mother would not give consent."

Messrs. Gaslight & Glyster

Will also introduce the pathetic Duet of
"Farewell to the Ward of St. Clement for ever."

To conclude with the celebrated Hornpipe called the

JACKALL's JIG

By LOTTO HENSERO

One of the Black Monkey tribe, who will be exhibited for a few nights only, as his Proprietor has determined to travel with him in a Puppet-show, with a collection of other animals of a similar nature.

The Managers beg also to state that they have another Play in Rehearsal, called

THE THIMBLE-RIG COMPANY.

The particulars of which will be printed in a few days.

Ipswich: Smith, Brown, Jones, and Robinson, Printers to the Establishment.

1958 ELECTION RETURNS TUESDAY NOVEMBER 4 9:00 PM — NYT CONCLUSION NBC TELEVISION NETWORK

43. *c.* 1845 ELECTION BILL
18¾″ × 6½″. Anon. Ipswich.
This mock playbill even has a bogus imprint.

T. Cook, Ipswich

44. 1958 ELECTION NOTICE
9″ × 5¼″. Richard Levine typ. Empire Typographers, New York.
These closely packed fat Egyptians, printed in blue, red and black are placed halfway up the folder which contains a notice of television advertising facilities on election night.

Election notices

NOTICE!
TO MUNICIPAL ELECTORS
OF THE
Township of Pickering

PUBLIC NOTICE is hereby given to the Electors of the Township of Pickering, that pursuant to statute in that behalf, I require the presence of said Electors at the

BROUGHAM HALL
FRIDAY, NOVEMBER 29, 1957

AT THE HOUR of 6:00 P.M. (Standard Time) for the purpose of nominating a Reeve, Deputy-Reeve and Five Councillors for the said Municipality for the year 1958 and for the nominating of School Area Nos. One and Two retiring trustees, and I further, give notice, that in case a poll is demanded and allowed in the manner prescribed by law, such polling place will be opened on SATURDAY, DECEMBER 7, 1957, in each of the sub-divisions in each of which a polling place will be opened and kept according to law, of which due notice will be given on Nomination Day. Every person interested is requested to take notice and govern themselves accordingly.

GIVEN UNDER MY HAND THIS 4TH DAY OF NOVEMBER, 1957.

L. T. JOHNSTON, Returning Officer

45. 1957 ELECTION NOTICE
18½″ × 16″. Pickering, Ont. This quite unselfconscious Canadian poster makes good use of mid-nineteenth century typefaces.

Fig. 43 shows an election bill in the form of a playbill. The practice of using such 'squibs' and other mock posters was fairly common in English electioneering.

The Canadian Municipal Electors Notice for the Township of Pickering in Ontario is a completely unconscious piece of pastiche-Victoriana, whereas the 'Kennedy for President' sticker shows a very modern use of nineteenth century grotesque typefaces.

KENNEDY
FOR PRESIDENT
CITIZENS FOR KENNEDY AND JOHNSON, 261 CONSTITUTION AVENUE, N.W., WASHINGTON, D.C.

46. 1960 ELECTION STICKER
3⅞″ × 8½″. Anon. Washington D.C.
Printed in red and dark blue and set in grotesques.

Rewards and Wanted notices

Two Guineas Bounty

In Addition to His MAJESTY's

Will be given immediately by the

Corporation of BRIDGNORTH

To the Firſt Fifteen *VOLUNTEERS*, who ſhall

Enter with

LIEUTENANT WILL^M ROSS, [2]

At his Rendezvous the *TUMBLING SAILORS*, for

the Service of the

Royal Navy.

Bridgnorth March 10th· 1795·

47. 1795 TWO GUINEAS BOUNTY
5″×6½″. Anon. Bridgnorth.
Recruiting notice for the Royal Navy during the
Napoleonic Wars. The provincial printer still
retains the long 's'.

WANTED,

FOR

A FAMILY IN THE COUNTRY,

A SENSIBLE WELL EDUCATED

Steady Woman,

Qualified to Superintend a Family,

OF STRICT MORALS, HEALTHY, AND GOOD HUMOURED,

BUT ABOVE CORRUPTION,

AND

A THOROUGH GOOD COOK.

BOTH AS TO

MEAT, PASTRY, PRESERVES, &c.

SHE will have a proper assistant in the kitchen, and every
reasonable encouragement given to her from the Family, according to her qualifications and integrity.

☞ Apply to Mrs. Howe, White-Lion St. Asaph; Mrs.
Salusbury, at the Bull Inn, Denbigh; Mrs. Turner, Grocer, in
Ruthin; and Mrs. Harrison, in Queen Street, Chester.

CHESTER, PRINTED BY J. MONK.

48. *c.* 1812 WANTED: STEADY WOMAN
6⅜″×5″. J. Monk, Chester.
This bookish notice, printed on a green paper uses
two modest little display letters. 'WANTED' is set in
2-line English Ornamented (now known as Fry's
Ornamented No. 2); and a line of open capitals is
used for 'A THOROUGH GOOD COOK'.

£200. Reward

WHEREAS

The *WAREHOUSE of Mr. William Radcliffe,*
COTTON MANUFACTURER,
ADJOINING TO HIS DWELLING-HOUSE IN THE HIGHER HILLGATE,
STOCKPORT, IN THE COUNTY OF CHESTER,

Was, between the Hours of **2** and **3** in the Morning
of FRIDAY the **20**th of March, instant,

Wilfully, maliciously, & feloniously

Set on Fire,

By some wicked and desperate Incendiaries, who
broke the Windows thereof, and threw in five Flam-
beaux or Torches, composed of Pitch, Tar, Oakum,
and Spirits of Turpentine; and some Waste Cops of
Cotton-weft, which had been dipped in similar
Spirits.
   The Villains left on the Outside of the said Warehouse, three Clubs or large
Sticks of a peculiar Sort, which may be the future Means of a Discovery.

A Reward of **£200.** will be paid to the Person
who may give such Information as may lead to the
Discovery and Conviction of the Principals con-
cerned in this diabolical Crime, upon Application to

J. LLOYD, *Solicitor.*

Stockport, March 21st, 1812.

LOMAX, PRINTER.

49. 1812 £200 REWARD
15″ × 12¼″. Lomax, Stockport.
An early example of a bill set throughout in Thorne's
fat faces.

Public Record Office

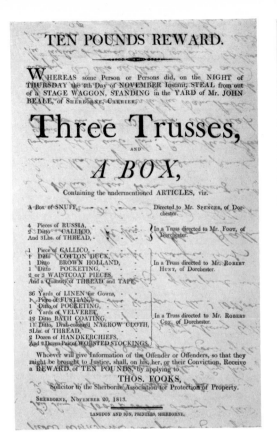

3 Guineas
REWARD.
WHEREAS
A SHEEP

Of **Mr. Hancock,** of *Ford*, was in the night between the 14th and 15th instant, **STOLEN** from *Horridge Down*, in the parish of *Milverton*. The Person or Persons who shall give such information, as may be the means of apprehending and bringing the Offender or Offenders to Trial and Conviction, will receive the above Reward. **PHILIP HANCOCK.**

FORD, near *Wiveliscombe*, 16th October 1829.

J. BAKER, PRINTER, WIVELISCOMBE.

50. 1813 TEN POUNDS REWARD
10″ × 6″. Langdon and Son, Sherborne.
This notice makes no concession to the display types already in use in London. The layout is reminiscent of a playbill or a programme of the time. 'Three Trusses' and 'A BOX' are set in Fry's Baskerville.

51. 1829 THREE GUINEAS REWARD
7″ × 8½″. J. Baker, Wiveliscombe.
Display typefaces are in full use here, headed by Thorowgood's fine Fat Face Italic.

Rewards and Wanted Notices

Presumably people's wants and losses have been advertised by one means or another since people could read or write. Printed notices shown here range from bribes to join the Royal Navy to rewards for losses of goods, chattels and livestock. Jobs are offered: for instance, a lady wants 'A thorough good cook of strict morals but above corruption'; (one wonders what inspired this *cri de coeur*). The 'Wanteds' are typographically not so vehement as the offers of rewards. Figs. 47 and 51 show the fantastic difference that thirty odd years made to the jobbing printer. The 'Two Guineas Bounty' is a simple and effective little bill in contrast to Fig. 51, where '3 Guineas' is set in Thorowgood's Fat Face Italic and the words 'A SHEEP' are in a very heavy Egyptian, coming probably from Vincent Figgins's foundry. This bill is a brilliant eye-catcher. Of even greater interest are Figures 48 and 49, both printed in 1812, but in completely different typographic styles. The charm of Fry's lozenge-decorated open capitals, used for the word 'WANTED' in the 'Steady Woman' notice, can hardly stand up to the competition of the fat face types used for '£200 REWARD' in the neighbouring bill.

52. 1861 REWARD NOTICE
12¾″ × 8¾″. Journal and Republican Steam-Press Print, Lowville N.Y.
A singularly unattractive condensed Egyptian is used for the heading of this bill. The text is set in a mixture of Clarendon and a semi-fat face, with a curious mixture of roman and italic for the words 'Road Company, with coupons etc'.

New York Public Library

$500 REWARD !
Bank Robbery !

The **BANK OF LOWVILLE** was entered by Burglars, on Saturday or Sunday night, and about $6,000 in Cash taken, as follows :

About $2400 in Gold. $800 in Silver, American Quarters and Halves, about $50 of which was Old Coin.

$1200 in mixed N. Y. State Money. $60 New England. $60 U. S. demand Treasury Notes.   20 in 5s, 3s and 1s on Bank of the People, Lowville, probably nearly all now out on that Bank.

$1500 in bills on the Bank of Lowville, about $600 of which was considerably torn or mutilated, and of which the following amounts were put up in sealed packages, and directed as follows ;

$374,   ROBERT HARVEY,   Boonville.
$250,   OWEN J. OWENS,   Turin.
$80   do   Boonville.

Also five Bonds of $1000 each, issued by the Sackets Harbor and Saratoga Rail Road Company, *with Coupons from 1857,* numbered 182, 196 197, 564 *and* 565.

☞ *All persons are forbid from negotiating the above Bonds.* Two Locks were picked--one Day & Newell's best--and a Safe cut Open.

☞ A REWARD of $500 will be given for the arrest of the Burglars and recovery of the property.
Lowville, N. Y., October 14, 1861.

J. L. Leonard,
President of the Bank of Lowville.

JOURNAL & REPUBLICAN STEAM-PRESS PRINT, LOWVILLE, N. Y.

53

Police notices

EXHIBITION
OF
INDUSTRY OF ALL NATIONS.

REGULATIONS
To be observed by Visitors to prevent Obstructions in the Park and Thoroughfares adjacent.

East Side.
Visitors Walking.

This Entrance will be reserved for the Visitors walking there, along the open Ground between the Ride and Carriage Road.

A broad Footway will be kept across the road within the Park, near Apsley-House Gates, by which persons entering the Park may cross to the Open Ground, leading to the Exhibition. They can return the same way on leaving the Exhibition.

Visitors walking may likewise enter by the other Entrances; but this one only will be Reserved exclusively for them without Interruption by Carriages.

South Side.
Carriages Setting Down.

Carriages going to this Entrance are to enter the Park by the New Gate, near Hyde Park Corner, or by Albert Gate, and form in line on the right-hand side of the road.

After setting down, if they are to wait, they will be placed by the Police upon the Open Ground to the West of the Exhibition between the Ride and Carriage Road, and are to remain there until called to take up. If they are not to wait they are to go away through the Kensington Gate or by the Road within the Park, as directed by the Police, and out of the Park at Albert Gate, or the new Gate near Hyde Park Corner.

Carriages Taking Up.

Carriages will be allowed by the Police to take up at the doors on the South Side, when it can be done so as not to interfere with the line of Carriages setting down, and they are to go away along the Road inside the Park, and out of the Park at Albert Gate, or the New Gate, near Hyde Park Corner.

West Side.
Carriages Setting Down.

Carriages going to this Entrance are to enter the Park at the Kensington Gate, and go along the Carriage Road upon the Ride; or they may enter the Park by the New Gates near Hyde Park Corner, or by Albert Gate, and drive along the Road within the Park to Kensington Gate, and there turn down the road upon the Ride to this Entrance. After setting down, if they are to wait, they will be placed by the Police upon the open ground to the West of the Exhibition between the Ride and Carriage Road, and are to remain there until called to take up. If they are not to wait they are to go away returning along the same Road as they came.

Carriages Taking Up.

Carriages will draw up as directed by the Police, at the Doors on the West Side, and go away along the Road up the Ride and out of the Park at Kensington Gate, or turning down the road within the Park towards Hyde Park Corner, go out of the Park at Albert Gate, or the New Gate near Hyde Park Corner.

North Side.
There are no Entrances for Visitors on this Side.

Carriages may draw up as directed by the Police, along the Road upon the Ride to the doors upon the North Side, and having taken up their Company go away, returning along the same Road and out of the Park at Kensington Gate, or turning there down the Road within the Park towards Hyde Park Corner, and go out of the Park at Albert Gate, or the New Gate near Hyde Park Corner.

If the line of Carriages going to the Exhibition should extend beyond the Gates by which they are to enter the Park, they will fall into line in the Streets approaching the Gates as directed by the Police. No Carriages can be allowed to stop in Piccadilly near the Gates entering Hyde Park or Constitution Hill Gate; across the entrance to a street, or at any place where an obstruction of the thoroughfare may be caused.

No persons can be allowed to remain at the doors of the Exhibition, or on the approaches to them. Servants belonging to the Carriages of Visitors are to remain in the places pointed out by the Police, or with their Carriages.

The Police will assist, as far as may be in their power, in calling up the Carriages, and in enabling persons to get to their Carriages where waiting.

Richard Mayne,
Commissioner of the Police of the Metropolis.

Whitehall Place, *April 26th, 1851.*

BY AUTHORITY—GOVERNMENT PRINTING OFFICE, LANGLEY-STREET, LONG ACRE.—1050. APRIL, 1851.

53. 1851 POLICE NOTICE
21″ × 15″. Government Printing Office, Long Acre, London.
Printed in black with a bold condensed Clarendon for 'Exhibition' and, for the subheadings, a combination of Thorne's Fat Face Italic and a heavy Egyptian, which is Caslon and Catherwood's 4-line pica Antique.

New Scotland Yard

CAUTION.

Whereas, it is understood that the Practice of

SELLING BEER

IN PRIVATE HOUSES,

Without a Licence, prevails to a considerable extent in this neighbourhood.

Now, I GIVE NOTICE and WARNING, that if the Occupier of any House erected on the Property of the late EDMUND WILLIAMS, Esq., of Maesruddud, be detected in the above illegal Practice, he will not only be proceeded against for the Penalty, but measures will be taken to forfeit the Lease under which the Premises may be held.

Dated this 8th October, 1851,

A. WADDINGTON,

SOLICITOR TO THE ESTATE.

H. HUGHES, PRINTER, BOOKBINDER, AND STATIONER, PONTYPOOL.

54. 1851 WARNING AGAINST SELLING BEER
10½″ × 8″. H. Hughes, Pontypool.
Bold typography with heavy sans serif and elongated fat faces, producing an ominously funereal appearance. The huge 'Caution' is from wood letter, but 'Selling Beer' is set in metal type.

Police notices

The police notices have a tendency to use heavy condensed letters. The 1851 Exhibition poster has a particularly fine Clarendon for the top line. This is a handsome bill. The printer certainly had no qualms about the readability of a twenty-five word line.

The vigorousness of the 'Caution Selling Beer' notice makes most of our contemporary notices look mighty feeble. It is made particularly effective by the contrast between the heavy sans serif wood letter, the elongated fat face used for 'Selling Beer' and the heavy Egyptian.

POLICE NOTICE.

STREET CROSSING SIGNALS.
BRIDGE STREET, NEW PALACE YARD.

CAUTION.   **STOP.**

The Semaphore Arms lowered, and by Night with a Green Light.

The Semaphore Arms extended, and by Night with a Red Light.

By the Signal "CAUTION," all persons in charge of Vehicles and Horses are warned to pass over the Crossing with care, and due regard to the safety of Foot Passengers.

The Signal "STOP," will only be displayed when it is necessary that Vehicles and Horses shall be actually stopped on each side of the Crossing, to allow the passage of Persons on Foot; notice being thus given to all persons in charge of Vehicles and Horses to stop clear of the Crossing.

RICHARD MAYNE,
Commissioner of Police of the Metropolis.

---

55. 1868 POLICE NOTICE
22″×11″. Government Printing Office, Long Acre, London.
Printed in black. The titling is a combination of condensed sans and Egyptian and a fat face. The body of the text is set in a debased and attenuated Egyptian.

New Scotland Yard

POLICE NOTICE

FIREWORKS

DISCHARGE IN STREETS, SALE TO CHILDREN, ETC.

The attention of the Public is called to the fact that it is an offence:—

(1) To let off fireworks in any thoroughfare or public place, or within 50 feet of the centre of any carriageway.

(2) To hawk or sell fireworks in the streets.

(3) To make bonfires in any thoroughfare or public place.

Shopkeepers and others are further warned that fireworks may not be sold to any child apparently under the age of 13.

The Police have instructions to enforce strictly the provisions of the Metropolitan Police Act and other Acts dealing with these matters.

Metropolitan Police Office,   **J. SIMPSON,**
New Scotland Yard, S.W.1.   *Commissioner of Police of the Metropolis*

---

56. 1960 POLICE NOTICE
13½″×8¼″. The Receiver, Metropolitan Police District, S.W.1.
Modern police notice with text set in a legible but undistinguished roman typeface.

New Scotland Yard

Police notices

The modern English and American police notices are faint echoes of the past. Half-tone photographs and finger prints are real innovations that may help to catch the criminals but do not add much to the typographic qualities of these notices.

PLEASE POST   Post Office Department   **PLEASE POST**
Office of the Inspector in Charge
Chicago 7, Ill.

(Taken in 1957)   Case No. 20414-F
July 7, 1960

WANTED
FOR MAIL FRAUD
WILLIAM G. DUDLEY

(No known aliases)

William G. Dudley   White; age 57; height 6′; weight 200 lbs.

The United States Marshal at Chicago, Illinois holds a warrant for the arrest of William G. Dudley who is wanted for using the mails in the execution of a scheme to defraud in the operation of the Trans-Continental Clearing House, a business brokerage service. Dudley and 18 co-defendants were indicted by a Federal Grand Jury at Chicago, Illinois, March 15, 1960.

Dudley was last known to be residing some place in Mexico and there is reason to believe that he makes secret trips to the United States.

If this man is seen any place within the territorial boundaries of the United States, please cause his immediate arrest and notify the undersigned, or the nearest Postal Inspector by telephone or telegraph collect.

Postal Inspector in Charge
Chicago 7, Illinois
Telephone HArrison 7-4820
Ext. 801

---

57. 1960 POLICE NOTICE
8″ × 8″. Post Office Department, Chicago, Illinois.
Text set in Linotype Modern and heading in a mixture of grotesques, and Caslon Titling for 'Wanted'. 'Post Office Department' with due respect for tradition, is set in a black letter.

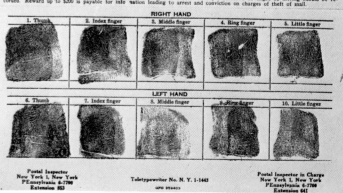

PLEASE POST   POST OFFICE DEPARTMENT   Fingerprint Classification
INSPECTION SERVICE
Case 44975-SD   OFFICE OF INSPECTOR IN CHARGE   15   O   31   W   100   14
January 6, 1961   New York 1, New York   I   29   W   OOI
F.B.I. No. 3 648 851

WANTED
FOR MAIL THEFT
MILTON EUGENE JOHNSON

DESCRIPTION: Negro; age 33, born Dec. 25, 1926, at Battle Creek, Mich.; height 6′; weight 200 lbs.; black hair; brown eyes; stocky build. (He may now have a mustache.) He was a heavyweight amateur boxer in Detroit and Battle Creek, Mich.
OCCUPATION: Taxi driver.
OFFENSE: Theft of mail on December 23, 1958, while he was officially employed at the General Post Office, New York 1, N.Y., during the 1958 Christmas period.

Photograph taken in 1952   Photograph taken in 1957

The United States Marshal for the Southern District of New York holds a warrant for the arrest of this offender. Johnson may seek employment as a taxi driver, bodyguard, or chauffeur. If he is located, please cause his immediate arrest and notify the nearest postal inspector or the undersigned by telephone, telegraph, or teletypewriter COLLECT. If Johnson is recognized and you are unable to cause his arrest, the license number and description of any automobile he might be driving should be recorded. Reward up to $200 is payable for information leading to arrest and conviction on charges of theft of mail.

RIGHT HAND

| 1. Thumb | 2. Index finger | 3. Middle finger | 4. Ring finger | 5. Little finger |

LEFT HAND

| 6. Thumb | 7. Index finger | 8. Middle finger | 9. Ring finger | 10. Little finger |

Postal Inspector   Teletypewriter No. N.Y. 1-1445   Postal Inspector in Charge
New York 1, New York   New York 1, New York
PEnnsylvania 6-7700   PEnnsylvania 6-7700
Extension 853   GPO 952403   Extension 641

---

58. 1961 POLICE NOTICE
8″ × 8″. Post Office Department, New York.
Modern police notice with heading in a condensed grotesque and text set in Old Style.

Almanacks

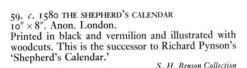

The first printed almanack was compiled and
produced between 1450 and 1461. The first
almanack actually printed in England was the
'Kalendar of Shepardes' which was translated
from the French and printed by Richard Pynson
in 1497. 'The Shepheards Kalender' shown here
has some very spirited woodcuts of the signs of
the zodiac, which occur through Francis Moore's
and most of the other almanacks to this day, for
almanacks quickly became established in content
and in typographic style. They were usually
printed in black and vermilion.

The most famous of the Stationers' Company's
almanacks was Francis Moore's *Vox Stellarum*,
which first appeared in 1697. The success of
Moore's Almanack rested largely on his forecasts
for each day of the following year. It has continued until the present day, widely known as
'Old Moore's Almanack'.

57

Almanacks

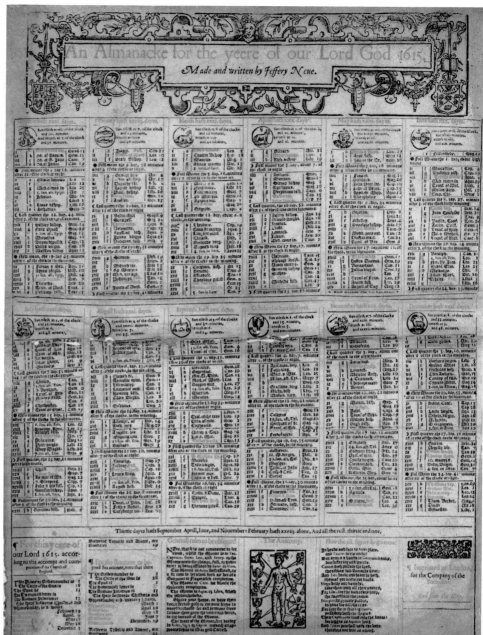

61. 1615 JEFFERY NEVE'S ALMANACK
16¼″ × 12″. Anon. London.
Printed in black and red, with zodiac diagram of a
man's body.

The two large almanacks shown here (Figs. 61 and 62), though over one hundred and fifty years apart, are very similar in appearance. Both divide up the months into two groups of six columns and both use a vermilion printing for a second colour and both have a diagram of the human figure, marked out with the signs of the zodiac. From the time of Queen Elizabeth I, the Stationers Company assumed the sole right to print and publish almanacks. This monopoly was challenged from time to time.

The earliest almanack printed in the United States appeared at Philadelphia in 1687. This was followed by *Poor Richard's Almanack*, published between 1732 and 1757 by Benjamin Franklin, under the pseudonym of Richard Saunders. *Poor Richard's Almanack* had a wide popularity and may have inspired the *American Almanack and Repository of Useful Knowledge*. This was produced by a man called Thomas, who lived at Dedham, Mass. His almanack was published in Boston between 1828 and 1861.

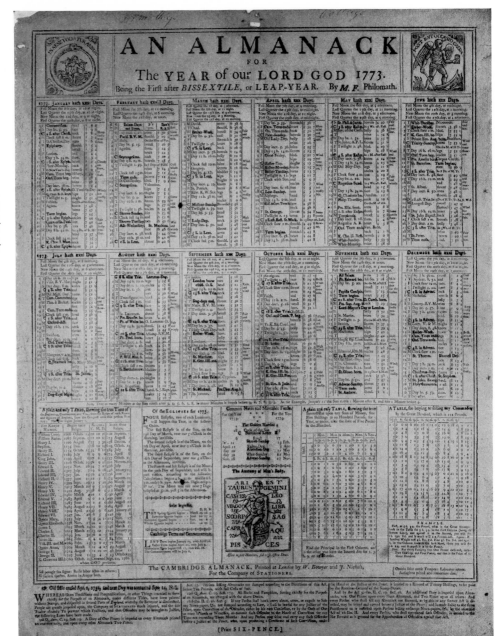

62. 1773 THE CAMBRIDGE ALMANACK
19½″ × 15″. W. Bowyer and J. Nichols, London.
Printed in black and vermilion. The form of almanack shown here remained in use for a very long
time. The top half contains the months, the bottom
half miscellaneous information about dates of
movable feasts, eclipses, rates of interest and a diagram showing the anatomy of the body, with signs of
the zodiac. Price sixpence.

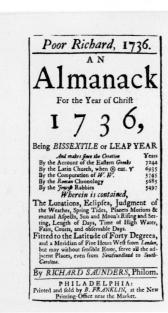

63. 1736 POOR RICHARD'S ALMANACK
5½″ × 2⅞″. B. Franklin, Philadelphia.
Title page and spread showing figure marked with
the signs of the zodiac.

New York Public Library

The fatal weapon was a blazing fpoke,
Which from the wheels of Sol's bright car he broke.
Stay, ftay thy hand, O Ariel! fpare the car;
We yield thee all the honors of the air.
Can fuch ftrong paffions fet thy breaft on flame,
And doft thou envy brave Pilater's name?
All—all is vain, by pow'rful vengeance mov'd,
Ariel regard's not how Rofiere was lov'd.

M	W	Remarkable Days, &c.	☉r.	☉f.	☽p.	Afpects, &c.
1	3	*lightning,*	4 37	7 23	♊12	
2	4	*heavy rain,*	4 37	7 23	27	
3	5		4 37	7 23	♋12	☿ great. elong.
4	6	Independence, 76.	4 38	7 22	27	
5	7	{7th after Trinity,	4 38	7 22	♌12	*Infult not*
6	F	{Bat. Green Spring, 81	4 38	7 22	27	
7	2		4 39	7 21	♍12	*another*
8	3	Can. Gwih's Ifl. 76.	4 39	7 21	28	
9	4	*clear,*	4 39	7 21	♎10	*for his want*
10	5		4 40	7 20	24	
11	6	*and very warm,*	4 40	7 20	♏ 7	*of a*
12	7		4 41	7 19	19	
13	F	8th after Trinity.	4 41	7 19	♐ 2	*talent*
14	2		4 42	7 18	14	
15	3	Days decreafe 16m.	4 43	7 17	26	*you poffefs :*
16	4	Stony Point taken, 79.	4 43	7 17	♑ 8	
17	5		4 44	7 16	20	♀ Stationary.
18	6	*rain,*	4 45	7 15	♒ 1	
19	7		4 46	7 14	13	
20	F	9th after Trinity.	4 46	7 14	25	☿ Stationary.
21	2	*then hot*	4 47	7 13	♓ 7	☉ enters ♌
22	3	*fultry weather,*	4 48	7 12	19	
23	4		4 48	7 12	♈ 1	
24	5	*more moderate,*	4 49	7 11	14	*he may have*
25	6	St. James's.	4 50	7 10	16	
26	7		4 51	7 9	♉ 9	*others,*
27	F	10th after Trinity.	4 52	7 8	23	
28	2	*clear*	4 53	7 7	♊ 7	*which you*
29	3	Day 14h. 12m.	4 54	7 6	21	
30	4		4 55	7 5	♋ 6	*want.*
31	5	*and pleafant.*	4 56	7 4	21	

Changes of the Moon.		Age of the Moon.								
		T.	28	W.	7	T.	15	F.	23	
		W.	29	T.	8	F.	16	S.	24	
D. H. M.		T.	1	F.	9	S.	17	27 25		
New ●	3 11 15 Morning.	F.	2	S.	10	20 18	13	M.	26	
Firft ☽	10 2 33 Morning.	S.	3	13 11	M.	19	T.	27		
Full ○	18 1 34 Morning.	6 4	M.	12	T.	20	W.	28		
Laft ☾	26 1 10 Morning.	M.	5	T.	13	W.	21	T.	29	
		T.	6	W.	14	T.	22			

M	☽ rife	☽ fou	T	
1	2 M 17	9 M 54	12	more admired their probity. He applaud-
2	3 18	10 56	1	ed their generous conduct. Perrin, faid he,
3	fets	11 59	2	cherifh thefe fentiments as long as you live.
4	8 E 14	1 E 2	3	The confcioufnefs of them will make you
5	8 54	2 1	4	happy; and they will draw down, from
6	9 33	2 55	5	Providence, a bleffing on your endeavours.
7	9 58	3 45	5	We fhall find the owner of this money; he
8	10 28	4 34	6	will recompenfe your integrity: to his re-
9	10 58	5 23	7	ward I will add a part of the money I have
10	11 30	6 12	8	faved: Lucetta fhall be yours; I will take
11	Morn	7 0	9	upon me to obtain her father's confent;
12	0 7	7 50	9	you are worthy of each other. If the mo-
13	0 45	8 40	10	ney, which you have depofited with me, is
14	1 30	9 30	11	not reclaimed, it belongs to the poor; you
15	2 18	10 19	12	are poor; in reftoring it to you, I fhall
16	3 7	11 8	12	think that I act in obedience to Provi-
17	4 4	11 54	1	dence, who, by your finding it, and lodg-
18	rifes	12 39	2	ing it with me, has already marked you as
19	7 E 52	0 M 39	3	an object of his favour.
20	8 25	1 23	3	The lovers retired, fatisfied with having
21	8 42	2 5	4	done their duty, and enlivened with the
22	9 8	2 45	5	hope of being yet united. The bag was
23	9 34	3 25	5	proclaimed in the rector's parifh: adver-
24	10 5	4 11	6	tifements of it were pofted up at Vitré,
25	10 35	4 57	7	and all the neighbouring villages. It was
26	11 13	5 46	8	claimed by many avaricious, and felfifh,
27	11 59	6 37	9	perfons; but none of them gave an accu-
28	Morn	7 35	10	rate account of the fum, the fpecie, and the
29	0 57	8 35	11	bag which contained it.
30	2 0	9 37	12	In the mean time the rector did not for-
31	3 1	10 39	1	get that he had promifed to efpoufe Per-
				rin's intereft. He took a little farm for

+ B

64. 1788 THE BALLOON ALMANACK
6½″ × 3½″. F. Bailey, J. Steele and J. Bailey, Philadelphia, Penn.
This almanack is set in a transitional typeface and admirably arranged in the form of a booklet, with woodcut frontispiece.
Historical Society of Pennsylvania

Almanacks

The Balloon Almanac of 1788 follows the conventional page layout, but has a spirited wood engraving on the cover. The *Town and Country Almanack* is eighteenth century in character, but for the shadow numerals used for '1821'. The line beginning 'From creation, . . .' is set in Binny and Ronaldson's pica Roman No. 1, marketed today by American Type Founders under the name of Oxford. This, incidentally, is the typeface in which D. B. Updike's *Printing Types* is set.

In the nineteenth century, calendars and almanacks were often used for trade purposes, sometimes printed on the back of trade cards. This practice continues to this day.

THE
BALLOON
ALMANAC,

For the Year of our LORD, 1788.

BISSEXTILE, or LEAP YEAR.

PENNSYLVANIA

Printed by F. BAILEY, J. STEELE, and J. BAILEY; and
sold by F. Bailey, *Philadelphia*, J. Bailey, *Lancaster*,
and J. Steele, at the Printing Office, *Octorara*.

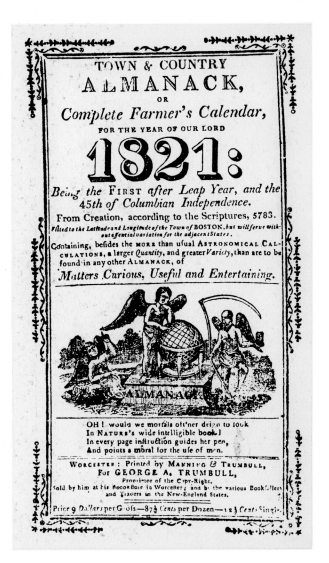

TOWN & COUNTRY
ALMANACK,
OR
Complete Farmer's Calendar,
FOR THE YEAR OF OUR LORD
1821:
Being the FIRST *after Leap Year, and the*
45th *of Columbian Independence.*
From Creation, according to the Scriptures, 5783.
Fitted to the Latitude and Longitude of the Town of BOSTON, but will serve without essential variation for the adjacent States.
Containing, besides the MORE than usual ASTRONOMICAL CAL-
CULATIONS, a larger *Quantity,* and greater *Variety,* than are to be
found in any other ALMANACK, of
Matters Curious, Useful and Entertaining.

OH! would we mortals oft'ner deign to look
In NATURE's wide intelligible book!
In every page instruction guides her pen,
And points a moral for the use of men.

WORCESTER: Printed by MANNING & TRUMBULL,
For GEORGE A. TRUMBULL,
Proprietor of the Copy-Right.
Sold by him at his Bookstore in Worcester; and by the various Booksellers
and Traders in the New-England States.

Price 9 Dollars per Gross—87½ Cents per Dozen—12¾ Cents Single.

65. 1788 THE BALLOON ALMANACK
Cover from the same almanack shown in Fig. 64.

66. 1821 ALMANACK.
6¼″ × 3½″. Manning and Trumbull, Worcester,
Massachusetts.
This title page shows a curious mixture of eighteenth
century decoration, in borders and rules and the
Thorne Shaded numerals for 1821. The pica roman
used for 'From Creation, etc' is from Binny and
Ronaldson's Foundry. This typeface, under the name
of Oxford, is issued by American Type Founders.

New York Public Library

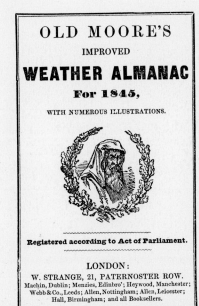

OLD MOORE'S
IMPROVED
WEATHER ALMANAC
For 1845,
WITH NUMEROUS ILLUSTRATIONS.

Registered according to Act of Parliament.

LONDON:
W. STRANGE, 21, PATERNOSTER ROW.
Machin, Dublin; Menzies, Edinbro'; Heywood, Manchester;
Webb & Co., Leeds; Allen, Nottingham; Allen, Leicester;
Hall, Birmingham; and all Booksellers.

67. 1845 OLD MOORE'S ALMANACK
4″ × 2½″ (single page). R. Allen, Nottingham.
Cover and spread. This is a 32-page
booklet, which in addition to the months
each having one page, illustrated by
small cuts, contains information on
window taxes, jokes, customs and
anniversaries, and also several pages of
advertisements for patent medicines.
Typographically not very adventurous
though an agreeable small bold Egyptian
is used for the headings.

MARCH, 31 DAYS.	
DESCRIPTION OF THE MONTH.—The month was dedicated by Romulus to Mars, from whom it was called March. In Saxon it was called Rethe or Rough monat; and Lenet or Length monat, from the lengthening of the days. Thence the name of Lent.	

1	S	St. David	WEATHER.—1 changeable; 2 wind; 3 fair; 4 frost; 5 cold; 6 and 7 fair; 8 stormy; 9 wind; 10 changeable; 11 frost; 12 fair; 13 rain; 14 fair; 15 wind; 16 frost; 17 stormy; 18 and 19 fair; 20 sleet; 21 stormy; 22 fair; 23 rain; 24 to 27 fair; 28 rain; 29 changeable; 30 and 31 fair.
2	Su	4 SUND. IN LENT.	
3	M	Otway born, 1651	
4	Tu	Lord Somers b. 1650	
5	W	Bat. of Berne, 1798	
6	TH	Bat. of Verona, 1799	
7	F	New M. 6h36m. p.m	
8	S	[Perpetua. M. M.	
9	Su	5 SUND. IN LENT	The cost of a hogshead of tobacco of 1200 lbs. varies from £14. to £25., the duty on which is £198.
10	M	J. Pinkerton d. 1825	
11	Tu	Sir B. West d. 1820	
12	W	Gregory	
13	TH	Nap. outl. 1815	
14	F	Camb. Term ends	In Norway there are 72,624 full owners of land, to 30,586 farmers, and 42,974 labourers. In France there are 10,296,682 owners. In Ireland there are only 40,000.
15	S	M.1st q. 1h52m. p.m	
16	Su	PALM SUNDAY	
17	M	St. Patrick	
18	Tu	Edward	
19	W	Newton died, 1726	The editor of an American paper requests those of his subscribers who never intend to pay, to give him notice as soon as possible.
20	TH	Young Nap. b. 1811	
21	F	Benedict. Good Fri.	
22	S	Goethe d. 1832	
23	Su	EAST. SUN. Full M.	
24	M	[8h 18m. a.m.	A BEAUTI-FUL IMAGE.—A deaf and dumb person being asked to give his ideas of forgiveness, took a pencil and wrote—"It is the sweetness which flowers yield when trampled upon."
25	Tu	Annunc. Lady Day	
26	W	P. Geo. Cam. b. 1819	
27	TH	Pe. of Amiens, 1802	
28	F	Gunpowd. intr. 1380	
29	S	Swedenberg d. 1772	
30	Su	Low SUND. Moon's	
31	M	[last qu. 5h0m. a.m	

APRIL, 30 DAYS.	
DESCRIPTION OF THE MONTH.—This month was under the auspices of Venus, among the Romans; hence it was frequently named Mensis Veneris; but its popular name was Aprilis. By the Anglo Saxons it was entitled Oster-monst, or "Easter month," probably from the frequency of the eastern winds.	

1	Tu	Qr. Sess. this week	WEATHER.—1 changeable; 2 showery; 3 changeable; 4 to 7 fair; 8 and 9 rain; 10 fair; 11 showery; 12 changeable; 13 wind; 14 & 15 fair; 16 showery; 17 and 18 fair; 19 changeable; 20 wind; 21 chang.; 22 fair; 23 cha.; 24 and 25 fair; 26 snow; 27 & 28 fair; 29 cha.; 30 snow.
2	W	Oxf. & Camb. T. beg.	
3	TH	Richard	
4	F	Ambrose	
5	S	John Stow d. 1605	
6	Su	2 SUN. AFT. EASTER	
7	M	[New M. 7h40m. a.m	
8	Tu	Mon. 1st co. b.c. 1069	
9	W	Lord Bacon d. 1626	GOOD AD-VICE.—"Resolve not to be poor. Whatever you have spend less. Poverty is a great enemy to human happiness: it certainly destroys liberty, and makes some virtues impracticable, and others extremely difficult."
10	TH	Cath. Rel. B. p.1829	
11	F	Canning born, 1770	
12	S	Rodney's Vic. 1782	
13	Su	3 SUN. AFT. EAST.	
14	M	M.1st q. 9h23m. a.m	
15	Tu	Mutin. at Spith. 1797	
16	W	Bat. of Cullod. 1746	
17	TH	Earthq. Calab. 1783	COMPARISON.—Why is a young lady of the present day like a careful housewife?—Because her waist is as little as she can make it.
18	F	Jud. Jeffries d. 1689	
19	S	Byron died, 1824	
20	Su	4 SUN. AFT. EAST.	
21	M	Full M. 7h12m. p.m	
22	Tu	R. Cromw. dep. 1659	
23	W	St. George	When you "pop the question" to a lady, do it with a kind of laugh, as if you were joking. If she accepts you, very well; if she does not, you can say "you were only in fun."
24	TH	Defoe died, 1731	
25	F	St. Mark. Duchess	
26	S	of Gloucest. b.1776	
27	Su	ROGATION SUNDAY	
28	M	M.l.qu. 11h19m. a.m	
29	Tu	Cons. of Portug. 1826	
30	W	Lon. Univ. com. 1827	

7

68. 1885 CALENDAR
11″ × 8¼″. Norris and Cokayne, Nottingham.
A trade calender published by the printers and
printed in six colours. Oriental influences are shown
by the title and design as a whole.

The *Norris and Cokayne Kalendar* for 1885, above, is a hotch-potch of Oriental motifs and roman typefaces aping Chinese characters. The asymmetry of this design foreshadows *l'Art Nouveau*, yet the calendarium itself is a model of clarity, set in a condensed Ionic type.

The two almanacks at the head of the opposite page, though only four years apart, show a widely differing approach. *Lambert's Family Almanack* follows the playbill tradition of symmetry and the widest possible use of types. *Goodalls Household Almanac* spurns the use of type, and lets the trade wood engraver have full rein, with what dire results can be only too clearly seen.

The Housewives' Almanack, printed in the 1920's is an imitation of the work of earlier times. It was produced at a time of a short-lived Romantic revival, inspired by such artists as Gordon Craig and C. Lovat Fraser. Francis Moore's tradition still lingers on in the modern 'Old Moore' (Fig. 73). The clogged typographic style of the cover has degenerated since earlier times. It is set in a mixture of Ultra Bodoni (the fat face), two grotesques, and Cloister Black (a somewhat feeble black letter). The Benham calendar uses Will Carter's typeface, Klang. The colourful John Roberts Press calendar uses grotesques and flat tint blocks with success (Figs. 72 and 74).

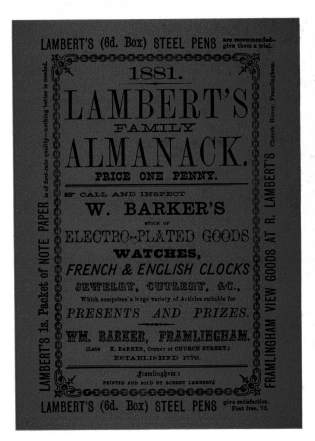

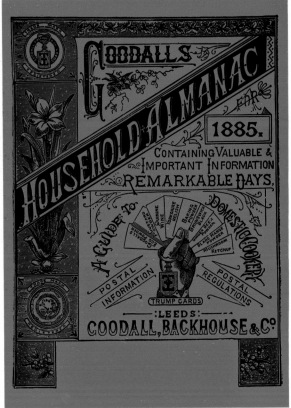

69. 1881 LAMBERT'S FAMILY ALMANACK
6¾" × 4¼". R. Lambert, Framlingham.
Printed in black on a lavender paper. The capitals used for the title show the degree of attenuation that the 'modern' face had reached by the 1880's. However, this almanack cover still has an unsophisticated richness, with its variety of typefaces.

70. 1885 GOODALLS HOUSEHOLD ALMANACK
5⅛" × 4⅛" (single page). Anon.
An elaborately wood engraved cover, showing a number of typographic innovations, including the sloped title and subhead – 'A guide to Domestic Cookery' drawn on a curve in the manner of the 'artistic' typography of the time. In the calendar pages, patent medicine advertising has crept in with such statements as 'Thousands snatched from the grave by taking . . .'; an appropriate sentiment for anyone anxiously watching the passing of days.

71. 1922 HOUSEWIVES' ALMANACK
8½" × 4" (approx.). Cloister Press, Heaton Mersey.
The cover and a double-spread from an almanack produced by C. W. Hobson in a style evocative of the past but no longer self-consciously archaic. Set in A.T.F. Garamond.

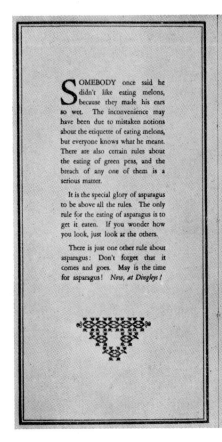

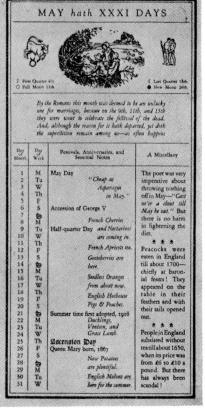

JANUARY

The rigidly poised day with the sun fixed as
steadily as an old coin in a showcase. Fencing wire
is hardly stiffer than the rime-blackened pond
rushes. Trees are wind-riven and the path on the
hill leads up to thinning snow.

SUNDAY		5	12	19	26
MONDAY		6	13	20	27
TUESDAY		7	14	21	28
WEDNESDAY	1	8	15	22	29
THURSDAY	2	9	16	23	30
FRIDAY	3	10	17	24	31
SATURDAY	4	11	18	25	

Benham

AND COMPANY LIMITED, PRINTERS
12 CULVER STREET, COLCHESTER
and at 3 Howard Street, London WC2

72. 1958 CALENDAR
6″ × 10¼″. Benham, Colchester.
This is a model of simplicity, decorated by a drawing
by John Nash, R.A. Printed in three colours. The
typeface used for the numerals is Klang.

73. 1961 OLD MOORE'S ALMANACK
6¾″ × 4⅛″. W. Foulsham and Co. Ltd, London.
Not exactly a typographic improvement on either
1701 or 1845 versions. This 64-page booklet is
packed with predictions and advice based on the
zodiac signs and the activity of the planets. The
cover is set in a mixture of black letter, fat face and
grotesque.

1961
1961

JOHN ROBERTS PRESS LTD   LETTERPRESS PRINTERS

JOROPRESS HOUSE
CLERKENWELL GREEN
LONDON EC1   CLERKENWELL 2583

October						October
Sunday	1	8	15	22	29	Sunday
Monday	2	9	16	23	30	Monday
Tuesday	3	10	17	24	31	Tuesday
Wednesday	4	11	18	25		Wednesday
Thursday	5	12	19	26		Thursday
Friday	6	13	20	27		Friday
Saturday	7	14	21	28		Saturday

74. 1961 ALMANACK
17⅞″ × 13⅜″. Bernard Roberts typ. John Roberts
Press, London.
This simple but vividly effective almanack was
printed in black, yellow, red and blue and is set in
Grotesques 215 and 216. The numerals are in Gill
Sans Bold

F

75. *c.* 1785 BOOKSELLERS' CATALOGUE
12″ × 9″ approx. Albany, N.Y.
Set mainly in Caslon's types, as shown by Isaiah
Thomas, printer of Worcester, Massachusetts, in his
sheet of 1705.

New-York Historical Society

Booksellers' lists and broadsheets

Booksellers' Lists earlier than 1800 were of little typographic interest. In the early years of the nineteenth century, booksellers made good use of printers' flowers and stock borders for their covers and title pages. The architectural settings that took the form of arched gateways (Figs. 76 and 78) gave a charming formality to these lists and the restrained use of small sizes of bold Egyptian typefaces and even bold black letter, and perhaps a single word, such as 'catalogue', as in J. Thorpe's list here, in a pica or nonpareil size of Thorne's or Figgins's Shaded capitals, gave a vitality to these pieces of printing that the seventeenth and eighteenth century job printer could never have attained. On this much smaller scale, the limited introduction of fat face and other display letters was just as successful as it was for playbill and poster. Booksellers announcements indeed soon followed the style of the playbill.

Booksellers' lists and leaflets

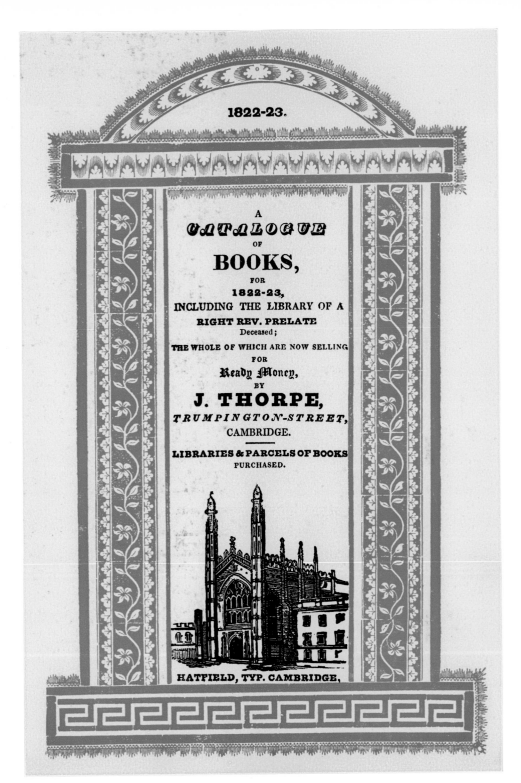

76. 1822–3 CATALOGUE OF BOOKS. COVER
7⅜″ × 4⅞″. University Press, Cambridge.
Printed in black and green, with a wood engraving
of the University Press. The elaborate border is
made up of 48-point units. The sloping shadow
letters combine happily with bold Didot and
Egyptians.

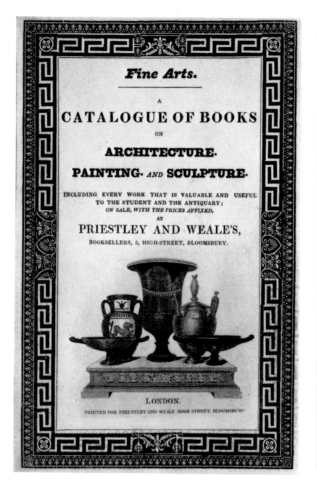

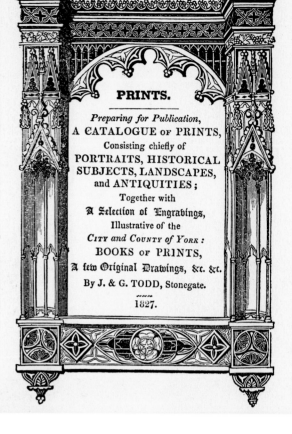

77. *c*.1823 CATALOGUE OF BOOKS. COVER
7⅛″ × 4½″. Anon. London.
The illustration is from a copper engraving, the text is letterpress printed. The same 'Greek key' border as in the previous illustration. The small bold Egyptian capitals alter the character of these otherwise bookish productions.

78. 1827 CATALOGUE OF PRINTS. COVER
4⅜″ × 2¾″. Anon. York.
The border was no doubt a stock ornament into which the printer locked up his type. Again the single word 'PRINTS', set in no larger than 9 point capitals gives emphasis and point to the rest of the layout.

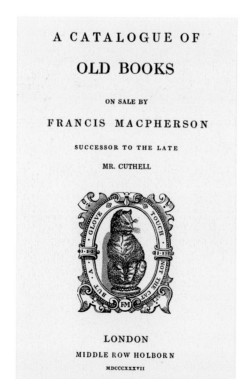

Booksellers' lists and leaflets

79. 1837 BOOKSELLERS' CATALOGUE
6¼″ × 3″. Anon. London.
Set in typefaces from Alexander Young and Sons, the Glasgow typefounders.

135,000 SETS, 270,000 VOLUMES SOLD.

UNCLE TOM'S CABIN

FOR SALE HERE.

AN EDITION FOR THE MILLION, COMPLETE IN 1 Vol., PRICE 37 1-2 CENTS.

" " IN GERMAN, IN 1 Vol., PRICE 50 CENTS.

" . " IN 2 Vols,. CLOTH, 6 PLATES, PRICE $1.50.

SUPERB ILLUSTRATED EDITION, IN 1 Vol., WITH 153 ENGRAVINGS,

PRICES FROM $2.50 TO $5.00.

The Greatest Book of the Age.

80. *c.* 1860 BOOKSELLER'S BROADSHEET
12½″ × 10″. Anon. U.S.A.
Booksellers by the mid-nineteenth century were for-
saking their reticence and launching out with bold
display.
Bella C. Landauer Collection, New-York Historical Society

Booksellers' broadsheets

**Booksellers' broadsheet
and
Booksellers' lists**

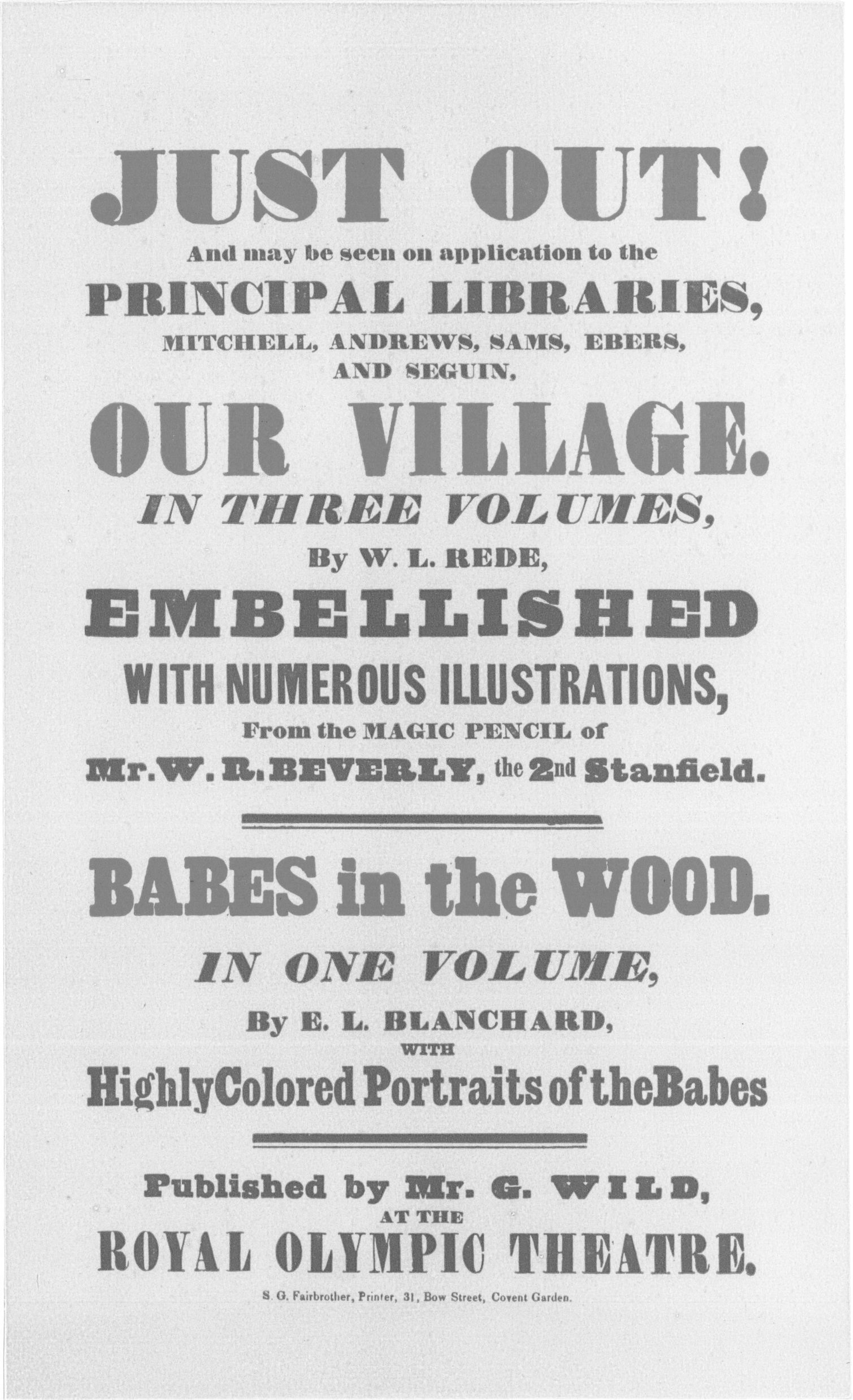

JUST OUT!

And may be seen on application to the

PRINCIPAL LIBRARIES,

MITCHELL, ANDREWS, SAMS, EBERS, AND SEGUIN,

OUR VILLAGE.

IN THREE VOLUMES,

By W. L. REDE,

EMBELLISHED

WITH NUMEROUS ILLUSTRATIONS,

From the MAGIC PENCIL of

Mr. W. R. BEVERLY, the 2nd Stanfield.

─────────────

BABES in the WOOD.

IN ONE VOLUME,

By E. L. BLANCHARD,

WITH

HighlyColored Portraits of theBabes

─────────────

Published by Mr. G. WILD,

AT THE

ROYAL OLYMPIC THEATRE.

S. G. Fairbrother, Printer, 31, Bow Street, Covent Garden.

81. *c.* 1860 BOOKSELLER'S BROADSHEET
$13\frac{1}{4}'' \times 8''$. S. G. Fairbrother, London.
Printed in blue and orange, this might be mistaken
for a playbill. There is a homogeneous quality given
by the limitation of typefaces to a fat face and a bold
Egyptian with the addition of a single line in condensed sans.

MEMENTO

Imprynted yn

Yᵉ Olde Streete of LONDON Towne

yᵉ greate Attraction

·yn·

Yᵉ Health EXHIBITION. Soᵛth Kensyng-
-ton ANNO·DOMINI: 1884.

atte yᵉ Signe of

Yᵉ LEADENHALLE PRESSE:

MAISTERS FIELD & TUER,

Artistic & Olde-style

PRINTERS & PVBLISHERS
Yᵉ LEADENHALLE PRESSE
50 Leadenhall Street,
LONDON, E.C.

☞ An'it please ye-Turn Over.

82. 1884 PUBLISHERS' LEAFLET
9¼″ × 7″. Leadenhall Press, London.
The publishers and printers of this leaflet were
Messrs Field and Tuer who were the leaders of the
'Antique Printing' movement of the 1880's. It was
consciously archaic, in reaction to the mechanical
complexity of the 'Artistic Printing' movement, with
its elaborate use of rules and borders.

KELMSCOTT PRESS, UPPER
MALL, HAMMERSMITH.

February 16th, 1897.

Note. This is the Golden type.
This is the Troy type.
This is the Chaucer type.

Secretary:
S. C. Cockerell, Kelmscott Press, Upper Mall,
Hammersmith, London, W., to whom all
letters should be addressed.

83. 1897 PRIVATE PRESS LIST
6⅝″ × 3½″. Kelmscott Press, London.
Four-page leaflet set in Golden type and showing
examples of William Morris's three type designs.
Printed in black and red.

❦ THE ERAGNY PRESS, THE
BROOK, HAMMERSMITH,
LONDON, W.
(No. 9). NOW READY.

[L] A BELLE
DAME
SANS
MERCI,
BY JOHN
KEATS,
(both versions). A booklet (demy
32mo.) printed in red and black and
decorated by Lucien Pissarro.
❦ The Rose cover paper is printed in
two colours.
❦ Two hundred copies have been
printed with the «Brook» type on
«Arches» linen hand-made paper,
at five shillings net, and ten on
Roman vellum, at one guinea net.

❦ N.B. No. 10 of the Eragny Press
books, «SONGS by BEN JON-
SON; A SELECTION FROM
THE PLAYS, MASQUES, &
POEMS WITH the EARLIEST
KNOWN SETTINGS OF CER-
TAIN NUMBERS», is in course
of printing, and will be published
in February.

85. 1905 PRIVATE PRESS LEAFLET
4¾″ × 2⅝″. The Eragny Press, London.
The Doves, the Vale and the Eragny all used re-
cuttings of the fifteenth century Venetian typefaces,
and they all made similar use of capital letters of the
text size for display and emphasis. The initial letter
here was cut by Lucien Pissarro and the typeface is
the Brook type that Pissarro also designed for his
press.

A CATALOGUE OF BOOKS
FROM THE LIBRARY OF THE
LATE GLEESON WHITE
PREFACED BY A TRIBUTE TO
HIS MEMORY BY PROF. YORK
POWELL OF CHRIST CHURCH
OXFORD

LONDON, W.:
A. LIONEL ISAACS,
16 SHAFTESBURY AVENUE
MDCCCXCIX.

84. 1899 BOOKSELLER'S CATALOGUE COVER
6½″ × 4″. Anon. London.
The asymmetry of l'Art Nouveau foreshadows the
New Typography of twenty-five years later.

M

Essrs. Houghton, Mifflin & Company take pleasure in announcing the adoption of the title 'The Riverside Press Editions' for their special, limited issues of books that are meeting with so much appreciation from collectors of fine printing both in this country and abroad. These volumes, though varying widely in subject, format, and style of treatment, are individually products of the most studious care in design and workmanship and are issued primarily as specimens of sound and thorough bookmaking as practiced at The Riverside Press. Following is a complete list of this series at the present time, together with an announcement of works now in preparation.

BOOKS ALREADY PRINTED

SONNETS AND MADRIGALS OF MICHELANGELO.
Translated by William Wells Newell.
300 *copies, published April* 14, 1900.
Price, $2.50, *net.*
Edition exhausted ten days after publication.

RUBÁIYÁT OF OMAR KHAYYÁM.
A reprint of FitzGerald's Second Edition, edited by William Augustus Brown.
300 *copies, published June,* 1900.
Price, $10.00, *net.*
Edition exhausted July, 1900.

OF FRIENDSHIP.
By Henry David Thoreau.
500 *copies, published June* 5, 1901.
Price, $2.00, *net.*
Edition exhausted before publication.

MR. BROWN'S LETTERS TO A YOUNG MAN ABOUT TOWN.
By William Makepeace Thackeray.
500 *copies, published September* 28, 1901.
Price, $3.00, *net.*
Edition exhausted October, 1901.

86. 1903 PUBLISHER'S LIST
$4\frac{1}{2}'' \times 2\frac{5}{8}''$ (single page type area). Bruce Rogers typ., Cambridge, Massachusetts.
Printed in black and vermilion. This pretty little list was designed by Bruce Rogers, one of the first to practice as a typographer in the twentieth century. His evocative talent as a 'pasticheur' was based on a sure knowledge of the history of printing.

At the Sign of Flying Fame.

LIST OF PUBLICATIONS.

BROADSIDES.
2 PENCE PLAIN,
4 PENCE COLOURED.

1. SONG. By Ralph Hodgson.
2. FEBRUARY. By Ralph Hodgson.
3. THE ROBIN'S SONG. By Richard Honeywood.
4. A PARABLE. By Lovat Fraser. Uncoloured.
5. CAPTAIN MACHEATH. By Lovat Fraser. Drawing, uncoloured.
   AT 4 PENCE.
6. THE LONELY HOUSE. By Lovat Fraser. Drawing in colours.

CHAP-BOOKS.
AT 6 PENCE.
1. EVE, and Other Poems. By Ralph Hodgson.
2. TOWN. An Essay. By Holbrook Jackson.
3. THE TWO WIZARDS, and Other Songs. By Richard Honeywood.
   AT 3 PENCE.
4. SIX ESSAYS in the XVIIIth Century. By Richard Honeywood.
   Postage on above, 1 Penny.

In the Press, other Chap-books, Broadsides, and Drawings, by James Stephens, Holbrook Jackson, Walter de la Mare, Ralph Hodgson, Richard Honeywood, and Lovat Fraser. All publications decorated throughout by Lovat Fraser.

87. 1913 PUBLISHER'S LIST
$12'' \times 4\frac{3}{4}''$. A. J. Stevens, London.
Broadside issued by Ralph Hodgson at the sign of the Flying Fame, with an illustration by Lovat Fraser, printed in black on a pink paper. The romantic movement, anticipated by the Leadenhall Press came to life under the hand of Lovat Fraser's decorations both to books and to ephemeral jobbing.

NONESUCH
AUTUMN BOOKS

LADIES' MISTAKES by James Laver	17s. 6d. & 6s.
COLERIDGE : Selected prose and poetry, 800 pages	8s. 6d.
WINTER HARVEST : Poems by Andrew Young	4s. 6d.
TENNYSON'S IN MEMORIAM : a limited edition	10s. 6d.
SHAKESPEARE : Seventh, and final, volume	£3 12s. 6d.
THE WEEK-END BOOK : 120th thousand	6s. & 8s. 6d.
BLAKE : Complete Writings, 1200 pages	12s. 6d.
DONNE : Complete poetry and selected prose, 800 pages	8s. 6d.
HAZLITT : Selected Essays, 800 pages	8s. 6d.
THE WEEK-END PROBLEMS BOOK	5s.

*T*ennyson's "IN MEMORIAM" has achieved again in these days its former reputation as one of the great poems of the language. The Nonesuch Press will centenarize the birth of Hallam by issuing at the beginning of December, in a singularly desirable limited edition, the threnody which Hallam inspired. The page will measure 7 by 11 inches, the paper will be Van Gelder, the type Blado italics, the binding Italian gold and black boards. And the price of this book, which is of more than 200 pages, and is certainly one of the finest of Nonesuch issues, will be only 10s. 6d. *There will also be a few copies bound in whole leather, having the title page decorated with gold leaf, at two guineas apiece. Specimen pages will be sent free to applicants.* ¶ The

88. 1933 PRIVATE PRESS LIST AND PROSPECTUS
$6\frac{1}{2}'' \times 3\frac{3}{4}''$. Francis Meynell typ. Fanfare Press, London.
'NONESUCH AUTUMN BOOKS' is set in Bardolph (known in Germany as Arpke Antiqua).

THE
OFFICINA BODONI

The Operation of a Hand-press during the first six years of its work

EDITIONES OFFICINAE BODONI
AT THE SIGN OF THE PEGASUS
PARIS · NEW YORK
MCMXXIX

CHANTICLEER

A
BIBLIOGRAPHY
OF   THE

GOLDEN
COCKEREL
PRESS

April 1921—1936 *August*

Introduction by Humbert Wolfe
Foreword & Notes by the Partners
Illustrations from the Books

PROSPECTUS

89. 1929 PUBLISHER'S ANNOUNCEMENT
7¼″ × 4″. Officina Bodoni, Verona, Italy.
Printed in black and vermilion by Giovanni Mardersteig at Verona, using typefaces cast from the original
matrices struck by Giambattista Bodoni at Parma
between 1790 and 1813.

90. 1936 PRIVATE PRESS LIST
7⅛″ × 4″. Robert Gibbings typ., London.
Set in Perpetua and printed in black and gold.

It was not until the private presses, such as the Doves and the Eragny had shown the way, that a reaction set in against the use of display letters, and the bookishness of booksellers' lists and publishers' announcements received a confirmation of the rightness of such an approach. The Doves, the Vale and the Eragny all used re-cuttings of the fifteenth century Venetian typefaces both for their books and their lists. Bruce Rogers at the Riverside Press and Giovanni Mardersteig at his Officina Bodoni in Verona continued in the same vein and it was not until the late 1920's that the effects of the Bauhaus and the New Typography began to be felt in this highly conservative field of ephemeral printing.

Booksellers' lists

91. 1928 PUBLISHER'S CATALOGUE' COVER AND TEXT
$6\frac{1}{4}'' \times 4\frac{1}{8}''$ (text page). Anon. London.
This cover and catalogue was designed by E.
McKnight Kauffer, an American artist who lived
for many years in England and had a profound
influence on poster art in England and the U.S.A.
between the two wars. The typeface used for display
on the text page is Rudolf Koch's Neuland.

92. c. 1928 PUBLISHER'S ANNOUNCEMENT
$5'' \times 7\frac{7}{8}''$. Bauhaus, Dessau.
This was issued by the Bauhaus, as one of a
series of publications dealing with the work
of that remarkable school. Sans serif typefaces, more often in lower-case than in
capitals, as here, and heavy rules were an
integral part of what was to become a
Bauhaus style.

Museum of Modern Art

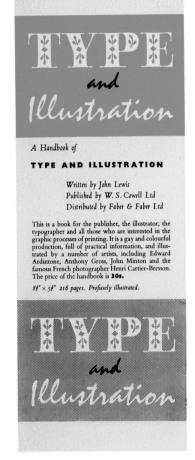

93. 1948–9 PUBLISHER'S LIST COVERS
8½″ × 2⅞″. Robert Harling typ., Shenval Press,
London.
Printed in black and two colours. The decorative
typeface is known as Macdonald. It is an unidentified
typeface, of about 1830.

94. 1956 PUBLISHER'S
ANNOUNCEMENT
7½″ × 3¼″ (area of tint). John Lewis
typ. W. S. Cowell Ltd, Ipswich.
Printed in black and two colours.
The displayed types used in reverse
are Saphir and Mistral.

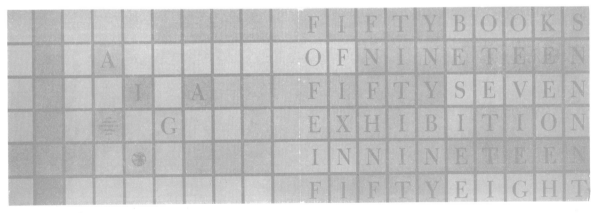

95. 1958 EXHIBITION BOOKLIST COVER
6″ × 18″. Bill English typ. Cons Lith. Corp., U.S.A.
Printed in black and three colours. The American
Institute of Graphic Arts makes use of type case grid
for title and imprint.

Booksellers' lists

Today, in lists such as those shown here,
display letters are made to speak for themselves
and to act as the main parts of arresting designs.

These lists make use of Victorian typefaces
in a very un-Victorian way. The typographic
revival of Victoriana after the second world
war was a reaction against austerity. Robert
Harling was one of the most fluent typographers
in this style.

For Sale notices

2.59

A
Particular or Inventory
OF THE
Real and Perſonal Eſtate
O F

JAMES EDMUNDSON, Eſq;

One of the

Late DIRECTORS of the *South Sea* Company,

Which he was poſſeſſed of or entitled unto in his own Right, or by any Perſon or Perſons in Truſt for him, on or about the Firſt Day of *June* 1720; together with ſuch Convey-ances, Transfers or other Alienations or Diſ-poſitions as have been made thereof, or of any Part thereof, by him or his Order, ſince that Time to this preſent 18th of *March*, 1721, in the beſt manner he is able to collect the ſame.

Together with the ABSTRACT *of the ſame.*

L O N D O N:
Printed for *Jacob Tonſon*, *Bernard Lintot*, and *William Taylor.* MDCCXXI.

96. 1731 A PARTICULAR (OR INVENTORY)
$9\frac{3}{4}'' \times 5\frac{1}{2}''$. Anon. London.
This notice refers to the seized property of one of the Directors of the South Sea Company. The types are probably of sixteenth century Dutch origin and possibly cut by Granjon.

Oxford University Press

For Sale and Auction Notices began in the style of the newspaper announcements. 'The Particular or Inventory' of the unfortunate James Edmundson, a director of the South Sea Company, is set very like a modern newspaper editorial, even with the first word of the text thrown into the margin in the same manner as the London *Daily Mail*'s front page column 'Comment'. The 'Jonathan Perry' bill shows the transition from the newspaper style of setting to the complete displayed poster. Fry's Ornamented typeface is still bookish in character, but the semi-fat face letters belong to the world of commerce. The heavily leaded text is set in a semi-bold 'modern' typeface. The judicious use of just one line of Fry's decorated type makes a very nice contrast with the semi-fat face italic used above and below it.

ELEGANT AND VERY EXCELLENT

FURNITURE,

Old Port Wine, Milking Cow, &c.

TO BE SOLD BY AUCTION,

By Jonathan Perry,

ON THE PREMISES,

At SEVERN HILL, close to SHREWSBURY,

On *MONDAY, TUESDAY & WEDNESDAY, the 16th, 17th & 18th of MAY,* 1814,

(To commence at Eleven each Day, and continue until the Day's Sale is ended);

THE WHOLE OF THE

Genteel and most valuable Household Furniture,

BELONGING TO COLONEL EGERTON;

COMPRISING

HANDSOME Four-post and Tent Bedsteads, with rich Morine and superfine Dimity Hangings, of modern Fashion; prime Dantzic Feather Beds of the first Quality, Hair, Flock, and Straw Mattresses, super Witney Blankets, Marseilles Quilts and Counterpanes, Childrens' Bedsteads and Bedding complete, Servants' Bedsteads and Hangings, with seasoned Feather Beds, Mattresses, and Bed Clothes; Spanish Mahogany Chamber Furniture of the finest Quality, in Wardrobes, Chests of Drawers, Night Tables, Dressing Tables, and Bason Stands; Japanned Washing Tables, Chamber Chairs, Swing Glasses, Bidettes, Bedsteps, and other Articles appropriate to Bed Rooms; a Drawing Room Suit of rich Chintz Curtains, lined, with elegant fringed Draperies, Cornices, and Appendages complete; Grecian Commode for Books, ebonized Chairs, Chaise Lounge, Ottomans; Mahogany Card, Pembroke, and Quartetto Tables; Dining Parlour Suit of handsome orange Morine Curtains and rich Draperies; Set of beautiful Mahogany Dining Tables, on best Castors, 9 Feet by 4 Feet 8 Inches; a Pair of neat Sideboards fitted up with Curtains, handsome Brass Rods and Pillars; twelve Mahogany Grecian Parlour Chairs, Wine Celleret, Deception Table, a rich Turkey Carpet, 14 Feet by 13 Feet 8 Inches (perfect as new), and other Articles appropriate to a Dining Room; various Miscellanies, including a neat and elegant Hall Lanthorn, Chamber Organ, Dinner Service, Tea China and Glass, Butler's Trays, Knife Boxes, Cheese Waggon, Supper Tray, a capital Lady's Saddle and Bridle (by Whippy), never used; Stair, Room and Bed Carpets, and Hearth Rugs; the general Routine of Kitchen Furniture, Culinary Vessels, &c.

Also, Twelve Dozen of superior OLD PORT WINE, (Vintage of 1804); and a Valuable Milking COW.

☞ The Auctioneer assures genteel Families, and the Public, that during his Experience of more than twenty Years, he has not had to dispose of such a Property in Furniture so deserving of their Notice as the present; every Article is truly excellent, and when seen must be admired.——To be viewed on *Friday* and *Saturday*, the 13th and 14th of *May*, by Tickets from the Auctioneer, of whom Catalogues may be had.

Sandford, Printer.

97. 1814 AUCTION SALE
$15\frac{1}{2}'' \times 9\frac{1}{2}''$. Sandford, Shrewsbury.
This elegant bill has a fair variety of semi-bold 'modern' typefaces though the word 'furniture' is in an old style letter. 2-line English Ornamented makes another appearance in the 'To be sold' line.

Oak Timber.

TO BE SOLD

At the GLOBE, in NETHER STOWEY,

On WEDNESDAY the 19th, Day of APRIL Inftant,

BY FOUR O'CLOCK,

FORTY
Large Oak Trees,

LOT 1. No. 1 to 10, both incluſive.

    2. - 11 to 20,   ditto.

    3, - 21 to 30,   ditto.

    4. - 31 to 40,   ditto.

THE TREES are in HOLFORD WOOD, near STOWEY, 3 Miles from COOMBWICH; 6 from WATCHET, and 12 from BRIDGWATER.

☞ JOHN WEBBER, of *Holford* aforeſaid, will ſhew the TIMBER.

Dated 12*th, April,* 1815.

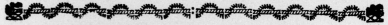

PILE, PRINTER, NORTON.

98. 1815 AUCTION SALE
7½″ × 5″. Pile, Norton.
Set in roman typefaces, in the typographic manner
of a hundred years earlier. 'Oak Timber' and 'Large
Oak Trees' are set in Moxon's Canon.

For Sale notices

To be SOLD, in Fee,

BY AUCTION,

AT THE

White Hart, in Glastonbury,

On Wednesday the 10th Day of January Inst.

By 4 o'Clock in the Afternoon,

In 1, 2, or 3 LOTS,

Two Gardens,

ADJOINING to, or near NORTH LOAD STREET, in *GLASTONBURY* aforesaid, late in the Possession of JOHN FRY REEVES, Esqr.

☞ MR. WILLIAM GODFREY, of NORTH LOAD STREET, or his SON, will shew the GARDENS; and Particulars may be known of MR. HANCOCK, of FORD, near *Wiveliscombe.*

Dated 2nd. JANUARY, 1827.

Piles: Book-sellers, Norton.

99. 1827 AUCTION SALE
6¼″ × 5″. Pile, Norton.
Set in fat faces and Thorne's Shaded for 'BY AUCTION',
and semi-bold, modern, vertically stressed types for
the body of the text.

The most striking comparison in the changing printing styles of the early years of the nineteenth century is shown by these two little bills from a printer in Dorset. Printed respectively in 1815 and 1827, they mark the biggest break in typographic styles that has happened since the beginning of printing. These two little bills, perhaps more than any other in this book, show the complete change of typographic language that happened in the early years of the nineteenth century. The 1815 one could have been printed two hundred years earlier without a significant change; the 1827 one could not have been printed even twenty years earlier, for the fat faces used in it were not invented, let alone available for a jobbing printer in Dorset. The 2-line shaded letter used for 'By Auction' only dates back to 1819, four years after Norton printed his first bill.

T. BURWELL,

Begs to invite the Attention of the Nobility, Gentry, Trades-People, and the Inhabitants of Cardiff and its Vicinity, to his very Superior and

EXTENSIVE STOCK

OF

PARISIAN,

London, Birmingham, Sheffield, and Tunbridge

WARES,

Fancy, Fashionable, and Useful:

Part of the same was opened in the Market-place on Saturday last, but now in the Shop lately occupied by Mr. Pardoe, where it will remain the whole of this Week.

THE STOCK CONSISTS OF

AN extensive and general assortment of Jewellery, of the most modern patterns, and superior quality; Silver and British Plate; Bracelets and Snaps, of the newest patterns; Tortoise-Shell, German Shell, Horn, and Ivory Combs, of every size, pattern, and quality; Flesh, Cloth, Hair, Tooth, Nail, and other Brushes; a large stock of Ladies' Work Boxes, Dressing Cases; Desks; Jewel and Netting Boxes, &c. &c. Tea Chests and Caddies, with Basins; Gentlemen's Dressing Cases, of all sizes; Desks, and Ne-plus-Ultras, of various sizes; Plated and Paper Castor Frames; Britannia Metal Goods, Toast Racks, Spoons, &c. Bronzed Goods and China ornaments, in the greatest variety; fancy Bellows; Riticules; Pope and Backgammon Boards; British and Foreign Toys; Ivory and Bone Wares; fine Town-made Cutlery; Coral and every other sort of Beads; Silk, and other Purses, of all sorts; Portfolios and Albums, of all sizes; Perfumery and Fancy Soaps; Smelling and toilet Bottles; Table, and various other Cushions; Busts of popular Characters; Table Mats; Watch Stands; Chimney Ornaments; and an almost innumerable quantity of other useful and fancy articles, too numerous to particularise in a Bill;—with respect to prices, the proprietor feels satisfied that every person of judgment, visiting the Bazaar, will be convinced that the late and present depression of trade, has reduced the prices of goods, of almost every description, to nearly half their real value.

THOMAS BURWELL,

Authorised agreeable to Act of Parliament.—Licensed Hawker, No 8. C.

J. & LL. JENKINS, PRINTERS, CASTLE-SRTEET, CARDIFF.

100. *c.* 1830 ANNOUNCEMENT OF SALE
$7\frac{1}{2}'' \times 6\frac{3}{8}$. J. and Ll. Jenkins, Cardiff.
Printed on an apple green paper and showing a very bold Egyptian for the word 'WARES'. Two varieties of shaded letters are shown with vertical and oblique slopes to the serifs, that used for 'Parisian' was Vincent Figgins's 2-line pica Antique shaded.

The heavy Egyptian typeface used for the word WARES in T. Burwell's bill justifies the statement that the Egyptian is the most brilliant typographical invention of the century.* The fat faces and Egyptians give these notices a punch that would have been a typographic impossibility if Robert Thorne had not thought of his original fat face.

*Nicolette Gray *19th Century Ornamented Types*. Faber 1938.

For Sale notices

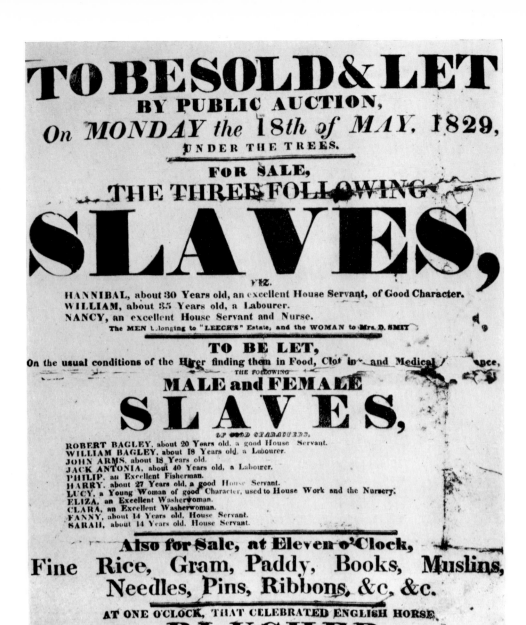

TO BE SOLD & LET
BY PUBLIC AUCTION,
On MONDAY the 18th of MAY, 1829,
UNDER THE TREES.

FOR SALE,
THE THREE FOLLOWING
SLAVES,
VIZ.

HANNIBAL, about 30 Years old, an excellent House Servant, of Good Character.
WILLIAM, about 35 Years old, a Labourer.
NANCY, an excellent House Servant and Nurse.
The MEN belonging to "LEECH'S" Estate, and the WOMAN to Mrs. D. SMIT

TO BE LET,
On the usual conditions of the Hirer finding them in Food, Clot in and Medical nce,
THE FOLLOWING
MALE and FEMALE
SLAVES,
OF GOOD CHARACTERS.

ROBERT BAGLEY, about 20 Years old, a good House Servant.
WILLIAM BAGLEY, about 18 Years old, a Labourer.
JOHN ARMS, about 18 Years old.
JACK ANTONIA, about 40 Years old, a Labourer.
PHILIP, an Excellent Fisherman.
HARRY, about 27 Years old, a good House Servant.
LUCY, a Young Woman of good Character, used to House Work and the Nursery.
ELIZA, an Excellent Washerwoman.
CLARA, an Excellent Washerwoman.
FANNY, about 14 Years old, House Servant.
SARAH, about 14 Years old, House Servant.

Also for Sale, at Eleven o'Clock,
Fine Rice, Gram, Paddy, Books, Muslins, Needles, Pins, Ribbons, &c. &c.

AT ONE O'CLOCK, THAT CELEBRATED ENGLISH HORSE,
BLUCHER,

101. 1829 AUCTION SALE
15″ × 12″ approx. Addison. Place unknown.
This leaflet announcing the sale of slaves presumably
comes from the United States of America, from one
of the southern states, or possibly from the West
Indies.

A
Committee Room
TO LET,
ENQUIRE OF
MR. CHARLES MOOR,
AGENT TO
JOHN FITZ-GERALD, Esq.
J. LODER, PRINTER AND BOOKSELLER, WOODBRIDGE.

102. c. 1832 TO LET
5¼″ × 7″. J. Loder, Woodbridge.
A simple notice, using five different typefaces in as
many lines, dominated by that typographic innovation, the bold Egyptian, used for the words 'TO LET'.

For Sale notices

GENTLEMEN'S
FURNISHING STORE
☞ **No. 8, HANOVER STREET,**
(Fourth Door from Court, opposite Concert Hall,)
BOSTON.

ARTHUR B. GOVE,

Offers to the public a large and complete assortment of

GENTS' FURNISHING GOODS

Of every description which has been selected with great care, and purchased
for CASH, and will be

SOLD AT LOWER PRICES,

Than they can be purchased at any other place. Among which may be found every
description of the most recent patterned

Handker'fs,	**Joinville Scarfs,**	**Shoulder Braces,**
Shirts,	**Hosiery,**	**Umbrellas,**
Bosoms,	**Suspenders,**	**Canes,**
Collars,	**Neck Stocks,**	**Under Shirts,**
Cravats,	**Neck Ties,**	**Drawers,**
Gloves,	**Scarfs,**	**Night Shirts,**
Night Caps.		**Bathing Caps,**

Smoking Caps, Hair Brushes, Cloth Brushes, Clothes Brushes, Tooth Brushes, Nail
Brushes, Lather Brushes, Hat Brushes, Pocket Knives, Dressing Combs,
Wallets, Purses, Porte Monaies, Pocket Mirrors, Cologne, Perfumery,
Hair Oil, Soap, &c. &c.

☞ Gentlemen in want of any of the above articles will find it to their advantage
to call at this place, where they will be guaranteed

Good Articles at Low Prices.
ARTHUR B. GOVE,
No. 8 Hanover Street, Boston.
Fourth Door from Court, opposite Concert Hall.

103. *c.* 1850 ANNOUNCEMENT OF SALE
13″ × 9″. Anon. Boston, Massachusetts.
The simplicity of T. Burwell's bill gives way to the
crowded typography of Arthur B. Gove's announcement. The decorated shadow letter used for 'BOSTON'
originates from the Cincinnati Typefoundry.
Oxford University Press

104. 1851 FOR SALE
25″ × 11″. East Burns Press, Boston, Massachusetts. Another combined notice of 'Sale and Inventory'. The typeface used for the word 'Library' is a curious variation of the Egyptian.

Oxford University Press

CATALOGUE
OF THE
LIBRARY
— OF A —
PRIVATE GENTLEMAN NOW IN EUROPE
EMBRACING
English, French, Italian and German Works
TO BE SOLD BY AUCTION.
On Tuesday, April 8th, 1851,
AT STORE No. 10 WATER STREET, BOSTON,
At 10 o'clock, A. M.
CLARK & HATCH, Auctioneers.

ENGLISH

1 History of Tom Jones, 9 vols.	103 Poems by N. P. Willis	202 Corneille's Works, 4 vols.	
2 Lardner's Cabinet Encyclopedia, 3 vols.	104 Sketches by do	203 Coress of Literature, 12 do	
3 Conversations with Goethe, from the German	105 Redburn or the First Voyage	204 Book of the People, 1 do	
4 Terrible Tractoration and other Poems	106 The Doom of Devorgoil, by Scott	205 Spirit of Memoir of St. Helena, 2 do	
5 Phantasmion	107 Alice, 2 vols.	206 French Review	
6 Smith's Am. Biography, 9 vols.	108 Pelham, 2 vols.	207 The Duchess, 2 vols.	
7 Combe's Tour in the U. States, 2 vols.	109 Devereux, 2 vols.	208 French Grammar	
8 Leopardo's History of England	110 The Alhambra, 2 vols.	209 Honest Man	
9 Bacon's Novum Organum	111 Bacon's Advancement of Learning	210 Master of Arms	
10 Mirum, &c.	112 Waverley Novels, 48 vols.	211 Genius of the 13th Century	
	113 Blackstone's Commentaries, 4 vols.	212 Physiology of Taste	
	114 Bolingbroke's Works, 5 vols.	213 Four Talismans	

TO YACHTSMEN AND PEOPLE OF TASTE.

TO BE DISPOSED OF
(With 15 Years remaining Lease,)
AN ELEGANT
COTTAGE ORNÉE,
At that select and Fashionable Watering Place,
SOUTHSEA, adjoining PORTSMOUTH.
IT IS
TO BE SOLD FURNISHED,
Just as it is, for £1,500,

With 2-stall Stable and Coach House; Dove Cote; Billiard Table; (of the most *recherché* description,) Pheasantry and Birds; Green House; Pictures, in all the Ground-Floor rooms; Flag Staff, (very complete and ornamental); Lawn; Shrubberies and Kitchen Garden; &c., &c.

Or it will be Let Furnished, for 8 Guineas a week,
FOR NOT LESS THAN SIX MONTHS.

In either case, possession can be had in a week or ten days.

It is within a few minutes walk of the Beach, Clarence Promenade, Reading Rooms, and Bathing Machines, Southsea Castle, &c., and has a full and commanding view of Spithead, and the Isle of Wight, to which, steamers pass to and fro every half hour.

For full and additional particulars, and Cards to view, apply to
Messrs. GREEN & STANLEY,
Estate and House Agents, 28, Old Bond Street, London; or
Mr. MARSH,
House Agent, Humbrook Street, Southsea, Hants.

105. 1857 FOR SALE
6⅛″ × 3¼″. Anon. Southsea, Hants.
This quiet little leaflet is in keeping with the house to be sold, a charming (it would seem) Regency cottage. The decorative letters for 'Cottage Ornée' are similar to those shown by the New York typefounder James Conner in 1859 and called 2-line small pica Ornamented No. 6. 'To be sold furnished' is set in H. W. Caslon's 2-line Tuscan Shaded, which Caslon first showed in 1854.

AUCTION SALE!
The Subscriber will sell at Public Auction at Groton, Vt., on
MONDAY, MAY 19, '90
AT 10 O'CLOCK, A.M. HIS
BLACKSMITH SHOP, TOOLS,
And Stock. A quantity of Nice White Ash Lumber, 1 nearly new
ROAD CART, & 1 GOOD SLEIGH.
——— Also the Following ———
HOUSEHOLD FURNITURE,
1 Crown Range, as good as new, with Pipe, 1 Box Stove and Pipe, Bureaus, Bedsteads, Tables, Crockery and Glass Ware, Carpets, and many other articles too numerous to mention.
TERMS, All sums under $10 Cash, and all over $10 three or six months with Bankable Notes.
These Goods must be sold as I am going West.
F. M. PAGE, AUCTIONEER.
H. E. FLEMING
Groton. Vt., May 8, 1890.
Wells River Job Print.

106. 1890 AUCTION BILL
15″ × 10¼″ approx. Wells River Job Print, Groton, Vermont.
A rich French Antique similar to the present-day Playbill is used for 'Auction Sale'; 'Blacksmith Shop, Tools' is set in an attenuated condensed Tuscan, an unhappy variation of a charming letter form.

Bella C. Landauer Collection, New-York Historical Society

MELTON

WOODBRIDGE 1½ MILES   IPSWICH 9 MILES

LOT 1

Announcement of Sale of the Freehold

DETACHED

SMALL HOUSE

KNOWN AS

POTASH FARM

In a most pleasant and convenient situation and forming an

Excellent Basis for Modernisation

Of colourwashed brick and tile construction with
THREE ROOMS, KITCHEN & SCULLERY ON
THE GROUND FLOOR & FOUR BEDROOMS
MAINS WATER, GAS & ELECTRICITY AVAILABLE
NEARLY HALF AN ACRE OF LAND

USEFUL BUILDINGS

Including Open Bay Shelters, Loose Boxes, Stables, Etc.

LOTS 2 & 3

The SURROUNDING LAND

in all some 9½ ACRES or thereabouts

To be offered for sale by Public Auction (unless previously sold privately) in THREE LOTS with

VACANT POSSESSION

on completion of the purchase by

DENNIS H. B. NEAL

At the Crown Hotel Assembly Room, Woodbridge

on

WEDNESDAY, 23ʳᵈ SEPTEMBER, 1959

At **3.30** p.m.

Particulars and Conditions of Sale from the Vendor's Solicitors Messrs. GROSS & CURJEL, The Thoro'fare, Woodbridge, (Tel. 97) or the Chartered Auctioneer, Church Street, Woodbridge (Tel. 62) and Messrs. NEAL & TUOHY, 18 High Street, Aldeburgh, (Tel. 46).

GEORGE BOOTH WOODBRIDGE LTD.

107. 1959 FOR SALE NOTICE
20⅛″ × 15¼″. George Booth, Woodbridge.
Printed in red and black with the liberal use of large
grotesque wooden letters. A good example of a well
laid out modern notice.

Modern auction bills do sometimes achieve
similar qualities to the early bills and though
most modern auction bills both in England and
the U.S.A. are not very distinguished, every
once in a while comes one that is both readable
and attractive to the eye. Such a one (Fig. 107)
is from a small print shop in the little Suffolk
town of Woodbridge.

Travel notices

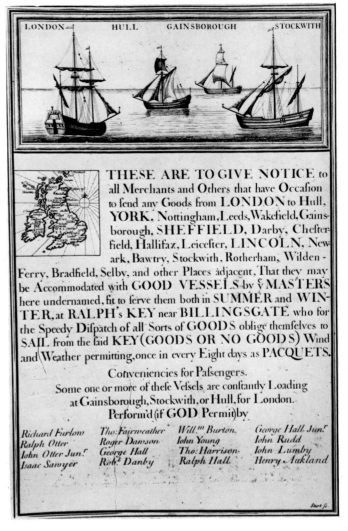

108. 1680 SAILING NOTICE
$7\frac{7}{8}'' \times 5\frac{1}{8}''$. Sturt sc, London.
Engraved notice.

Pepysian Library, Cambridge

The earliest printed travel notices that I have seen are those in a scrap book of Samuel Pepys entitled *Vulgaria* and now in the Pepysian Library at Magdalene College, Cambridge. These are all from the seventeenth century, which in England was remarkable for the poor quality of the letterpress printing. For notices of any importance, the only alternative to the slovenly letterpress work was to use engravings. The engravings were as good as the letterpress printing was bad, though the exquisite little engraving of ships (Fig. 108) gives little idea of the seas encountered on this stormy North Sea coast; the phrase 'Perform'd (if God permit) by . . .' is ominous.

Fifty years later, the work of the letterpress printers was no better, though the chap-book style of illustration, as in the Birmingham stage coach bill lends some vitality to the undistinguished letterpress. The baggage weight allowance quoted was some thirty pounds less than the usual air travel allowance today.

The 'Boston, Plymouth and Sandwich Mail Stage' bill is a fine example of transitional typography, with a charmingly archaic engraving of early nineteenth century New England and an extremely elegant turn-out of a light coach and four horses. The semi-bold modern typefaces used have a close affinity to those cut by William Martin for William Bulmer at the Shakespeare Printing Office in London (Fig. 113).

The printer's use of Thorne's Shaded Fat Face for 'Messageries Royales' and 'The Union' (Figs. 119 and 120) lends sparkle to these little notices. Nothing much has been written of the virtues of these shadow letters. They are typographically highly ingenious and provide an interesting contrast to the normal fat face letters. They must have been produced in emulation of engraved letters.

The contrast between letterpress and copperplate is shown by comparing these two illustrations with Fig. 122. Interesting shadow letters are shown in the Cheltenham notice. Here the engraver is influenced by the typefounder.

85

BIRMINGHAM STAGE-COACH,

In Two *Days* and a half; begins *May* the 24th, 1731.

SET out from the *Swan-Inn* in *Birmingham*, every *Monday* at six a Clock in the Morning, through *Warwick*, *Banbury* and *Alesbury*, to the *Red Lion Inn* in *Alderfgate ftreet*, *London*, every *Wednefday* Morning: And returns from the faid *Red Lion Inn* every *Thurfday* Morning at five a Clock the fame Way to the *Swan-Inn* in *Birmingham* every *Saturday*, at 21 Shillings each Paffenger, and 18 Shillings from *Warwick*, who has liberty to carry 14 Pounds in Weight, and all above to *pay One Penny a Pound*.
Perform'd (if God permit)

By Nicholas Rothwell.

The Weekly Waggon fets out every *Tuefday* from the *Nagg's-Head* in *Birmingham*, to the *Red Lion Inn* aforefaid, every *Saturday*, and returns from the faid Inn every *Monday*, to the *Nagg's-Head* in *Birmingham* every *Thurfday*.

Note. *By the faid Nicholas Rothwell at Warwick, all Perfons may be furnifhed with a By Coach, Chariot, Chaife, or Hearfe, with a Mourning Coach and able Horfes, to any Part of Great Britain, at reafonable Rates: And alfo Saddle Horfes to be had.*

---

109. 1731 STAGE COACH NOTICE
7¼″ × 4″. Anon. Birmingham.
The use of spirited engravings in such a leaflet as this for the 'Birmingham Stage Coach' shown here was some compensation for the inadequate typefaces and poor presswork. The indiscriminate use of italics is typical of this period.

Oxford University Press

Travel notices

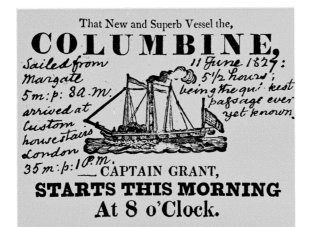

That New and Superb Vessel the,

COLUMBINE,

Sailed from Margate 5 m: p: 8 a.m. arrived at Custom house stairs London 35 m: p: 10 p.m.

11 June 1829: 5½ hours; being the quickest passage ever yet known.

CAPTAIN GRANT,

STARTS THIS MORNING At 8 o'Clock.

---

111. 1827 SAILING NOTICE
2″ × 2⅝″. Anon. Margate.
A contemporary hand has written on this: 'Sailed from Margate 5m: p: 8 a.m. arrived at Custom house stairs London 35m: p: 1 p.m. 11 June 1827: 5½ hours; being the quickest passage ever yet known.'

THE Oxford, Bath, *and* Briftol MACHINE,

On Steel Springs, in one Day, twice a Week,

Licenfed by the Rev. the Vice Chancellor;

BEGAN Flying the Second Day of *April*, 1770: Sets out from the STAR Inn in the *Corn Market*, OXFORD, every *Monday* Morning at Four o'Clock; to the *King's Arms* in *Broad Street*, *Bath*: Returns from *Bath* to *Oxford*, on *Wednefday* Morning at Four o'Clock; goes down to *Bath* on *Thurfdays*, and up again on *Saturdays*, at the fame Hour. Infide Paffengers to pay One Guinea each; Half at taking their Places, and the reft on getting into the Coach. To be allowed 20lb. Weight for Luggage; and pay One Penny a Pound for all above. Children in Lap, and Outfide Paffengers Half Price and no Luggage allowed. *Performed by*
EPHRAIM SPERINCK, and Co.
For the Conveniency of Paffengers, this Machine meets the *London* Coaches at *Oxford* every Journey, and the *Exeter* Machine at *Bath* every *Thurfday*.

---

110. 1770 STAGE COACH NOTICE
6″ × 4¾″. Anon. Oxford.
Typographically an improvement on the Birmingham Stage, this also makes full use of italics for place names, etc. Set in Caslon's types throughout.

Oxford University Press

STEEL YARD, Upper Thames Street.

KENNET & AVON
CANAL CONVEYANCE
TO AND FROM
LONDON & BRISTOL;
AND BY STEAM TO
Dublin, Cork, and Waterford.

BETTS and DREWE return their acknowledgments for the Favors they have received, and beg to apprize the Public, that they have established *FLY BARGES*, which leave the STEEL YARD, Upper Thames Street, London, and QUEEN STREET WHARF, Bristol, daily; *and will perform the Passage in Four or Five Days, and all intermediate places in proportionate times—unavoidable detentions excepted.*

B. and D. hold themselves responsible for Goods committed to their care, according to the NOTICE and CONDITIONS SUBJOINED, which are publicly exhibited at their Offices and Wharfs; where they receive and deliver Goods.

The Proprietors give PUBLIC NOTICE, that they will not hold themselves answerable or accountable for Fire, or for any Loss or Injury the Goods may sustain, by any accident to their Barges on the Rivers, and Navigation of whatever Nature or Kind soever, (neglect excepted,) or for any Article, unless the same shall be entered by the Book-keeper, or marked, as received by one of them, on the Book or Paper of the Porter or other Person who may deliver it.

They will not be accountable for any Money, Plate, Watches, Rings, Jewels, Writings, Glass, China, Marble, Prints, Paintings, or other Valuables, unless entered as such, and an Insurance paid above the common rate of carriage, according to the Value, upon delivery to them.

Any Claim for Loss or Damage, that is not made within three Days after the Delivery of the Goods, will not be allowed.

Leakage arising from Bad Casks or Cooperage will not be accounted for.

All Goods which shall be delivered for the purpose of being carried, will be considered as *general Liens*, and subject, not only to the Money due for the Carriage of such particular *Goods*, but also to the *general Balance* due from the respective Owners to the Proprietors of the said Conveyance.

Further particulars may be obtained by applying as above, or to R. PARKER, *Darlington Wharf, Bath*; JAMES LONG, *Bradford, Wilts*; D. PHIPPS, *Devizes*; BETTS and DREWE, *Wharf, Newbury*; and *Gas Wharf, Reading*; and Mr. MASON, *Windsor*.

LONDON, January, 1827.

N. B.—*The above Wharfingers are not accountable for Fire, or Damage arising from High Tides.*

---

112. 1827 CANAL NOTICE
6⅜″ × 5⅝″. Anon. London.
Notice giving details of fly barges which took four to five days to journey from London to Bristol.

BOSTON,
Plymouth & Sandwich
MAIL STAGE,

CONTINUES TO RUN AS FOLLOWS:

LEAVES Boston every Tuesday, Thursday, and Saturday mornings at 5 o'clock, breakfast at Leonard's, Scituate; dine at Bradford's, Plymouth; and arrive in Sandwich the same evening. Leaves Sandwich every Monday, Wednesday and Friday mornings; breakfast at Bradford's, Plymouth; dine at Leonard's, Scituate, and arrive in Boston the same evening.

Passing through Dorchester, Quincy, Wyemouth, Hingham, Scituate, Hanover, Pembroke, Duxbury, Kingston, Plymouth to Sandwich. *Fare,* from Boston to Scituate, 1 doll. 25 cts. From Boston to Plymouth, 2 dolls. 50 cts. From Boston to Sandwich, 3 dolls. 63 cts.

N. B. Extra Carriages can be obtained of the proprietor's, at Boston and Plymouth, at short notice.— STAGE BOOKS kept at Boyden's Market-square, Boston, and at Fessendon's, Plymouth.

LEONARD & WOODWARD.

BOSTON, *November 24,* 1810.

113. 1810 MAIL COACH NOTICE
9½″ × 6⅜″. Anon. Boston, Massachusetts.
This handsome bill is set in typefaces very similar to those issued by the London typefounder, Thorne.
New York Public Library

BOSTON AND ALBANY
MAIL STAGE.

PHŒNIX LINE.
THROUGH IN TWO DAYS.

Leaves S. W Willard's, City Coffee House, No. 336 North Market-street, Albany, and Babcock's City Hotel, Troy, every Monday, Wednesday and Friday, at 1 o'clock A. M. by the way of Williamstown and Greenfield, to Boston. Returning, leaves Boston every Monday, Wednesday and Friday.

☞ Seats taken at S. W. Willard's, City Coffee House, No. 336 North Market-street, Albany; at Babcock's City Hotel, Troy; I. Newton's Greenfield and A. Brigham's, Boston Fare to Greenfield, $3,00—Fare to Boston, $6,00

☞ All Baggage at the risk of the owner.

L. NEWELL. ALBANY.
J. S. KEELER. TROY. } AGENT.

ALBANY MAY 14, 1830.

114. 1830 MAIL COACH NOTICE
3¼″ × 2¼″. Anon. Albany, N.Y.
A nice mixture of Egyptian, fat face and italic shaded, and practically the same stock cut used by the New York printer in Fig. 115.

Bella C. Landauer Collection, New-York Historical Society

COACH LINE,
FOR
PHILADELPHIA,
VIA
STATEN ISLAND,
Through in One Day.   Fare $5

THIS Coach will take up and set down its patrons at their lodgings in either city, and will leave New-York from the East side of the Battery at half-past 6 o'clock A. M. in the Steam Boat

NAUTILUS,

via Staten Island, New-Brunswick, Princeton and Trenton, and arrive in Philadelphia, at half-past 6 o'clock, P. M.

For Seats, apply at No. 118 BROADWAY, opposite the City Hotel, the evening previous, to secure a seat.

M. BERGEN,
J. DRAKE, } *Agents.*

For JOHN GULICK & SONS and R. L. HOWELL, Proprietors.

₊ Goods and Baggage at the Owners' Risk.

Nov. 4th, 1820.

115. 1820 COACH NOTICE
4⅜″ × 2⅝″. Anon. New York.
A curious back-sloping italic for 'Staten Island' makes an interesting contrast with the forward-sloping 'Philadelphia'.

Bella C. Landauer Collection, New-York Historical Society

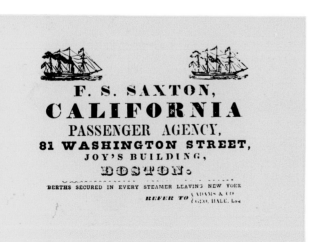

F. S. SAXTON,
CALIFORNIA
PASSENGER AGENCY,
81 WASHINGTON STREET,
JOY'S BUILDING,
BOSTON.

BERTHS SECURED IN EVERY STEAMER LEAVING NEW YORK
REFER TO ADAMS & CO
GEO. HALE, Esq

116. c. 1840 TRAVEL AGENCY SLIP
3″ × 4″. Anon. Boston, Massachusetts.
The cuts of the two steamships were cast on the equivalent of a 36-point body.

New York Public Library

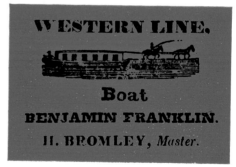

WESTERN LINE.
Boat
BENJAMIN FRANKLIN.
H. BROMLEY, *Master.*

117. c. 1840 CANAL BARGE SLIP
1⅜″ × 2″. Anon. U.S.A.
The same small bold Egyptian capitals are here used for 'BENJAMIN FRANKLIN' as in Fig. 116 in the fourth line, but here set solid.

New York Public Library

OMNIBUS.
To first London *4th July 1829*

G. SHILLIBEER, induced by the universal admiration the above Vehicles called forth
at PARIS, has commenced running one upon the *Parisian mode*, from

PADDINGTON to the BANK.

The Superiority of this Carriage over the ordinary Stage Coaches, for Comfort and Safety,

All the Passengers being Inside,

And the Fare charged from PADDINGTON to the BANK being

ONE SHILLING,

And for Half the Distance,

ONLY SIXPENCE,

Will, the Proprietor trusts, ensure for him that decided support, which in the
conducting of this Vehicle, it will always be his anxious endeavour to deserve.

HOURS OF STARTING:
From Paddington Green to the Bank, at 9, 12, 3, 6, and 8 o'clock.
From the Bank to Paddington, at 10, 1, 4, 7, and 9 o'clock.

Howlett & Brimmer, Printers, 10, Frith Street, Soho.

118. 1829 OMNIBUS NOTICE
$4\frac{7}{8}'' \times 7\frac{1}{8}''$. Howlett & Brimmer, Soho.
Thorowgood's Fat Face in two sizes and in roman
and italic gives emphasis to the notice of this
omnibus, run in the 'Parisian mode'.

Oxford University Press

REDUCED FARES!!!

MESSAGERIES ROYALES,
Rue Notre Dame des Victoires, à Paris.

NEW ENGLISH DILIGENCES TO PARIS,

Every Morning and Evening at Six o'Clock,
FROM
THE WHITE BEAR, PICCADILLY, LONDON,
Also from the Cross Keys, Wood Street, Cheapside,
THE only Offices in London corresponding with the above *Company,* and where
Places can be secured to

PARIS, DOVER, CALAIS,

AMIENS,	OSTEND,	TOURS,	GENEVA,	BAYONNE,
ABBEVILLE,	CAMBRAY,	TOULOUSE,	MOULINS,	TURIN,
BRUSSELS,	VALENCIENNE,	LYON,	STRASBOURG,	MILAN,
LILLE,	BORDEAUX,	DIJON,	MARSEILLE,	&c. &c.

Packet-boats are always ready, at *Dover,* for the conveyance of Passengers booked through—
out; but persons wishing to stop on the road, are allowed to do it, and resume their journey at
pleasure, without any extra expence, provided it is mentioned when the place is taken.

A New ENGLISH LIGHT COACH leaves CALAIS every Morning at 10 o'clock, through *Boulogne,*
Montreuil, Abbeville, Amiens, &c. and performs the journey in *thirty-six hours.* The Fares by this
Coach are:

From London to Paris { Inside .... 3*l.* 14*s.* 0*d.* } *Passage by Sea included.*
{ Cabriolet ...... 3*l.* 2*s.* 0*d.* }
{ Outside .... 2*l.* 14*s.* 0*d.* }

Another ENGLISH LIGHT COACH leaves CALAIS every Afternoon at 5 o'clock, through *Boulogne,*
Montreuil, Abbeville, Poix, Beauvais, &c. and arrives at PARIS in 30 hours. The Fares are as
follows:

From London to Paris { Inside .... 3*l.* 14*s.* 0*d.* } *Passage by Sea included.*
{ Cabriolet ...... 3*l.* 2*s.* 0*d.* }

At Calais, apply to Mr. *Tarnier,* Director, at the Coach Office, *Messe-Maurice's Hotel,* Rue de
Prison, from whence Coaches set out every Day for the places above mentioned.

The Coach puts up at the *Paris Hotel, Dover,* kept by *Victor Poidevin,* and also at the *Ship Inn.*

There are also Coaches, three times a day, from the *White Bear* to
DOVER, RAMSGATE, MARGATE, DEAL, CANTERBURY, CHATHAM, ROCHESTER,
AND GRAVESEND.

NOTICE.—*Persons sending Parcels to the Continent are requested to annex a written
Declaration of the contents and value; also the name and direction of the Person who sent it.*

•* A Waggon to Dover three times a Week.

☞ *The Public are respectfully cautioned against the misrepresentations at the Black
Bear, and their pretending to Book through to Paris, for which they have no authority; the
Royal Messageries having no other Offices, in London, than the WHITE BEAR, Piccadilly,
and the Cross Keys, Wood Street, Cheapside.*

119. *c.* 1830–40 STAGE COACH NOTICE
$7\frac{1}{4}'' \times 4\frac{1}{4}''$. Anon. London.
The combination of woodcuts and restrained use of
display letters and rules gives this little bill some
distinction.

Oxford University Press

LONDON AND PARIS COACHES.

THE UNION
SAFE COACHES,
FROM THE
UNION AND ANTWERP HOTELS,
Gun and Castle Inns,
AND
45, SNARGATE STREET,
DOVER,

Every Morning at 8 and 10 o'clock, and Evening at 6;
TO THE
White Bear, Piccadilly;
BLOSSOMS' INN, LAWRENCE LANE,
Cheapside;
BELL AND CROWN, HOLBORN;
AND 11,
Gracechurch Street, London;
From whence they return every Morning at half-past 7,
and 11 o'clock; and Evening at 7.

*From Dover to London without changing Coaches
or Coachmen.*

Chitty, Back, Gilbert, Sanders, and Co. *Proprietors.*

120. *c.* 1830–40 STAGE COACH NOTICE
$6\frac{1}{4}'' \times 3\frac{3}{4}''$. Anon. London.
The elongated shadow letter used for 'THE UNION'
balances effectively the sloping capitals used for
'DOVER'. Set throughout in French typefaces.

Oxford University Press

Public Meeting

RESPECTING

GLOUCESTER, WORCESTER,

Kidderminster, Stourbridge, Dudley,

AND

BIRMINGHAM

RAILWAY.

TO THE

HIGH BAILIFF

OF THE BOROUGH OF

KIDDERMINSTER.

SIR,

WE, the undersigned, request that you will call an early MEETING of the Inhabitants of this Town, and any other PERSONS in this NEIGHBOURHOOD feeling interested, to take into consideration the Plan of a RAIL ROAD by Mr. WOODDESON, Civil Engineer, to communicate with the **LONDON RAIL ROAD** at **BIRMINGHAM;**—and **CAMBRIAN RAILWAY** at **GLOUCESTER ;**—the particulars of which will be explained by that Gentleman, who is now in this Town, and will attend such Meeting.

JOHN GOUGH, Jun.
PARDOE, HOOMAN, & PARDOE
J. MORTON
JOSEPH NEWCOMB
WATSON, SON, & BADLAND
G. & H. TALBOT & SONS
JOHN GOUGH & SONS
THOS. HALLEN.

In compliance with the above highly respectable Requisition, I hereby appoint a Meeting, for the purpose therein mentioned, to be held at the Guildhall, in the said Borough, on FRIDAY Next, the 22d inst. at Eleven o'Clock in the Forenoon.

S. BEDDOES,

Kidderminster, Nov. 19th, 1833.   *HIGH BAILIFF.*

THOMAS PENNELL, PRINTER, HIGH-STREET, KIDDERMINSTER.

121. 1833 RAILWAY NOTICE
13½″ × 8″. Thomas Pennell, Kidderminster.
The notice is set in a combination of Egyptian and
fat faces, with a particularly graceful early fat face
for the word 'RAILWAY'.

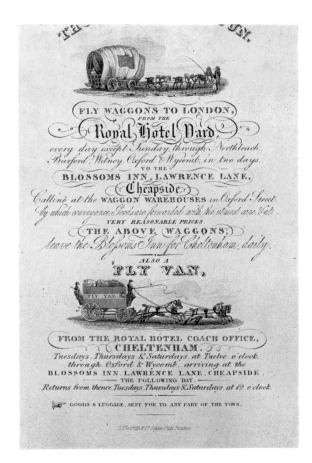

122. *c.* 1830 FLY WAGGON NOTICE
6½″×4″. S. Y. Griffith and Co., Cheltenham.
This notice has unfortunately been mutilated at the
head. It is, however, worth showing for the delicacy
of the engraved lettering which is in such contrast to
the robust typography of the day.

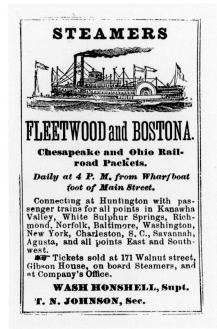

123. *c.* 1879 STEAMSHIP NOTICE
3″ × 2″. Anon. Boston, Massachusetts.
Letterpress card for Chesapeake and Ohio
Railroad Packets.

124. *c.* 1880 OMNIBUS NOTICE
3¼″ × 2″. A. Sims, Nailsworth.
The back of a letterpress card for Clothiers' Arms
Commercial Inn.

Saturday, Aug. 4.

EXCURSION

TO THE

NORE

COMBINING

A View of the Mouth of the Thames and Medway, His Majesty's Fleet, &c.

On Saturday Next

THE

ALBION,

THE FLOATING PALACE,

Capt. READ, will start from off the Tower Stairs at a quarter before Eight, and return early in the Evening, on which occasion, there will be a Grand

Concert and Ball,

PROFESSIONAL

DANCING, RECITATIONS, &c.

ACCOMPANIED BY A

FULL MILITARY BAND.

It will be the endeavour of the Managers to give the same degree of satisfaction in this Excursion, as they had the honor of doing to a select and respectable Company last Year.

TICKETS 5s. EACH, CHILDREN HALF PRICE,

To be had at the Margate Packet Office, Fenchurch Street; and for other References and Particulars, see Small Bills.

Nichols, Printer, Earl's Court, Cranbourn Street, Soho.

125. *c.* 1830 SAILING EXCURSION NOTICE
12″ × 8″ approx. Nichols, Soho.
This very rich piece of typography makes good use of the heavy bold Egyptians and fat faces. The decorated swelled rule is particularly noteworthy. The variation in the form of the lower case 'a's suggests that the Egyptians may well be wood letters. Printed on yellow paper.

Oxford University Press

The use of decorative and plain swelled rules which were first produced by Richard Austin in 1797 and later by both Figgins and Thorowgood provided both decorative and unifying qualities to these heavily weighted bills.

The 'Nore Excursion' bill is a magnificent example of the splendours of the fat faces of Thorne and Thorowgood. These fat faces also appear with effect in the series of railway notices, starting with the one from the oldest railway in the world, the Stockton and Darlington railway. Many of these bills are very charming, such as the 'Working Men's Temperance Society's Excursion to Hull' where the use of a kind of Tuscan letter for the top line gives real movement to the typography (Fig. 131).

STOCKTON & DARLINGTON RAILWAY.

The Public are respectfully informed that the

RAILWAY COACH

BETWEEN
SAINT HELEN'S AUCKLAND & SHILDON,

Will commence to run daily, on Monday, the
10th. of September, 1838, (Sundays excepted)

TWO ADDITIONAL TRIPS

to and from the above places, as under:—

From St. Helen's at 10 o'clock | From Shildon at 11 o'clock.
do.   do.   at 2 do | do.   do.   at 3 do.

FARES:—INSIDE 6d.—OUTSIDE 3d.

THE OTHER LONG TRAINS WILL START AS USUAL.

By Order of the Committee,

JOHN GRAHAM, *Inspector.*

NEW SHILDON. September 5th 1838.

P. FAIR, PRINTER AND BOOKBINDER, BISHOP AUCKLAND

---

126. 1838 RAILWAY NOTICE
7″ × 5½″ approx. P. Fair, Bishop Auckland.
Thorowgood's Fat Face Italic, noticeable for its
capital 'A' with the blobbed terminai, and the rich
bold Egyptian give plenty of life to this little bill.

Curator of Historical Relics British Transport Commission

OXFORD, WORCESTER, AND WOLVERHAMPTON RAILWAY.

EXCURSION

At Reduced Fares,

FROM EVESHAM TO

BLENHEIM,

THE

SEAT OF THE DUKE OF MARLBOROUGH.

ON WEDNESDAY NEXT, THE 22ND JUNE,

Tickets, at Reduced Fares, will be issued by the Train leaving
Worcester at 7 30 a.m., Returning from the Handborough Station
(within 2 Miles of Blenheim) at 6 50 p.m. A number of Con-
veyances will pe provided at the Station.

*An early application for Tickets should be made as only a limited
number will be issued.*

Fares to Handborough and Back:
FIRST CLASS   **SECOND CLASS**

6s. 6d.   4s. 6d.

By Order, W. T. ADCOCK.

JUNE 16TH, 1853.

Printed by J. Stanley, Sidbury Place and Wyld's Lane, Worcester.

---

127. 1853 RAILWAY EXCURSION NOTICE
7½″ × 4½″ approx. J. Stanley, Worcestershire.
Decorated letters did not often make their appearance
in railway posters. The one used for 'BLENHEIM'
is the 4-line Rounded Ornamented issued by H. W.
Caslon in 1844.

Curator of Historical Relics, British Transport Commission

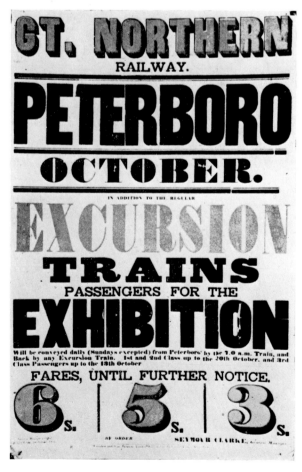

---

128. 1881 RAILWAY EXCURSION NOTICE
15″ × 10″ approx. Waterlow and Sons, London.
Poster printed in three colours, using two versions
of shaded letter, each printed in black and a second
colour.

Curator of Historical Relics, British Transport Commission

EXPEDITIOUS CONVEYANCE PER RAILWAY.

LIPSCOMB'S

(Late BURNETT's)

WAGONS,

From the WHITE HORSE, Friday Street,
Cheapside; and OLD WHITE HORSE
CELLAR, Piccadilly, London;

To Winchester, Southampton, Isle of Wight, Jersey, Guernsey,

AND ALL PLACES ADJACENT,

EVERY AFTERNOON:

To Romsey, Ringwood, Wimborne, Poole, Lymington, Lyndhurst,

Christchurch, Wareham, Swanage, Corfe Castle,

ETC.

TUESDAY, THURSDAY and SATURDAY AFTERNOON, arriving at
these Places the following Days, (Sunday excepted.)

The Proprietor will not be account for any Parcel above the value of £5, unless booked, and
paid for accordingly.——No L. ng-glass, or Glass of any other Description, China or Earth-
enware, insured against any acci-

EXTRA WAGONS for the Conveyance of Gentlemen's Goods to any Part of the Kingdom.

[WARREN, Printer, Winchester.

---

129. *c.* **1840 CARRIER'S NOTICE**
7¼″ × 5¾″. Warren, Winchester.
Printed in black and set in a combination of fat
faces and Egyptians.

Travel notices

Great Western Railway.

EPSOM RACES.

On MONDAY, MAY 25th, 1868,

LEWIS'S

EXCURSION TRAIN

WILL RUN TO

LONDON

From Shrewsbury at 10-55 a.m.
Wellington at 11-15 a.m.

FARES FOR THE DOUBLE JOURNEY.

COV. CARRIAGE 12/-

FIRST CLASS 24s.

Returning on the following Thursday, May 28th, from the Paddington
Station London at 10-30 a.m.

The Tickets are not transferable, and only available and from the Stations named upon them, and by the TRAINs specified in the Bills, Passengers using them by any other TRAIN will be charged the full Ordinary Fare. Passengers are allowed One Package of personal Luggage, Free, but it must be distinctly understood that it is at their own risk. Bills and every information to be had at the Stations and from

DAVID LEWIS, Agent,

MAY, 1868. Excursion Office, 7, Pride Hill, Shrewsbury

130. 1868 EXCURSION NOTICE
8″ × 4¾″. Anon. Shrewsbury.
The lively contrast between the delicate decorative
type for 'Excursion Train' (pica 2-line Ornamented
No. 4 from the Caslon Type Foundry after 1854)
and the massive semi-Tuscan capitals for 'LONDON'
give distinction to this bill.

CHEAP TRIP TO HULL

ON EASTER TUESDAY, APRIL 2nd, 1872.

THE COMMITTEE OF THE SCARBOROUGH

WORKING MEN'S TEMPERANCE SOCIETY

Respectfully announce that they have arranged with the North Eastern Railway Company to run a Grand

EXCURSION TRAIN

TO THE POPULOUS TOWN OF

HULL

FROM

Scarborough, Filey, & Burlington,

ON EASTER TUESDAY, APRIL 2nd, 1872.

Recreation is necessary to the comfort and happiness of the people. Temperance Societies seek to promote healthy amusements as well as sobriety; and surely there cannot be a more agreeable mode of spending the Holidays---at Easter especially---than having an Excursion to some neighbouring town for a short relaxation from the cares and anxieties of business.

Pleasure Parties will be amply repaid, for there is something attractive at almost every turn. A ramble round the spacious Docks, Wharfs, Quays, and Steamboat Jetties, is worth a visit; these are probably the largest in the Kingdom. In the Market Place, near the South End, stands the noble equestrian gilded Statue of William III, erected in 1735. At the entrance of Junction Street is an elegant Doric Column, upwards of 72 feet in height, erected at a cost of £1,250, and known as the Wilberforce Monument, being a tribute to that great statesman and philanthropist, who was a native of Hull, and whose Statue surmounts the pillar. The Public Buildings in the town are numerous and elegant, to describe which would occupy considerably more space than the limits of this bill will allow.

Leave SCARBRO' at 7 a.m.; FILEY at 7-20 a.m.; BURLINGTON at 8 a.m.

FARES TO HULL AND BACK (COVERED CARRIAGES):

Scarborough and Filey, 2s. 6d.; Burlington, 1s. 6d.

CHILDREN UNDER TWELVE YEARS OF AGE, HALF-PRICE

THE TRAIN WILL RETURN FROM HULL AT 5 P.M.   NO LUGGAGE ALLOWED.

To prevent confusion and facilitate the departure of the train the Booking Offices at Scarborough, Filey, and Bridlington Railway Stations will be open on Saturday, March 30th, from 6-30 to 8 p.m., for the sale of Tickets; and on the morning of April 2nd, previous to departure of the train.

W. W. COOPLAND, PRINTER, SCARBORO'.

131. 1872 RAILWAY EXCURSION NOTICE
10″ × 7½″ approx. W. W. Coopland, Scarborough.
Once again the massive splendour of a bold Egyptian typeface provides a foil for the unusual version of the Tuscan letter used for the top line and the delicate little cut of the train.

Curator of Historical Relics, British Transport Commission

The 'Palo Alto' bill shows some decline in the quality of the type faces, but I can forgive it everything for the charming cut of the wood-burning locomotive (Fig. 132).

The use of typefounder's stock blocks such as in Fig. 132 enabled the jobbing printer, from the beginning of the nineteenth century, to compete with the more versatile engraver. When the blocks were engraved by artists of the calibre of the Bewicks and Luke Clennell in England and Alexander Anderson in America, the job printer got off to a flying start.

The typefounders were not slow in providing the jobbing printers, in both America and Britain with a wide variety of stock blocks for their travel notices. The age of steam certainly seems to have inspired the trade engravers to produce some most spirited little cuts, ranging from very small ones actually cast on type-size bodies. The little train shown in the Hull Excursion bill is very similar to one shown by Miller and Richard in their 1887 type specimen book, cast on a 2-line English body. The Mackellar, Smiths and Jordan cut in Fig. 132 is from a stock stereo, reproduced from a wood engraving.

☞ SEE MAP INSIDE. ☜

PALO ✳ ALTO!

THE BUSINESS AND RESIDENCE TOWN
OF THE
LELAND STANFORD, JR., UNIVERSITY.

1,000 BEAUTIFUL LOTS,
AT AUCTION, ON THE GROUNDS,
THURSDAY, MAY 3rd, 1888,
AT 12 O'CLOCK, M.

✳ SPECIAL EXCURSION ✳

Trains will leave: San Francisco; Fourth and Townsend Streets, 10 A.M., sharp; Valencia and 26th Streets, 10.10 A.M., sharp.

$1.00 — ROUND TRIP TICKETS — $1.00

San Jose; S. P. R. R. Depot, (Broad Gauge) 10.30 A.M., sharp.

50 Cts. — ROUND TRIP TICKETS, — 50 Cts.

TERMS OF SALE, ONE-THIRD CASH.
Balance in Equal Payments, in 12 and 18 Months.   Interest, 8 per Cent. per Annum

N. C. CARNALL & CO.

WM. BUTTERFIELD,
Auctioneer.

624 Market Street,
San Francisco.

132. 1888 RAIL EXCURSION NOTICE
12″ × 8½″. Anon. San Francisco.
Sixteen or seventeen different typefaces seem an undue number for one notice. The wood engraving is a stock block from the Mackellar, Smiths and Jordan Typefoundry of Philadelphia, with the words 'Palo Alto' dropped in, in type. The sans serif types are most feeble in comparison with the Egyptians.

Oxford University Press

LONDON, CHATHAM, & DOVER RAILWAY.

Dover Regatta.

THURSDAY, AUGUST 24, 1871.

A SPECIAL TRAIN

WILL RUN TO **DOVER** AS UNDER FROM

Chatham	... at 8 55 a.m.	Teynham	... at 9 30 a.m.
New Brompton	... „ 9 0 „	**Faversham**	... „ 9 40 „
Rainham ...	... „ 9 7 „	Selling ...	... „ 9 50 „
Newington	... „ 9 14 „	**Canterbury**	... „ 10 5 „
Sheerness	... „ 8 38 „	Bekesbourne	... „ 10 13 „
Queenboro'	... „ 8 43 „	Adisham ...	... „ 10 20 „
Sittingbourne	... „ 9 22 „		

The Special Train will return from DOVER HARBOUR at 9.30 p.m., and DOVER PRIORY at 9.32 p.m.

RETURN TICKETS

At Single Fares for the Double Journey,

BY THIS TRAIN ONLY.

RETURN TICKETS AT SINGLE FARES

WILL ALSO BE ISSUED

To **DOVER** from **RAMSGATE** and all intermediate Stations up to and including **WHITSTABLE**, by the Train leaving RAMSGATE at 7.50 a.m., available to return by the Special Train leaving DOVER at 7.5 p.m.

The Tickets will be available to return on the day of issue only, and by the Trains named above.
No Luggage allowed.   *Children under Twelve half-price.*
August 16th, 1871.   **J. S. FORBES, Managing Director.**

S.E.B.—105.—7U.   Printed at the Company's Works, Victoria Station, Pimlico.

LONDON BRIGHTON & SOUTH COAST RAILWAY.

SMITHFIELD CLUB

CATTLE SHOW WEEK.

CHEAP VISIT

TO THE

GRAND AQUARIUM

AT

BRIGHTON.

Wednesday & Friday, Dec. 10th & 12th.

A CHEAP TRAIN

To BRIGHTON

FROM

LONDON BRIDGE 9.0 a.m.,

Calling at **CROYDON 9.15 a.m.,**

Returning from Brighton 7.30 p.m.

Fares to Brighton & back, including admission to the Aquarium.

First Class.	Covered Carriages.
# 8s.	# 4s.

Children under Twelve years of age, Half-price.
Passengers with Luggage charged Ordinary Fares. Tickets not Transferable; only available to and from the Stations named thereon, by the above-named Train, and on the date of issue.

London Bridge Terminus,
November, 1873.   (BY ORDER) **J. P. KNIGHT, General Manager.**

{15,000—11-11-73}.

Waterlow & Sons, Printers, Great Winchester Street, E.C.

---

133. 1871 EXCURSION NOTICE
7″ × 4″. Company's Printing Works, Pimlico.
Printed in black on a lavender-coloured paper. 'Dover Regatta' is set in Miller and Richard's 4-line Skeleton Antique.

134. 1873 EXCURSION NOTICE
6¾″ × 4¼″. Waterlow and Sons, London.
Printed in black and red on a lemon-yellow paper and set in a grotesque, Egyptian, modern, and (for Grand Aquarium) 2-line Great Primer Antique.

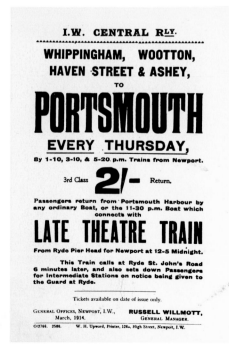

I.W. CENTRAL RLY.

WHIPPINGHAM, WOOTTON, HAVEN STREET & ASHEY,

TO

PORTSMOUTH

EVERY THURSDAY,

By 1-10, 3-10, & 5-20 p.m. Trains from Newport.

3rd Class **2/-** Return.

Passengers return from Portsmouth Harbour by any ordinary Boat, or the 11-30 p.m. Boat which connects with

LATE THEATRE TRAIN

From Ryde Pier Head for Newport at 12-5 Midnight.

This Train calls at Ryde St. John's Road 6 minutes later, and also sets down Passengers for Intermediate Stations on notice being given to the Guard at Ryde.

Tickets available on date of issue only.

GENERAL OFFICES, NEWPORT, I.W.   **RUSSELL WILLMOTT,**
March, 1914.   **GENERAL MANAGER.**

O/2766. 2500.   W. H. Upward, Printer, 126A, High Street, Newport, I.W.

135. 1914 RAILWAY NOTICE
15″ × 10″. W. H. Upward, Newport, I.o.W.
A notice devoid of any typographical distinction.
Curator of Historical Relics, British Transport Commission

Travel notices

The Anchor Line notice shows the depths of typographic depravity that the influences of 'free drawn, artistic lithography' had wreaked on the work of the letterpress printer. In contrast, William Fenton's omnibus notice (Fig. 137) is a deliberate and most successful evocation of mid-Victorian printing, in a truly typographic idiom.

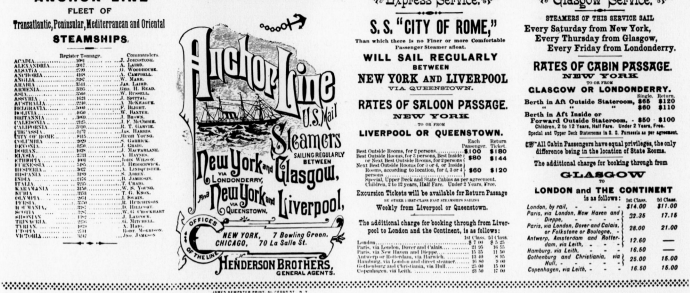

136. *c.* 1885 STEAMSHIP NOTICE
5½″ × 12½″. James Kempster Print. Cedar St. N.Y.
An 8-page folder with wood engraved title page, set in a variety of typefaces, including an italic sans serif for the 'Glasgow to London and the Continent' timetable.

New York Public Library

137. 1956 OMNIBUS NOTICE
13¾″×18″. William Fenton typ. W. S. Cowell Ltd., Ipswich.
Printed in black and red on yellow paper within a border of printers' ornaments. This is an intentionally evocative design, using Victorian typefaces, including Sans Serif Shaded and Expanded Egyptian, from Stephenson Blake's Caslon Letter Foundry.

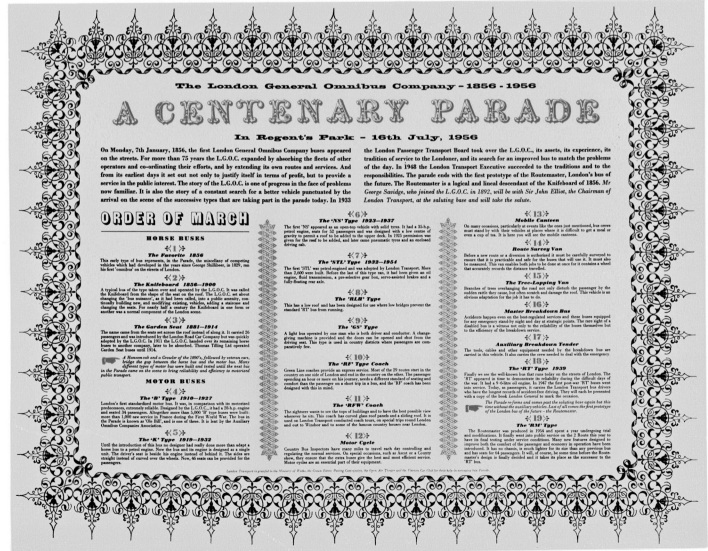

Travel notices

Modern railway notices are as a rule not of very much interest, though the 'Husking Bee' bill from the New Haven Railroad makes good use of the narrow playbill form and the very large wood letters. The Railway Museum poster is avowedly evocative but makes a brilliant use of 'period' typography. Today it would seem that the organizing design ability of someone like Zéró (Mr Hans Schleger) is needed to achieve what an untutored compositor could do with ease in the early years of the nineteenth century. Zéró's fine poster for the Railway Museum owes much to a handsome bill advertising the 'Coach called the Experiment, which commenced travelling on Monday 10th October 1825'. The two-hour journey cost passengers 1s., with no more than 14 lb. of baggage. This bill is on show in the York Museum.

138. 1958 RAIL EXCURSION NOTICE
18″ × 6¼″. Anon. New York.
Printed in black on orange. A welcome return to the vitality of the early nineteenth century bills – even though this was printed within the last few years.

ZÉRÓ

Visit The
Railway
⚬━❧✦❦━⚬
MUSEUM
◆ YORK ◆

In the Railway Museum at York will be found *ITEMS* as cannot be discovered elsewhere in the Realm, including such rare EX-HIBITS as a Brass Plate on which is inscribed '*Take Notice*: *This Engine is the property of Alexander Tracy of Cambridge*'. On View are hundreds of Relics from the Past : – Buttons, Tickets, Engravings, Uniforms, Train Staffs, Paintings & Signals.

ON MONDAY, TUESDAY,

THE LARGE EXHIBITS SECTION - includes Engines resplendent in their *Original Livery*; superb Examples of Engineering Craftsman-ship, displayed for the *Edification and Amusement of Persons* visiting the Exhibition. Also included is the *HETTON Travelling Engine* by Mr. Stephenson, the Oldest Rail Way Locomotive in the Museum.

WEDNESDAY, THURSDAY
FRIDAY,

In no other Place is there Presented to the Public Eye such a Panorama of Railway History.

& SATURDAY

ENTRANCE to *the* EXHIBITION can be made between the hours of 10 o'clock in the Morning & 5 in the Afternoon. *VISITORS* pay 6d each children 3d *for* admission to the *hall* containing the *Large Exhibits*. ADMISSION for *Organised* Parties on *Sundays* by Arrangement.

PUBLISHED BY THE BRITISH TRANSPORT COMMISSION (B.R.)   PRINTED AT THE BAYNARD PRESS

139. 1960 RAILWAY EXCURSION POSTER
40″ × 25″. Zéró typ. Baynard Press, London.
Printed on a bright yellow paper in black and five colours.

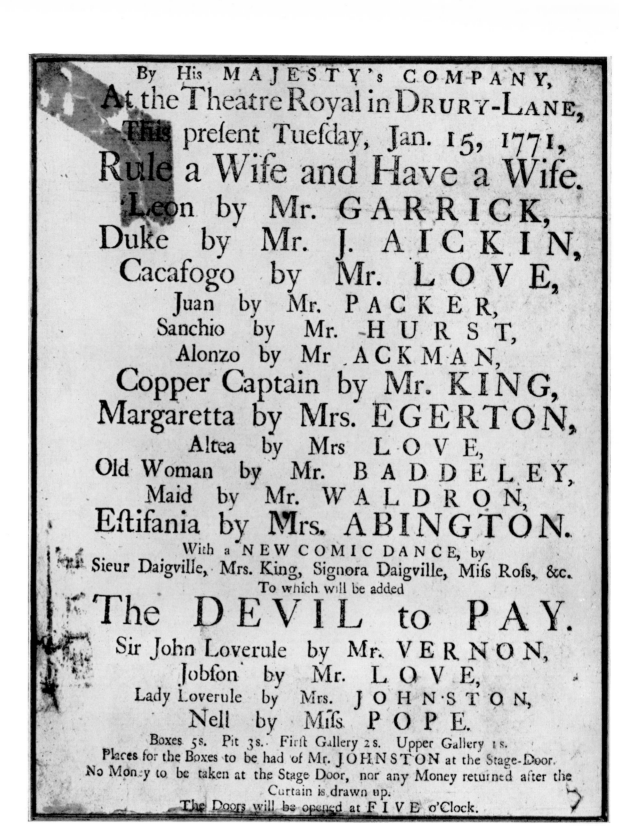

By His MAJESTY's COMPANY,
At the Theatre Royal in DRURY-LANE,
This present Tuesday, Jan. 15, 1771,
Rule a Wife and Have a Wife.
Leon by Mr. GARRICK,
Duke by Mr. J. AICKIN,
Cacafogo by Mr. LOVE,
Juan by Mr. PACKER,
Sanchio by Mr. HURST,
Alonzo by Mr ACKMAN,
Copper Captain by Mr. KING,
Margaretta by Mrs. EGERTON,
Altea by Mrs LOVE,
Old Woman by Mr. BADDELEY,
Maid by Mr. WALDRON,
Estifania by Mrs. ABINGTON.
With a NEW COMIC DANCE, by
Sieur Daigville, Mrs. King, Signora Daigville, Miss Ross, &c.
To which will be added
The DEVIL to PAY.
Sir John Loverule by Mr. VERNON,
Jobson by Mr. LOVE,
Lady Loverule by Mrs. JOHNSTON,
Nell by Miss POPE.
Boxes 5s. Pit 3s. First Gallery 2s. Upper Gallery 1s.
Places for the Boxes to be had of Mr. JOHNSTON at the Stage-Door.
No Money to be taken at the Stage Door, nor any Money returned after the
Curtain is drawn up.
The Doors will be opened at FIVE o'Clock.

140. 1771 PLAYBILL
9″ × 7″ approx. Anon. London.
Apparently set in Jackson's typeface, this clearly set
out bill for David Garrick's performance at Drury
Lane in *Rule a Wife and Have a Wife* and also *The
Devil to Pay* makes good use of the contrast between
capitals and small letters.
Andrew Block

Entertainment notices

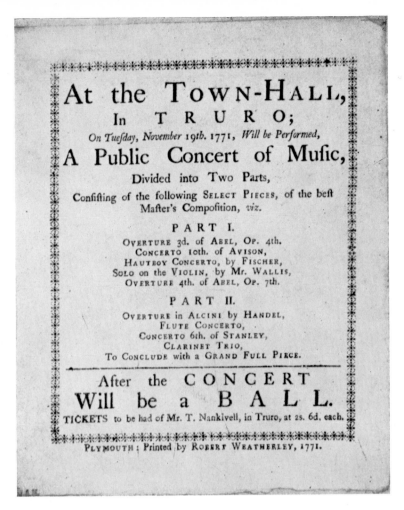

At the TOWN-HALL,
In TRURO;
On Tuesday, November 19th. 1771, Will be Performed,
A Public Concert of Music,
Divided into Two Parts,
Consisting of the following SELECT PIECES, of the best
Master's Composition, viz.

PART I.
OVERTURE 3d. of ABEL, OP. 4th.
CONCERTO 10th. of AVISON,
HAUTBOY CONCERTO, by FISCHER,
SOLO on the VIOLIN, by Mr. WALLIS,
OVERTURE 4th. of ABEL, OP. 7th.

PART II.
OVERTURE in ALCINI by HANDEL,
FLUTE CONCERTO,
CONCERTO 6th. of STANLEY,
CLARINET TRIO,
To CONCLUDE with a GRAND FULL PIECE.

After the CONCERT
Will be a BALL.
TICKETS to be had of Mr. T. Nankivell, in Truro, at 2s. 6d. each.

PLYMOUTH: Printed by ROBERT WEATHERLEY, 1771.

God save the King!
WOODBRIDGE
FESTIVAL.
IN HONOUR OF THE
CORONATION OF KING GEORGE THE FOURTH,
THURSDAY, JULY 19th, 1821,
A Public Dinner
Will be given to 500 Old People and Children, on the Lawn of GEORGE THOMAS, Esq. precisely
at One o'clock; and at Three o'clock the following
Rustic Sports and Amusements
WILL COMMENCE:
A JUMPING MATCH,
By Twelve Men, or not less than Eight,
Each man to jump in a good 4-bushel sack (to be provided by himself) the distance of 100 yards,
for a Hat, which will be given to the winner.
A Grinning Match,
THROUGH HORSE COLLARS, FOR A QUARTER-OF-AN-HOUR,
By Six Men, for a Pair of Shoes, (each Man to provide himself with a Collar) which will be
given to the winner, and 2s. 6d. to the second best.
A SPINNING MATCH,
By Three Old Women, for a Pound of Tea, (each Woman to provide herself with a Wheel) the
Wool will be furnished by the Stewards, and the prize adjudged by a competent person.
A BOBBING MATCH,
By Six Boys, for Five Shillings,
Six earthen pans will be provided by the Stewards, and Sixpence deposited in each with some
Flour, and the Boy who shall first take out the Sixpence with his mouth (having his hands tied
behind him) shall receive the above Prize, and the second boy, doing the same shall receive 2s. 6d.
A Jingling Match,
BY NOT LESS THAN TEN MEN,
For a good Cheese, and 2s. 6d. the Man who catches the Jingler to receive the first Prize, but if
the Jingler is not caught in half-an-hour, he is to receive both prizes. Each man is to be blind-
folded, and placed at equal distances from the Jingler before starting.
A CLIMBING MATCH,
For a Hat placed on the top of a Pole, the first person that reach the top to be entitled to the Hat.
A WHEELBARROW RACE,
BY SIX MEN BLINDFOLDED, FOR A PAIR OF SHOES,
The above Prizes will be determined by the Stewards, appointed for that purpose.
The Names of Persons for the above Sports, to be entered at Mr. GALL's, Druggist, on or before Wednesday Evening.
N. B. No Person will be allowed to go inside the Ropes during the time of Dinner, except such as are appointed to keep the
ground clear.
[J. LODER, Printer, Bookseller, and Stationer.]

141. 1771 CONCERT NOTICE
7″ × 5½″ approx. Robert Weatherley, Plymouth.
The border of printers' ornaments in this very
'bookish' notice, and some of the typefaces come from
William Caslon's Foundry.
Oxford University Press

142. 1821 DINNER NOTICE
13″ × 8¼″. J. Loder, Woodbridge.
2-line English Ornamented for 'Woodbridge', probably Thorne's, and Thorowgood's magnificent Fat
Face Italic for 'Festival' and an open gothic give
variety without too much dis-array to the design.

Entertainment notices

Early playbills were all set in a bookish style and
in the typefaces then in use for bookwork. The
only variations that the printer could produce
were by spacing, using borders and ringing as
many changes as possible on his limited reper-
toire of type, by using his founts of capitals and
small capitals and lower case, both in roman and
italic. The little bill of 'A Public Concert of
Music in Truro Town Hall' is beautifully laid
out with a quite subtle use of letter spacing in
the lines of capitals. David Garrick's bill (Fig.
140) is rather less elegant than the Truro bill,
but its printer has produced a remarkably good
bill from fairly scanty typographic sources.

The transition from the bookish layouts to
rich black display arrangements took place with
some speed, for the moment Robert Thorne
placed his first fat face types on the market,
printers all over the place saw the obvious
advantage of these robust and vigorous types.
One day they were setting bills that looked like
book title pages, and the next, or so it would

seem, they were shouting their wares in great
fat black letters.

The intermediate stage can be seen in the
American bill (Fig. 143). The 'Boston Theatre'
makes use of an elegant semi-fat face and
also of an inline black letter for 'Battle of
Bunker Hill'. A more stunted version of this
inline black letter appears in two other bills here
(Figs. 142 and 144), for the song 'Here's to the
Maiden' in the Grand Lodge State of New York
bill and 'Rustic Sports and Amusements' in the
Woodbridge Festival bill.

The black letter must seem a curious choice
for display in such things as playbills. It was one
of the happier typographic productions of the
Regency period and whether used as fat face
black letters or as inline types, it has all the
gaiety that Regency Gothic architecture has and
no possible connection with liturgical or legal
printing which, one would think, would be its
more usual provenance.

BOSTON THEATRE.

THE BATTLE OF BUNKER HILL, FOR THIS NIGHT ONLY.

The Grand Washington Transparency, for the fourth time..........Tekeli, for the last time this season.

THIS EVENING, (WEDNESDAY,) APRIL 5th, 1820,

Will be performed, (first and only, time for several years,) the Patriotic Play, in 5 acts, called the

Battle of Bunker Hill.

"Let the Rallying Word through all the Day, be, LIBERTY OR DEATH,"

Of Rome's and Cato's fall, the World has rung :
Why not Columbia's rising fame be sung ?
If Rome her Brutus, and her Cato boast,
Her Washington, and Warren, each a host,
Columbia owns ; with thousand names beside,
The least of which, would swell the Roman Pride.

Gen. Warren,	Mr. Pelby.	Sir William Howe,	Mr. Holland.
Gen. Prescott,	Mr. Adamson.	Gen. Gage,	Mr. McCulley.
Gen. Putnam,	Mr. Dykes.	Harman,	Mr. Baker.
Abercrombie,	Mr. Williams.	American Soldier,	Mr. Spooner.
Elvira,	Mrs. Young.	Anna,	Miss Jones.

ACT FIRST........SCENE FIRST.

A VIEW OF STATE STREET..............LORD PERCY AND BRITISH SOLDIERS,

Returning, fatigued and disordered, from Lexington..................Act Second, CHAMBER....GENERAL WARREN discovered *Reading a Letter,* which announces the DEFEAT AT LEXINGTON...........Act Third,

A View of the American Camp.....Act Fourth, A View of Bunker Hill....Bunker Hill Fortified.

THE BATTLE....CHARLESTOWN IN FLAMES !

The BRITISH march towards the Hill, to the Music of " *Yankee Doodle*"....Three times they make the Assault, and each time are driven back....After the third Repulse, WARREN descends and Addresses the AMERICANS....The BATTLE is renewed, GENERAL WARREN *receives a Mortal Wound, and Dies for his Country !*

End of the Play, an Interlude, (fourth time,) in which will be Displayed, A GRAND HISTORICAL and EMBLEMATICAL.

TRANSPARENCY.

DELINEATING the IMPORTANT EVENTS in the MILITARY and CIVIL LIFE of the ILLUSTRIOUS WASHINGTON.

IN THE BACK OF WHICH, IS

a Whole Length Figure of WASHINGTON ; at his feet, Civil and Military Emblems ; and on each side, the Ensigns of his Country......On the Cornice of the Pedestal, is inscribed : *"Born February 22d, 1732 ;"*......On the Plinth : *"Died December 13th, 1799."*

IN THE CENTRE OF THE FRIZE, AND SUPPORTED BY THE COLUMNS, IS A KEY STONE, ON WHICH IS WRITTEN :

"First in War, First in Peace, and First in the Hearts of His Fellow Citizens.".............Under, in the Horizon, are the *Thirteen Stars,* Emblematic of the *Thirteen Original States.*

The Standard of Liberty ! Addressed to the Armies of the United States, - - - by *Mrs. Williams.*

To which will be added, (last time this season,) the Grand Melo Drama, in 3 acts, called

TEKELI.

Count Tekeli.	Mr. Williams.	Edmund,	Mr. Baker.	Conrad,	Mr. Pelby.
Wolf, *(his friend.)*	Mr. Charnock.	Frank,	Mr. Holland.	Maurice,	Mr. Adamson.
Brasdefer,	Mr. Bray.	Count Caraffa,	Mr. McCulley.	Isidore,	Mr. Jones.
Alexina,	Mrs. Powell.	Christine,	Miss Jones.	Officer,	Mr. Spooner.

☞ Due notice will be given of the second performance of *Raymond and Agnes*...Also, of the fourth representation of *Cinderella.*

☞ TIME OF RISING THE CURTAIN IS ALTERED TO QUARTER BEFORE SEVEN O'CLOCK.

143. 1820 PLAYBILL
10″ × 7¼″. Anon. Boston, Massachusetts.
Traditional typography with a sparing use of fat
face and the 'open' gothic.

Oxford University Press

Entertainment notices

The use of colour in playbills was not very common, though the circus bills of Polito and others made good use of it. The most restrained use of a second printing that I have ever seen is in the 'Madame Vestris' bill (Fig. 145), where the bill is printed entirely in black, but for the one word 'OLYMPIC'. What drove the compositor to this extravagance I cannot imagine, yet it is strangely effective and the interchange of the heavy Egyptian capitals and the fat face italic echoed by the little italic Egyptians provides movement.

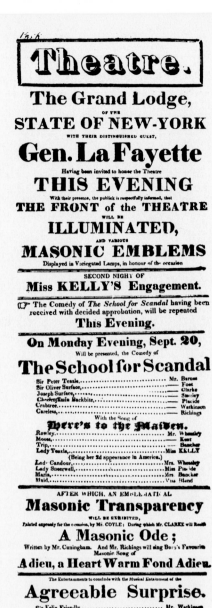

MADAME VESTRIS
Royal Olympic Theatre.

THIS EVENING, MONDAY, NOVEMBER 28th, 1836.
Will be presented, Seventeenth Time, a Burletta, entitled The

BARRACK ROOM.

The MUSIC SELECTED & ARRANGED by Mr. TULLY.---Madame VESTRIS' SONGS by Mr. BARNETT
The Marquis de Cruzac,   Mr. F. MATTHEWS,
Colonel Ferrier,   - - - - - Mr. JAMES VINING,
Captain Valmont,   Mr. SELBY,   Bernard,   Mr. J. BLAND,
Batiste, Mr. HUGHES,   Michel, Mr. HITCHINSON,   Notary, Mr. PINSENT,
Officers, Messrs. MORRIS, MORGAN and DAVIS.
Clarisse de Cruzac, - - - - - Madame VESTRIS,
In which Character she will sing
"WHAT CAN MEAN THIS REGAL GIFT?" AND
"WAKE, WAKE, THOUGH I AM LATE."
After which, the Burletta of A

HANDSOME HUSBAND.

Mr. Wyndham, — Mr. CHARLES MATHEWS,
Mr. Henry Fitzherbert, — Mr. JAMES VINING,
Stephen, Mr. KERRIDGE.
Mrs. Twisden, Mrs. MACNAMARA,   Mrs. Melford, Miss FITZWALTER,
Mrs Wyndham, — — — Madame VESTRIS.
To which will be added, Twenty-Fifth Time, a Burletta, in One Act, entitled

HE WOULD BE AN ACTOR.

Mr. Currant, Mr. W. VINING,   Edward Sinclair, Mr. SELBY,
Griffith Morgan, Mr. WYMAN,   Dicky Darling, Mr. OXBERRY,
Motley, Mr. CHARLES MATHEWS, in which he will sing
"The Pleasures of Acting," and the Welsh Ballad of "Jenny Jones."
Becky Morgan, Mrs. ORGER.
To conclude with the highly popular Burlesque Burletta, in One Act, entitled

Olympic Devils.
Or, ORPHEUS & EURYDICE!
INFERNALS.

Pluto, — (King of "Oh, no, we never mention it," an Imp-erious Deity) — Mr. J. BLAND,
Proserpine, — — (his Queen "by Jupiter!" an Imp-rovident Housewife) — Mrs. KNIGHT,
Minos, (Lora low Chancellor) { Mr. TULLY,
Rhadamanthus, (Vice Chancellor) } Imp-artial Judges { Mr. DAVIS,
Æacus, (Master of the [hot] Rolls) { Mr. HUGHES,
Clotho, — — { { Miss JACKSON,
Lachesis, — — { Three Imp-enetrable Spinsters "all of that Parish," } Miss A. JACKSON,
Atropos, — — { { Miss R. IRELAND,
Tisiphone, Megara, & Alecto, (Three Imp-lacable Furies) Miss BARTLETT, Mrs. T. IRELAND, & Miss RANDOM,
Cerberus, — (Head Porter, an Imp-udent Dog) — Mr. MORRIS,
Charon, — (a Wherry Ferry Funny Fireman-Waterman, and Imp-orter of Spirits) — Mr. WYMAN,
Leader of Pluto's Band, (an Imp-osing Professor, with an Imp-romptu Performance) by OLD SCRATCH, from Fiddler's Green, who is Imp-eratively engaged on this occasion.
Ixion, — Mr. MORGAN,   Sisyphus, — Mr. PINSENT
SUPERNALS.
Phœbus Apollo, (a shining Character) Mr. KERRIDGE,   Pan, (a Pan-tomimic Character) Mr. COLLIER,
Silenus, — (a Drunken Character) — Mr. W. VINING,
IMMORTAL MORTALS.
Orpheus, — — (a Charming Musician) — — — Madame VESTRIS,
Eurydice, — — (his Departed Wife) — Mrs. ANDERSON,
First Bacchante, Miss FITZWALTER,   Second Bacchante, Miss CRAWFORD,   Third Bacchante, Miss NORMAN.

145. 1836 PLAYBILL
13¾″ × 8¼″. Anon. London.
The unlikely introduction of vermilion for just one
word adds sparkle to this well-balanced bill with its
fat faces and very bold Egyptians.

144. 1824 PLAYBILL
21″ × 5″. Anon. New York.
A traditional bill using modern semi-fat faces.

Oxford University Press

103

146. 1844 PLAYBILL
$28\frac{3}{4}'' \times 8\frac{1}{2}''$. Phillips and Co., Brighton.
The woodcut had cracked badly before this was printed; over a dozen display types are used here.

Egyptian Hall, Piccadilly.

THE

MISSOURI

LEVIATHAN,

WITH THE LARGEST AND MOST INTERESTING COLLECTION OF

North American Antediluvian Animal Remains in the World,

Is now Exhibiting in the Upper Saloon of the above Hall, from 10 o'Clock A.M. until 10 P.M.

This magnificent Collection has been disinterred by the Proprietor, in various parts of the State of Missouri, sixteen hundred to two thousand miles from New York City; and is the fruit of many years' laborious, highly expensive, and frequently dangerous excursions in the wilderness of the "far West."

The Missouri Leviathan, between whose legs the Mammoth, and even the mighty Iguanodon may easily have crept, is universally acknowledged by men of science to be the greatest phenomenon ever discovered in Natural History. On viewing this vast relic, which after lying prostrate in the bosom of the earth for thousands of years, now standing erect in all its grandeur, the beholder will be lost in wonder and astonishment at its immensity and perfect preservation.

Disinterred 1840,

After five months' labour,

In N. lat. 40°, W. long. 95°

30 feet in length, nearly

15 feet high.

Tusks, from point to point, 21 feet.

A LECTURE,

AT THREE O'CLOCK, DAILY.

Mr. A. KOCH, the discoverer of the above rare and unique Collection, will deliver Lectures and give statements of Indian traditions, connected with various Specimens contained in this Collection; he will also show Specimens and make statements, which bear indisputable evidence that the human race existed coeval or contemporary with the Tetracaulodon, Missourium, Mastodon, and many other extinct animals.

Admission ONE SHILLING. No additional Charge for the Lecture.

** Mr. KOCH is generally present, to give explanations to visitors.

Pamphlets, containing a Catalogue of the whole Collection, and giving a description of the Missouri Leviathan, with its supposed habits, Indian traditions, &c. &c. can be had at the door of the Sa'oon.

E. Fisher, Printer, 33, Cannon Street, City.

147. *c.* 1845 EXHIBITION AND LECTURE NOTICE
$8\frac{3}{4}'' \times 5\frac{3}{4}''$. E. Fisher, London.
The crisply cut wood engraving had already filled up in the original. Subtle little cuts like this need better presswork than such notices received.

Playbills

It is remarkable that these nineteenth century playbills have survived, for they were printed on paper of almost tissue thinness. As the century progressed, both in America and in England, the typography became more complicated and an even greater variety of typefaces was used. The 'Pine Street Theatre' bill (Fig. 150) shows a pleasant mixture of woodcut, decorated letters and the useful (for these tall, narrow bills) Slim-black, used for 'Uncle Tom's Cabin'. The theatre bills never attained the richness and colour shown by the circuses, such as Astley's (Fig. 152) or the variety of typefaces in such a bill as the Circus Royal (Fig. 151) where no less than twenty-seven faces were used.

LAST THREE NIGHTS

Of the present Engagement of those popular American Artistes,

MR. and MRS. BARNEY WILLIAMS,

THE ORIGINAL
IRISH BOY and YANKEE GAL.

Mr. BENJAMIN WEBSTER,
MR. WRIGHT,
AND
MADAME CELESTE.

THIS EVENING, THURSDAY, JULY 24th, 1856,
Will be presented (51st Time) the Greatly Successful New Adelphi Drama, in 2 Acts,
BY W. J. SORRELL & J. LANGFORD, ESQRS. CALLED

LIKE AND UNLIKE.

	Sir Arthur Redgrave,		MR. GARDEN,
Harry Mowbray, Esq.,	(of Buck Park, Yorkshire)	Mr. BENN. WEBSTER,
Mr. Arthur Leslie,	(his Cousin)	Mr. CHARLES SELBY,
Mr. Peter Potter,	(of Manchester)	Mr. WRIGHT,
	Louis,	Mr. MORELAND,
Lisette,		MADAME CELESTE,
A Lady,		******

Six Months are supposed to elapse between the Acts.

CHARACTERS IN ACT II.

Harry Mowbray, Esq.,		Mr. BENN. WEBSTER,
Mr. Arthur Leslie,		Mr. CHARLES SELBY,
Mr. Peter Potter,		Mr. WRIGHT,
The Count Kromowskie,		Mr. PAUL BEDFORD,
	François,	Mr. HENRY,
Madame Ventadour,		Miss WYNDHAM,
The Countess Kromowskie,		MADAME CELESTE,
Lisette,		******
Toinette,		Miss LAIDLAW.

On FRIDAY, July 25th,

Will be presented, the Highly Successful Adelphi Drama of the

FLYING DUTCHMAN!

Captain Peppercoal,	(formerly Captain of a Trade Ship)	Mr. CHARLES SELBY,
Lieutenant Mowdrey,	(a Young Sea Officer)	Mr. J. G. SHORE,
Peter Von Bummel,	a Cockney Dutchman and Dabbler in the Law,	Mr. WRIGHT,
	alias a Benighted Shepherdess,	
Toby Varnish,	His Friend; a Physical Marine Painter and a Bear—not the Great Bear,	Mr. BEN. WEBSTER,
Tom Willis,	(Mate of the "Enterprize")	Mr. PAUL BEDFORD,
Mynheer Von Swiggs,	(Purser of the same) Mr. SANDERS, Smutta, (a Slave) Mr. MORELAND,
Vanderdecken,	Captain of the Phantom Ship, "The Flying Dutchman,"	MADAME CELESTE,
Rockalda,	(an Evil Spirit of the Deep)	Mr. JAMES BLAND,
Lisette Vanhelm (Niece to Peppercoal) Miss MARY KEELEY, Lucy, (her Attendant) Miss KATE KELLY.

After the First Piece, EACH NIGHT, (13th & 14th Times) the successful Tragedy in One Act,
Freely Adapted from Mr. THOMAS WILLIAMS'S Translation of
Signor JOSEPH MONTANELLI'S reproduction of Monsieur ERNEST
LEGOUVE'S imitation of EURIPIDES, and called

MEDEA;
Or, A Libel on the Lady of Colchis.

Creon,	(A Corinthian Manager)	Mr. JAMES BLAND.
Orpheus,	(A Widowed Minstrel)	Miss MARY KEELEY,
Jason,	(A Classical Lothario)	Miss WYNDHAM,
	Glaucè, (A Grecian Daughter) Mr. PAUL BEDFORD	
Medea,	(The Lady of Colchis)	Mr. WRIGHT,
Manto, (A Ruler of the Spirits) Miss ALDRIDGE, Panacèa, (A Terrified Domestic) Miss LE LACHEUR.
Polyphemus, Apollodorus, (Medea's Incumbrances, Responsibilities, & Victims) Miss H. MANNING, Miss STOKER.

For a Handbook to the Tragedy, see the Flyleaf of this Bill.

To be followed by, the Original and screaming Comic Drama, entitled The

CUSTOMS OF THE COUNTRY.

Mr. Manners,	Mr. CHARLES SELBY,	Sparkle,	Mr. PARSELLE,	Frank,	Mr. MORELAND,
Mrs. Manners,	Miss ARDEN,	Milly,	Miss KATE KELLY,
Melissa, (a Yankee Gal from "Down East")	Mrs. BARNEY WILLIAMS,

Her Original Character - with the Popular and Eccentric Song of

"MY MARY ANN,"

To conclude with the admired Comedy of

BORN TO GOOD LUCK

Count Malfi.	Mr. CHARLES SELBY,	Count Manfredi,	Mr. PARSELLE;
Florenzi,	Mr. J. G. SHORE,	Rufo, Mr. GARDEN, Carlos, Mr. HASTINGS,
Paddy O'Rafferty,	(Fourth Time in England)	Mr. BARNEY WILLIAMS

In which character he will sing "Flaming O'Flannigan" and Dance an Irish Jig.

Pedro,	Mr. MORELAND,	Chairman, Mr. PAGE,
Countess Molinga,	Mrs. CHATTERLEY—(Her First Appearance at this Theatre)
Margaretta,	Miss LAIDLAW,	Nina, Miss MARY KEELEY.

On SATURDAY, July 26th, for the
BENEFIT of MR. and MRS.
BARNEY WILLIAMS,
FIRST TIME IN THIS COUNTRY,
OUR GAL,

In which Mrs. BARNEY WILLIAMS will sustain her
Original Character, and sing
"Bobbing Around" and "My Mary Ann."
With OTHER ENTERTAINMENTS in which

Mr. BARNEY WILLIAMS,   Mr. BEN. WEBSTER,
Mr. WRIGHT,   Mr. PAUL BEDFORD,
And   MADAME CELESTE   will appear.

Private Boxes £2 2s.   Stalls 5s.   Boxes 4s.   Pit 2s.   Gallery 1s.
Doors open at half-past 6, to commence at 7 o'clock.   [Second Price at 9 o'clock.

"Nassau Steam Press," W. S. JOHN N, 60, St. Martin's Lane, Charing Cross.

---

148. 1856 PLAYBILL
18½″ × 7¼″. Nassau Steam Press, Charing Cross.
Double playbill, printed in black and using Egyptian,
fat faces and a very handsome 12-line Ionic for
'MEDEA'.

149. 1849 PLAYBILL
21″ × 7¼″. Herald Print, New York.
'Christy's Minstrels' displayed in bold sans serif and Egyptian.

Bella C. Landauer Collection, New-York Historical Society

150. 1859 PLAYBILL
12½″ × 4¼″. Anon. New York.
Elongated Egyptians and a Condensed Modern (for 'Uncle Tom's Cabin') give a severe air to this American playbill, and neither the decorated letters used for 'HOWARD' nor the final injunction not to whistle, shout, etc. relieves the feeling of Puritanism.

Bella C. Landauer Collection, New-York Historical Society

151. *c.* 1840 CIRCUS BILL
28¾″ × 9¾″. J. W. Peel, Lambeth.
Circus Royal at the New Road, Marylebone, also
used Mr Peel to print their bills. Here in contrast to
the Astley bill he makes a prodigal use of his type
stock with over twenty display faces, including
curious shaded letters for 'Lubinand Annette'.

152. 1844 CIRCUS BILL
28¾″ × 8¾″. J. W. Peel, Lambeth.
The bill for Astley's Royal Amphitheatre of the Arts
is printed in black and orange, and using only eight
different display types, including Thorowgood's
4-line Pica Italian Etruscan for 'Steed Meg'.

153. *c.* 1840 CIRCUS BILL
$11\frac{3}{4}'' \times 12\frac{1}{4}''$. Anon. Germany.
Polito advertised the visit of his circus from London
with a rich use of decorative types. These Polito bills
come from the Fillenham Collection at the British
Museum.

British Museum

A SIX HEURES DU SOIR

C'EST LE MOMENT QUE L'ON DONNE

LE REPAS AUX ANIMAUX,

A LA SUPERBE MENAGERIE DU SIEUR POLITO,

Aux Allées de Meilhan.

M. POLITO a l'honneur de prévenir le Public qu'à la demande
générale sa Ménagerie ne quittera pas Marseille jusqu'au trois mai
prochain; elle sera tous les jours visible depuis 10 heures du matin
jusqu'à 9 heures du soir et à 6 heures après midi l'on donne à
manger aux animaux.

154. *c.* 1840 CIRCUS BILL
$6'' \times 4\frac{3}{4}''$. Anon. France.
Small bill for Polito's circus with a
restrained use of shadow letter.

British Museum

Birch, Wambold AND Backus' SAN FRANCISCO MINSTRELS

"THE TROUBLE COMMENCES AT EIGHT."

ENTERTAINMENT A LA SALON—PART PREMIER.

Overture, arranged by W. S. Mullaly ..San Francisco Minstrels
Ballad—"When the Whip-poor-will is Calling"..C. S. Fredericks
Comic Ditty—"A Doleful Tale"...............Charley Backus
Ballad—"Little Sweetheart Come and Kiss Me .."D. S. Wambold
Comic Song—"Mother says I Musn't"..........Billy Birch
Ballad—"Mother, bear me to the Window"... Beaumont Read
FINALE, "Champagne Galop," "She's a Gal of Mine,"
and "Railroad Overture," with all the Effects....
SAN FRANCISCO MINSTRELS

PART SECOND—"The Virginians," by Thackeray.

"LET ME BE!"

Double Song and Dance, by the inimitable
JOHNSON and POWERS.

Favorite Ballad, "Touch the Harp Gently,
my Pretty Louise"....Beaumont Read

THE YOUNG ACTORS!

Billy Birch and Charley Backus.

BURLESQUE PRIMA DONNA
By the GREAT RICARDO.

The Alabama Triplets!

Messrs. JOHNSON, POWERS & GIBBONS.

Flute Solo, with Variations ..Mr. J. G. Withers

To conclude with Shakespeare's m at Mirthful Comedy, in 1 Act, (the only
original text,) entitled the

Merry Wives of Windsor

Mrs. Ford, a gentle and loving wife..................
Mr. Charley Backus
Mrs. Page, very weak, but liable to be aroused........
Mr. Ricardo
Mr. Page, a model of a husband, who loves quietude...
Mr. Billy Birch
Mr. Ford, a gentle disposition, but not always........
Mr. Chas. Gibbons
Shallow, mentally...................
Mr. J. Johnson
Slender, not in appetite ....Mr. Geo. Powers

Metropolitan Print, Gerald Building, Broadway & Ann St., N. Y.

155. 1873 PLAYBILL
$10\frac{3}{4}'' \times 3\frac{1}{4}''$. Metropolitan Print, New York.
A small bill using a variety of elongated
typefaces with a particularly attenuated type
for 'Merry Wives of Windsor'.

Oxford University Press

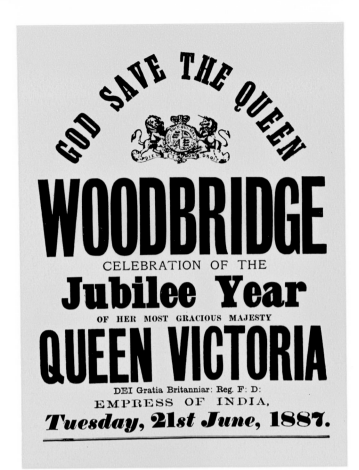

156. 1887 JUBILEE CELEBRATIONS NOTICE
7½" × 6". Anon. Woodbridge.
An austere use of condensed sans serif and Egyptian typefaces reflects something of latter-day Victorian England. Top of bill only shown. The parabolic arch, however, formed by 'God Save the Queen' conveys a festive air, with great typographic economy.

Entertainment notices

Colour crept into bills before the end of the century. The Woodbridge Celebration Bill for the Marriage of George V and Queen Mary was a formidable production for a provincial printer, printed in about seven colours on a black paper. After this there was a quick decline in the typography, and indeed there was, up until the end of the second world war, nothing of typographic note in playbills. Typefaces became more and more debased. There were occasional posters such as those drawn by the 'Beggarstaffs' for the Lyceum, and by Lovat Fraser for the Beggar's Opera that were attractive to look at, but of no typographic interest. The modern revival of interest in typography had its effect on some Music and Art Festivals, resulting in much stimulating ephemeral printing.

157. 1893 CELEBRATION NOTICES
16½" × 7". G. Booth, Woodbridge.
This bill was printed in several colours by letterpress on black paper. The celebrations were for the marriage of the future King George V and Queen Mary.

Entertainment notices

The Henry Irving playbill, still retaining the character of bills of fifty or sixty years earlier has a certain sadness attached to it. This was truly a farewell performance, for the promise of a farewell performance 'for six nights only' was only partially fulfilled. The great actor-manager died in Bradford on Friday, 13th October, five days after the date of this bill.

The Gillot poster for 'Le Musée de la Jeunesse' shows only too well the degradation letter-forms attained during the *Art Nouveau* epoch. In the early years of the nineteenth century the French started using lithography for commercial and ephemeral printing; ever since this introduction of freely drawn letters, there has been a slackening of the standards set by the discipline of the copper plate or metal types.

The vernacular of the New Typography that has made such inroads into American and, to a lesser extent, British printing has had little effect on entertainment notices. The 'Klavier Konzert' programme from Regensburg shows how effective such a typographic treatment can be, as does the Catholic Church notice, (Fig. 165) which is also from Germany. I have included two exhibition posters from the U.S.A. (Figs. 166 and 167) to make up for the inadequacies of their modern theatrical bills.

158. 1905 PLAYBILL
28″ × 8½″. Anon. Bradford, Yorks.
This bill, set in the style that had lasted from the 1830's and printed in black and red, uses heavy wood letters for 'Henry Irving', and French Antique for 'Theatre Royal'.

Andrew Block

159A. 1909 MINIATURE PLAYBILL
5½″ × 3½″. Waddingtons, Leeds.
Printed in blue, yellow, green and black for the type,
using divided ink ducts so that the colours could all
be printed as one operation. This miniature playbill
for the Sunderland Empire was for postcard use.

159B. 1940 MINIATURE PLAYBILL
5″ × 3″. Taylor, Wombwell, Yorkshire.
Printed in blue and red for the Granville Theatre of
Varieties at Walham Green, London.

Entertainment notices

160. 1885 EXHIBITION BILL
9″ × 6″. A. Lahure des. Paris.
Lithographed in six colours, with drawn lettering
based on contemporary typefaces.

161. 1960 CONCERT POSTER
15½″ × 12″. Anon. Regensburg, Germany.
Modern concert poster carrying the wood-letter
Futura type for 'Klavier Konzert' right to the edges
of the sheet.

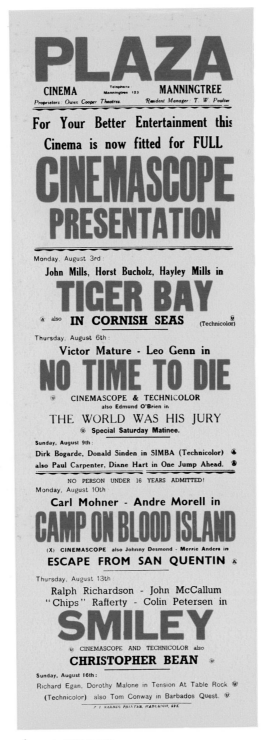

PLAZA

CINEMA   Telephone Manningtree 123   MANNINGTREE

Proprietors: Owen Cooper Theatres   Resident Manager: T. W. Poulter

For Your Better Entertainment this Cinema is now fitted for FULL

CINEMASCOPE PRESENTATION

Monday, August 3rd

John Mills, Horst Bucholz, Hayley Mills in

TIGER BAY

(A) also **IN CORNISH SEAS** (Technicolor)

Thursday, August 6th:

Victor Mature - Leo Genn in

NO TIME TO DIE

(U) CINEMASCOPE & TECHNICOLOR

also Edmund O'Brien in

THE WORLD WAS HIS JURY

(U) Special Saturday Matinee.

Sunday, August 9th:

Dirk Bogarde, Donald Sinden in SIMBA (Technicolor) (A)

also Paul Carpenter, Diane Hart in One Jump Ahead. (A)

NO PERSON UNDER 16 YEARS ADMITTED!

Monday, August 10th

Carl Mohner - Andre Morell in

CAMP ON BLOOD ISLAND

(X) CINEMASCOPE also Johnny Desmond - Merrie Anders in

ESCAPE FROM SAN QUENTIN (A)

Thursday, August 13th:

Ralph Richardson - John McCallum
"Chips" Rafferty - Colin Petersen in

SMILEY

(U) CINEMASCOPE AND TECHNICOLOR also

CHRISTOPHER BEAN (U)

Sunday, August 16th:

Richard Egan, Dorothy Malone in Tension At Table Rock (U)

(Technicolor) also Tom Conway in Barbados Quest. (U)

P. J. BARBER, PRINTER, HADLEIGH, SFK.

162. 1959 CINEMA BILL
$29\frac{3}{4}'' \times 9''$. Barber, Hadleigh, Suffolk.
This bill for a small East Anglian village cinema is
completely in the tradition of the mid-nineteenth
century in overall size and shape and typographical
format. Printed in red and black on yellow paper.

---

163. 1959 PLAYBILL
$19'' \times 11\frac{1}{2}''$. King's Theatre Steam Printers, London.
This is a consciously archaic poster, printed in
black and red.

MILLBROOK STREET FAIR DANCE

FRIDAY
AUG. 19

164. 1960 DANCE POSTER
$12\frac{1}{2}'' \times 10''$. Anon. Millbrook, Ontario.
Modern Canadian dance poster, with a lively
condensed Tuscan for 'STREET FAIR'.

**Catholic Church
and Exhibition notices**

165. 1960 CATHOLIC CHURCH POSTER
$16\frac{1}{4}'' \times 11\frac{5}{8}''$. Anon. Germany.
Printed in black and red from Standard or Akzidene
Grotesk in black and in reverse. Note that the large
letters have been fitted much closer together than
would have been possible in a typeset poster; presumably this has been printed by offset or silk-
screen.

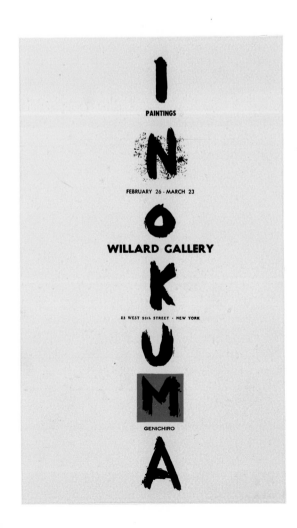

166. 1959 POSTER
$14\frac{1}{8}'' \times 8\frac{1}{2}''$. Inokuma des. New York.
Gallery poster printed in black and orange.

Museum of Modern Art

Exhibition notice

167. 1959 POSTER
24″ × 14¼″. Rai Komai des. The Composing Room
Inc. and Mastercraft Litho and Printing Co., New
York.
Printed by lithography in black, blue, red and orange.
A background pattern is made up of a repeat over-
printing of the last line of copy.

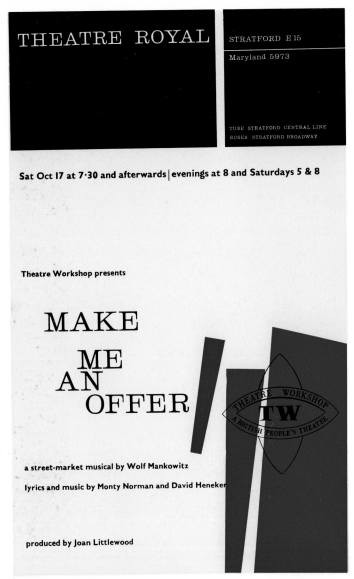

168. 1959 PLAYBILL
16½″ × 11″. Westerham Press, Kent.
This bill is a reversion to the engraved style notice
of the seventeenth and eighteenth centuries. The
typeface used is the oldest English display letter,
Union Pearl, dating from 1692. The drawing of
Long John Silver is by Paul Sharp.

169. 1959 PLAYBILL
20″ × 12″. George Mayhew des. G. & B. Arts,
London.
No concession to tradition, Theatre Workshop's
poster is printed in black and purple and is clearly
the production of a typographic designer and not a
jobbing printer.

Entertainment notices

The little cinema at Manningtree has a bill that
has much of the character of the nineteenth-
century playbill. Provincial cinemas in England
still use the narrow playbill form and often the,
by now, traditional colours of red and black on
yellow paper (Fig. 162).

Modern theatre bills both for Broadway and
the West End are usually beneath contempt.
However, attempts are being made by one or two
managements to produce more attractive bills
either in the traditional manner or making use
of a more modern idiom (Figs. 168 and 169).

Sporting posters

In their presentation, sporting posters were rather like playbills. This short section is of interest mainly for the consistency of character in the sequence of race bills, starting in 1789 and ending with the Arthur Ontario bill of 1960.

ROYAL
VAUXHALL GARDENS

TO NIGHT,
Wednesday, Aug. 18th,
Mr. Wardell's
BENEFIT,
VARIOUS NOVELTIES AND
NASSAU
BALLOON ASCENT
BY THE
VETERAN GREEN,
Being his LAST but TWO Farewell Ascents.

On this Occasion the Doors will be Opened at 6. Ascent at 7.

Thursday, August 19,
A
GRAND GALA
Admission - 2s. 6d.
Doors Open at 8.

On FRIDAY,
A GRAND
BAL MASQUE.
Gentlemen's Tickets - 10s.
Ladies 5s.
Doors Open at 10.

Mr. J. Nathan, Castle Street, Leicester Square, is Appointed Costumier.
H. Green, Printer, 64, Blackman Street, Borough.

171. *c.* 1844 AERONAUTIC POSTER
21″ × 7″ approx. H. Green, Borough, London.
This shows a happy variety of faces including three varieties of Tuscan; that used for 'Vauxhall Gardens' is 2-line Tuscan Shaded; 'Benefit' is in 2-line Ornamented No. 3 and 'Grand Gala' is in 3-line pica Tuscan. 'Veteran Green' is set in Rounded Open. All these typefaces were shown by H. W. Caslon in his 1854 type specimen.

Oxford University Press

172. *c.* 1850 AERONAUTIC POSTER
7¼″ × 4½″ approx. Balne, Gracechurch St., London.
The use of lower-case (for 'Double Ascent', etc.) renders this long line very legible.
Oxford University Press

Greenwich, 11th June, 1825.

LOSS
OF
Mr. GRAHAM,
THE AERONAUT.

From the Statement beneath, it will be perceived that the above named Gentleman, in affording Amusement and Gratification to the Inhabitants of Greenwich and its vicinity, by his Ascent on Monday last, and thereby in some degree benefiting the Town, has Sustained a

Loss of £50.11s.2d.

and it having been Suggested to him by several Gentlemen of the place, that provided the same was made known and accompanied by an appeal to the well known liberality of the Public here, they were convinced it would have the effect of at least alleviating, if not altogether clearing him of so great a Loss. He therefore upon these conditions respectfully informs the Public, that Subscriptions for that purpose will be received at Mr. COLES, Bookseller London Street, Greenwich, and at the BAR OF THE MITRE TAVERN.

EXPENDITURE.	RECEIPT.
£. 91 : 12 : 2	£. 41 : 1 : 0

Printed by J. COLE, London Street, Greenwich.

170. 1825 AERONAUTIC POSTER
7¼″ × 6¼″. J. Cole, Greenwich.
The somewhat misleading wording refers not to loss of life, but to out-of-pocket expenses.

Oxford University Press

ROYAL GARDENS, VAUXHALL,
The Proprietors having received numerous applications and suggestions to display their Royal Nassau Balloon in conjunction with a Balloon of the ordinary size, they have determined, previous to the close of the Season, to give a GRAND DAY AND EVENING FETE, combining the unprecedented Attraction of the
Double Ascent & Night Entertainment
NEXT TUESDAY, 28th of AUGUST.

ROYAL NASSAU BALLOON, To be conducted by Mr. GREEN.

The ASCENT of both Balloons will take place exactly AT THE SAME MOMENT, and the different currents of the atmosphere be rendered clearly perceptible by the direction taken by each machine.

There will be Seats for TEN PERSONS in the Car of the NASSAU BALLOON, and One vacant Seat in the Car of Mr. GREEN'S CORONATION BALLOON.

CORONATION BALLOON, To be conducted by Mr. H. GREEN,

Immediately after the Ascents, the Evening Entertainment will commence; and in order to render the whole Entertainment of equal grandeur, the Evening Amusements will be on an extended scale, including a grand New Piece of Illumination, viz.
AN ILLUMINATED BALLOON, FORTY FEET IN HEIGHT, FORMED ENTIRELY OF LAMPS!
Doors open at Half-past Four.—The Two Balloons to start at Half-past Five.—The Fire Works at Half-past Ten.
Admission to the whole, 1s. 6d.; or, after the Ascent, ONE SHILLING.
PARTIES CAN DINE IN THE GARDENS. [Balne, Printer, 38, Gracechurch Street

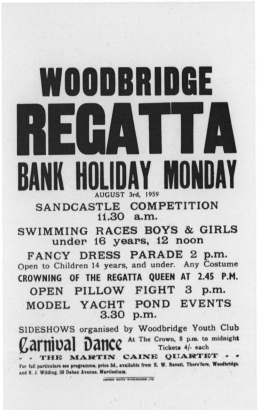

173. 1846 REGATTA POSTER
15″ × 10″. J. Loder, Woodbridge.
Printed in several colours and using a divided duct.
In style it would seem to be ten or fifteen years
behind the times, but it comes from a small provincial
town.

174. 1959 REGATTA POSTER
18″ × 12¼″. Geo. Booth, Woodbridge.
Letterpress poster, printed in blue and compares
unfavourably with the Woodbridge Regatta poster
of 1846. The effectiveness of the wood letters at the
top is reduced by the rather thin Latin Antique used
below for 'SWIMMING RACES', etc.

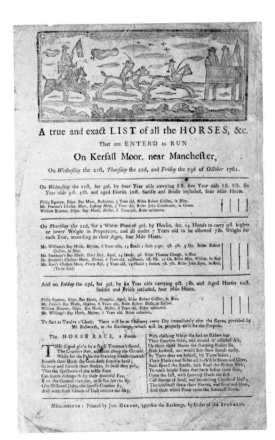

175. 1761 RACE BILL
11¼″ × 6½″. Jos. Harrop, Manchester.
A very archaic woodcut is matched by old style
typefaces.

176. 1789 RACE BILL
12″ × 7½″. Benham and Strange, Kingston.
The woodcut is still very primitive; the type matter
is set in Fry's Baskerville.

177. 1820 RACE BILL
12″ × 7″. W. Meggy, Great Yarmouth.
The combination of woodcut and type remains, but the bookish layout and typefaces are replaced by a bolder display and fat face types.

178. 1829 RACE BILL
10″ × 7¼″. Sloman, Great Yarmouth.
A much simpler layout, with telling use of a much larger size of upper and lower-case fat face for 'Nelson Stakes'.

179. 1833 RACE BILL
9¾″ × 7¼″. J. Barnes, Great Yarmouth.
Fat faces here are lighter and Egyptian capitals in roman and italic carry the main typographic burden.

180. 1849 RACE BILL
10⅛″ × 7½″. Pannifer, Ipswich.
A vigorous little bill, printed in black and red, making effective use of condensed typefaces.

GREAT SPORTING NOVELTY

The Proprietor of the STADIUM having FOR MANY YEARS, *and upon every occasion* strenuously urged in all his writings the importance, not only of extending the *knowledge* of Swimming, but of *making it one of the Duties which ought not to be neglected in Education*, and approving of the laudable efforts made by the recently Established *National Swimming Society*, to promote the cultivation of the Art of Swimming, in order to encourage their endeavours has determined to give, on

Thursday, Sept. 20, 1838.

A

STADIUM FÊTE

AT

CREMORNE HOUSE, KING's ROAD,

CHELSEA,

IN ORDER TO EXHIBIT A

SWIMMING RACE,

ON THE

RIVER THAMES,

in *two* Heats :—*each* from the Stadium Grounds to Battersea and back to Chelsea by *two Classes*; *each* to start, by the Discharge of Artillery, from

SIX to EIGHT AQUATIC JOCKEYS,

From Flag Staffs with the same *Colors* of the *Caps* worn by the jockeys, and who will compete for *four pieces of plate*, given as a stimulus to this highly useful Society, by the Proprietor of that

UNIQUE, SPLENDID, AND TRULY ROMANTIC

ESTABLISHMENT.

The whole of its beautiful and extensive grounds, as also its elegant suites of apartments will be thrown open to visitors, who are invited to witness, and are at liberty to join in (under Standing Regulations of course) A

GRAND ASSAULT OF ARMS,

Or, FENCING DISPLAY;

AS ALSO,

CARROUSEL RIDING,

GYMNASTICS,

AND

OTHER MANLY and SKILFUL EXERCISES,

By *Amateurs* and *First-rate Professors*, as well as by the *Masters* and *Pupils* of that

FASHIONABLE ARENA;

Under the Arrangements made, LADIES, can view the Race *without infringement on Decorum* provided they do so FROM the *Stadium* Grounds.

A SUPERIOR BAND WILL ATTEND,

AND REFRESHMENTS SUPPLIED AT MODERATE CHARGES.

Doors will open at one o'clock, and the Racing will begin soon after two o'clock.—Tickets, 2s. 6d. each, recommended to be purchased before Wednesday the 19th instant, for they will be charged Five Shillings each, after 12 o'clock, at noon, on that day.—Tickets can be obtained at Messrs EBERS and Co., Bond Street; Mr. SAMS, Booksellers, Pall Mall; Mr. HEWITT, Confectioner, 188. Regent Street,; Mr. BLAKE'S, at the Lowther Rooms, King William Street, Strand; at GARRAWAY'S, City; The NATIONAL SWIMMING SOCIETY'S MACHINE, Surrey Canal; and at the STADIUM CREMORNE HOUSE, KING'S ROAD, Chelsea; where RIFLE and PISTOL SHOOTING, AR-CHERY, &c. are *practised* and *taught* as usual; as also *Instructions are given* in CARROUSEL RIDING, and similar *preparation* for *joining* TOURNAMENTS, about to be revived.

Messrs; A. & R. De BERENGER, under the advice of their Father, the Proprietor of the Stadium, will undertake to fit up Carrousel Rings and Gymnasia in Parks or other Grounds, and will, henceforth, Manufacture and supply all the Implements used in such or similar exercises.

N.B. The London & Westminster Company, will employ extra Steamers to Chelsea, to Start from Hungerford at one o'clock, and at two o'clock.—Omnibusses every half hour.

J. W. PEEL, Printer, 9, New Cut, Lambeth.

182. 1960 RACE BILL
17″ × 10″. Anon. Arthur, Ontario.
Canadian race bill in traditional style.

Sporting posters

181. 1838 SPORTING POSTER
14¼″ × 4⅛″. J. W. Peel, Lambeth.
Printed in blue on a yellow paper and set in a variety of decorated display faces, including Thorowgood's Canon Ornamented No. 2 for 'STADIUM FÊTE' and, for the same type founder, 2-line English Perspective for 'SWIMMING RACES'.

THE
ACCURATE DIMENSIONS
OF THE
QUEEN CHARLOTTE,
OF 120 GUNS,

FROM OFFICIAL DOCUMENTS.

This beautiful Ship was built in His Majesty's Dock-Yard, at Deptford, and is to be launched from thence on Tuesday, the 17th of July, 1810, at Two o'Clock in the Afternoon.— She is supposed to be the finest Vessel ever built in the River Thames, being Twenty-six Feet Six Inches more in length than the Monument on Fish-Street Hill is in height!

[N. B. The Dock-Yard will be open at TEN o'Clock in the Morning.]

	FEET.	IN.
Length on the Range of the Lower Gun-Deck from the Rabbit of the Stem to the Rabbit of the Stern Post - - - - - -	190	0
Length from the Aft Part of the Fife-rail to the Fore Part of the Figure-Head -	228	6
Length of the Keel for Tonnage - - - - -	156	5
Breadth Moulded - - - - -	51	7
Breadth Extreme - - - - -	52	4
Breadth to the Outside of the Main Wales - - - - -	53	3
Depth in the Hold - - - - - - -	22	4
Perpendicular Height from the Underside of the False Keel to the Upper Part of the Figure-Head - - - - -	53	6
Perpendicular Height from the Underside of the False Keel to the Upper Part of the Taff-rail	63	4
Length of the Foremast - - - - - -	113	0
Diameter - - - - - -	3	2
Length of the Mainmast - - - - - -	123	0
Diameter - - - - -	3	4½
Length of the Maintopmast - - - -	61	0
Length of the Main Yard - - - -	102	0
Diameter - - - - -	1	11
Length of the Bowsprit - - - - -	75	4
Diameter - - - - -	3	1½
Draught of Water {Afore - - - - -	23	11
{Abaft - - - - -	24	10
Burthen in Tons - - - - - 2,278		

The masts are composed, as usual, of several pieces, but the bowsprit, contrary to that of any first rate in the Navy, is a single stick of New England timber, of the above extraordinary dimensions, and is the object of universal admiration. So beautiful a piece of timber was perhaps never seen in England. It is very closely grained, and so clean, that there is scarcely a knot in the whole length. The proportions of this fine ship are so happily adapted, that, although of such immense magnitude, she does not appear large at a distance, and it is only when on board that her stupendous size becomes striking.— The figure-head of her Majesty, and the Royal Arms over the stern, have attracted particular attention. They are plain, grand, impressive, and capitally executed.

Published by JOHN FAIRBURN, 146, Minories;

And sold by G. CURLING, Butt Lane, Deptford; G. ALLEN, Stockwell Street, Greenwich; and by all other Booksellers, &c. at Deptford, Greenwich, Woolwich, &c. &c.

183. 1810 SHIP LAUNCHING PROGRAMME
9½″ × 7″. John Fairburn, Minories, London.
This programme is at first sight more like an inventory. The semi-bold italic at the top is probably from Caslon and Catherwood's Foundry.

Programmes, Menus and Wine Lists

I have limited this section to the outside pages of theatrical programmes, and functions such as dinners, congresses, sporting events, festivals and exhibitions. The survey covers only 150 years, but nevertheless embraces a great variety of typographic styles. The programme for the launching of the *Queen Charlotte* looks more like an auctioneer's inventory than a programme. The layout of the first paragraph set in an italic semi-bold face is interesting because of the indention following the first line. The Hunt programme (Fig. 184, engraved by Bewick) is more reminiscent of a dance programme than anything so robust as beagling. The nineteenth century programmes shown here reflect the changing fashions in design, but not until the Bauhaus productions does one find any signs of originality.

The Martha Washington dance programme shows the most odd diversity of typographic styles. The cover is a free and informal design with some wretched letterforms; the inside is the essence of formality (Fig. 186).

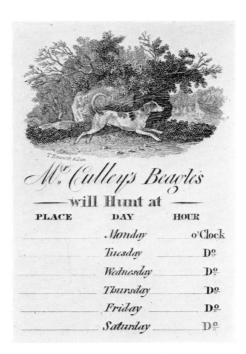

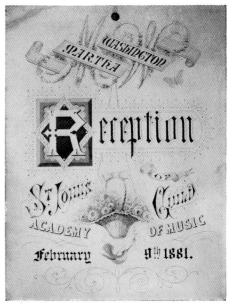

184. *c.* 1815 HUNT PROGRAMME
3¼″ × 2¼″. T. Bewick and Son, Newcastle-upon-Tyne.
This beautifully engraved card may well have been
done by Thomas Bewick himself, who was an
engraver upon copper before he ever engraved wood.

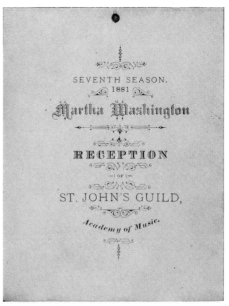

186. 1881 DANCE PROGRAMME
4½″ × 3½″. Komer Lee Bank Note Co., New York.
Engraved cover and opening page showing a marked
disparity of styles.

Programmes

185. 1847 OPERA PROGRAMME
9½″ × 6″. Palmer and Clayton, Fleet St., London.
This programme is for Jenny Lind's appearance in
La Sonnambula at Her Majesty's Theatre in the
Haymarket. Typographically unexceptional, it might
almost be the cover of a parish magazine.

St Bride's Printing Library

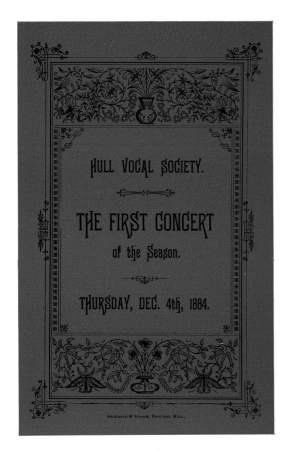

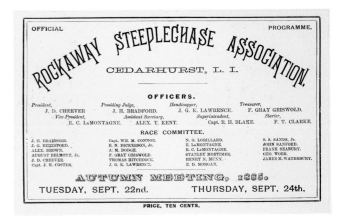

189. 1885 RACE PROGRAMME
$4\frac{1}{2}'' \times 7''$. Anon. Cedarhurst, Long Island, U.S.A.
The same broken-backed typeface used by the Hull
Vocal Society appears within a year on a Long Island
race track.

187. 1884 CONCERT PROGRAMME
$8'' \times 5\frac{1}{4}''$. Archibald and Stoole, Hull.
Lovingly executed for *The Printers' International
Specimen Exchange*. The typefaces used are a sorry
reflection of Oriental influence on 'Artistic' printing.

188. 1884 DINNER ENTERTAINMENT PROGRAMME
$6\frac{3}{4}'' \times 5\frac{1}{2}''$. W. H. Vauhan typ. Eccles, Eastcheap,
London. The asymmetry of the Leicester Free Style,
which lacks the restraint of *L'Art Nouveau*.

190. 1886 PROGRAMME
$6'' \times 2\frac{3}{4}''$. Jones and Cuthbertson, London.
Lithographed in five colours, including gold.

191. *c.* 1928 SCHOOL INVITATION
5⅞″ × 13¾″. H. Bayer typ. Bauhaus, Dessau.
Printed in black, red and buff with a half-tone of the
school buildings, with programme of events.
Museum of Modern Art

Programmes

192. 1954 FESTIVAL EXHIBITION BOOKLET
6¾″ × 5¼″. Alvin Lustig typ. Marchbanks Press, New
York.
Printed in black and blue on an oatmeal coloured
chipboard – this piece of festival literature uses
display grotesque types with power and effect.

The Hull Vocal Society's cover was lovingly
executed for *The Printers' International Specimen
Exchange.* The typefaces used are a sorry reflection of oriental influence on 'Artistic' printing.
The same letterforms can be seen in the Rock-
away Steeplechase card. This typeface, with its
plunging tails to the letters A, H, K, R, comes
from the Cincinnati Typefoundry of Horace
Wells.

The London Operative Millers' programme
has a smell of the *Art Nouveau.* The semi-
Oriental motifs and the despicable typefaces all
contribute their depressing quota to the 'refined'
typography of the 1880's.

The Bauhaus brings order and a rigid formality of design into their School Programme.
The vertical and horizontal axis provides an
utterly satisfying arrangement, which is repeated in Fig. 192 where Alvin Lustig's simple
cover for '2 pittori 3 scultori' is made doubly
attractive by the use of a rough chipboard. This,
unfortunately, is a quality one cannot easily
reproduce here.

Programmes

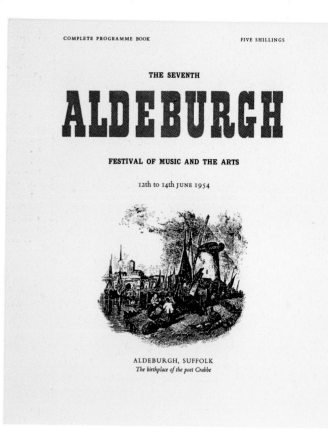

THE SEVENTH

ALDEBURGH

FESTIVAL OF MUSIC AND THE ARTS

12th to 14th JUNE 1954

ALDEBURGH, SUFFOLK
The birthplace of the poet Crabbe

194. 1954 FESTIVAL PROGRAMME
$9\frac{3}{4}'' \times 7\frac{1}{4}''$. John Lewis typ. Benham, Colchester.
Printed in black and red, set in Latin Antique with
a drawn letter for 'ALDEBURGH' based on the typefaces
French Antique or Playbill.

193. 1957 MUSIC RECITAL PROGRAMME
$10'' \times 4\frac{1}{2}''$. Allan Fleming typ. Cooper and Beatty,
Toronto.
Printed in black and light brown on a grey card. The
elaborate cartouches used here are a reflection of
earlier engraved programmes. Set in A.T.F. Caslon.

THIRTEENTH
ALDEBURGH
FESTIVAL
OF MUSIC AND THE ARTS

11-26 JUNE 1960

COMPLETE
PROGRAMME
BOOK

196. 1960 EXHIBITION CATALOGUE COVER
$9'' \times 9''$. F. H. K. Henrion typ. London.
Printed in four colours and set in a grotesque with
'staggered' letters for 'HENRION'.

195. 1960 FESTIVAL PROGRAMME
$9\frac{3}{4}'' \times 7\frac{1}{4}''$. John Lewis typ. Benham, Colchester.
Printed in black, red and blue from heavy grotesque
typefaces.

Programmes

integration

An exhibition

197. 1949 EXHIBITION CATALOGUE COVER
11⅜″ × 8⅞″. Will Burtin des. Chicago.
Printed in black, vermilion, cobalt blue and grey, this
cover was for an exhibition programme at the Art
Director's Club, Chicago.
Museum of Modern Art

The 1957 programme of the Bach Society of Toronto is printed in black and light brown on a grey card. The elaborate cartouches used here are a reflection of earlier engraved programmes. This is a pleasant and successful example of a design produced to give something of a period flavour without in any way being a pastiche. The Aldeburgh Festival programme covers (separated by six years, but by the same designer) show different ways of handling large display letters. All the printed literature for the first seven years of the Aldeburgh Festival, which centres round the music and person of Benjamin Britten, was somewhat Victorian in character;

intentionally so, as Aldeburgh is essentially a Victorian watering place, even though it was the birthplace of the poet Crabbe, whose poems provided the theme for Britten's opera *Peter Grimes*.

Henrion's design for a catalogue of his own exhibition achieves its effect by the simplest of methods, by overprinting flat tint blocks in different colours. Simplicity is carried a stage further by Will Burtin where his exhibition catalogue cover is a pure white board except for the narrow band of primary colours and black, set in perfect equilibrium.

Menus and Wine Lists

PRIX DES VINS

Chez Barbaux et Basillac,

Rue Notre-Dame-des-Victoires.

Bourgogne.		Du Midi.	
Mâcon, vieux	2 fr.	L'Hermitage, rouge.	4 fr.
Baune	2	Idem, blanc	4
Pomard	2	Côte-Rotie	4
Volnay	2	St. Perrey, rouge	4
Vosne	2	Idem, blanc	4
Nuits	2	Rivesaltes	4
Meursault	2	Collioure	4
Champagne.		**Bordeaux.**	
Mousseux rouge	3	Saint-Julien	4
Mousseux blanc	3	Saint-Emilien	4
Non-mousseux	3	Sauterne	4
Rosé, mousseux	3		
Vin d'Ailly	3		
Ptisane	3		

VINS DE LIQUEURS.

Tokay	6 fr.	Alicante	6
Lunel	6	Malaga	6
Frontignan	6	Madère	6

On fournira des paniers de douze Bouteilles.

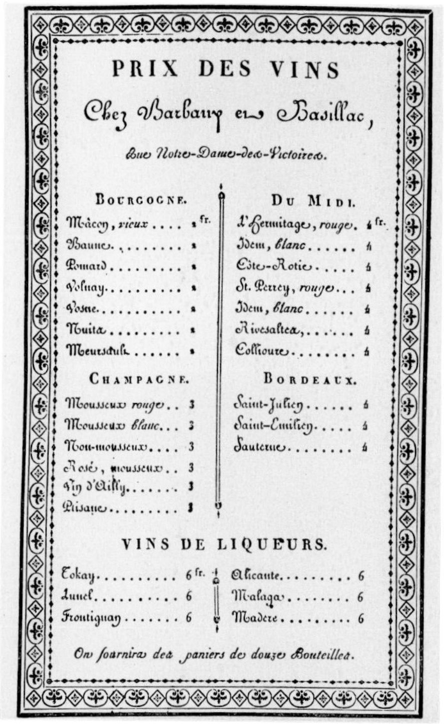

198. 1820 WINE LIST
$7\frac{3}{8}'' \times 4\frac{3}{8}''$. Gillé, Paris.
This wine list was shown as a specimen by Gillé in his typebook. The formal border is typical of the Bodoni and Didot style of typography.

THE KING'S THEATRE.

M. DUBOURG

Most respectfully informs the NOBILITY, the SUBSCRIBERS to, and FREQUENTERS of, the OPERA, that he has made arrangements to supply

THE REFRESHMENTS

in this Theatre, on the style they are provided at the most elegant Cafés and Confiseurs in Paris, from whence he has imported a variety of

" BONBONS,"

entirely new in this country, which may be had at the following Prices:—

		s.	d.
Bonbons enveloppés	(l'once)	1	0
Fruits candis de toute espèce	,,	1	0
Drajées, idem	,,	0	9
Pastilles ,,	,,	0	9
Pains à la Vanille	,,	1	0
Pistaches à Liqueurs	,,	1	0
Pâtes de Jujubes	,,	0	6
Sucre de Pommes riche	(le bâton)	1	0
Plaisirs et Histoire de l'Amour	(la pièce)	1	0
Bonbons envelloppés dans de la musique	,,	0	6
Surprises	,,	2	6
Bracelets	,,	2	6
Bijoux	,,	1	0
Petits Gâteaux assortis	,,	0	2
Cup of Coffee		0	6
Cup of Tea		0	6
Glass of Jelly		1	0
Glass of Hot Jelly		1	0
Ginger Beer		0	6
Soda Water		0	6
Capillaire		0	6
Orgeat		0	6
Lemonade		0	6
Cheriade		0	6
Cream Ice		1	0
Water Ice		1	0
Punch à la Romaine		1	0
Glass of Ice Water		0	2

The above Refreshments may be procured in the Box Entrance Saloon; the Gallery Coffee Room; or ordered to the Boxes through the respective Box-Keepers.

Balls, Routs, Dinners, and Suppers supplied, on Terms which may be arranged with M. DUBOURG, *at the* Café du Salon de l'Opéra; *or, at his* Restaurant, 63, Haymarket.

200. 1833 BILL OF FARE
$6\frac{1}{4}'' \times 3\frac{3}{8}''$. Anon. London.
The King's Theatre bill of fare makes an effective contrast with the small Egyptians and Thorne's Shaded letter used for 'M. Dubourg'.

VAUXHALL
ROYAL GARDENS,
1826.

16 Day of June 1826

The Company are respectfully acquainted that the Waiters are ordered not to charge in their Bill any Article they may place on the Table that shall remain untouched.

If any Person experience inattention or incivility from the Waiters, it is hoped application will be made at the Bar, that they may be reprimanded, or, if requisite, dismissed.

REFRESHMENTS.	s.	d.
Pâté à la Perigueux	15	0
Ditto	10	6
Ditto....Quail	6	0
A Chicken	4	0
A pulled Chicken	5	0
Dish of Ham	2	0
Ditto	1	0
Dish of Beef	1	0
Plate of Collared Beef	1	6
Dish of Potted Meat	1	6
Tart	1	6
Cheesecake	0	6
Custard	0	6
Heart Cake	0	4
Shrewsbury Cake	0	2
Biscuit	0	1
Jelly	0	9
Plate of Olives	1	0
Plate of Sugar	0	6
Lemon	0	6
Lettuce	0	6
Cucumber	0	6
Cruet of Oil	0	6
Egg	0	2
Slice of Cheese	0	3
Pat of Butter	0	2
Slice of Bread	0	1
Pot of Stout	1	0
Pair of Wax Lights	2	0

The Pastry and Confectionery are furnished by Mr. FARRANCE.

Box No Holton } Waiter's Name.

The Proprietors respectfully request the Company will see that every Bottle of Wine, brought by the Waiters, has the Seal of The London Wine Company:— *the Bar being answerable for the quality, if the Bottles are sealed as above; the Company ought, therefore, to examine the Seal, and see the Cork drawn in their presence.*

WINES.	s.	d.
Port	6	0
Sherry	6	0
Bucellas	6	0
Lisbon	6	0
Vidonia	6	0
Madeira	8	6
Sauterne	8	6
Barsac	8	6
Claret	9	6
Old Hock	12	0
Champagne	12	0
Burgundy	13	0
Arrack, ℔ Quart	12	0
Ditto, ℔ Pint	6	0
Ditto, ℔ Half Pint	3	0

£

*** *All the Wines have been furnished by the London Wine Company, 141, Fleet Street.*

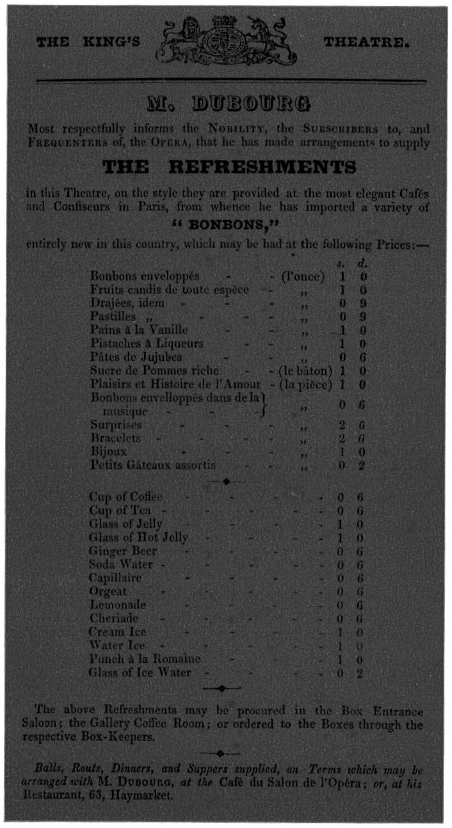

199. 1826 BILL OF FARE WINE LIST
$10'' \times 3''$ approx. Anon. London.
Thorowgood's Fat Face for the heading is in keeping with the posters and playbills used at Vauxhall, as is the long narrow shape of this bill.

Oxford University Press

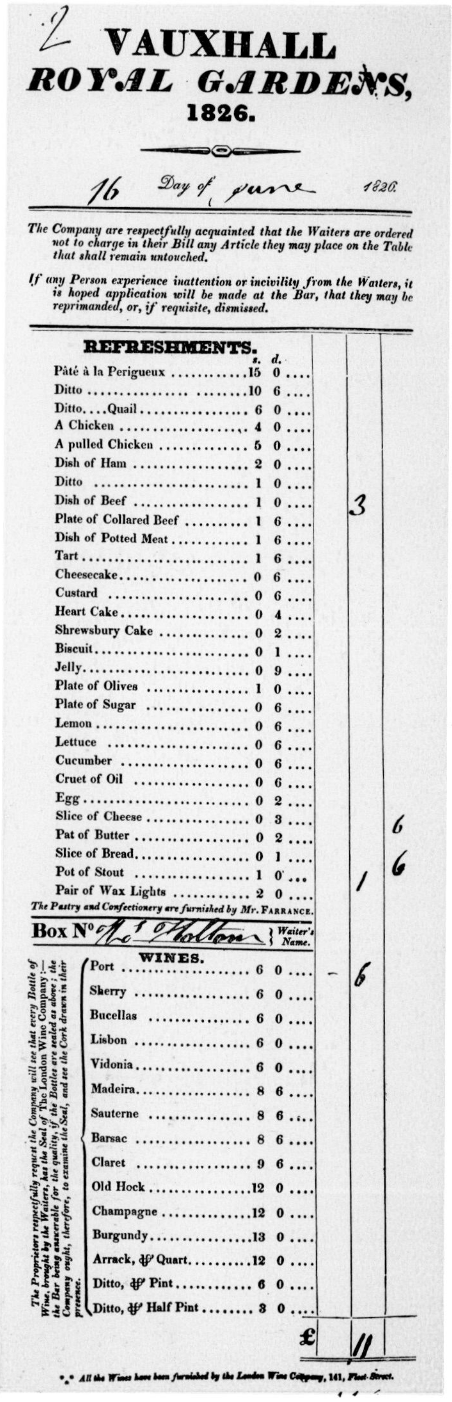

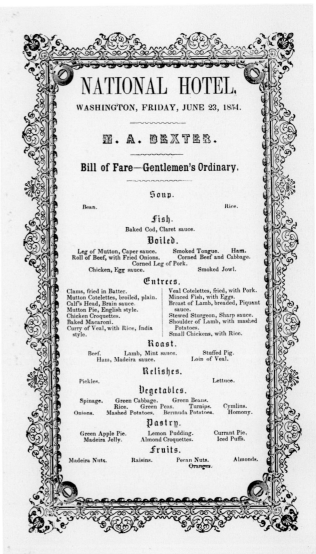

201. 1854 MENU AND WINE LIST
6¾″ × 4¼″. Sickels and Reading, Philadelphia.
'Girard House' is in an outlined twig letter, which originated from Vincent Figgins's Foundry in 1845 (without the outline); and an early showing of an extended Egyptian for 'Gentlemen's Ordinary'.

202. 1854 MENU
6½″ × 5″. Anon. Washington D.C.
Signs of typographic decay, with a wretched elongated 'modern' type for 'NATIONAL HOTEL' and a border of elaborate feebleness. The letterspaced gothic type for 'Soup, Fish' etc. is the final futility.

203. 1894 MENU
8½″ × 3¼″ each. Ring and Brymer, London.
This menu for 'The Voluntary Early Closing Association' is printed in gold, green and black and has a printed credit on it saying that it is 'perfumed by Rimmel'. L'Art Nouveau in character, the asymmetry of the cover is not made use of for the menu, which is set in a light sans serif and old style typefaces.

Menus and Wine Lists

Menus and wine lists tend to fall into two basic categories, the list of foods or drinks with their prices or the set meal with the courses shown separately. The use of borders was established by Gillé (Fig. 198) and has continued in use until today. By the early eighteen hundreds Bewick was producing stock blocks for headings and surrounds. At the end of the century, letter forms and decorations were becoming very debased, as can be seen in the stock blocks from Philadelphia (Fig. 206).

PROGRAMME OF MUSIC

TO BE PERFORMED DURING THE TABLE D'HÔTE
FROM 6 TILL 9 O'CLOCK

1. MARSCH............ "Bummler"............ *Josef Gung'l.*
2. OVERTURE............ "Algérienne"............ *O. Métra.*
3. WALZER............ "Amélie"............ *H. C. Lumbye.*
4. SELECTION............ Herold's Opera,
"Le Pré aux Clercs"............ *Meyer Lutz.*
5. MAZURKA............ "Douce Amie"............ *J. Richard.*
6. DUETTO, Harp and Pianoforte ... Pacini's Opera,
"Fidanzata Corsa, No Maleditto"............ *Bochsa.*
(Messrs. Stratford and Ripley.)
7. OVERTURE............ "Nabucodonosor"............ *Verdi.*
8. WALZER............ "Journalisten"............ *Strauss.*
9. FANTAISIE sur les Puritains............ *V. Robillard.*
10. MEDITATION Bach 1er Prélude pour Violin
et Violincello............ *Ch. Gounod.*
(Messrs. Ripley, Saunders, and Goff.)
11. HARP SOLO, Air Varié "Home, Sweet Home" *Stratford.*
(Mr. R. H. Stratford.)
12. VALSE............ "La Châtelaine"............ *N. Bousquet.*
13. OVERTURE............ "Apollo"............ *Bonnisseau.*
14. QUADRILLE............ "H.M.S. Pinafore"............ *C. Godfrey.*
15. GALOP............ "Prestissimo"............ *Emile Waldteufel.*

Musical Director ... Mr. J. Ripley.

WYMAN AND SONS, PRINTERS.

Visitors will oblige by carrying away this Menû
and recommending the Establishment to their friends

MACLURE & MACDONALD, LITHrs TO THE QUEEN, LONDON & GLASGOW.

The Holborn Restaurant
THE GRAND SALON ‡ 218, HIGH HOLBORN

LINCOLNS INN BUFFET THE GRILL ROOM

TABLE D'HÔTE FROM 6 TO 8.30. P.M. Price 3/6

Menû for Wednesday, Sept. 11, 1878.

POTAGES,
Purée de Legumes.
Consommé au Macaroni.

SOUPS.
Purée of Vegetables.
Consommé with Macaroni.

POISSONE.
Hareng grillé à la Maître d'Hôtel.
Cabillaud, Sauce aux Huîtres.

FISH.
Grilled Herring à la Maître d'Hôtel.
Cod, Oyster Sauce.

ENTREES.
Ris de Veau en Caisse.
Lièvre à la Chasseur.

ENTREES.
Sweetbreads in Cases.
Hare à la Chasseur.

ROTI.
Côtes de Bœuf au Raifort.

ROAST.
Ribs of Beef with Horseradish.

ENTREMETS.
Tourtes des Prunes.
Beignets Soufflés.
Gelée au Vin.

SWEETS.
Plum Tarts.
Beignets Soufflés.
Wine Jelly.

POUDINGS GLACES.
Fromage. Salade à la Française.

ICE PUDDINGS.
Cheese. French Salad.

DESSERT.
Poires. Noix. Melons.
Pommes. Amandes et Raisins.
Olives. Raisins.

DESSERT.
Pears. Walnuts. Melons.
Apples. Almonds and Raisins.
Olives. Grapes.

Single places or separate tables for parties of three or more may be previously engaged
and will be reserved until Seven o'Clock.
The dining Salons may be reached without passing the Public Buffet either by the separate
entrance in the Holborn Lobby or the Lincolns Inn Entrance in Little Queen Street.
CLOAK ROOMS FOR LADIES AND GENTLEMEN
Gentlemen are respectfully requested to examine their Bills before paying the waiter

MACLURE & MACDONALD, LITHrs TO THE QUEEN, LONDON & GLASGOW.

204. 1878 MENU
$7\frac{5}{8}'' \times 8\frac{3}{4}''$. Maclure and Macdonald lith. & Wyman,
London.
Printed in black on a pale blue paper. The borders
are lithographed, but the actual menu has been
printed by letterpress.

BILL OF FARE.

LISTA DE LA COMIDA.

DINNER.

SOUP. (SOPA.)   FISH. (PESCADO.)

Macaronie

BOILED. (COCIDOS.)

Stewed Beef
Corned Beef & Cabbage

ROAST. (ASADOS.)

Mutton
Fowl

Menus and Wine Lists

205. 1879 BILL OF FARE
$7\frac{3}{4}'' \times 4\frac{5}{8}''$. Rufus Adams, Pine Street, New York.
Printed in black on a pink paper for the steamship
Atlas. (Mail steamer to the South Pacific.)

206. 1897 MENU HEADINGS
9″×6⅝″. Mackellar, Smiths and Jordan Co.,
Philadelphia, shown in their typebook of that year.

Stock Blocks for menus and wine lists

All these stock stereos show the influence of the signwriter and nothing of the typographer, which is perhaps natural enough, for by this time there was no such typographic vernacular, as had guided the printers in England and the U.S.A. during the first half of the eighteenth century. A period of typographic decay had set in. The 'commercial artist' provided 'artwork' to prefabricate the job for the printer. It was not until many years after the private presses had shown what sensitive hands could do with type, that typographers – not printers – turned their attention to jobbing work. The Curwen Press, first under Harold Curwen and later under the guidance of the brothers Simon, was one of the first printing houses in England to concern itself seriously with the quality of jobbing printing. Oliver Simon made a wide use of formal borders and introduced the Didot style typeface Walbaum into England. Walbaum is a typeface that still usefully serves the needs of the jobbing typographer today.

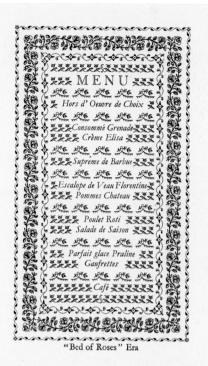

"Bed of Roses" Era

The Second Dinner
of the Double Crown Club

The Café Royal
December 11th, 1924

Chairman
Holbrook Jackson

Designer
Gerard T. Meynell

Guest
Emery Walker

Toast
To the memory of
Claude Garamond

Discussion
Type Faces of To-day

M E N
E U

Hors d' Oeuvre de Choix
✳
Consommé Grenade
Crème Elisa
✳
Suprême de Barbue
✳
Escalope de Veau Florentine
Pommes Chateau
✳
Poulet Roti
Salade de Saison
✳
Parfait glace Praline
Gaufrettes
✳
Café

"Get joy into your printed things—cheerily" Era

207. 1924 MENU
6″ × 3⅜″ each. Gerard Meynell typ. Westminster
Press, London.
Menu designs for the second dinner of the Double
Crown Club, by the editor of 'IMPRINT' the first
influential typographic journal.

208. 1944 MENU
4½″ × 4½″. Curwen Press, London.
Double Crown Club menu, printed in black and
dark brown.

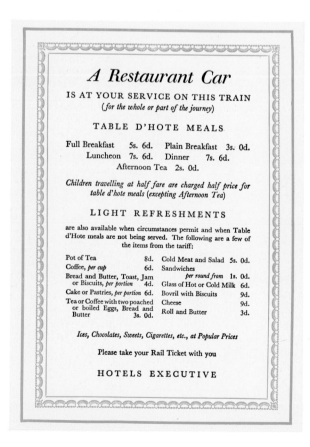

209. c. 1947 MENU
6½″ × 4½″. Curwen Press, London.
Printed in black and red and set in Walbaum, Baskerville with Times Roman figures.

Menus and Wine lists

The Double Crown Club is a typophile's dining club that has done much to foster an interest in fine printing. A collection of their menus from 1924, when they were founded, until today would offer a fair comment on the conservative attitude of the Club's members to ephemeral printing.

PHILIP JAMES
will speak
on

Recent
French Book
Illustrations

followed by a discussion

MENU

Hors d'œuvre assorti

Pascal Maison

Coupe glacée

Café

210. 1945 MENU
4⅜″ × 6⅞″ (inside spread). Baynard Press, London.
Printed in black and blue and set in Baskerville.

108th DINNER DOUBLE CROWN CLUB

The President in the Chair

MARCH 15th 1951 AT KETTNERS MENU

Pâté Maison
Consommé Double
✠

Demi Poussin Rôti
Pommes Château
Petits Pois au beurre
✠

Poire Belle Hélène
Café
✠

211. 1951 MENU
6⅝″ × 4″. Berthold Wolpe typ. Curwen Press, London.
Printed in black and red, with the headings set in
Albertus.

menu

212. 1957 MENU AND WINE LIST
$9\frac{1}{2}'' \times 8\frac{1}{2}''$ cover and $7'' \times 3\frac{1}{2}''$. Royal
College of Art, London.
Printed in black and red for cover,
and black on yellow paper for the
inside, set throughout in Gill Sans.
The cover folded to make a three-
sided box; into this the single leaf
of the menu was dropped.

principal guest Gerard Hoffnung

menu watercress soup
roast turkey chestnut stuffing
chipolatas roast potatoes brussels sprouts

christmas pudding rum sauce
mince pies
coffee

wines margaux 1953
hermitage la chapelle 1953
beaujolais

toasts H.M. the Queen.

the President of the J.C.R. will introduce
the guests and propose their health

the principal guest will respond for the
guests and propose the health of the College

the Principal will reply for the College

menu

christmas dinner 1957

These menus (Figs. 212 and 213) designed by
students at the Royal College of Art are colourful. Their origins may lie in the work of the
Bauhaus but they have a liveliness not often
shown in the typographic work of that famous
school. The Harvey's wine list is an attempt at
the marriage of two cultures. Here, nineteenth
century display letters are incorporated in a
mid-twentieth century asymmetric layout. The
decorations used in this list show what a perfect
foil wood engravings are to type.

132

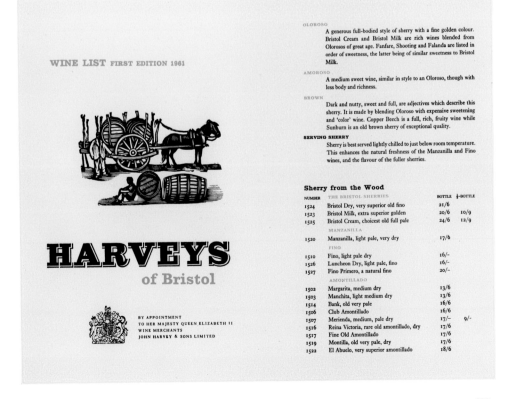

213. 1958 MENU
6¾″ × 6″. Royal College of Art, London.
The cover of this menu was printed in black, blue
and yellow on a smooth white board. The inside in
blue and black on an antique surfaced mustard-
coloured paper. The typeface is Walbaum Medium.

214. 1961 WINE LIST
7″ × 4″. John Lewis typ. Millbrook Press, Southampton.
Printed in black and vermilion, set in Ehrhardt and
for the cross-headings New Clarendon Bold. The
engraving is by David Gentleman.

WINE LIST FIRST EDITION 1961

HARVEYS
of Bristol

BY APPOINTMENT
TO HER MAJESTY QUEEN ELIZABETH II
WINE MERCHANTS
JOHN HARVEY & SONS LIMITED

OLOROSO
A generous full-bodied style of sherry with a fine golden colour.
Bristol Cream and Bristol Milk are rich wines blended from
Olorosos of great age. Fanfare, Shooting and Falanda are listed in
order of sweetness, the latter being of similar sweetness to Bristol
Milk.

AMOROSO
A medium sweet wine, similar in style to an Oloroso, though with
less body and richness.

BROWN
Dark and nutty, sweet and full, are adjectives which describe this
sherry. It is made by blending Oloroso with expensive sweetening
and 'color' wine. Copper Beech is a full, rich, fruity wine while
Sunburn is an old brown sherry of exceptional quality.

SERVING SHERRY
Sherry is best served lightly chilled to just below room temperature.
This enhances the natural freshness of the Manzanilla and Fino
wines, and the flavour of the fuller sherries.

Sherry from the Wood

NUMBER	THE BRISTOL SHERRIES	BOTTLE	½-BOTTLE
1524	Bristol Dry, very superior old fino	21/6	
1523	Bristol Milk, extra superior golden	20/6	10/9
1525	Bristol Cream, choicest old full pale	24/6	12/9
	MANZANILLA		
1520	Manzanilla, light pale, very dry	17/6	
	FINO		
1510	Fino, light pale dry	16/-	
1526	Luncheon Dry, light pale, fino	16/-	
1527	Fino Primero, a natural fino	20/-	
	AMONTILLADO		
1502	Margarita, medium dry	13/6	
1503	Manchita, light medium dry	13/6	
1514	Bank, old very pale	16/6	
1506	Club Amontillado	16/6	
1507	Merienda, medium, pale dry	17/-	9/-
1516	Reina Victoria, rare old amontillado, dry	17/6	
1517	Fine Old Amontillado	17/6	
1519	Montilla, old very pale, dry	17/6	
1522	El Abuelo, very superior amontillado	18/6	

Tollgate tickets

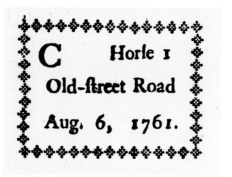

215A and B. *c.* 1761 TURNPIKE TICKETS
$1\frac{3}{8}'' \times 2''$ and $1\frac{1}{8}'' \times 1\frac{3}{8}''$. Anon. London.
These two delicate little tickets make a good use of fleurons.

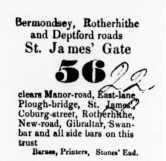

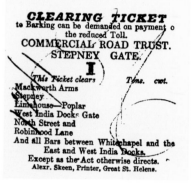

216A and B. *c.* 1830 TOLLGATE TICKETS
$\frac{3}{4}'' \times 1\frac{3}{4}''$ and $1\frac{5}{8}'' \times 1\frac{3}{4}''$. Alex. Skeen, Gt St Helens.
The use of a small bold Egyptian for 'CLEARING TICKET' gives distinction to the ticket on the right.

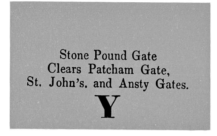

217A and B. *c.* 1840 TOLLGATE TICKETS
$1\frac{3}{8}'' \times 1\frac{1}{4}''$ and $\frac{7}{8}'' \times 1\frac{3}{8}''$. Potter, Kingsland and Barnes, Stone's End, London.
Thorowgood's Fat Face doing splendid duty for '56'.

Oxford University Press

Tickets: Travel

Tickets, both for travelling and entertainment, present a teasing typographical problem. Early travel tickets, whether for coach, tollgate, train or steamer were printed on paper, often coloured, and until the early years of the nineteenth century, were set in 'book' typefaces, with a judicious use of rules, borders and fleurons.

The early days of rail travel overlapped the coach and tollgate period. It was not until the 1840's that the card tickets were introduced, in exactly the size they are used on British Railways today. The introduction of fat face, Egyptians and grotesques provided the printer of tickets with an exciting new typographic language. Sometimes it must have gone to their heads, for on the old London, Brighton and South Coast Railway they combined Expanded Egyptians with grotesques, mixed up founts of different sizes, and even introduced capitals into lower case lines. (Fig. 229).

218. 1832 RAILWAY TICKETS
$4\frac{3}{4}'' \times 7\frac{1}{2}''$. Anon. Liverpool.
Printed in black on brown paper, using Thorowgood's Fat Face Italic and a vigorous border to separate each ticket.

Railway tickets

The Railway Museum at York, has, in its 'Small Exhibits Section', an interesting collection of printed ephemera, including some very early tickets with one for the Stockton and Darlington Railway dating from 1842, using Thorowgood's Fat Face Italic.

219. 1844 RAILWAY PASS TICKET
$2\frac{1}{2}'' \times 4''$. Anon. London.
Printed letterpress, in black from a heavy black letter and a bold Egyptian.

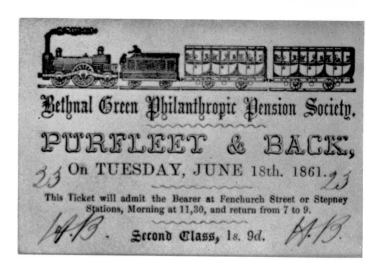

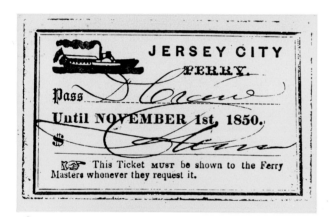

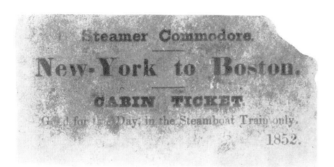

220. 1852 STEAMER TICKET
s/s Anon. New York.
Printed in black on a white card.

New York Public Library

222. 1861 RAILWAY EXCURSION TICKET
2″ × 3¼″. Anon. England.
Printed in black and pink from black letter, an open Tuscan and decorated with stereos of a wood engraving, cast on a 48-point body.

221. *c.* 1850 STEAMSHIP TICKET
1″ × 3″. Anon. New York.
Printed in black on tinted paper.

New York Public Library

223. 1864 SEASON TICKET
2⅝″ × 3½″. Anon. London.
Engraved ticket printed in green on a buff card.

Oxford University Press

224. 1850–70 RAILWAY TICKETS
1″ × 2″ each. Anon. England.
Six tickets printed in black on different coloured cards for Leeds and Thirsk Railway, Durham and Sunderland Railway, St Helens Railway, Thetford and Watton Railway, Oxford, Worcester and Wolverhampton Railway and London and South Western Railway.

Curator of Historical Records, British Transport Commission

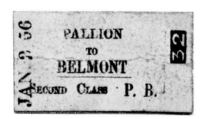

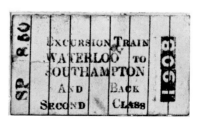

225. 1853 STEAMER TICKET
s/s Anon. Boston, Massachusetts.
Printed in black on a white card.

New York Public Library

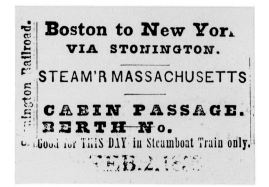

Boston to New Yor.
VIA STONINGTON.

STEAM'R MASSACHUSETTS

CABIN PASSAGE.
BERTH No.
Good for THIS DAY in Steamboat Train only.
FEB. 2. 1853

LondonSteam Omnibus
Company, Ltd.

MARBLE ARCH
TO
NOTTING HILL.

Free Trial Admit Bearer.
Leave Marble Arch
at 3 p.m.

London Steam Omnibus
Company, Ltd.

MARBLE ARCH
TO
NOTTING HILL.

Free Trial Admit Bearer.
Leave Marble Arch
at 3 p.m.

226. 1871 TURNPIKE TICKET
3″ × 2⅛″. Anon. Liskeard, Cornwall.
Here a ticket is in the form of a receipt.

Oxford University Press

LISKEARD TURNPIKE.

Sheviock Gate.

22 day of August 1871

	No. of Horses	s	d
Horses, &c., drawing			
Carriage	- - -		
Chaise	- - -		
Phaeton	- -c-		
Gig	- - -		
Waggon	- - -		
Cart	- - -	1	6
Van	- - -		
Dray	- - -		

This Ticket frees Craftbole and
Cremil Gates.

228. c. 1880 OMNIBUS TICKET
3½″ × 1½″. Anon.
On pink card, set in Latin
Antique and a condensed
grotesque.

Tickets

The L.B. and S.C. Railway used various typographic eccentricities in an attempt to defy forgers; such as in 'Kemp Town', combining Expanded Egyptian initials with a condensed grotesque and for 'Tunbridge Wells', the most odd mixture of Elongated Roman initials and ascending letters, such as the 'b's and 'd's; and using small capitals in place of descending letters such as the 'g'.

South Eastern Railway.
SOLDIERS TICKET
204
C
DOVER
TO
LONDON
Covered Carriages.

227. 1866 RAILWAY TICKET
2¼″ × 1¼″. Anon. England.
Soldier's ticket, printed in black
and pink.

Oxford University Press

229. c. 1880 RAILWAY TICKETS
1″ × 2″ each. Anon. England.
Six tickets printed in black on different coloured cards for London, Brighton and South Coast Railway and North British Railway.

Curator of Historical Records, British Transport Commission

L. B. & S. C. RY.
Available on the DATE of issue ONLY.
This Ticket is issued subject to the Regulations
& Conditions stated in the Company's Time
Tables & Bills.
LONDON ROAD BRIGHTON
Series 7] TO [Series 7
KEMP TOWN k.t.
4234
1½d. THIRD CLASS. 1½d.

L. B. & S. C. RY.
Available on the DATE of issue ONLY.
This Ticket is issued subject to the Regulations
& Conditions stated in the Company's Time
Tables & Bills.
STOATS NEST Nr COULSDON & CANE HILL
No 51 TO
PURLEY
8892
1½d. THIRD CLASS. 1½d.

L. B. & S. C. RY.
Available on the DATE of issue ONLY.
This Ticket is issued subject to the Regulations
& Conditions stated in the Company's Time
Tables & Bills.
CHELSEA & FULHAM
TO
CLAPHAM JUNCTION c.j.
4236
4d. FIRST CLASS. 4d.

L. B. & S. C. RY.
WEST BRIGHTON
DOWN TO DOWN
Tunbridge Wells
5055
2s.6d. Third Class. 2s.6d.
[See Back

NORTH BRITISH RAILWAY
No 88
EDINBURGH TO NEWCASTLE
SECOND CLASS & OUTSIDE

L.B. & S.C.Ry.
STEYNING
TO
HENFIELD EN
1540
Parliamentary
Henfield (See Back

The top ticket:

THE 42nd ST., MANHATTANVILLE & ST. NICHOLAS AVE. RY. CO.

ELECTRIC LINE. BOULEVARD BRANCH.—Transfer. WILLIAM JAY, Receiver.
It is *agreed* by the party accepting this ticket that it is *good only at place of transfer*—for this *current trip* and *date* and *before time punched*—and is void if presented at any other time and place. Subject to the Rules of the Company. *Not Transferable.*

Issued by Conductor No. 190

17237

110th St or 125th St. at MANHATTAN ST | 86th St | 10th AVE 71st SP | 42nd ST AT 7th AVE | 10th AVE AT 42nd ST | 3d Ave | DRY DOCK R R AT 1st AV & 34th ST

1 15 30 45
2 15 30 45
3 15 30 45
4 15 30 45
5 15 30 45
6 15 30 45
7 15 30 45
8 15 30 45
9 15 30 45
10 15 30 45
11 15 30 45
12 15 30 45

1 2 3 4 5 6 7 8 9 10 11 12 13 14 15
Jan. Feb. Mar. Apr. May June July Aug. Sept. Oct. Nov. Dec.
16 17 18 19 20 21 22 23 24 25 26 27 28 29 30 31

230. 1901 RAILWAY TICKET
$1\frac{3}{4}'' \times 5''$. Anon. New York.
This ticket, printed in black on a green board, is an early example of a time-date-place check.

Tickets: Travelling and Cloakroom

231. 1961 RAILWAY TICKET
Anon. London.
Printed in black and red (for 'child') on cream card for British Railways.

2nd-SINGLE   SINGLE 2nd
Woodbridge to
Woodbridge   Woodbridge
Wickham Market   Wickham Market
WICKHAM MARKET
(E)   0/6   FARE   0/6   (E)
For conditions see over   For conditions see over

0324   0324

232. 1909 RAILWAY TICKET
$7\frac{1}{8}'' \times 3''$. Anon. Canada.
Canadian Pacific Railway ticket printed in black on a tinted card with date and station check points punched. Set mostly in grotesque.
Oxford University Press

233. 1957 RAILWAY TICKET
$6\frac{1}{4}'' \times 1\frac{3}{4}''$. Anon. San Francisco.
Printed in black on tinted papers and overprinted in various colours. Set throughout in sans serif.

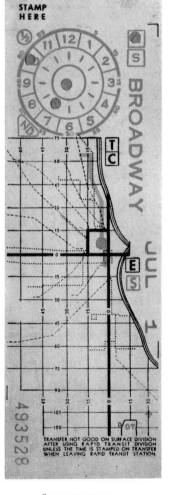

234. 1958 SUBWAY TICKET
$6\frac{1}{4}'' \times 2''$. Anon. Chicago.
Printed in black and red on newsprint, with a clockface for punching.

235. 1879 NATIONAL FAIR CLOAKROOM TICKET
1½″ × 2¾″. J. P. Spindle, Washington D.C.
Printed in black on orange coloured card with a very
attenuated French Antique for 'Grand Stand'.

236. 1894 HOTEL CLOAKROOM TICKET
2″ diam. Anon. London.
This roundel was printed in dark blue on a light blue
card by lithography.

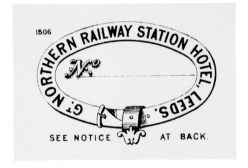

237. c. 1900 HOTEL CLOAKROOM TICKET
2″ × 1¼″. Anon. Leeds.
This convention of a clasped belt, on which was set
the name of the hotel, dates back at least to the time
of Thomas Bewick.

Cloakroom Tickets

Cloakroom and Public Convenience tickets
provide an interesting typographical survey of
changing styles. The W.C. Tickets in Fig. 238
come from Dr John Johnson's collection in the
Sanctuary of Printing at the University Press,
Oxford. As Dr Johnson so often said 'Nothing
is too humble or too insignificant . . .' Typographically these cloakroom tickets are of some
interest, ranging as they do from the City of
Edinburgh's use of a Bold Latin Antique to
Hastings Corporation's French Antique. For
plain speaking, however, the Crystal Palace has
it – with a good bold grotesque.

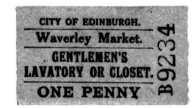

238. c. 1905 W.C. TICKETS
Average size 2¾″ × 1¼″. Williamson,
Ashton-under-Lyme, etc.
Oxford University Press

Cloakroom tickets

239. *c.* 1880 LUGGAGE LABELS
$1\frac{1}{4}'' \times 2\frac{1}{4}''$. Anon. York and Glasgow.
The Caledonian Railway label has a successful combination of Egyptian and sans serif typefaces. The old North Eastern Railway has an effective label for 'Rochdale' using a heavy fat face and rather an elegant Egyptian for 'L. & Y. via Goole'.

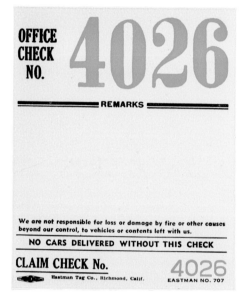

240. 1957 CAR PARK TICKETS
$3''$, $3\frac{1}{2}''$ and $3''$ wide. Eastman Tag Co., Richmond, California, U.S.A.
These three car park tickets, each printed in two colours show different typefaces for the large numerals, which are all based on nineteenth century types.

241. 1957 AIR LINE BAGGAGE TICKETS
$3''$, $3''$ and $2\frac{1}{2}''$ wide. Anon. U.S.A.
These Air Line baggage (claim) tickets are each printed in black and red. On the word 'SWISSAIR' there is an effective use of a tint to break down the black, this leaves the words 'NEW YORK' to dominate the design. The overprinting on the pink card of 'NEW YORK' in red on the Pan American ticket is less effective. The Pittsburg ticket is less elegant than the other two, but it serves its purpose effectively with the use of a condensed grotesque.

140

For the BENEFIT
OF A
GENTLEMAN OF RANK,
AT THE
ANCIENT MUSIC ROOMS,
TOTTENHAM STREET,
On Monday Evening, the 29th of APRIL,
WILL BE
A GRAND CONCERT
Of VOCAL and INSTRUMENTAL MUSIC,
By the most EMINENT PERFORMERS.
TICKETS 10s 6d Each.

242. *c.* 1750 CONCERT TICKETS
$2\frac{1}{2}'' \times 4\frac{3}{8}''$. Anon. London.
William Caslon's typeface is used for the well letter-
spaced capitals.

243. 1778–9 THEATRE TICKET
$2\frac{1}{2}'' \times 3''$. Anon. London.
Engraved ticket for Drury Lane.

Oxford University Press

Tickets: Functions and Exhibitions

Entertainment tickets were, at least in the
eighteenth century, usually engraved, but by the
early years of the nineteenth century, the display
letters of the letterpress printer were in full use.
Not only the fat faces but also a rather frivolous use of black letter was typical of both
English and American printers at this time.

245. *c.* 1800 CONCERT TICKET
$2\frac{1}{4}'' \times 3''$. T. Bewick, Newcastle-upon-Tyne.
The word 'NASON' appears at the head of this engraved ticket – whether this is the engraver's name
or whether it should read 'MASON', I do not know.
There is no record of Bewick having an apprentice
of either name, so it probably refers to a Masonic
concert.

244. *c.* 1750 THEATRE (BENEFIT) TICKET
$3\frac{3}{4}'' \times 4''$. Anon. London.
Engraved cartouche with mask and musical instru-
ments surround the beautifully disposed copy.

Oxford University Press

246. *c.* 1835 THEATRE TICKET
$2\frac{3}{4}'' \times 3\frac{1}{4}''$. Anon. London.
A lively use of bold Egyptians with a single line of
gothic giving sparkle to what might otherwise have
been rather a severe ticket.

141

247. *c.* 1830 THEATRE TICKET
$2\frac{1}{2}'' \times 4''$. George Cruikshank, London.
This engraved ticket for a box at Her Majesty's Theatre is a most delicate piece of engraving. George Cruikshank was a versatile artist, though much of his work at this time was of a coarse nature – for political lampoons, etc.

250. 1842 THEATRE TICKET
$2\frac{1}{2}'' \times 3\frac{1}{2}''$. Anon. New York.
In contrast to the previous label ticket, this shows a New England Puritanism in arrangement and economy of decoration.

Oxford University Press

248. 1834 CONCERT TICKET
$2\frac{3}{8}'' \times 4''$. Anon. London.
Thorne's Shaded, a bold Egyptian and a gothic type lend variety to 'Mr Dando's Evening Concert'.

Oxford University Press

251. 1859 CONCERT TICKET
$2\frac{1}{2}'' \times 4\frac{3}{8}''$. Anon. London.
A typographic ticket, showing the marked influence of the engraver.

Oxford University Press

252. 1874 OPERA HOUSE TICKET
$2\frac{1}{4}'' \times 4\frac{1}{4}''$ approx. Anon. U.S.A.
This letterpress ticket has been punched in the manner of a bus ticket at the month, date and day. The very small shaded letters used for 'COMPLIMENTARY' is of interest, as I doubt if any English typefounders produced such a small version of Thorne's Shaded.

Bella C. Landauer Collection, New-York Historical Society

249. 1840–1 THEATRE TICKET
$3\frac{3}{8}'' \times 4\frac{3}{4}''$. Anon. Philadelphia.
This ticket has a more ponderous style of engraving, with a full complement of swashes and a particularly evil gothic letter for 'New National Theatre'.

Oxford University Press

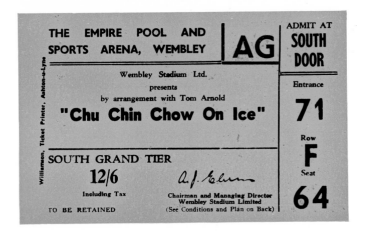

253. 1953 THEATRE TICKET
$2\frac{3}{4}'' \times 4\frac{1}{4}''$. Williamson, Ashton-under-Lyme.
Printed in black on pink paper and divided into
compartments apparently to no purpose.

254. 1949 OPERA TICKET
$2\frac{1}{4}'' \times 4\frac{1}{4}''$. John Lewis typ. W. S. Cowell Ltd, Ipswich.
The fat faced italic and Figgins' Shaded used for
the 'Children's Opera' give this ticket a flavour of
the 1830's.

255. 1957 THEATRE TICKET
$3'' \times 5''$. Royal College of Art, London.
Printed in black and red and set in the revived
Egyptian Expanded.

256. 1957 THEATRE TICKET
$1\frac{1}{2}'' \times 3\frac{1}{4}''$. Anon. Los Angeles.
Printed in black and yellow and set throughout in
sans serif types.

Theatre, Opera and Concert tickets

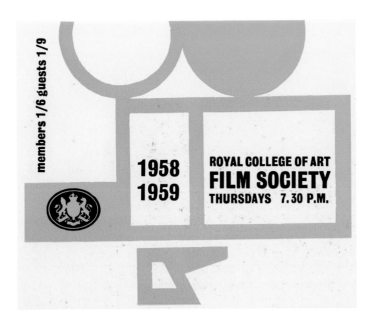

257. 1958-9 THEATRE TICKET
$3\frac{1}{4}'' \times 3\frac{3}{4}''$. Royal College of Art, London.
Printed in black and purple and set in Grotesque
No. 9.

The opera ticket for the 1949 Aldeburgh Festival,
with its use of Figgins Shaded for 'Children's
Opera' echoes Mr Dando's ticket of 1834, where
the same face is used for 'London Tavern'. The
brass rules which add so little to the 'Chu Chin
Chow on Ice' ticket (what an extraordinary
thing to put on ice!) are used as a basic part of
the design in Figs. 255 and 257 and provide
for the first an efficient and for the other a very
lively arrangement.

Tickets for functions such as Coronations,
Festivals and Balls clearly need a certain de-
corous and decorative formality which would
appear such an easy achievement for the engraver and such a difficult one for the printer
using only type and ornament. Yet with a
judicious use of ornament or borders, and a
combination of black letter and script, as in
Fig. 261 a surprisingly rich little card emerges.

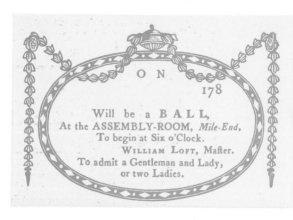

Tickets: Functions and Balls

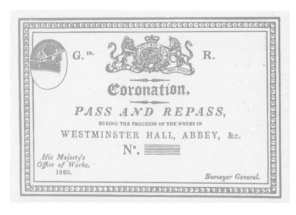

263. 1843 GALLERY TICKET
$2\frac{1}{2}'' \times 3\frac{7}{8}''$. C. H. Billings del. G. G. Smith sculpt.
Boston, Massachusetts.
This charming engraved ticket has all the rococo
delicacy of a hundred years earlier.

Oxford University Press

264. *c*. 1810 BALL TICKET
$3'' \times 4\frac{3}{4}''$. T. Bewick, Newcastle-upon-Tyne.
This ticket was for a masquerade dance and is signed
by T. Bewick, who also engraved the same scene
upon wood.

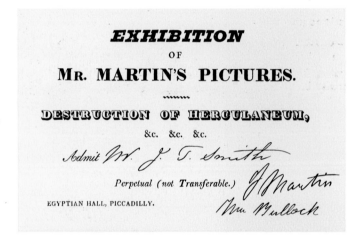

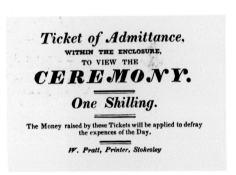

266. *c*. 1820 CEREMONY TICKET
$2\frac{1}{8}'' \times 3\frac{1}{4}''$. W. Pratt, Stokesley.
Whatever the 'ceremony' may have been, it is very
boldly displayed in Thorowgood's Fat Face Italic
with its alternative sorts (A, M, N, Y) with blobby
terminals.

265. 1822 EXHIBITION TICKET
$2\frac{3}{8}'' \times 3\frac{7}{8}''$. Anon. London.
Three display typefaces used in as many lines. James
Martin's exhibition had his painting 'Destruction
of Herculaneum' as the highlight.

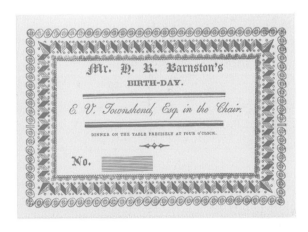

267. *c*. 1800 BALL TICKET
$2\frac{1}{4}'' \times 3\frac{3}{4}''$. T. Bewick, Newcastle-upon-Tyne.
This engraving of a rustic dance shows the steeple
of St Nicholas's Church, Newcastle. Mr Kinloch
was a noted Northumbrian dancing master.

268. 1823 BIRTHDAY PARTY INVITATION
$2\frac{1}{2}'' \times 3\frac{7}{8}''$. Anon. London.
Printed in blue on a white card, with an effective
combination of borders, which in company with the
type come from Thorowgood's foundry.

269. 1832 BALL TICKET
$7\frac{3}{8}'' \times 5\frac{5}{8}''$. John Mottram sculpt., London.
Engraved ticket for a Ball at the Guildhall, with a seal in the top left corner.

Tickets: Functions and Balls

In both the Test Match and Fancy Dress Ball tickets, on page 148, the use of heavy wood letters and very large sans serifs gives vitality to tickets that would otherwise be of little typographic interest.

Jack Lenor Larsen's Exhibition ticket (Fig. 280) is clearly intended to simulate the standard Broadway theatre ticket though it is for a textile and fashion display. The fashion district is close to the theatrical – in many ways.

The frivolous use of black letter, as for 'Mr Barnston's' is typical of English printers at this time (Fig. 268). Though gothic types have been used consistently for odd words in legal and liturgical printing, the early eighteen hundreds saw the introduction of a gothic fat face and its use for a number of purposes where its clumsy, spiky form added sparkle not only to book pages, but to a lot of jobbing work.

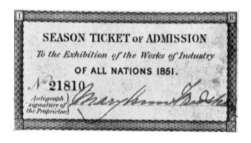

270. 1851 EXHIBITION TICKET
$1\frac{3}{8}'' \times 2\frac{5}{8}''$. Anon. London.
Engraved ticket with 'engine' turned borders. It seems curious that engraving should be used for such a mundane little season ticket.

Oxford University Press

271. 1851 BALL TICKET
$4'' \times 6''$. Anon. London.
Lithographed in several colours this ticket is Germanic in its baroque feeling and may well have been drawn by a German craftsman.

272. c. 1910 EXHIBITION TICKET
2¼″ × 1¾″. Anon. London.
Printed in black on green paper from grotesques,
Latin Antique and a line block.

273. 1890 RACE MEETING TICKET
3½″ × 4⅝″. Anon. Ascot.
Printed in black and gold from line blocks.

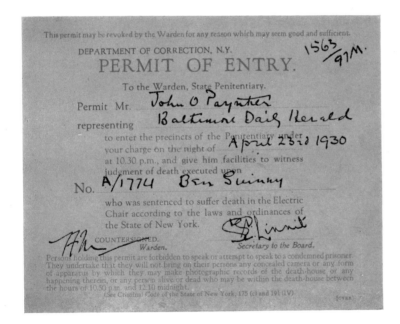

275. 1930 EXECUTION TICKET
4″ × 4¾″. Anon. London.
Ticket printed in green and red on a light green
card, this is actually a copy of the New York Department of Correction Permit of Entry. It was produced
as a very macabre piece of advertising for the play
Smoky Gill at Wyndhams Theatre in London.

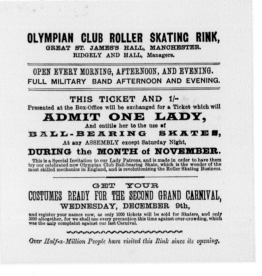

274. c. 1910 SKATING RINK TICKET
3½″ × 3¼″. Anon. Manchester.
Printed in black on pink paper and set in a variety of
condensed and extended typefaces, including the
effective Latin Antique for 'Admit one Lady', etc.

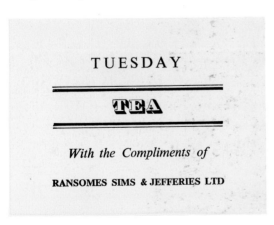

276. 1957 TEA TICKET
1½″ × 2″. W. S. Cowell Ltd, Ipswich.
Printed in black and purple with Figgins' Shaded used
for 'Tea'; this was cut by Anthony Bessemer in 1825.

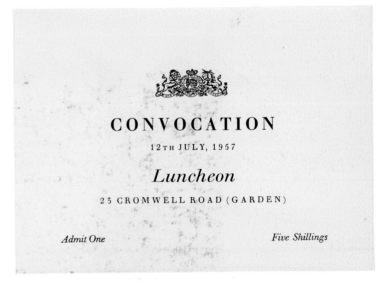

277. 1957 LUNCHEON TICKET
2¼″ × 3¾″. Royal College of Art, London.
Severely classical use of Walbaum suits the formality
of the occasion.

278. 1957 FOOTBALL TICKET
$1\frac{1}{4}'' \times 2''$. Anon. New Haven, Connecticut.
Printed in black and red on a buff card. The heavy Egyptian used for 'Yale Bowl' gives this little ticket some distinction.

279. 1958 EXHIBITION TICKET
$\frac{7}{8}'' \times 1\frac{3}{4}''$. Toledo Ticket Co., Toledo, Ohio.
Printed in black on purple card and set throughout in sans serif.

280. 1957–8 EXHIBITION TICKET
$1\frac{1}{4}'' \times 3\frac{1}{2}''$. Anon. New York.
Printed in black and brown on lemon yellow card.

281. 1958 EXHIBITION TICKET
$1'' \times 2\frac{1}{8}''$. Bell Punch Co., London.
Printed in black on pinkish card, set in sans serifs and a bold Latin Antique for '1/-'.

282. 1958 TEST MATCH TICKET
$5\frac{1}{4}'' \times 2''$. Lord's, London.
Printed in red and black on a lemon yellow card. The overprinting from wood letters of '4' is reminiscent of the 1860's.

283. 1958 DANCE TICKET
$4\frac{3}{8}'' \times 3\frac{3}{4}''$. Royal College of Art, London.
Printed in black on a blue card, the heavy wood letters used for '12s 6d' provide the main motif for the design, apart from the bandleader's rubber stamp.

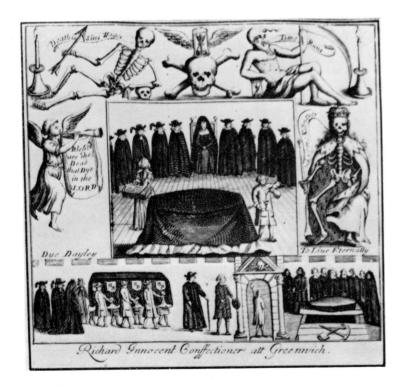

284. *c.* 1685 FUNERAL INVITATIONS
(various). Anon. Greenwich, and London.
Three engraved funeral invitations, showing the full
panoply of death.

Pepysian Library

Invitation and Announcement cards

Funerals, weddings, christenings, dinners, dances and other functions have little in common with each other except the printed invitation card. In 1685 the funeral cards were of a Puritanical severity with due acknowledgement to draped mourners and *memento mori*. When Mrs Loasbey died in 1736 (Fig. 286), on the invitation 'to accompany her corpse', the Company of Upholsterers gave her the full panoply of Winged Time with scythe and hour-glass and the three Fates, Clotho, Lachesis and Atropos to send her on her way. What a contrast to the austerity of our age, where Jan Tschichold announces the birth of a friend's child with superb and asymmetric economy (Fig. 292).

285. 1685 FUNERAL INVITATION
$1\frac{1}{2}'' \times 3\frac{3}{8}''$. Stanton Harcourt, Oxon.
Printed by letterpress, with details filled in by hand.

Oxford University Press

286. 1736 FUNERAL INVITATION
$9\frac{1}{2}'' \times 10\frac{3}{4}''$. N. N. Coypel des. Ja. Chereau sculpt.,
London.
Printed from a copper engraving. This elaborate
illustration was printed with a blank centre, the
wording for each funeral would have to have been
engraved and printed separately.

287. 1746 FUNERAL INVITATION
$6'' \times 8\frac{1}{2}''$. Anon. London.
Wood engraved surround with typeset centre. Nicks
have been cut in the centre to accommodate the
furniture that held the type in position.

Oxford University Press

Funeral invitations

Funeral invitations

288. *c.* 1820 FUNERAL INVITATION
4″ × 5″. J. Gillé, Paris.
I assume this is a Gillé production; the types and borders are similar to those shown in his type specimens. Printed in black on a yellow card.

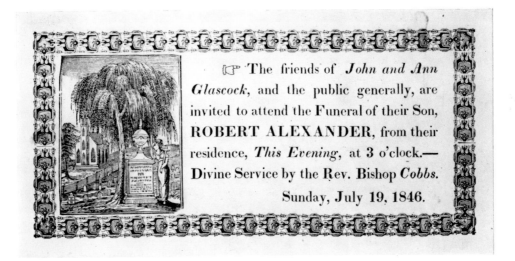

289. 1846 FUNERAL INVITATION
6½″ × 3″. Anon. New England.
This invitation is framed in an unusual border, which comes from the wood engraving of the rather ill-drawn damsel leaning on an urn with a little New England Church in the background.

Bella C. Landauer Collection, New-York Historical Society

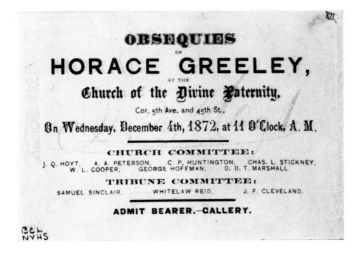

290. 1872 FUNERAL INVITATION
2½″ × 3¾″. Anon. New York.
This is typographically undistinguished, but for the outline fat face used for 'OBSEQUIES'.

Bella C. Landauer Collection, New-York Historical Society

OLIVER SIMON

29 April 1895 · 18 March 1956

Founder of the Double Crown Club

291. 1956 ANNOUNCEMENT OF DEATH
¾″ × 1¾″. University Press, Cambridge.
This austere little announcement was circulated to the members of the Double Crown Club.

olga + hans fischli

katharina

* **25. VII. 1935**
olga susanna

**klinik hirslanden zürich
+ meilen**

292. 1935 ANNOUNCEMENT OF BIRTH
$5\frac{3}{4}'' \times 1\frac{1}{2}''$. Jan Tschichold typ. Zurich.
Printed in black and vermilion, and laid out by one
of the pioneers of the New Movement in typography.
Museum of Modern Art

Christening and Wedding announcements

To Valiant & Christopher Bradshaw

a son

NOEL ANTHONY

born 00.02 hrs 22.iii.56

11 Ornan Road London N. W. 3

293. 1956 ANNOUNCEMENT OF BIRTH
$3\frac{1}{4}'' \times 2\frac{1}{2}''$. C. Bradshaw, typ. London.
Printed in black and blue on a hand press.

Mr and Mrs Basil Spence

request the pleasure of the company of

at the marriage of their daughter

Gillian

to

Mr Anthony Blee

*in the Chapel of the Cross, Coventry Cathedral
on Saturday, 7th February 1959 at 2.00 p.m.
and afterwards
at the Leofric*

R.S.V.P. One Canonbury Place, London N.1

294. 1959 WEDDING INVITATION
$4\frac{3}{8}'' \times 3''$. W. S. Cowell Ltd, Ipswich.
Set in Alfred Fairbank's beautiful Bembo Narrow
Italic, and printed in grey on a white card.

295. 1680 DINNER INVITATION
8″ × 6″ approx. Anon. London.
This elaborate invitation card comes from the
Pepysian Library. Space is left for day and hour, so
presumably Nath. Meystnor often invited his friends
or patrons to dine with his students – and perhaps on
the products resulting from their tuition.

Pepysian Library

Invitations and Announcements:
Functions, Dinners, Balls etc.

As for functions, Nathaniel Meystnor must
have had some faith in his student's labours to
send out invitations to the Quality to come and
dine off them; or perhaps it was just a way of
getting rid of 'burnt offerings and bloody
sacrifices'. Whatever joys or horrors the meals
may have provided, the engraved card is a delight.

The early eighteenth century letterpress invitations are rather stodgy and remained so until
the French typefounders such as Gillé produced
the charming borders and frivolous types
(Fig. 288) so appropriate for ephemeral work.
This framed approach was often used a century
later by the Double Crown Club for their
Dinner Announcements.

296. *c.* 1685 DINNER INVITATION
6½″ × 5¼″ approx. Anon. London.
This engraved invitation has the printed injunction
'Please pay ye bearer hereof 2s. 6d.'. It shows a press
for copperplate printing and pressman warming the
plate.

Pepysian Library

SIR,
YOU are desired to be at a Committee of
Almoners in *Christ's-Hospital*, on
ffryday next, being the 28th day of *Aprill*
1710 at three of the Clock in the after
noon precisely.

297. 1710 COMMITTEE MEETING INVITATION
3½″ × 5″. Anon. London.
Printed by letterpress with wood engraved device.

British Museum

SIR,
YOUR WORSHIP is desired to be at *Guildhall*
on *Sunday* next, at Nine of the Clock in the Forenoon, being the 12th Day of *January*, 1772, in your Scarlet
Gown, to proceed from thence to St. *Laurence's* Church,
to receive the holy Communion with the Lord-Mayor.

John Greig.

298. 1772 INVITATION TO HOLY COMMUNION
4½″ × 5⅜″. Anon. London.
Printed by letterpress, with wood engraved
coat of arms.

299. 1762. INVITATION TO A MEETING
7" × 5½". Anon. New York.
This engraved card with its richly decorated rococo
frame illustrates the artist's idea of the Hand-in-
Hand Fire Company at work in an unidentified
New York street.

New York Public Library

Invitations: Dinners and Functions

Independence Ball.

Be gone dull care,————
Make room for mirth and glee.

The compliments of the Managers to
Mr̃ Arthur Bronson & Lady . and
respectfully solicit & Your attendance at the
house of **Z. Larnard's**, *in Rutland,*
on the 4th July next, at 1 o'clock, P.M.

A. EAMES,
G. STERETT,
V. HICKOX,   } MANAGERS.
O. PIERCE,

Rutland, June 5th 1827.

300. 1827 BALL INVITATION
2¼″ × 3″. Rutland, Vermont.
The formality of copperplate is given some life by
W. Thorowgood's Great Primer Open Black Letter,
used for 'Independence Ball' and the surprising
introduction of an italic fat face for 'Z. Larnard's'.

New York Public Library

For invitation cards, the combination of black
letter, whether solid, open or shaded, and a
copperplate script type of the style of the 'English' hand of Bickham and other eighteenth
century writing masters gave the letterpress
printers' work something of the look of an engraving. The 'Independence Ball' card (Fig. 300)
with quite economical typographic means
achieves an effect of quality, and even the
violent intrusion of an italic fat face, used for
'Z. Larnard's', does not destroy this.

The same kind of script typeface can be seen
in the invitation issued by 'The Directors of the
Limited Editions Club' (Fig. 310). This typeface, unrelieved by black letter or anything else,
is a little monotonous. This could have been
enriched by even such a small decorative border
as the Curwen Press used to frame the 'Faculty
of Royal Designers for Industry' card, set in
Walbaum Italic (Fig. 311).

Borders and printers' flowers are invaluable,
for they provide the printer with an easy means
of framing his invitations, etc. The rich flowery
border used for 'The London Silk Congress' in
1951 is exactly the same as that used by J. Last,
Haymarket Leather Merchant, for his trade
card in 1840 (Figs. 312 and 389).

The illustrations on pages 162 and 163 show
that there are other ways of tackling the problems of designing invitation cards. The painter
Julian Trevelyan draws very freely his invitation
to an annual boat race party, whereas graphic
design students at the Royal College of Art
make use of bold sans serif typefaces, asymmetric
arrangements and brightly coloured cards for
their party, dinner and film-show invitations
(Figs. 320–2).

301. 1824 DINNER INVITATION
9¾" × 7". Oliver and Samson fc. Haymarket, London.
Elaborate engraved card, printed in black.

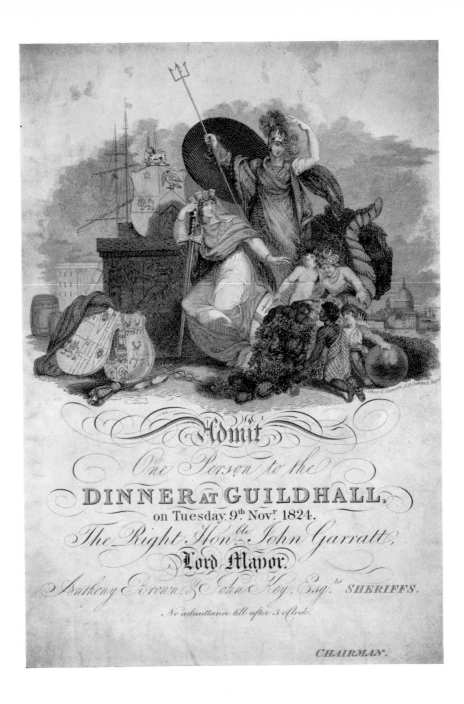

302. *c.* 1840 ORPHANAGE ANNOUNCEMENT
2" × 3¼". Anon. London.
The fat face gothic and the heavy Egyptian add
interest to this poignant little card.

303. 1887 DINNER INVITATION
2¾" × 4¼". Anon. London.
Printed in blue, purple and gold on a lavender
coloured card, this is an example of 'artistic' printing.

Invitations: Dinners and Functions

304. 1884 SOIREE INVITATION
8″ × 5½″. W. H. Carman, Ashby-de-la-Zouche.
Printed in blue, red and gold from type and ornaments.

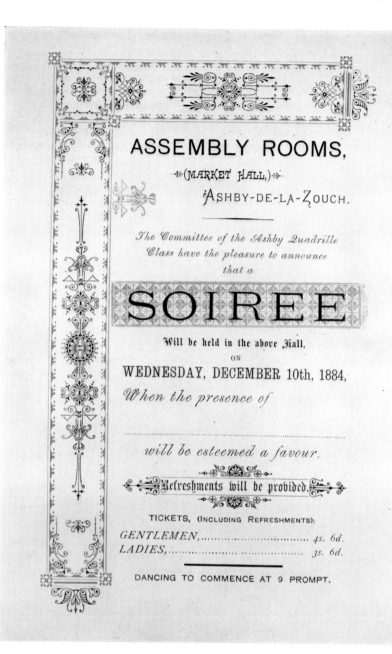

ASSEMBLY ROOMS,
(MARKET HALL,)
ASHBY-DE-LA-ZOUCH.

The Committee of the Ashby Quadrille
Class have the pleasure to announce
that a

SOIREE

Will be held in the above Hall,
ON
WEDNESDAY, DECEMBER 10th, 1884,

When the presence of

....

will be esteemed a favour.

Refreshments will be provided.

TICKETS, (INCLUDING REFRESHMENTS):

GENTLEMEN, ... 4s. 6d.
LADIES, ... 3s. 6d.

DANCING TO COMMENCE AT 9 PROMPT.

THE
Double Crown Club

¶ The 53rd Dinner of the Club will be held in the Hall of Exeter College, Oxford, by kind permission of the Rector and Fellows, at 7.30 on January 10th, 1936 (not January 15th as previously announced). The Chair will be taken by Mr. Hubert J. Foss, and after Dinner there will be a visit to Dr. John Johnson's collection of ephemera in the Sanctuary of Printing at the University Press, Walton Street, Oxford.

¶ Members intending to be present should inform the Dinner Secretary, Holbrook Jackson, at the National Trade Press Ltd., Drury House, Russell Street, W.C.2, giving name of guest (if any), and enclosing cheque, not later than January 7th. Dinner 10/6 per head.

305. 1936 DINNER CARD
5⅝″ × 3¼″. Oxford University Press, London.
Printed in black and red and set in Fell types in a border of fleurons.

Double Crown Club 127th Dinner

The 127th Dinner will be held at Kettners Romilly Street
on Wednesday December 8 at 7.15 for 7.30 pm
Christian Barman will read a paper on the work of

FRANK PICK

Please send cheques (Members 16s per head, Guests 18s per head) and
name of guest, if any, to Desmond Flower, 37-38 St Andrew's Hill
EC 4 not later than Wednesday December 1st

306. 1947 DINNER CARD
3″ × 4″. Curwen Press, London.
Set in Walbaum with shaded grotesque, *c.* 1830, for
'FRANK PICK', who did so much for the advertising of
the London Underground Railway between the wars.

62nd dinner

of the Double Crown Club will

be held 13 October 1937 at the

Cafe Royal at 7 for 7 15 pm

Mr Christian Barman

will read a paper on

Design in Timetables

Members intending to be present should
inform the Dinner Secretary, Holbrook Jackson
at the National Trade Press Ltd, Drury House
Russell Street WC2, giving name of guest
if any, and enclosing cheque (10s 6d per head)
not later than 11 October

307. 1937 DINNER CARD
4¾″ × 2¾″. Kynoch Press, Heaton Mersey.
Set in a condensed grotesque and Plantin in an off
centre manner.

Dinner invitations

DCC | 80

The 80th Meeting of the
Double Crown Club
will be held at
Kettner's Restaurant
Romilly Street, W.1
Thursday, April 19, 1945
12.45 for 1 o'clock

MEMBERS *intending to attend
should inform the Hon. Dinner
Secretary, Holbrook Jackson,
Drury House, Russell Street,
W.C.2 (by April 12th) giving
name of guest and enclosing
cheque. Lunches 12/6.*

PLEASE NOTE DINNER ON MAY 17th

Philip James
will speak
on

Recent
French
Book
Illustrations

*followed by a
discussion*

Francis Meynell

in the Chair

APR | 19

308. 1945 DINNER CARD
7¾″ × 4¾″. Shenval Press, Hertford.
Set in Slimblack, Monotype Bodoni and Baskerville
italic.

Double Crown Club

Dinner 151

The 151st Dinner will be at Kettner's on Wednesday, 28 October 1959 at
7 p.m. for 7.30 Ian Parsons will speak on

Dragon's Blood, Tissue Paper and String
British Printing today as it strikes an old fashioned Publisher

Please notify the Hon. Dinner Secretary, Desmond Flower, Cassell &
Company Ltd., 35 Red Lion Square, London, W.C.1, of your intention to
dine, with or without guest, and send him your cheque for 25s. (guest
27s. 6d.) not later than Wednesday, 21 October

Provisional dates for further dinners in 1959-60, all with guests are: Tuesday, 8 December; Wednesday,
17 February; Tuesday, 26 April

309. 1959 DINNER CARD
3″ × 4½″. Westerham Press, Kent.
Set in Eric Gill's Joanna, a typeface newly released
for general jobbing work.

The Directors of The Limited Editions Club

request your presence at

A Dinner Party

to celebrate the Twenty-first Birthday of the Club,

the Fiftieth Birthday of its founder,

and the inauguration of the Aldine Awards

with the first "Aldus" presented

to Mr. Bruce Rogers

in celebration of his Eightieth Birthday

The Roof of the St. Regis Hotel, New York

The eleventh of May, 1950

Black tie, please
Aperitif at 7:45, dinner at 8:45
R.S.V.P. (see Notes overleaf)

310. 1950 DINNER INVITATION
$6\frac{1}{2}'' \times 5\frac{1}{2}''$. Anon. New York.
Printed in black and set in a 'copper plate' script
typeface.

**FACULTY OF
ROYAL DESIGNERS
FOR INDUSTRY**

The Master and Members of the
Faculty of Royal Designers for Industry in this
the Bicentenary year of its parent body,
the Royal Society of Arts, request through

the pleasure of the company of

at a Reception
on Thursday, July 8th 1954, at the
Royal Society of Arts, John Adam Street
Adelphi, London, W.C.2

Evening Dress and Decorations   8.45 p.m.
R.S.V.P. *to the Secretary*
8 John Adam Street, Adelphi
London, W.C.2

There will be a short programme of songs by MISS NANCY EVANS
and of poetry reading by MISS MARGARET RAWLINGS

311. 1954 RECEPTION INVITATION
$7\frac{1}{2}'' \times 4''$. Curwen Press, London.
Set in Walbaum and Walbaum italic.

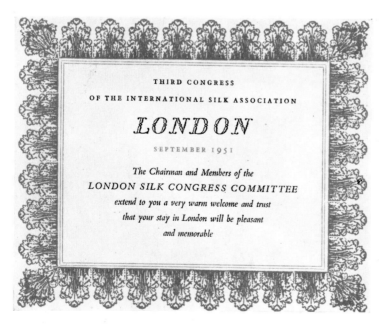

THIRD CONGRESS
OF THE INTERNATIONAL SILK ASSOCIATION
LONDON
SEPTEMBER 1951
The Chairman and Members of the
LONDON SILK CONGRESS COMMITTEE
extend to you a very warm welcome and trust
that your stay in London will be pleasant
and memorable

312. 1951 CONGRESS CARD
$4\frac{3}{4}'' \times 6''$. John Lewis, typ. Chiswick Press, London.
Printed in black and blue and set in Bembo, and
in June for 'London'; the border is reproduced from
that used by Wm. Savage for the title page of *The
Art of Decorative Printing*, 1820.

THE MASTER
OF CORPUS CHRISTI COLLEGE

At Home
CORPUS CHRISTI DAY
9 June 1955

The Master's Lodge
Corpus Christi College
Cambridge

10 P.M.
R.S.V.P.

313. 1955 AT HOME CARD
$2\frac{3}{4}'' \times 4''$. University Press, Cambridge.
Set in Goudy Old Style and Garamond italic.

The Council and Principal of the Royal College of Art

request the pleasure of your company at the

CONVOCATION DAY CEREMONY

to be held at 2.45 pm on Thursday, July 12th, 1951 in the Hall of

The Royal College of Music, Prince Consort Road, SW7

The Rt. Hon. R. A. Butler, MP will give the Address

314. 1951 CONVOCATION INVITATION
4½″ × 5″. Royal College of Art, London.
Printed in black and pink and set in Walbaum
Medium and a drawn letter.

1855   1955

THE DIRECTORS OF CHATTO & WINDUS

request the pleasure of the company of

Mr Edward Bawden

at 23 Knightsbridge, S.W.1

on Wednesday, July 6th

to celebrate the Centenary of the firm

9 p.m.
Buffet Supper

R.S.V.P.
42 William IV Street,
London, W.C.2

315. 1955 SUPPER INVITATION
3¼″ × 4¼″. Anon. London.
Printed in black and blue and set in Bembo and
Blado italic.

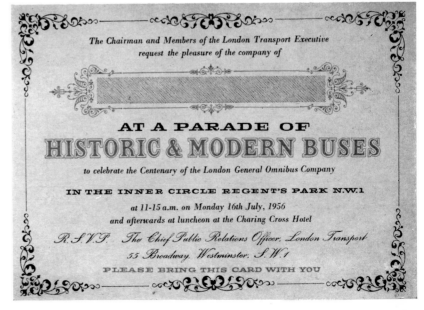

The Chairman and Members of the London Transport Executive
request the pleasure of the company of

AT A PARADE OF
HISTORIC & MODERN BUSES

to celebrate the Centenary of the London General Omnibus Company

IN THE INNER CIRCLE REGENT'S PARK N.W.1

at 11-15 a.m. on Monday 16th July, 1956
and afterwards at luncheon at the Charing Cross Hotel

R.S.V.P. The Chief Public Relations Officer, London Transport
55 Broadway, Westminster, S.W.1

PLEASE BRING THIS CARD WITH YOU

316. 1956 DISPLAY INVITATION
4″ × 5¾″. W. Fenton, typ. W. S. Cowell Ltd, Ipswich.
Printed in black and red on a yellow card, this card
reflects the flavour of the display.

M

317. 1957 DINNER INVITATION
$2\frac{3}{4}'' \times 5\frac{1}{2}''$. Allan Fleming, typ. Cooper and Beatty,
Toronto.
Printed in black and blue on a cream ground and
set throughout in small capitals.

318. 1958 DINNER INVITATION
$3\frac{1}{2}'' \times 4''$. J. P. Ascherl des. Huxley House, New York.
Printed in black on a cream card and set in Palatino.

319. 1960 PARTY INVITATION
$6'' \times 4''$. Julian Trevelyan des. London.
A freely drawn card, printed in brown.

162

320. 1957 PARTY CARD
5¼″ × 2″. Royal College of Art,
London.
Printed in black on a yellow card.

banana boat song
      calypso carnival
island in the sun

textile party : fancy dress : jass : calypso
friday sixth december: seven thirty-eleven
5s single 7/6 double: free drink and buffet

christmas dinner

1957

Wednesday 4th December

7.30 for 8 pm

Dress optional

21 CROMWELL ROAD SW7

321. 1957 DINNER INVITATION
8″ × 2⅝″. Royal College of Art, London.
Printed in black and red and set in Gill Sans.

322. 1957 FILM SHOW INVITATION
1¼″×6¼″. Royal College of Art, London.
Printed in black and set in Gill Sans with an 8-line
wood letter for 'F'.

Students of the Graphic Design School Royal College of Art invite you to a

FILM SHOW 4 pm Friday 6th December
in the main hall **21 Cromwell Road SW7**

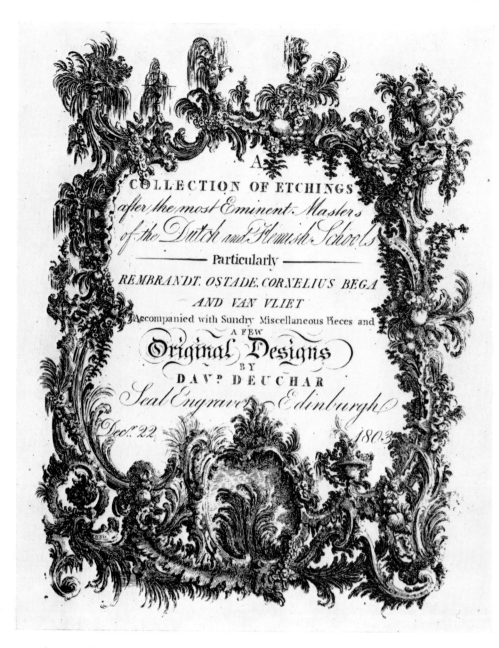

323. 1803 EXHIBITION CARD
$6\frac{1}{2}'' \times 5''$. D. Deuchar. Edinburgh.
This richly rococo engraving might well have been
produced thirty or forty years earlier.

Oxford University Press

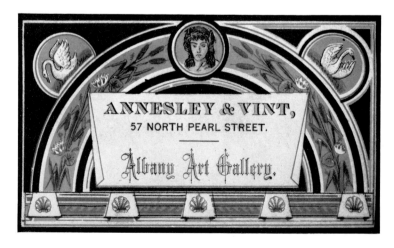

324. 1879 GALLERY CARD
$2\frac{3}{8}'' \times 4''$. Anon. U.S.A.
Printed by lithography, in four colours.

325. *c.* 1900 EXHIBITION CARD
$4\frac{3}{8}'' \times 3\frac{1}{4}''$. Graham Robertson des. Virtue, London.
Printed by letterpress in four colours, presumably
from a poster design for the same exhibition.

326. *c.* 1928 EXHIBITION CARD
$5\frac{1}{8}'' \times 3\frac{1}{2}''$. Herbert Bayer typ. Bauhaus, Dessau.
Printed in black and vermilion and set throughout
in sans serif typefaces.
Museum of Modern Art, New York

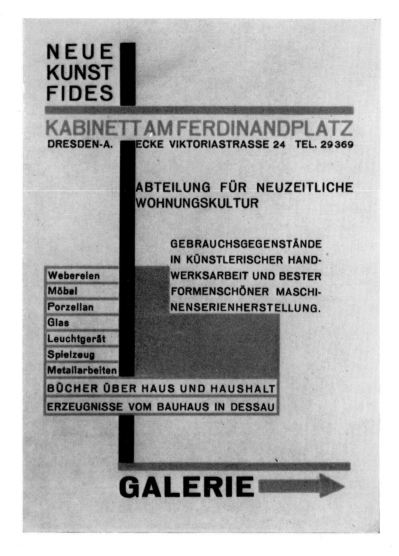

Exhibition cards

Art Exhibition, Museum and Gallery cards are one example of printed ephemera where the best productions of today are at least as exciting as the pretty designs of the past; even designs such as that of David Deuchar, seal engraver of Edinburgh, where inside his rococo border he uses a mixture of English copperplate hand, open roman capitals and a readable black letter.

After the typographic horrors of the late nineteenth century, where even a card for the Pre-Raphaelites has the most abysmal lettering, Herbert Bayer's card for the Bauhaus exhibition has a brave, bold, if heavy handed, kind of logic about it. The Moholy-Nagy card is more inspired. These cards were to set a lasting fashion that persists to this day, though with periodic interruptions from printers with more classic or baroque ideals. The Anglo-Saxon race at least has no great stomach for logic in design or in anything else. So we find aseptically clean post-Bauhaus designs, such as Herbert Spencer's red, yellow and black card (Fig. 335), side by side with the Arts Council's Hogarth exhibition card, which is a return to the sombre formality of the Gillé border, enriched with a panel of colour. Oliver Simon, at the Curwen Press, worked much in this vein and with much skill. In opposition to such conventions, Dr Sandberg, at the Stedelijk Museum in Amsterdam, breaking every canon of conventional typographic usage, sometimes achieves quite brilliant results. The final word on design should be with the younger print designers, the students at such schools as the School of Architecture and Design at Yale and the Royal College of Art in London, where would-be typographers are flexing their muscles, often with a success that must make older designers a little envious.

327. 1935 EXHIBITION CARD
4″ × 7¼″. Vytiskla, Brno. Czechoslovakia.
The only reason for going so far from our
self-imposed geographical limitations is
that this card is for an exhibition of L.
Moholy-Nagy's work and that it owes so
much to the Bauhaus, where Moholy-
Nagy was a teacher.

Museum of Modern Art, New York

künstlerhaus, brno, koblížná 41   od 1. do 16. června 1935

výstava

l. moholy-nagy

oleje na plátně, aluminiu, silberitu, galalitu, neolitu, trolitu, celuloidu, akvarely, kresby, obrazy
montované, fotomontáže - fotoplastiky, fotogramy, fotografie, snímky divadelních scén a výstav,
práce typografické a mnohé jiné

vernisáž v sobotu 1. června o 17.30 hodině . úvodní slovo promluví **dr. bedřich václavek**

u příležitosti výstavy uspořádána jest v pátek dne 7. června v 21. hodině v kinu »lucerna«
v brně-žabovřeskách projekce experimentálních filmů profesora l. moholy-nagy

marseille . světelná hra černá-bílá-šedá . cikáni ve velkoměstě . znějící abeceda

úvodní přednáška: **fr. kalivoda**

instalace výstavy: architekt fr. kalivoda

štočky zapůjčil mezinárodní časopis pro optickou kulturu »telehor«, brno, plotní 37   vytiskla »typia«, brno, cejl 21

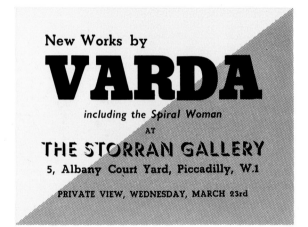

New Works by

VARDA

including the Spiral Woman

AT

THE STORRAN GALLERY

5, Albany Court Yard, Piccadilly, W.1

PRIVATE VIEW, WEDNESDAY, MARCH 23rd

328. 1938 GALLERY CARD
4½″ × 6″. Anon. London.
Printed in black and green and set in Rockwell and
Gill Sans.

MODERN MASTERS
JUNE 12TH — JUNE 24TH

PICASSO	MATISSE
BONNARD	ROUAULT
SOUTINE	UTRILLO

etc

THE STORRAN GALLERY
5, ALBANY COURT YARD, PICCADILLY, W.I.

329. 1939 GALLERY CARD
4½″ × 6″. Anon. London.
Printed in black and red on yellow and set in Gill
Sans.

THE   HANOVER   GALLERY

LUCIAN
FREUD

Private view Tuesday 6 May at 3 o'clock until 14 June

32A St George Street Hanover Square London W1

330. *c.* 1949 GALLERY CARD
4″ × 5″. Anon. London.
Printed in black and green and set in a condensed
grotesque and Times New Roman

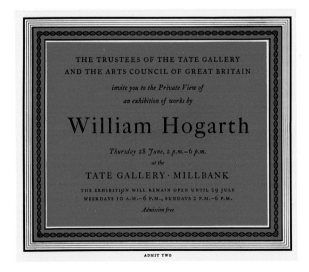

THE TRUSTEES OF THE TATE GALLERY
AND THE ARTS COUNCIL OF GREAT BRITAIN

invite you to the Private View of
an exhibition of works by

William Hogarth

Thursday 28 June, 2 p.m.–6 p.m.
at the
TATE GALLERY · MILLBANK

THE EXHIBITION WILL REMAIN OPEN UNTIL 29 JULY
WEEKDAYS 10 A.M.–6 P.M., SUNDAYS 2 P.M.–6 P.M.
Admission free

ADMIT TWO

331. 1951 GALLERY CARD
5⅜″ × 6¾″. Curwen Press, London.
Printed in black and red and set in Caslon Old Face.

332. *c.* 1950 EXHIBITION CARD
7" × 4½". Lund Humphries, Bradford
Printed in black and pink, with the artist's signature
and design printed from a block. Set in Garamond.

Exhibition cards

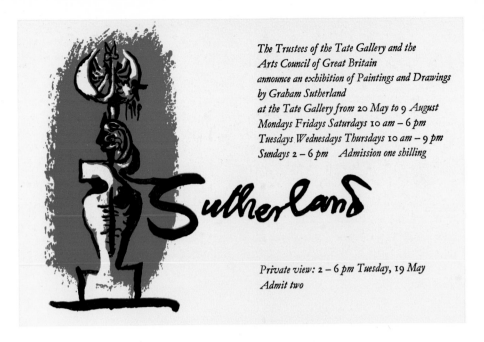

The Trustees of the Tate Gallery and the
Arts Council of Great Britain
announce an exhibition of Paintings and Drawings
by Graham Sutherland
at the Tate Gallery from 20 May to 9 August
Mondays Fridays Saturdays 10 am – 6 pm
Tuesdays Wednesdays Thursdays 10 am – 9 pm
Sundays 2 – 6 pm   Admission one shilling

Sutherland

Private view: 2 – 6 pm Tuesday, 19 May

Admit two

THE ARTS COUNCIL OF GREAT BRITAIN
invite you to the Private View of

SPLENDID OCCASIONS

*An exhibition of prints and panoramas illustrating
four centuries of public rejoicing and ceremonial in many countries
on Tuesday 8th May from 2–6 pm at the Arts Council Gallery
4 St James's Square, SW1*

*The exhibition will remain open until 9th June
Mondays, Wednesdays, Fridays and Saturdays from 10–6 pm
Tuesdays and Thursdays from 10–8 pm
Admission Free*

Lund Humphries cordially invite you

to visit an exhibition of

post-war printing design from fourteen countries

PURPOSE AND PLEASURE

12 Bedford Square London WC1

11–28 June 1952

Monday to Friday 11–6, Saturday 10–1

Admission Free

334. 1952 EXHIBITION CARD
2¼" × 4½". Herbert Spencer typ. Lund Humphries,
Bradford.
Printed in black and red on yellow and set in Gill
Sans, Tea-chest and an unidentified ornamented
typeface.

333. 1951 EXHIBITION INVITATION
4⅝" × 6". M. Dufton des. Shenval Press, Hertford.
Printed in green and pink and set in Bembo.

TYPOGRAPHICA

You are cordially invited

to visit an exhibition

of typography and design by

Herbert Spencer

at the Zwemmer Gallery

26 Litchfield Street

Charing Cross Road London WC2

23–31 October 1953

335. 1953 TYPOGRAPHY EXHIBITION CARD
4"×8". Herbert Spencer des. Lund Humphries,
Bradford.
Printed in black, yellow and red by offset lithography.
Set in Gill Sans.

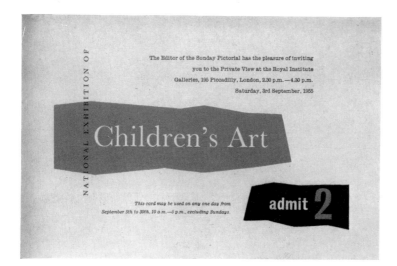

336. 1955 EXHIBITION CARD
$3\frac{3}{8}'' \times 6\frac{1}{8}''$. Anon. London.
Printed in black and brown on grey card and set in
Ionic, Baskerville and Grotesque No. 9.

337. 1958 EXHIBITION CARD
$5\frac{3}{4}'' \times 8''$. Anon. London.
Printed in white, black and cerise on a grey
card and set in a condensed grotesque and Ionic.

GEORGE STUBBS: REDISCOVERED ANATOMICAL DRAWINGS

An exhibition of the drawings recently found at Worcester, Massachusetts,
will be held at the Arts Council Gallery, 4 St. James's Square, SW1, until
December 13. It will be open on Monday, Wednesday, Friday and Saturday
from 10 to 6 and on Tuesday and Thursday from 10 to 8.

ADMIT TWO TO PRIVATE VIEW, FRIDAY 21 NOV 2–6

338. c. 1956 EXHIBITION CARD
$1\frac{5}{8}'' \times 6''$. David Thomas typ. Shenval Press, Hertford.
Printed in black and set in Modern No. 1.

339. c. 1956
EXHIBITION CARD
$1\frac{7}{8}'' \times 7\frac{3}{8}''$. W. H. J.
Sandberg, typ. Am-
sterdam.
Printed in dark blue
and orange; designed
by the director of the
Stedelijk Museum.

do you leave without seeing the   vous partez sans avoir vu les
150 van gogh's
stedelijk museum paulus potterstraat 13, amsterdam
open|ouvert 10-5 on sundays|dimanche 1-5

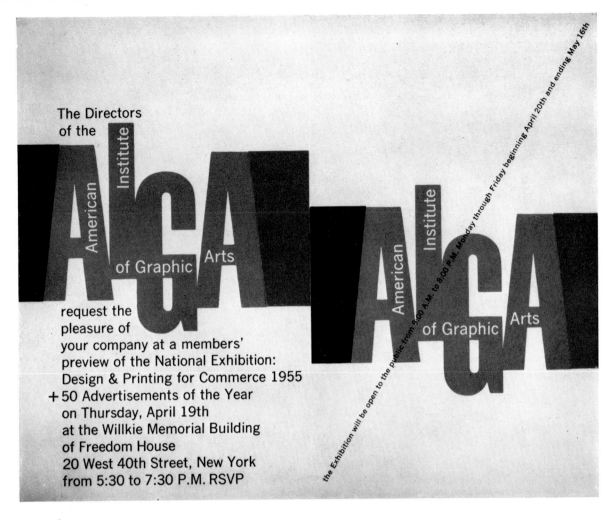

340. 1956 EXHIBITION CARD
5½″ × 10½″. Anon. New York.
The American Institute of Graphic Arts card is
printed in black, khaki and vermilion and set
throughout in Intertype News Gothic, with its Bold
Condensed for 'AIGA'.

341. 1959 EXHIBITION CARD
8½″ × 13¾″. Royal College of Art, London.
This concertina card folds to show part of the inside
illustration and copy. Printed in vermilion on the
outside and mustard and black inside. Set in
Grotesque 215.

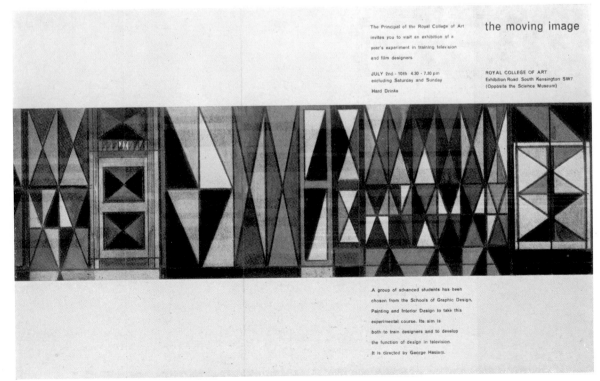

342. 1953 EXHIBITION CARD
3″ × 11¼″. Herbert Spencer des. Lund Humphries, Bradford.
Printed in black and red and set in Gill Sans and a condensed grotesque.

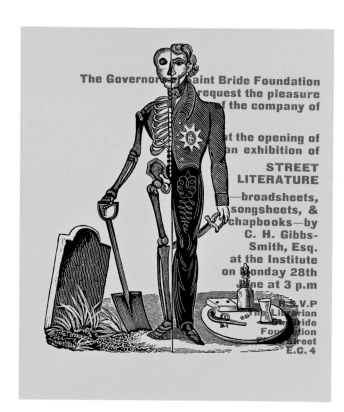

343. 1956 EXHIBITION CARD
4¾″ × 4¼″. Charles Hasler typ. London.
Printed in black and red on lemon-yellow board and set in Venus.

344. 1958 LECTURE CARD
15½″ × 3⅛″. Royal College of Art, London.
This three-fold card (outside only shown here) is (in the original) printed in black, yellow and purple and is set in a condensed grotesque.

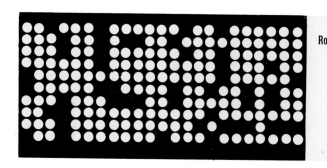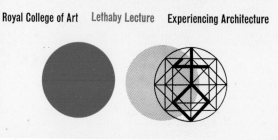

345. 1958 EXHIBITION CARD
$5\frac{1}{2}'' \times 6\frac{1}{2}''$. Royal College of Art, London.
Printed in black, yellow and blue and set in
Gill Sans italic and Grotesque No. 9.

Invitations to exhibitions

The Council and Principal of the Royal College of Art
have the honour to invite you to an
OPEN-AIR EXHIBITION OF SCULPTURE
by Recent Sculptors of the College
in the Gardens of the Natural History Museum, Cromwell Road, S.W.7
on Friday, 11 July 1958, at 3.0 pm

The Exhibition will be open until 31 July. 10.0 am—6.0 pm weekdays. 2.30 pm—6.0 pm Sundays.

YOU ARE CORDIALLY INVITED
TO A PRIVATE VIEW
OF PAINTINGS BY

Stuart Brisley
Astrid Balinska - Jundzill
Raymond Fawcet

AT 13 KENSINGTON GORE S.W.7

347. 1960 EXHIBITION CARD
$3\frac{1}{8}'' \times 2''$. John Griffiths typ. London.
Printed in black on white card and set in Grotes-
que No. 9 and Venus Light Condensed typefaces.

Bella C. Landauer Collection, New-York Historical Society

The School of Graphic Design has much
pleasure in inviting you to see the work
of the students who are taking their Diploma
in Engraving, Illustration and Graphic Design.

Graphic Design Diploma Exhibition 1959

Royal College of Art (main building)   Wednesday, Thursday and Friday
Exhibition Road, SW7   June 17, 18 and 19
                                         10 a.m. to 5.30 p.m.

346. 1959 EXHIBITION CARD
$3'' \times 5''$ Royal College of Art, London.
Printed in black and blue and set in Grotesque 215.

348. 1957 EXHIBITION CARD
$3\frac{1}{8}'' \times 6''$. Cooper and Beatty, Toronto.
The Paul Rand card is printed in red and black
and set in American Typefounders' Spartan.

you are cordially invited to an exhibition of the graphic work of PAUL RAND, May 12-23, in

the executive offices of COOPER & BEATTY, LIMITED, 196 Adelaide St. West, Toronto, 11-6 pm

FRANCIS DODSWORTH Gold & Silver Wye
Drawer at the Shipp & Anchor in Lombard=street
neere Gracious=street maketh & seleth all sorts of
Gold, Silver, & Silk Laces, & Fringes, Gold & Silver
Thred of all sorts, & other things very reasonable.

349. *c.* 1680 TRADE CARD
6¾″ × 5⅞″. Anon. London.
Engraved card for a gold and silver wire drawer and
gold and silver thread manufacturer.
Pepysian Library

Trade Cards

The tradesmen's cards of the eighteenth century represent a brilliant little sideline of the graphic arts. The baroque and rococo motifs used in the architecture, furniture and ceramics of the day found their way into this much smaller compass. Here the engravers released their curious swirling asymmetric forms into a wild mad world of their own. Pastrycook, haberdasher, coalman, nightman (who emptied the privies), apothecary, ship's chandler and even seminaries for young ladies were advertised in this exquisite manner. Many extremely skilful artists designed and engraved these cards, including the painter William Hogarth.

Not many trade cards have survived from earlier than Pepys's time. Sir Ambrose Heal* mentions one of about 1620. At a time when in England the standard of letterpress printing was at a low ebb, it was natural that tradesmen should turn to the engraver for these little pieces of self-advertisement.

The early engraved cards usually followed the design of the shop signs that used to hang outside the shops. In 1762, in England, the hanging signs were abolished by law, presumably because they were a possible menace to passers-by.

* Ambrose Heal: *London Tradesmen's cards of the Eighteenth Century.* Batsford 1925.

350. *c.* 1680. TRADE CARD
$6\frac{1}{8}'' \times 4\frac{7}{8}''$. Anon. London.
Engraved card for a surgical instrument maker.

Pepysian Library

351. *c.* 1700 TRADE CARD
$4\frac{1}{2}'' \times 2\frac{3}{8}''$. Anon. London.
Engraved card for a stationer.

British Museum

Trade Cards

352. *c.* 1700 TRADE CARD
$6'' \times 3\frac{1}{4}''$. Anon. London.
Printed by letterpress, from type and a woodcut.

British Museum

This same law ordered that all houses had to be numbered. The tradesmen had little appreciation for such a prosaic way of showing their addresses and still remained faithful to such round-about descriptions as 'Mr Dighton, snuffmaker at the City of Seville, next door to the King's Head Tavern at Chancery Lane end in Fleet Street'. Or Thomas Williams the Nightman, who describes his address as 'At his yard and stables, No. 50, Four doors from Windmill-Street, Tottenham-Court-Road'.

The engraved trade cards up until the early years of the nineteenth century had for their subjects shop signs, either heraldically treated, with a panel of lettering, or the sign set in a classical, baroque, rococo or Chinoiserie frame, or an illustration of their wares again set in a frame.

When the repetition of the sign was finally dropped, the design tended to show a display of goods, though arms, effigies and other emblems were used. In turn these were replaced by either a picture of the trade being performed (such as a gold-beater at work) or an illustration of the shop or factory.

353. *c.* 1720 TRADE CARD
5⅜″ × 3¾″. Anon. London.
Printed in black from a wood engraving, with lettering engraved in relief.

British Museum

354. *c.* 1720 TRADE CARD
5¾″ × 3¾″. Anon. London.
Printed in black from a wood engraving, with lettering engraved in relief.

British Museum

355. *c.* 1720 TRADE CARD
3¾″ × 3⅝″. Anon. London.
Printed by letterpress from a wood engraving and type, within a border of printers' flowers.

British Museum

Trade cards

These trade cards from one of the albums in the Bagford Collection in the British Museum (Figs. 350–62) are very vividly engraved, both on wood and copper. It is interesting to note that in such cards as that for Samuel Bridger, Clock Engraver, the letterforms are those of the engraver. On many of the cards, though the letters are actually engraved, they are doing their, sometimes quite inadequate, best to imitate type. (Figs. 353–4).

The variety in these engraved cards is infinite. There is the charmingly decorative one of the gunmaker (Fig. 367) set in a richly rococo frame, with views of highwaymen holding up a coach and illustrated with crossed guns, wildfowler, drums, flags, pikes and other warlike instruments. And as a contrast, the quite severe card of John Bell, famous printer-publisher, in good copperplate hand decorated with a few swashes. Or Thomas Bewick's dainty ladylike card, with his name set in an oval frame decorated with ribbons and roses. This would seem to be a surprising choice for so robust and open air a character. The card Bewick engraved for The King's Arms at Ross is much more typical of his work. This is of particular interest as it is so very similar to his relief wood engravings but is engraved intaglio on copper.

The engraver, whose card is shown in Fig. 374, may well be a connection of a certain Rollinson who was credited with engraving some decorative buttons for George Washington, for the coat that he wore on the day of his inauguration as President.

Trade cards and engraved wrappers and labels were probably printed from steel plates, in the way that the Cruikshank and Phiz illustrations for Dickens were done. Where there is no plate mark, a plate larger than the trimmed size of the paper or card was used. Each print was dried in tissue paper between drying boards and afterwards put in glazing boards in a hydraulic press for twenty-four hours. This had the effect of flattening the raised printed line. The speed of production was about 500 a day. The apprentice rate for this work only fifty years ago was 10½d per hundred.

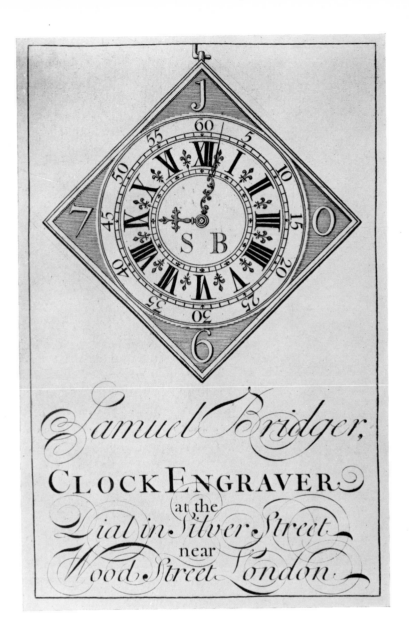

356. 1760 TRADE CARD
5¾″ × 3¾″. Anon. London.
Engraved card showing a very finely engraved clock face with the date 1760 on it.

British Museum

357. *c.* 1740 TRADE CARD
4⅝″ × 3½″. Anon. London.
Wood engraved card for a cap maker. Printed in black.

British Museum

358. *c.* 1740 TRADE CARD
5¾″ × 3¾″. Anon. London.
Printed by letterpress from type and a wood engraving. In the original, translations of the text are given both in French and in Dutch.

British Museum

JOHN PAYNE, at the Black Spread-Eagle in *Ludgate-Street*, near St. *Paul*'s Church, Sells all sorts of Knives, Pen-knives, Scissors, and Rasors of the best Make ; fine Canes, Whips, Spurs, Tobacco-Boxes, and fine Snuff-Boxes; Combs, Buttons, Buckles, and Tables ; fine Steel or Silver Works, and other Curiosities, at Reasonable Rates, by Wholesale or Retale. And all Sorts of fine SNUFF.

A Lexander Hames at the *Black Swan* on *Snow-hill*, over against the *Saracen's Head*, being Tayler and Salesman, Maketh and Selleth all forts of Mens and Boys Apparel ; likewife felleth all forts of Cloths, Searges, Shalloons and Callamancoes at reafonable Rates.

359. *c.* 1740 TRADE CARD
$5\frac{1}{4}'' \times 3\frac{1}{4}''$. Anon. London.
Printed in black by letterpress, from wood engraving and type, for a clothier.

British Museum

360. *c.* 1760 TRADE CARD
$4\frac{3}{8}'' \times 3\frac{1}{8}''$. Anon. London.
Wood engraved card, printed in black, presumably for a coat maker or tailor though there is no lettering to indicate the origin of this very attractive card.

British Museum

Trade cards

Richard Meares Mufical Inftrument maker is Remov'd from ý Golden Viol in Leaden-Hall Street to ý North Side of St Pauls Church-yard, at ý Golden Viol & Haut-boy. Where he sells all sorts of Mufical Inftruments. Books & Songs, with Tunes Rul'd Paper &c. as alfo ý beft sorts of Cutlery-Wares, at reasonable rates.

361. *c.* 1760 TRADE CARD
$3\frac{3}{4}'' \times 3''$. Anon. London.
Engraved card for a musical instrument maker.

British Museum

362. *c.* 1750 TRADE CARD
$2\frac{3}{4}'' \times 3\frac{1}{4}''$. Anon. London.
Wood engraved card for a glove maker. Printed in black.

British Museum

THOMAS WILLIAMS,

NIGHTMAN and CARMAN,

At his YARD and STABLES,

No. 50, Four Doors from WINDMILL-STREET,

TOTTENHAM-COURT-ROAD,

KEEPS CARTS and HORSES for emptying *Bog-Houses*, likewife *Drains* and *Sefs-Pools*, with the utmoft Expedition; and by a ftrict Attention to Bufinefs himfelf, Performs what he undertakes, with the utmoft Care and Decency, and on the moft reafonable Terms.

Rubbifh taken away on the fhorteft Notice.

Thofe who pleafe to favour him with their Orders, may depend on having them faithfully executed, and the Favour gratefully acknowledged by their humble Servant,

THOMAS WILLIAMS.

363. *c.* 1770 TRADE CARD
4¾″ × 5⅝″. Anon. London.
Letterpress card for a nightman and carman. Set in Fry's Baskerville.

Oxford University Press

Trade cards

William Lewis, Tallow-Chandler,

At the SUN in *Oxford Road,* near *Soho-Square* ;

KEEPETH Carts and Horfes for Carriages of Sand, Gravel, Slop, Rubbifh, &c. Alfo keeps Night-Carts and Men for emptying of Bogg-Houfes ; which Employ his Men perform with the utmoft Expedition and Care, giving greater Satisfaction (as to Quantity) than any others of that Profeffion, having Carriages that carry one, two, or three Loads at a Time.

Himfelf or Men to be heard of every Day at the following Places :

The Golden Anchor, in Clare-ftreet, Clare-market ;
The Golden Horfe, Theobald's-Row, Red-lion-fquare ; and at
The Cock and Harp, Jermyn-ftreet, St. James's.

Attendance is given at the above-mentioned Places from Eight in the Morning till Twelve at Noon, and afterwards at Home.

☞ For the better Encouragement to WATCHMEN, that detect Nightmen in fhooting their SOIL in the Streets, or in Tottenham Court-Road, I promife to give a Reward of Twenty Shillings, upon Conviction of the Offender.

364. 1754 TRADE CARD
3¼″ × 4¾″. Anon. London.
Letterpress card for a tallow chandler, set in Caslon's types.

Oxford University Press

:·MICHAEL ELLIS,

SHOEMAKER,

At the Sign of the Boot, *in* Cannon-ftreet,

Succeffor to the late Mr. EDDIS,

MAKES and SELLS all Sorts of Mens and Boys Shoes and Boots ; likewife all Sorts of Ladies Silk and Stuff Shoes and Pumps, Slippers and Clogs, in the neateft Manner, and at the loweft Prices.

Likewife all Sorts of Childrens Pumps.

365. *c.* 1775 TRADE CARD
3½″ × 5″. Anon. London.
Letterpress card for a shoemaker. Set partly in Caslon's types and enclosed in a border of fleurs-de-lis.

Oxford University Press

Thomas Allen,

SILK - DYER,

(At No. 29.)

In Leaden-Hall Street, oppofite St. Mary Axe,

LONDON.

CLEANS and Dyes all Sorts of Silks, Stuffs, Furniture of Beds, Wrought Works, &c. after the beft Manner.

366. *c.* 1735. TRADE CARD
2″ × 3⅝″. Anon. London.
Letterpress card for a silk dyer. Set in Caslon's type, and enclosed in a border from the same type foundry.

367. *c.* 1735 TRADE CARD
6″ × 4¾″. Anon. London.
Engraved card for a gunmaker, with an elaborate rococo frame.

Oxford University Press

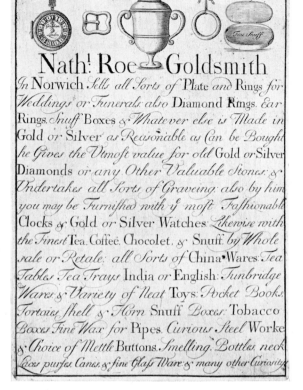

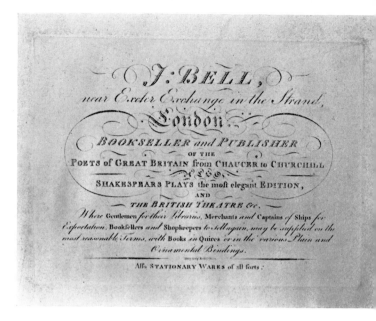

368. *c.* 1780 TRADE CARD
$7'' \times 5''$. Anon. Norwich.
Engraved card for a goldsmith, possibly engraved
by his own metal workers.

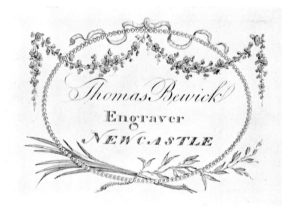

370. *c.* 1770 TRADE CARD
$2\frac{1}{4}'' \times 3''$. T. Bewick. Newcastle-upon-Tyne (presumably by himself).
Bewick's own card (from the Bewick Sale) engraved
on copper or steel.

371. *c.* 1790 TRADE CARD
$2\frac{3}{4}'' \times 4\frac{1}{2}''$. F. Malpas sculpt. London.
Engraved card for a nightman and carman. The
nightman was responsible for emptying the privies.

Oxford University Press

Trade cards

372. *c.* 1790 TRADE CARD
$2\frac{7}{8}'' \times 4\frac{1}{2}''$. T. Bewick, Newcastle-upon-Tyne.
Card engraved on copper by the great wood engraver,
for Wall, The King's Arms Inn, Ross-on-Wye. This
card is signed 'T. B. dirext'.

373. *c.* 1810. TRADE CARD
$2\frac{1}{4}'' \times 3\frac{1}{8}''$. Huntley sculpt. New Bond Street,
London.
Engraved card for chair manufacturer. The shaded
letter reflects the style that the typefounder Thorne
was soon to make popular.

Oxford University Press

374. *c.* 1820 TRADE CARD
$2\frac{1}{4}'' \times 3\frac{1}{2}''$. Rollinson, New York.
Engraved card for engraver and printer.

Bella C. Landauer Collection, New-York Historical Society

375. *c.* 1790 TRADE CARD
$1\frac{5}{8}'' \times 2\frac{3}{8}''$. Anon. Plymouth.
Engraved card for a mercer and draper.

376. *c.* 1790 TRADE CARD
$2\frac{1}{2}'' \times 3\frac{1}{2}''$. Wiseman sculpt. Widegate Street, London.
Engraved card for a cabinet and chair manufactory.

Oxford University Press

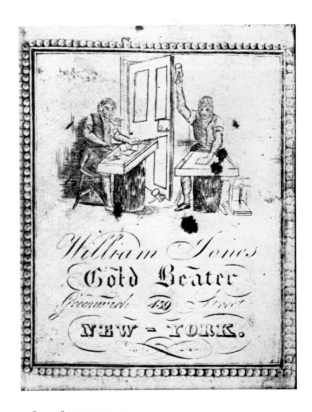

377. *c.* 1820 TRADE CARD
$2\frac{3}{8}'' \times 3\frac{1}{2}''$. Anon. Leicester.
Engraved card for a dealer in stilton cheese.

378. *c.* 1820 TRADE CARD
$4'' \times 3\frac{1}{2}''$. Anon. New York.
Engraved card for a gold beater.

Bella C. Landauer Collection, New-York Historical Society

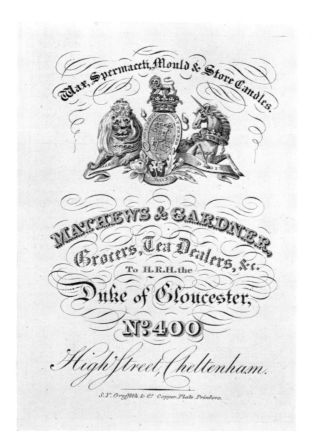

379. *c.* 1825 TRADE CARD
$4\frac{1}{4}'' \times 2\frac{3}{4}''$. S. Y. Griffith, Cheltenham.
Engraved card for grocer, tea dealer etc. with the
Royal coat of arms by the same engraver as the
Fly Waggon notice, Fig. 122.

380. *c.* 1820 TRADE CARD
$5\frac{1}{4}'' \times 3\frac{1}{2}''$. Ryley del. Skelton fc. London.
Engraved card for sadler, cap and whip maker.

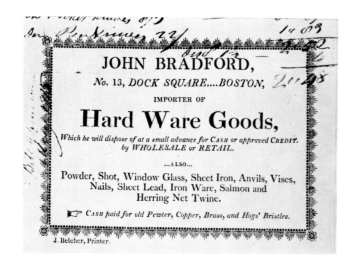

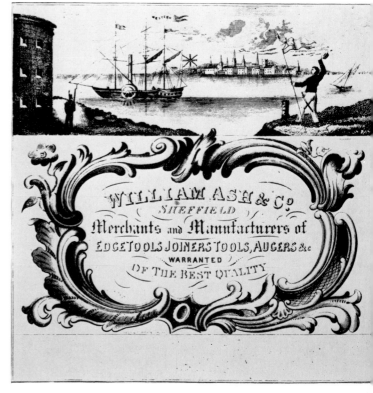

381. *c.* 1820 TRADE CARD
$3\frac{1}{4}'' \times 4\frac{1}{2}''$. J. Belcher. Boston, Massachusetts.
Letterpress card set in the same border as the ex
libris labels on pages 186–7.

382. *c.* 1840 TRADE CARD
$4'' \times 4''$. Anon. Sheffield.
Engraved card for merchants and manufacturers of
edge tools, etc. in Sheffield. The picture depicts the
Great Western – the first paddle-steamer to make
regular voyages across the Atlantic.

Oxford University Press

383. *c.* 1825 TRADE CARD
$2\frac{1}{2}'' \times 2\frac{3}{4}''$. Anon. London.
Engraved card for a linen draper.

384. *c.* 1840 TRADE CARD
$2\frac{1}{4}'' \times 3\frac{1}{2}''$. Weston sculpt. Bath.
Engraved card for a cook and confectioner.

385. *c.* 1840 TRADE CARD
$1\frac{5}{8}'' \times 2\frac{1}{2}''$. Anon. Bath.
Engraved card for tea dealer and grocer.

386. 1842 TRADE CARD
$4\frac{3}{4}'' \times 5\frac{3}{4}''$. F. Wolstenholme sculpt. Sheffield.
Engraved card for 'Mr Wolstenholme's Commercial
and Classical Academy, Furnival Street, Sheffield.'
The flourishes and scrolls here are a development
of the writing master's craft, as shown in Bickham's
Universal Penman.

Oxford University Press

Trade cards

387. *c.* 1825 TRADE CARD
2¼″ × 3⅛″. Anon. Leeds.
Letterpress card for hotel and tavern, set in a wood
engraved oval.

Trade cards

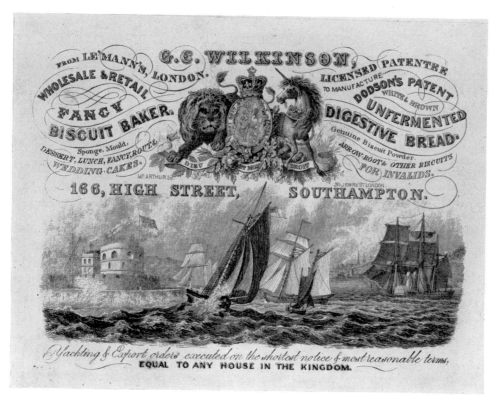

388. *c.* 1845 TRADE CARD
3⅜″ × 4⅝″. McArthur sculpt. 30 Jewry Street,
London.
Engraved card for a biscuit maker in Southampton,
with the Royal coat of arms and a view of Southampton Water.

389. *c.* 1840 TRADE CARD
4⅛ × 5¼″. Anon. London.
Letterpress card for a manufacturer of portmanteaux
etc. The border was produced by Caslon and Liver-
more in 1830 and named 4-line pica No. 10. The
text is set in a condensed Clarendon.

390. *c.* 1840 TRADE CARD
2⅞″ × 4¼″. Anon. New York.
Engraved card for an apothecary, with the street
number (7) placed on a pestle and mortar.

Bella C. Landauer Collection, New-York Historical Society

391. *c.* 1880 TRADE CARD
5½″ × 6¼″ approx. Anon. Cincinnati, Ohio.
Letterpress card for a bell founder. Set in fifteen
different typefaces.

Bella C. Landauer Collection, New-York Historical Society

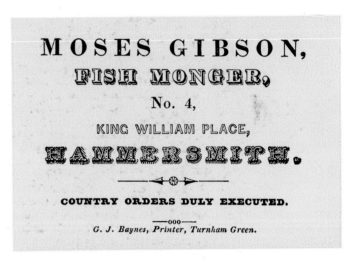

392. *c.* 1850 TRADE CARD
2″ × 2¾″. G. J. Baynes, Turnham Green.
Letterpress card for a fishmonger. The six lines are
set in six different typefaces, and in a style of fifty
years earlier.

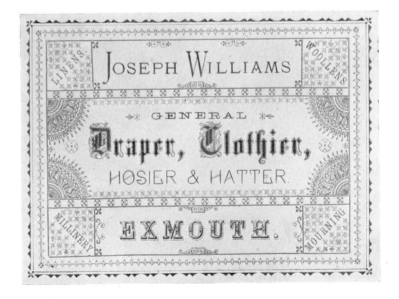

393. 1885 TRADE CARD
3¼″ × 4⅜″. J. G. Williams typ. Smith, Chipping
Norton.
Letterpress card in the 'artistic' style for draper
and clothier. Printed in black, red and green.

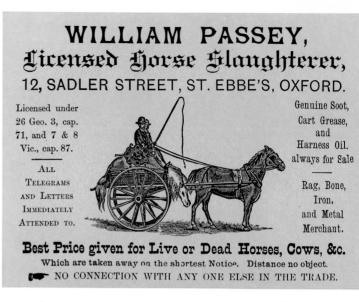

394. *c.* 1890 TRADE CARD
$3\frac{1}{4}'' \times 4\frac{1}{2}''$. Anon. Oxford.
Letterpress card for horse slaughterer. Printed on a
green card with woodcut.

Trade cards

The interdependence of engraving and letter-press printing is revealed by many of these cards, when in some cases they are emulating type forms and in others they are anticipating the typefaces the printer will be using in a very few years. The shaded letter that the English and American typefounders marketed with so much success in the nineteenth century can be seen in the New York gold beater's card (Fig. 378); in the Soho furniture manufacturer's card and also in the New York printer's card (Figs. 373–4).

The superb figure-skating techniques of so many engraver-writing masters is shown in the card for Mr Wolstenholme's 'Commercial and Classical Academy'. (Where did classics end and commerce begin?) The *putto* at the top is a splendid example of inspired doodling. So much for the engravings. The letterpress cards range from very plain statements, to the use of typographic flowers and borders for frames. In Fig. 392 Moses Gibson returns the compliment of the engraver with Thorne's shaded letter and similar engraver-style capitals. J. Last's card has a plummy richness with a florid 48-point border and a typographic combination of heavy Egyptians, fat faces and shadow black letter that has all the splendour of a page from a Gothic Missal (Fig. 389). This is the same border as William Savage used for the title page in his *Art of Decorative Printing*.

The nineteenth century cards show a sharp decline, though 'Neely's Apothecary in New York' is enchanting, with its view of clapboard houses and crinolined figures. The influence of 'Artistic Printing' can be seen in Fig. 393 with a monstrous outlined black letter for 'Draper, Clothier' and of *l'Art Nouveau* in 'Ward's Patent Sanitary Coffin' (Fig. 397).

Modern cards vary from the still ubiquitous copperplate engraved calling card to letterpress ones that are both formal and informal. A pleasant example of the former is that of the bookbinder Roger Powell, and of the latter that for John Reid, Toronto car dealer. In this card, the formal copperplate is used for the representative's name and a condensed grotesque for address, telephone and trade.

Trade cards are a subtle reflection of the manners of an age and the characters of their owners.

395. 1893 TRADE CARD
$2\frac{3}{4}'' \times 4''$. Anon. Hailsham.
Letterpress card for hotel. Printed in red
and blue.

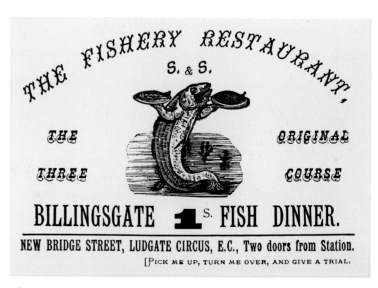

396. *c.* 1900 TRADE CARD
$2\frac{3}{4}'' \times 4''$. Anon. London.
Letterpress card for fish restaurant with
woodcut.

Martin Simmons

455 EAST 57TH STREET, NEW YORK 22

PLAZA 1-3463

representing

W. S. COWELL LIMITED

LETTERPRESS AND LITHOGRAPHIC
PRINTERS AND DESIGNERS

BUTTER MARKET IPSWICH

ENGLAND

also

23 PERCY STREET LONDON W.I

398. 1957 TRADE CARD
$3\frac{5}{8}'' \times 2\frac{1}{4}''$. W. S. Cowell Ltd, Ipswich.
Letterpress card for printer. Printed in red and
black and set in Bembo.

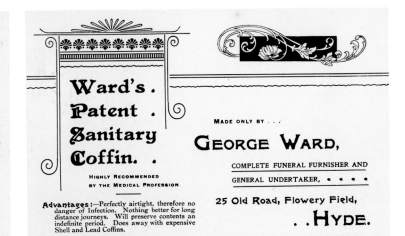

397. *c.* 1910 TRADE CARD
$2\frac{3}{4}'' \times 4\frac{1}{2}''$. Anon. Hyde.
Letterpress card for undertaker. Printed in
black and red with *l'Art Nouveau* decorations.

ARTHUR H. GRAY

Assistant University Printer

UNIVERSITY PRESS, CAMBRIDGE

ENGLAND

399. 1956 TRADE CARD
$\frac{5}{8}'' \times 1\frac{7}{8}''$ University Press, Cambridge.
Letterpress card for printer and set in Bembo italic
and Perpetua small capitals.

ROGER POWELL

BOOKBINDERS

The Slade, Froxfield, Petersfield, Hants.

Tel. Hawkley 29

400. 1955 TRADE CARD
$1\frac{3}{8}'' \times 2\frac{5}{8}''$. Anon. Petersfield.
Letterpress card printed in red and black for book-
binder and set in Bembo.

401. 1958 TRADE CARD
$1'' \times 2''$. John Bateson typ. Toronto.
Letterpress card for Canadian graphic designer.

402. 1959 TRADE CARD
$1\frac{1}{4}'' \times 2\frac{1}{2}''$. Allan Fleming, typ. Cooper and Beatty,
Toronto.
Letterpress card printed in blue and black.

403. 1958 TRADE CARD
$1\frac{5}{8}'' \times 3\frac{1}{4}''$. Anon. New York.
Letterpress card printed in black and orange on
lavender coloured card.

Stationers' and Ex Libris labels

The first stationer's label shown here is from the Pepysian Library at Cambridge. This was used as a wrapper for playing cards. Most stationers' labels are on a smaller scale. Miniature objects have a certain special appeal. A full-rigged ship model the size of a penny is clearly a thing to marvel at, that such a beautiful and intricate thing can be made so small. There is almost as much pleasure in printed miniatures such as those minute books that William Pickering produced. But all these objects are contrived for us to wonder at, whereas the stationers' and booksellers' labels are small for a purpose. If they were not very small, customers might well object to having them inserted in their books. Inevitably these tiny labels are engraved. The *Ex Libris* labels have rather more justification for their inclusion on the inside covers and fly leaves of books and so can be of less modest proportions; and they can be composed more easily of type and ornaments. Fleurons and borders play a most important part in these labels. The same border comes up in places as far apart as Manchester and St Helena, and a very similar one is used by James Mosley for his 1958 'Change of Address Card'. (Figs. 405, 410 and 432).

404. *c.* 1680 STATIONER'S LABEL
7¾″ × 3¼″. Anon. London.
Engraved label used for the cover of a packet of playing cards; the illustration is a pun on the stationer's name. A pretty decorated Tuscan style of letter is used for the initials A. F.

Pepysian Library, Cambridge

405. *c.* 1790 EX LIBRIS LABEL
s/s Anon. St Helena.
Label in border, produced by V. Figgins, as a double-pica flower, No. 15.

186

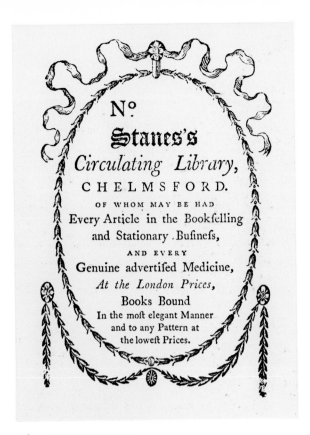

No.

Stanes's

Circulating Library,

CHELMSFORD.

OF WHOM MAY BE HAD

Every Article in the Bookſelling
and Stationary Buſineſs,

AND EVERY

Genuine advertiſed Medicine,

At the London Prices,

Books Bound

In the moſt elegant Manner
and to any Pattern at
the loweſt Prices.

406. *c.* 1790 EX LIBRIS LABEL
$3\frac{1}{2}'' \times 2\frac{1}{4}''$. Anon. Chelmsford.
Letterpress label set in a delicate wood engraved
frame.

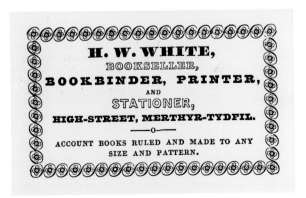

TREBLE'S

Circulating Library,

PEMBROKE & TENBY.

This Book is requested to be returned at the Expira-
tion of the limited Period, for the Accommodation of the
Subscribers.

408. *c.* 1815 EX LIBRIS LABEL
s/s Anon. Pembroke, S. Wales.
Fry's semi-bold typefaces were soon in wide use for
all kinds of ephemera.

MANCHESTER

New Circulating Library.

No. *1801*

9 DAYS ALLOWED.—FORFEIT *2* *d*

It is requested that no Person will damage any Book belonging
to the Library, by turning down or tearing the Leaves; writing on
the Margin; or any otherwise defacing or injuring the Books. All
Damages will be particularly noticed, and the Offenders fined,
agreeable to the Sixteenth Law of the Library.

410. *c.* 1790 EX LIBRIS LABEL
s/s Anon. Manchester.
Label set in same border as Fig. 405.

**THIS BOOK
IS THE PROPERTY OF
J. SPURWAY,**
Circulating Library,
HONITON;
Which when read, is earnestly requested to be
returned, for the general Accommodation
of SUBSCRIBERS.

407. *c.* 1810 EX LIBRIS LABEL
s/s Anon. Honiton, Devon.
Label set in Fry's Shaded and Great Primer, for
'Circulating Library'.

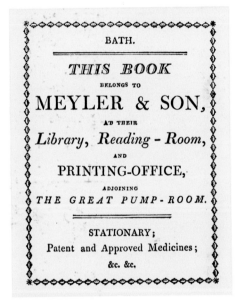

BATH.

THIS BOOK

BELONGS TO

MEYLER & SON,

AT THEIR

Library, Reading - Room,

AND

PRINTING-OFFICE,

ADJOINING

THE GREAT PUMP - ROOM.

STATIONARY;

Patent and Approved Medicines;

&c. &c.

409. *c.* 1790. EX LIBRIS LABEL
$3\frac{5}{8}'' \times 2\frac{5}{8}''$. Meyler, Bath.
Label with Fournier border and 'THIS BOOK' set in
Fry's Nonpareil 2-line shaded.

H. W. WHITE,
BOOKSELLER,
BOOKBINDER, PRINTER,
AND
STATIONER,
HIGH-STREET, MERTHYR-TYDFIL.
ACCOUNT BOOKS RULED AND MADE TO ANY
SIZE AND PATTERN.

411. *c.* 1840 EX LIBRIS LABEL
s/s H. W. White, Merthyr Tydfil.
The border comes from Thorowgood. It was first
shown in 1825. Two varieties of open letter are
used on this pretty little label.

412. 1800–1830 BOOKSELLERS' LABELS
s/s Plymouth, Devon.
Two letterpress labels with borders.

Oxford University Press

Stationers' and Ex Libris labels

413. *c.* 1880 STATIONER'S LABEL
5″ × 4″. Anon. London.
A label showing within a frame eight different
varieties of display letter including a 'rustic' letter
for 'Steam Navigation'. This label was fixed to a
green marbled paper case.

Oxford University Press

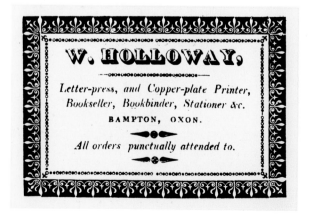

414. *c.* 1830 EX LIBRIS LABELS
1¼″ × 2⅞″. W. Holloway, Bampton.
The reverse border, Thorne's Shaded letter and the
open swelled rules all add to the richness of these
two little labels.

Oxford University Press

415. 1830–1890 STATIONERS' LABELS
s/s Edinburgh etc.
A group of engraved labels.

Oxford University Press

416. *c.* 1810 EX LIBRIS LABEL
1¾″ × 2¾″. Graham. Alnwick.
Engraved by T. Bewick, who seems to have worked
for all the local printers.

417. *c.* 1810 EX LIBRIS LABEL
1¾″ × 2⅜″. J. Catnach, Seven Dials, London.
Device wood engraved by T. Bewick and used by
Catnach for labels and probably billheads. Bewick
did a lot of work for Catnach who was a Northumbrian like the engraver.

419. *c.* 1950 EX LIBRIS LABEL
3″ × 3″. Anon. England.
Engraved by Reynolds Stone.

418. 1800–1850 STATIONERS' LABELS
s/s Plymouth, Devon.
A group of engraved labels.
Oxford University Press

420. *c.* 1938 EX LIBRIS LABEL
3″ × 2¾″. Curwen Press, London.
Drawn by Claudia Freedman and printed in brown
ink on a blue paper.

421. *c.* 1950 EX LIBRIS LABEL
s/s Anon. England and U.S.A.
These two little labels were engraved by Reynolds
Stone.

422. *c.* 1820 EX LIBRIS LABEL
s/s Anon. Boston, Massachusetts.
Printed in black from engraved plates.

New York Public Library

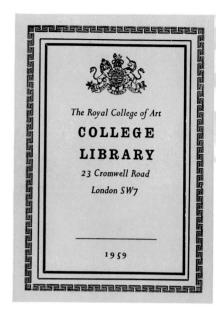

423. 1958 EX LIBRIS LABEL
2¾″ × 1¾″. University Press, Cambridge.
Letterpress label within a border, set
in Bembo.

424. 1959 EX LIBRIS LABEL
3⅛″ × 2⅛″. Royal College of Art, London.
Letterpress label, printed in black and
purple within a Greek key border, set in
Perpetua and Clarendon.

426. 1960 EX LIBRIS LABEL
s/s Ashley Havinden des. Shenval Press, Hertford.
Printed in black and green and set in Gill Extra
Heavy.

425. *c.* 1940 EX LIBRIS LABEL
s/s Anon. Salt Lake City, Utah.
Printed in black from type and ornaments.

New York Public Library

Change of Address cards and Compliments slips

Change of address cards vary from what is little
more than a bald piece of newspaper setting to
Alan Fletcher's use of a photographic reproduction of screw-on plastic letters. Compliments
slips might well provide typographers with scope
for experiment. So far they tend to follow well-
worn conventions.

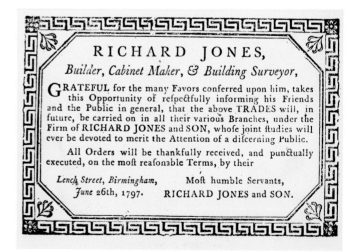

427. 1735 CHANGE OF ADDRESS CARD
2¼″ × 4¾″. Anon. London.
Set in Caslon's Great Primer.

Oxford University Press

428. 1797 CHANGE OF ADDRESS CARD
2⅜″ × 3½″. Anon. Birmingham.
Set in Baskerville's Brevier typeface with a reverse
Greek key border.

Mr John Minton

HAS REMOVED FROM 5 SHAFTESBURY VILLAS W.8

and is now installed at

9 APOLLO PLACE S.W.10 TEL: FLAX 0453

429. *c.* 1955 CHANGE OF ADDRESS CARD
3″ × 3⅝″. John Brinkley typ. London.
Printed in black and red and set in Walbaum.

DAVID AND ROSALIND GENTLEMAN

have moved to

51 GLOUCESTER CRESCENT
LONDON NW1

(not yet on the telephone)

430. *c.* 1955 CHANGE OF ADDRESS CARD
2⅜″ × 2⅞″. D. Gentleman des. London.
Printed in black and green from type and a wood
block and set in Walbaum Medium.

C and **CM**

Photographers Limited

Our telephone number is Grosvenor 4508

J Cowderoy G B Moss
A E C Evans S L Moss

Jervis Court
Princes Street
Hanover Square
London W 1

431. 1960 ADDRESS CARD
3″ × 4¼″. W. Fenton des. W. S. Cowell Ltd,
Ipswich.
Printed in black on a grey card. C & M Photographers
stress their telephone number by a silhouette of a
telephone. The verso of the card shows a map of
their location.

432. 1958 CHANGE OF ADDRESS CARD
3¼″ × 3¾″. James Mosley typ. London.
Printed in black on a red card and set in new castings
of Figgins' and Thorowgood's typefaces and borders.

433. 1960 CHANGE OF ADDRESS CARD
7¾″ × 4¾″. Alan Fletcher, typ. London.
Printed in black and red from line and half-
tone blocks and type. The large numerals are
from photoprints of screw-on plastic lettering,
used for numbering houses.

TO

John Lewis Esq

with the
compliments
of
Robert Harling

10 HERTFORD STREET
LONDON W1
Grosvenor 3477

With the compliments of
WILL CARTER

12 CHESTERTON ROAD
CAMBRIDGE

434. *c.* 1950 COMPLIMENTS SLIP
6″ × 2″. R. Harling typ. Shenval Press, Hertford.
Printed in black and set in Perpetua.

435. *c.* 1950 COMPLIMENTS SLIP
2¾″ × 1¾″. Rampant Lions Press, Cambridge.
Printed in black and terra cotta red and set in Bembo.

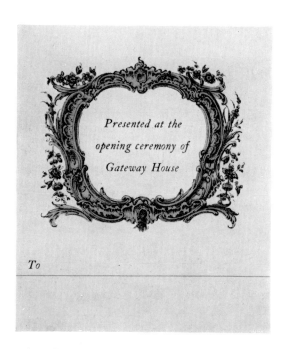

*Presented at the
opening ceremony of
Gateway House*

To

With Compliments

The Curwen Press Ltd
NORTH STREET, PLAISTOW, E.13
GRANGEWOOD 3411–4

436. 1958 COMPLIMENTS SLIP
3⅞″ × 3⅛″. W. S. Cowell Ltd, Ipswich.
Printed by offset in four colours.

437. *c.* 1950 COMPLIMENTS SLIP
3⅝″ × 2″. Curwen Press, London.
Set in Walbaum and printed in black.

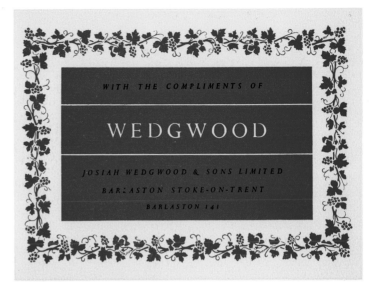

438. *c.* 1957 COMPLIMENTS SLIP
$1\frac{5}{8}'' \times 3''$. Royal College of Art, London.
Printed in black and blue and set in Times New
Roman.

439. *c.* 1955 COMPLIMENTS SLIP
$3\frac{1}{8}'' \times 4\frac{1}{2}''$. W. S. Cowell Ltd, Ipswich.
Printed in black and Wedgwood blue. The border is
from one of Wedgwood's early pattern books.

440. 1960 COMPLIMENTS SLIP
$1\frac{7}{8}'' \times 3\frac{3}{4}''$. Monotype Corporation Ltd, London.
Printed in black and brown and set in Grotesques
150 and 215.

441. 1959 COMPLIMENTS SLIP
$2'' \times 4''$. John Sewell typ. London.
Printed in black and purple and set in a condensed
grotesque.

Compliments slips

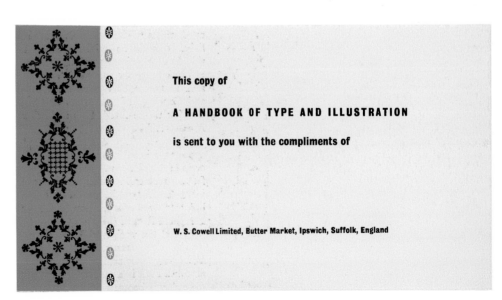

442. 1956 COMPLIMENTS SLIP
$3\frac{5}{8}'' \times 5\frac{1}{2}''$. W. S. Cowell Ltd, Ipswich.
Printed in black and burnt sienna and set in
Grotesque No. 9. The arabesques are by
Fournier le Jeune and were part of the cover
design of the Handbook.

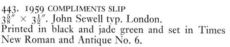

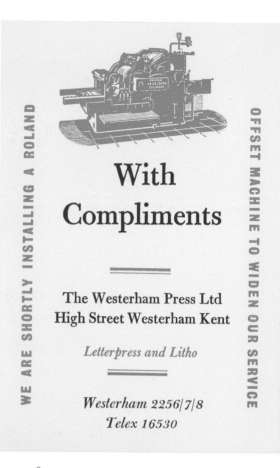

443. 1959 COMPLIMENTS SLIP
$3\frac{5}{8}'' \times 3\frac{1}{2}''$. John Sewell typ. London.
Printed in black and jade green and set in Times
New Roman and Antique No. 6.

444. 1958 COMPLIMENTS SLIP
$4\frac{1}{4} \times 2\frac{1}{2}''$. Westerham Press, Kent.
Printed in black, red and brown on a buff paper;
set in Baskerville, Bulmer and Grotesque No. 9.

Receipts, Order Forms and Billheads

Billheads, etc., are a continuation of the trade card, and owe their charm to the vanities and quirks of their owners, and the engravers and printers who worked for them. Printed receipts, on the other hand, are rather more formal, though not always without pictorial and typographic interest.

The Trinity House receipt, *c.* 1680 (Fig. 445), is pleasantly set in an italic typeface and decorated with a spirited engraving of the St Agnes light. It would be quite a pleasure to receive this. In these printed receipts, the recurring use of black letter for the word 'received' can be seen in the stock receipt for the 'Governor and Company of Merchants of Great Britain Trading to the South Seas and other Parts of America ...'

The same ubiquitous black letter makes its appearance in various guises in the first decade or so of the nineteenth century; sometimes as a fat face type and at other times in a shadow or inline form. It can be seen in the Shipley Wharf bill, combined with a heavy fat face and a slim Elongated Roman (Fig. 451).

Income tax receipts today are not particularly appealing documents, but the 1814 Lady-Day Receipt for 'Income Tax and Land Tax' is very prettily set out in a semi-fat face, with a delicate swelled rule beneath the heading (Fig. 448).

From the seventeenth century onwards, both engraved and typographic headings were used for these forms and letterheads. The English copperplate hand came into its own at about the time William Bickham published his *The Universal Penman*. The invoice shown here (Fig. 455) appeared in that book.

The letterforms used in the engraved billheads made use of a combination of the English hand, the black letter and the open, decorated or Tuscan letters, providing a rich and excitingly varied combination.

The engraved and so-called 'English' hand shown by Bickham had completely ousted the Chancery italic by the end of the eighteenth century. The engravers, working on what might be considered a debased letter form, nevertheless showed great dexterity in their control of swirls and flourishes, and indeed established a style of lettering that exists in letterheadings and calling cards to this day. This was the hand that clerks learned to use with such patent skill, and it was also the hand in which countless schoolboys penned their 'hundred lines' of *Manners Maketh Man* and other salutary little homilies. In Fig. 456, Thomas Seddon, Bookseller of Philadelphia, used the same engraved script and penned his bill to George Washington in the same clerkly hand.

Receipts

THe day of One Thousand Six Hundred

Received here at of Master of the good Ship, called the of of the Burden of Tons, per Ton, bound for the duty due for the Maintenance of One Light-House upon Agnes One of the Islands of Scilly

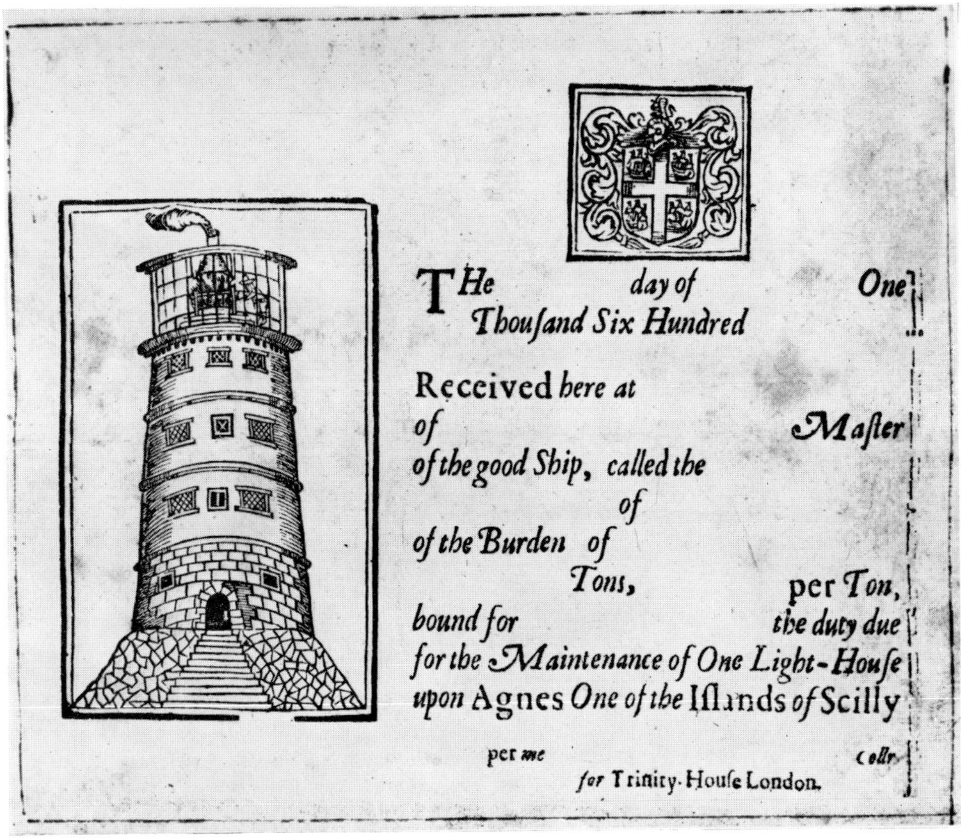

per me Collr for Trinity-House London.

445. 1680 LIGHT DUES RECEIPT
$5\frac{1}{8}'' \times 6\frac{1}{2}''$. Anon. London.
Trinity House Receipt for duty paid for the 'Maintenance of One Light-House upon Agnes, one of the Islands of Scilly'.
Trinity House

STOCK.

London, the 21st Day of Octob. 1730

REceived of The Masters & Wardens of the Stationers Comp the Sum of Fifty five Pounds 19s & 2d being in full for Fifty Four Pounds in the Capital and Principal Stock of the Governor and Company of Merchants of Great-Britain, Trading to the South-Seas, and other Parts of America, and for Encouraging the Fishery, &c. this Day Transferr'd in the said Company's Books, unto the said The Masters & Wardens of the Stationers Company £55:19.2

Witness, By Lewis Vanden Enden

R 829 C Drew

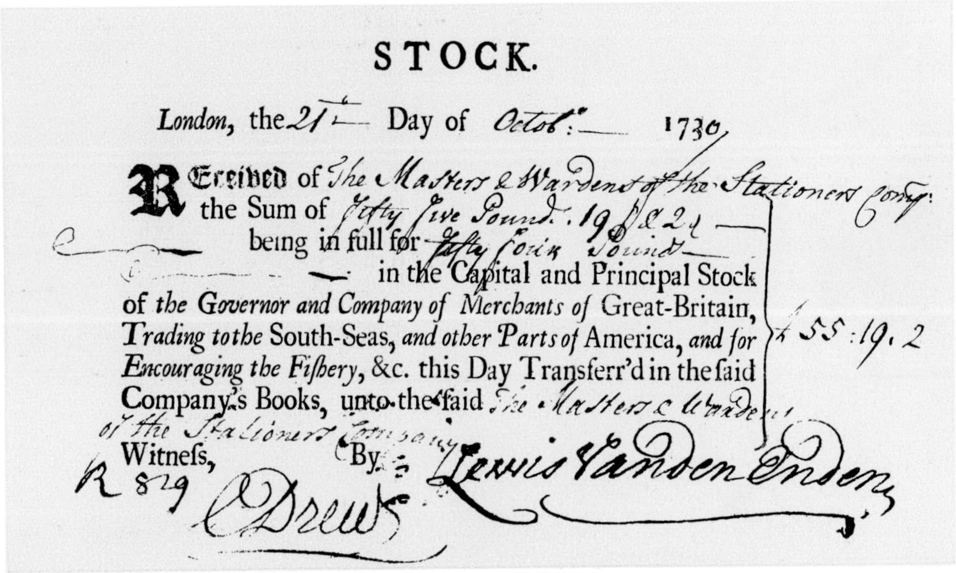

446. 1730 STOCK RECEIPT
$3'' \times 5''$. Anon. London.
Letterpress receipt set in roman and italic with black letter for 'Received'.
Oxford University Press

REceived the twenty ninth day of June 1750 ~~174~~ of the Rev. Mr Geo. Beaumont two Shillings and Six pence being the First Payment for one Copy of my Help to the Art of Swift Writing, which upon the Payment of the further Sum of two Shillings and Six pence, I promise to deliver in Sheets when Printed.

Witness my Hand Wm Tiffin. 537.

447. 1750 RECEIPT
$1\frac{5}{8}'' \times 5''$. Anon. England.
Letterpress receipt from writing master for an advance payment on *Help to the Art of Swift Writing*.
Oxford University Press

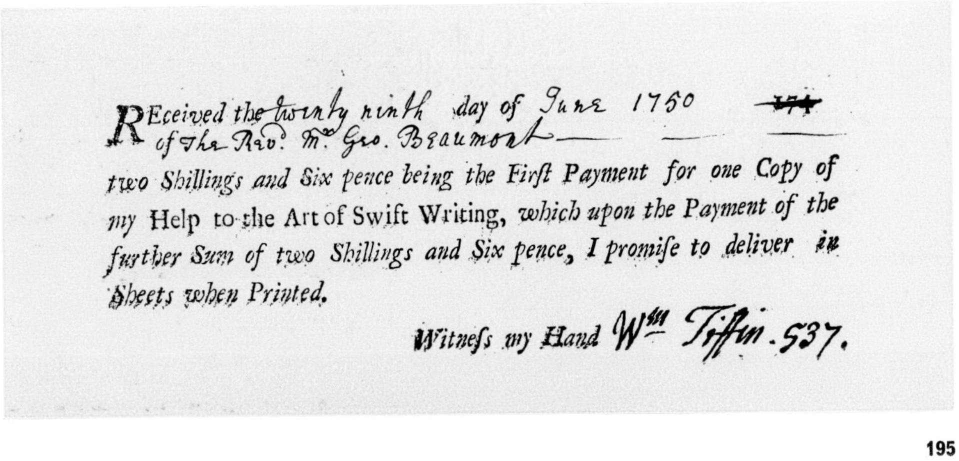

From Lady-day, 1814 to Lady-day, 1815

Received 16 of May 1815 of Mr. *pricmore*

£.

Half-a-Year's Property and Income Tax, due 6th of April

A. Landlord, ... 2   0   0
B. Tenant, ... 1   10   0
D. Income, ...

£3   10   0

Josiah Rainbow, Gosford-Street Ward, Collector.

Rollason & Reader, Printers.]

448. 1815 INCOME TAX RECEIPT
3″ × 5¼″ Rollason and Reader, London.
Letterpress receipt set in Fry and Steele's new
modern typeface.

No. 847   RECEIPT FOR RACE HORSE DUTY.

INLAND   REVENUE.

RECEIVED this 19th day of April 1865,
of Capt. King (in a/c)
the Sum of Three Pounds, Seventeen Shillings, being the Excise Duty for the Year ending
31st December, 1865, on the Race Horse, known and described as Salpinctes 3yrs.

£3 : 17 : 0

Receiver of Race Horse Duty.

London: Printed by W. P. Griffith, for Her Majesty's Stationery Office. 11 64.

N.B.—This Receipt is to be produced to the Receiver of Race Horse Duty, or to any person duly authorized
by him, on demand, before the Horse named herein runs at any Race.

449. 1865 INLAND REVENUE RECEIPT
3½″ × 7¼″. W. P. Griffith, London.
Letterpress receipt for Race Horse Duty. Printed in
black on green paper.

INCOME TAX & LAND TAX

Year	Assessment or Reference Number	Sch. and Inst. or Land Tax or PAYE	Name of Person Assessed (Schedules D and E) or of Employer (PAYE) Description of Property (Schedules A and B and Land Tax)	Paid by Cheque, Money Order or Postal Order			Paid by Cash or Stamp Card		
				£	s.	d.	£	s.	d.
59/60 9/10	P345/5110	PAYE		1	4	—	—	—	—

Date Stamp   Con. No.

A/c

RECEIVED the above payment.

Collector   DA 059650

See notes overleaf

450. 1960 TAX RECEIPT
3″ × 8⅛″. H.M. Stationery Office, London.
Letterpress Income Tax receipt, printed on blue
paper.

By permission of the Controller, Her Majesty's Stationery Office

SHIPLEY WHARF.

NEWPORT PAGNEL, 184

Mr.

Bought of WILLIAM SAUNDERSON.

	tons.	cwts.	qrs.	bus.	price	£	s.	d.
Old Shipley, durable hard								
Shipley, blazing hard								
Ditto, bright cementing								
Slack, for lime and brick burning								
Moira Coal								
Wednesbury Ditto								
Common Coal								
Cokes								
Oil Cake								
Salt								
Lime								
Cement								
Slate								
Brick								
Tiles								
Timber								
Deals								
Lath								
Grindstones								
Carriage								

Two-pence per Cwt. will be taken off if paid for within six weeks of delivery.

£

Tite, Printer, Bookseller, and Binder, John-Street, Newport Pagnel.

SHIPLEY WHARF.

NEWPORT PAGNEL, 184

Mr.

Bought of WILLIAM SAUNDERSON.

	tons.	cwts.	qrs.	bus.	price	£	s.	d.
Old Shipley, durable hard								
Shipley, blazing hard								
Ditto, bright cementing								
Slack, for lime and brick burning								
Moira Coal								
Wednesbury Ditto								
Common Coal								
Cokes								
Oil Cake								
Salt								
Lime								
Cement								
Slate								
Brick								
Tiles								
Timber								
Deals								
Lath								
Grindstones								
Carriage								

Two-pence per Cwt. will be taken off if paid for within six weeks of delivery.

£

451. 1844 COALS ORDER FORM
4⅝″ × 9¼″. Tite, Newport Pagnel.
The heading is set in Thorowgood's Fat Face;
'Bought of' in open black letter and 'William
Sanderson' in Wilson's Elongated Roman.

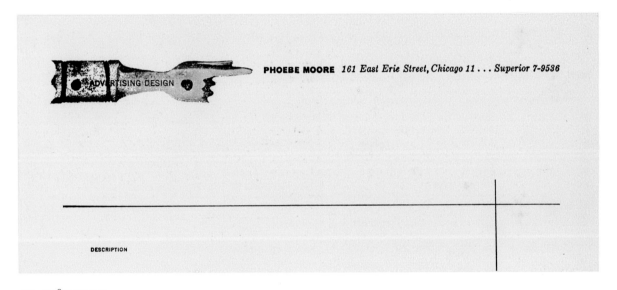

452. 1958 BILLHEAD
s/s Phoebe Moore typ. Chicago.
Designer's billhead printed in black and gold.

453. 1958 RECEIPT
2½″ × 3½″. John Sewell typ. London.
Printed in black and red and set throughout in
Grotesque No. 8.

454. *c.* 1700 ENGRAVED BILL
1½″ × 7½″. Anon. London.
A somewhat tentative version of the English copperplate hand with an ornamental initial.

Engraved invoices and billheads

Typical features of the eighteenth and early
nineteenth century engraved billheads were the
'English' copperplate hand, shadow and decorated roman capitals, and black letter in various
forms. The use of swashes increased and became
wilder and wilder. As time went on the engraved
illustrations included shop signs (Fig. 458),
classical figures and urns, ships, casks, bales and
Chinamen (for tea importers). Views of places of
business appear with the façade of Messrs King's
shop in Covent Garden (Fig. 459) and Mr
Udall's little Regency cottage (Fig. 463). Rarely
can a billhead, showing a tradesman's premises,
have had a more charming engraving than this
rose-bowered cottage.

Economy in printing and engraving was clearly
the object of the Boston China, Glass, Crockery
and Japanned Warehouse of Samuel Sumner
(Fig. 457), who in 1797 had the effective money-
and space-saving idea of limiting the engraved
part of his billhead to a very small area, leaving
all the paper to the right of his engraving free
for writing.

The three delicate engraved headings (Figs.
460–2) might well come from the same engraving shop – but there is no signature to any of
them. It would indeed seem likely that the two
Rotherham bills are from the same engraver;
the manner of enclosing the street names inside
the swirling foot of the 'R' of Rotherham is one
indication of this.

455. 1739 ENGRAVED INVOICE
8¾″ × 5¼″. Champion scr. London.
A specimen page from Bickham's *The Universal
Penman.*

Engraved billheads

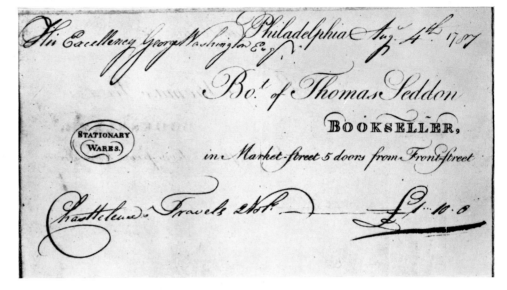

456. 1787 BOOKSELLER'S BILLHEAD
3½″ × 7¾″. Anon. Philadelphia.
Thomas Seddon's bill to George Washington is
typical of the simple engraved heading. The word
'Bookseller' is in a shaded or inline letter.

Bella C. Landauer Collection, New-York Historical Society

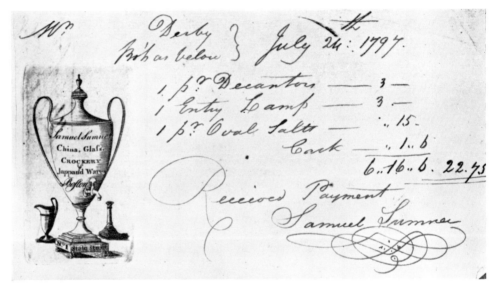

457. 1797 CHINA SHOP BILL
3½″ × 6¾″ (2¾″ × 1½″ engraved area). Anon. Boston,
Massachusetts
This billhead is unusual in that the name and
address are confined to the limits of the engraved urn.

Bella C. Landauer Collection, New-York Historical Society

458. 1792 HOSIER'S BILLHEAD
3¼″ × 6⅝″. C. L. Hannel sculpt. London.
The engraving of the lamb no doubt represents the
sign that would have hung outside the shop.

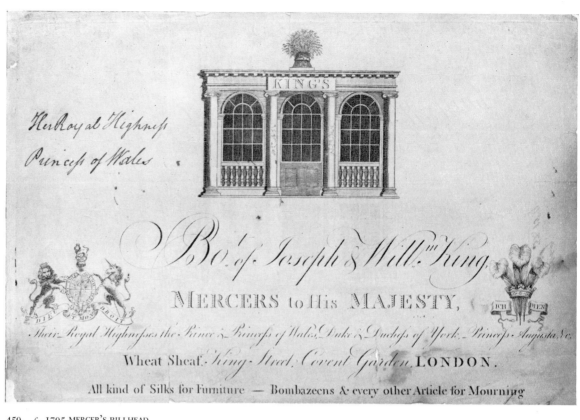

459. *c.* 1795 MERCER'S BILLHEAD
6½″ × 10″. Anon. London.
This bill, made out to 'Her Royal Highness Princess of Wales,'
has an engraving of William King's shop-front in Covent Garden.

460. *c.* 1800 WINE
MERCHANT'S BILLHEAD
2½″ × 6″. Anon.
Rotherham.

Oxford University Press

461. *c.* 1800.
DRAPER'S BILLHEAD
2½″ × 7½″. Anon.
Rotherham.
The engraving is of
Earnshaw's shop and
is similar to Fig. 460.

Oxford University Press

462. *c*. 1800 GROCER'S BILLHEAD
2¼″ × 6″. Anon. Lympstone.
The engraver here shows, to the best of his ability, both sides of Mr Titcher's import trade.

Engraved billheads

463. *c*. 1840 HABERDASHER'S BILLHEAD
s/s Anon. London.
A beautifully engraved bill, the lettering being throughout in the 'English' hand. Any possible monotony is relieved by the precise little engraving of Mr Udall's shop.

464. 1821 DRAPER'S BILLHEAD
3½″ × 8¾″. T. Welch sc. Lamb's Conduit Street, London.
The classical figure is of 'Hope'. The engraver's flourish cannot disguise his misuse of gothic capitals for the word 'LONDON'. He uses a remarkable open decorated gothic for 'Linen Draper and Mercer' but here makes a more proper use of the minuscule.

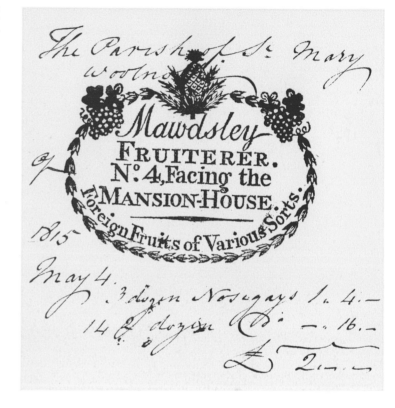

Her Royal Highness
Princess Charlotte London,

180

Bought of THOMAS HILL,
GLOVE MANUFACTURER,
To Her MAJESTY, and Their Royal Highnesses the PRINCESSES,
No. 8, COCKSPUR-STREET, *near the Haymarket.*

1804

465. 1804 GLOVE MANUFACTURER'S BILLHEAD
$1\frac{7}{8}'' \times 5\frac{1}{4}''$. Anon. London.
Letterpress billhead made out to H.R.H. Princess
Charlotte. The open capitals used for 'GLOVE MANU-
FACTURER' are the Nonpareil 2-lines from Caslon and
Catherwood's Typefoundry.

466. 1815 FRUITERER'S BILLHEAD
$2\frac{1}{2}'' \times 3''$. Anon. London.
Printed in green from a wood engraving. The letters
are engraved and not typeset.

Letterpress billheads

The letterpress billheads begin with a simple
arrangement, often asymmetric, of roman and
italic types, though in Fig. 465 there is one line
in Caslon's open letter with elegant little blobbed
terminals to the letters 'A', 'M' and 'N'. The Old
Kent Road Fishmonger, J. Pummell, shows in
his little bill the influence of the engraver on
letterpress printing (Fig. 467). And Mawdsley,
the Mansion House Fruiterer, though using a
letterpress printer, relied entirely on a relief
engraved wood-block both for the decoration
and the wording (Fig. 466).

467. 1832 FISHMONGER'S BILLHEAD
$1\frac{3}{8}'' \times 4''$. Anon. London.
Letterpress billhead, in many ways influenced by the
style of the engraver. The shadow letter used for
'FISHMONGER' is an italic version of Thorne's Shaded.
'Bought of' is from a typefounder's stock stereo.

468. *c.* 1820 POULTERER'S BILLHEAD
1½″ × 4½″. Kent sculpt. High Holborn, London.
Engraved bill with shadow lettering and English
copperplate. Both the illustrations of the wild fowl
and the lettering are done with much delicacy.

Engraved letterpress billheads

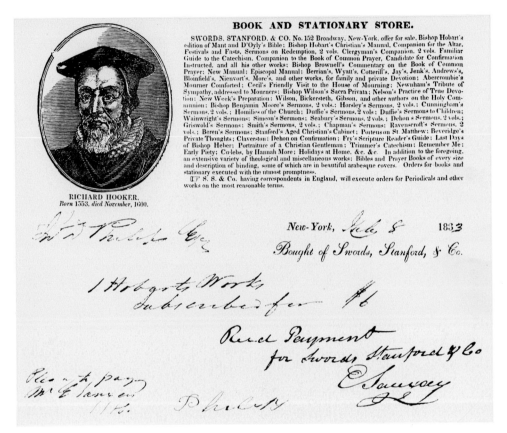

469. 1833 BOOK AND STATIONERY STORE BILLHEAD
6″ × 6¾″. Anon. New York.
Letterpress bill with wood engravings.

Bella C. Landauer Collection, New-York Historical Society

470. 1839 LINEN DRAPER'S BILLHEAD
4″ × 6¼″. Anon. Bath.
Letterpress bill with Thorowgood's Fat Faces and an
open 2-line Nonpareil for 'Linen drapers etc.'

Oxford University Press

Letterpress billheads

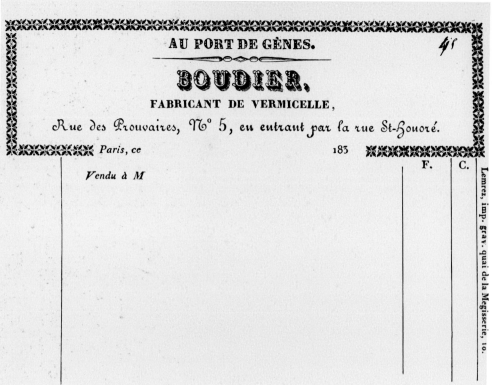

471. 1838 GROCER'S BILLHEAD
6⅝″ × 6¾″. Lemrez, Paris.
Printed by letterpress.

472. 1837 GROCER'S BILLHEAD
4¼″ × 6″. Lemrez. Paris.
Printed by letterpress.

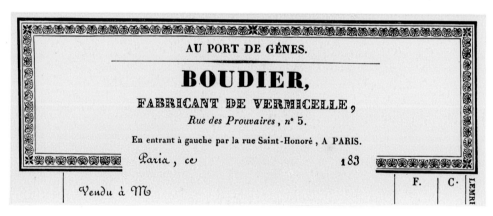

473. 1840 PRINTER'S BILLHEAD
1¾″ × 6″. J. Wilson. London.
Impeccably simple letterpress bill with the most
careful placing of the typographic components.

Engraved and letterpress billheads

474. 1844 DRAPER'S BILLHEAD
3″ × 6″. Anon. Richmond.
The engraver's combination of the English copperplate hand, gothic and decorated letters has degenerated into a surfeit of swirls and flourishes.

The two French bills (opposite page) are included in this mainly Anglo-Saxon collection to show the use of borders and decorated letters. They are from the same shop, and owe much to the great French typefounder, J. Gillé, whose specimen book, issued in 1818, is full of such bills as these with a wide use of borders. The printer has rung clever changes with his decora-ted and plain letter forms. In Fig. 473, J. Wilson's Printing Office has an asymmetric arrangement and a most thoughtfully judged positioning of the few typographic elements. This simple bill is given strength by the bold typefaces used; Egyptian for 'Printing Office', a semi-fat faced italic for 'J. Wilson' and a heavy black letter for 'Printing'.

475. 1840 INNKEEPER'S BILLHEAD
4½″ wide. Anon. Sheffield.
A simple billhead, given some distinction by the use of the open and shadow letters for 'Sheffield' and 'Bridge Inn'.

Oxford University Press

Lithographed billhead

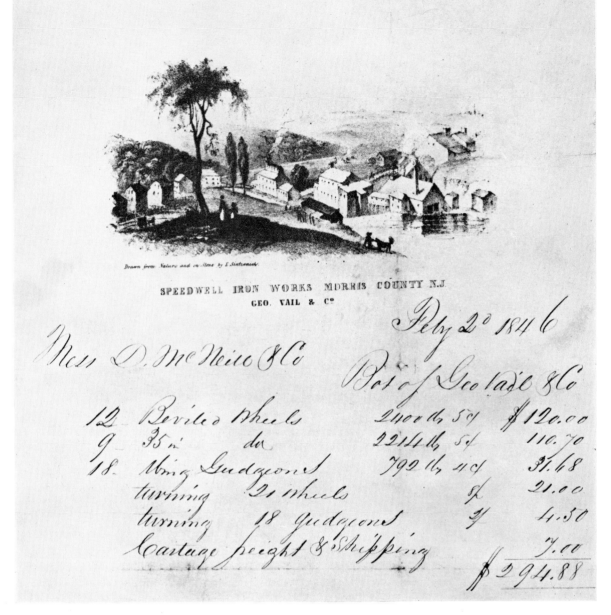

476. 1846 IRONWORKS BILLHEAD
4¼″ × 7″. E. Sintzenich del. New Jersey.
Lithographed billhead.

Bella C. Landauer Collection, New-York Historical Society

Letterpress billhead

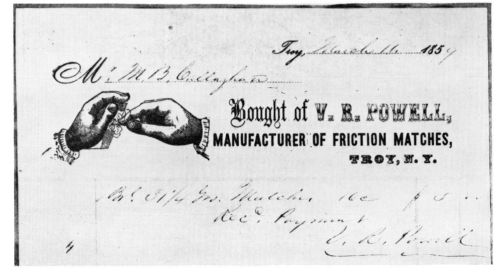

477. 1859. MATCH MANUFACTURER'S BILLHEAD
2″ × 6½″. Anon. Troy, New York.
The decorated letter used for 'V. R. Powell' originates
from Miller and Richard's Edinburgh typefoundry
and was known as '2-line Small Pica Ornamented
No. 8'.

Bella C. Landauer Collection, New-York Historical Society

Letterpress billheads

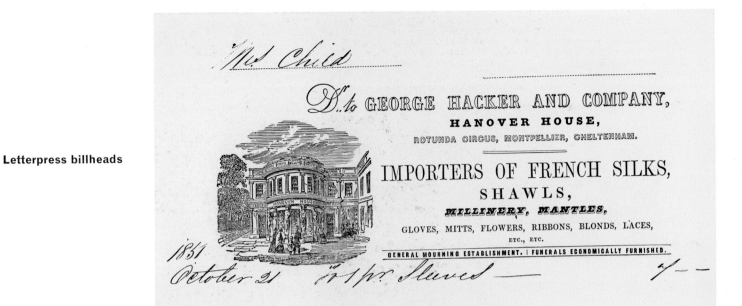

478. 1851 DRAPER'S BILLHEAD
2½″ × 6½″. Bonner sc. Cheltenham.
Letterpress billhead; the nine lines of copy are set in ten different types. The illustration is from a wood engraving.

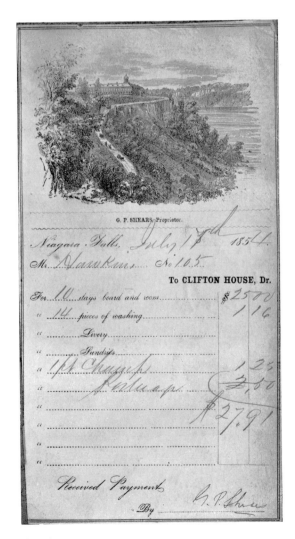

480. 1854 HOTEL BILLHEAD
8¾″ × 4¾″. J. W. Orr sc. Niagara Falls.
Bill set throughout in a script typeface except for a few words in a Clarendon.

479. 1850 HOTEL BILLHEAD
4″ × 7″. J. W. Orr sc. Washington D.C.
Bill mainly set in a Clarendon.

The two mid-nineteenth-century hotel bills (shown here) from Washington D.C. and Niagara Falls were both illustrated by the same wood engraver, and possibly printed by the same printer. They make use of the unusual combination of the English script and Clarendon, with the addition, in the Washington bill, of a not very distinguished shaded letter (Figs. 479 and 480.)

481. 1879 POTATO MERCHANT'S BILLHEAD
3″ × 8″. Anon. Birmingham.
Bill printed in black from type and a wood engraving
of a locomotive. The outlined Tuscan letter used for
'BY CALEB LEWIS' was issued by the Caslon Letter
Foundry in 1856.

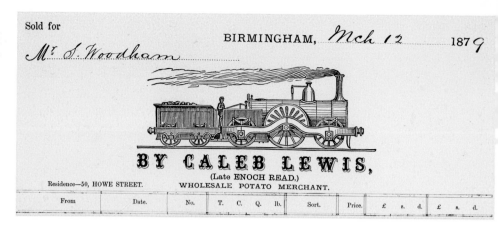

| Sold for | | | | | BIRMINGHAM, *Mch 12* | | | 1879 |

Mr S. Woodham

BY CALEB LEWIS,
(Late ENOCH READ.)
Residence—50, HOWE STREET.   WHOLESALE POTATO MERCHANT.

From	Date.	No.	T.	C.	Q.	lb.	Sort.	Price.	£	s.	d.	£	s.	d.

482. 1870 PRINTER'S BILLHEAD
2¾″ × 7¼″. R. C. Ibbs. Kimbolton.
Letterpress bill made out to the '1st Hunts Foot
Volunteers'. The words 'Paper-Hanger' are set in
Long Primer Ornamental No. 3 from the Baltimore
Type Foundry. It was first issued by them in 1851
so this may be an English copy.

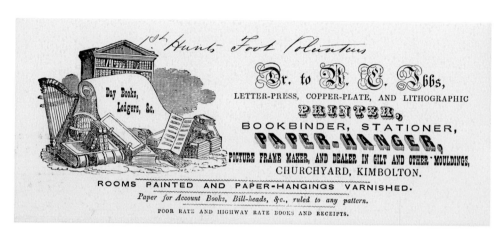

1st Hunts Foot Volunteers

Dr. to R. C. Ibbs,
LETTER-PRESS, COPPER-PLATE, AND LITHOGRAPHIC
PRINTER,
BOOKBINDER, STATIONER,
PAPER-HANGER,
PICTURE FRAME MAKER, AND DEALER IN GILT AND OTHER MOULDINGS,
CHURCHYARD, KIMBOLTON.
ROOMS PAINTED AND PAPER-HANGINGS VARNISHED.
Day Books, Ledgers, &c.
Paper for Account Books, Bill-heads, &c., ruled to any pattern.
POOR RATE AND HIGHWAY RATE BOOKS AND RECEIPTS.

483. 1872 PRINT PUBLISHER'S BILLHEAD
4″ × 8″ Anon. New York.
Bill from the famous lithographer and print dealer,
set largely in an over-ligatured roman typeface.

Bella C. Landauer Collection, New-York Historical Society

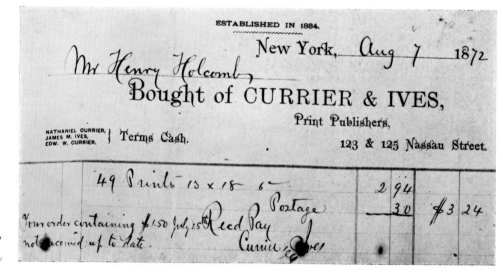

ESTABLISHED IN 1834.

New York, *Aug 7* 1872

Mr Henry Holcomb

Bought of CURRIER & IVES,
Print Publishers,

NATHANIEL CURRIER,
JAMES M. IVES,   } Terms Cash.
EDW. W. CURRIER.

123 & 125 Nassau Street.

484. 1883. SHIPPING COMPANY LETTERHEAD
1″ × 3¼″. Anon. Hong Kong.
A commendably austere letterheading in a bold
Egyptian and a rather condensed black letter.

HONG KONG.

Peninsular and Oriental Steam Navigation Company,

17 Sept 18 83

Letterpress and lithographic
billheads

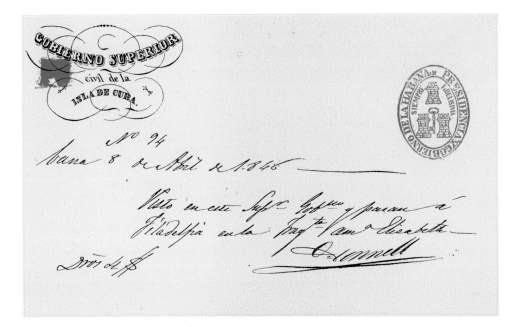

485. 1846 GOVERNMENT NOTEPAPER
5″ × 8″ (paper area). Anon. Cuba.
Engraved letterhead, set to the left of the paper and
printed in black, with the Presidency stamp in red.
The seal, also in red, is no longer intact.

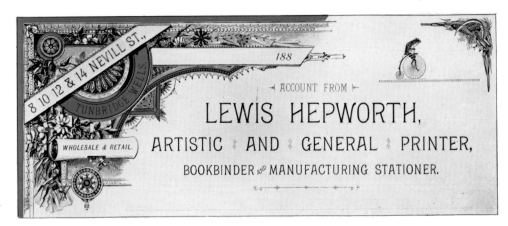

486. 1885 PRINTER'S LETTERHEAD
3¼″ × 7⅞″. Lewis Hepworth. Tunbridge Wells.
Printed in black and four colours by letterpress from
wood engravings and type.

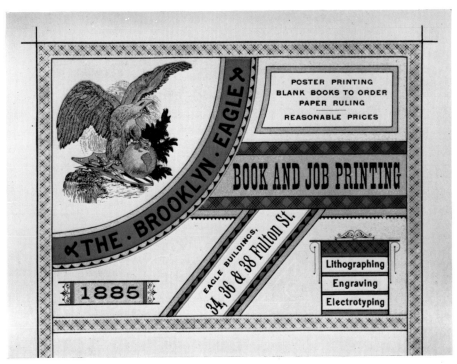

487. 1885 PRINTER'S LETTERHEAD
4⅝″ × 6¾″. Brooklyn Eagle Press, Brooklyn.
Printed in five colours and gold by lithography.

Letterpress billheads

488. *c.* 1900 STATIONER'S LETTERHEAD
$2\frac{1}{2}'' \times 7\frac{1}{2}''$. Anon. Wells, Norfolk.
This letterhead was still in daily use in 1950. Its mixture of design metaphors is only exceeded by the indifferent quality of the original presswork.

489. 1913 PRIVATE PRESS LETTERHEAD
$2\frac{1}{2}'' \times 7\frac{1}{4}''$. C. Lovat Fraser des. A. J. Stevens, London.
Printed in red from type and line block. The 'Flying Fame Press' was set up by the artist Claud Lovat Fraser in co-operation with Ralph Hodgson and Holbrook Jackson to publish broadsheets and chapbooks.

490. *c.* 1935 DECORATOR'S LETTERHEAD
$1\frac{1}{2}'' \times 3\frac{1}{2}''$. E. McKnight Kauffer typ. Lund Humphries, Bradford.
Printed in dark grey and grey-green and set in Corvinus Bold and Corvinus Bold Italic.

Both the engraved and the typographic letterheads of the first half of the nineteenth century had charm and dignity. The typographic letterheads, as the century progressed, varied from the complexity of that of Mr Ibbs, Printer and Paperhanger (Fig. 482) to the straightforward typography of the famous print publishers, Currier and Ives (Fig. 483). By the 1880's the simplicity of the work of both American and British printers was beginning to give way to 'Artistic Printing', a movement that swept through the printing shops of both America and England. This was the last independent stand of the compositor, who made up for his lack of typographic sense by his dexterity in using ornamental rules and borders.

Letterpress billheads

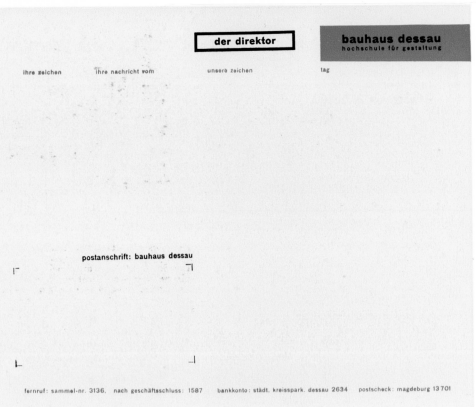

491. 1930 ART SCHOOL LETTERHEAD
$3\frac{1}{2}'' \times 7\frac{1}{4}''$. Bauhaus, Dessau. Germany.
Printed in black and red.

492. 1930 ART SCHOOL LETTERHEAD
$3\frac{1}{2}'' \times 7\frac{1}{4}''$ Bauhaus, Dessau.
Printed in black and red.

The modern bill and letterhead has its origins in all these past movements, including *l'Art Nouveau*, and the revival of interest in typography that came in with the private press movement, and in the work of the Bauhaus school of typographers.

These two letterheadings from the Bauhaus (Figs. 491–2) were a complete innovation when they were produced. It has taken nearly a quarter of a century for such a typographic approach to be generally accepted.

In the last two decades a spring cleaning of house stationery has occurred throughout businesses and industries on both sides of the Atlantic. Liberated once again from the formality of a central axis of design, typographers and printers have produced, amongst the spate of inevitable mediocrity, much work of inspired freshness and vitality. Yet there are still many who remain faithful to a classic style, with a judicious use of crests and trade marks. Printers on the whole are conservative, and the University Presses are more so than most. However, the letterheads used by designers are on the whole even more modest, less flamboyant than any others. Maybe because, more than their clients, they realize that the prime purpose of typography is communication.

Letterpress billheads

493. *c.* 1940 SCHOOL LETTERCARD
8⅜″ × 7⅞″. Max Bill typ. Zürich.
Designed to fold with ruled space for recipient's
address.

Museum of Modern Art

494. 1936 PRINTER'S LETTERHEAD
2½″ × 7½″. Jan Tschichold typ. Lund Humphries.
Bradford.
Printed in black and red and set in Gill Sans in
various weights. This was one of the first design
jobs that Tschichold undertook when he came to
England.

495. 1947 DESIGNER'S LETTERHEADING
3⅝″ wide. Robert Harling typ. Hague and Gill.
Ditchling. Set in one of Eric Gill's prettiest typefaces,
Joanna Italic.

trudi stössel

schule für gymnastik und rhythmik

trudi stössel
schule für gymnastik und rhythmik

telefon 28.946
postscheck VIII 17544

trudi stössel   zürich   freiestrasse 56

freiestrasse 56   parterre   telefon 28.946

sprechstunden täglich   11—12 uhr
ausgenommen mittwoch 13—15 uhr

bill · zürich

lund humphries

Percy Lund Humphries & Co Ltd . 12 Bedford Square w.c. 1

Printers
Publishers
Binders

London: Telephone: Museum 7676
           Telegrams: Lund Museum 7676 London

Bradford: The Country Press
           Telephone 11311 (three lines)
           Telegrams: Typography Bradford

Robert Harling: 10 Hertford Street London W1 and GRO 3477

R. & R. CLARK
LIMITED

BRANDON STREET EDINBURGH

Telephone :
21221-2-3

Telegrams :
Clark, Edinburgh

496. 1947 PRINTER'S LETTERHEAD
$1\frac{1}{2}'' \times 3''$. R. & R. Clark, Edinburgh.
Printed in black and brown and set in Perpetua.

Fine Letterpress and Lithographic Printers

W . S . COWELL LTD

8 BUTTER MARKET, IPSWICH, ENGLAND

TELEPHONE : IPSWICH 56781·TELEGRAMS : LITHOCOWL·IPSWICH

497. *c.* **1948** PRINTER'S LETTERHEAD
$\frac{7}{8}'' \times 3\frac{1}{2}''$. John Brinkley des. W. S. Cowell Ltd,
Ipswich.
Engraved letterhead; the shadow letter derives from
Thorne's Shaded, which this printer used in 1818.

Fonderie de Caractères Haas S.A. Munchenstein-Bâle

Fabrique de filets en cuivre · Galvanoplastie · Atelier de gravure

498. 1948 TYPEFOUNDER'S LETTERHEAD
$\frac{3}{4}'' \times 4\frac{3}{4}''$. Anon. Munchenstein-Bâle.
Printed in dark green and red. The word 'HAAS' is
set in Profil and Haas Caslon.

Fry, Drew & Partners

c/o UNIVERSITY COLLEGE, IBADAN
Telephone: Ibadan, 212
Telegrams: Fridrew, Ibadan

175 IGBOSERE ROAD, LAGOS
P.O. Box 2185
Telephone: Lagos 21984
Telegrams: Fridrew, Lagos

Senior Partners
E. Maxwell Fry, C.B.E. F.R.I.B.A.,   Jane B. Drew, F.R.I.B.A.
Frank S. Knight, A.R.I.B.A., Norman C. Creamer, A.R.I.B.A.
J. Robin Atkinson, M.A., A.R.I.B.A. (West Africa)

Partners
Peter B. Bond, A.R.I.B.A.,   Robert D. Byng, A.R.I.B.A.

And at Accra, Ghana and 63 Gloucester Place, London W1

499. 1947 ARCHITECT'S LETTERHEAD
$2'' \times 7\frac{1}{4}''$. Herbert Spencer typ. Lund Humphries,
Bradford.
Printed in black and red and set in grotesque and
Gill Sans.

The New York Public Library

Astor, Lenox and Tilden Foundations

FIFTH AVENUE AND 42ND STREET
NEW YORK 18, N. Y.

500. 1957 PUBLIC LIBRARY LETTERHEAD
$1'' \times 3\frac{1}{2}''$. Anon. New York.
Printed in black and the first two lines are set in
a nineteenth century gothic.

Lithographed and letterpress billheads

University Printer
BROOKE CRUTCHLEY

University Press
Cambridge

Telephone: CAMBRIDGE 4226
Telegrams: UNIPRESS CAMBRIDGE

501. 1947 UNIVERSITY PRESS LETTERHEAD
¾″ × 4¼″. John Dreyfus typ. University Press,
Cambridge.
Printed in black and set in Perpetua.

DIRECTORS: OLIVER SIMON, O.B.E. — HERBERT SIMON — O.R.G. WILLIAMS

THE CURWEN PRESS LTD

NORTH STREET, PLAISTOW, LONDON, E.13
GRANGEWOOD 3411 (4 lines)
CABLES: NEWRUCPRES STRAT LONDON

502. 1953 PRINTER'S LETTERHEAD
1¼″ × 5½″. Curwen Press, London.
Printed in black and red and set in Ehrhardt and
Van Krimpen's Open Titling.

The Lakeside Press
R·R·DONNELLEY & SONS COMPANY

350 EAST TWENTY-SECOND STREET · CHICAGO 16

TELEPHONE CALUMET 5-2121

503. 1959 PRINTER'S LETTERHEAD
2″ × 4¾″. R. R. Donnelley, Chicago.
Printed in black and red, with the top line in
American Type Founders' Cloister Black.

Department of Art   Yale University School of Art and Architecture   New Haven, Connecticut

504. 1957 UNIVERSITY (DEPARTMENT OF ART)
LETTERHEAD
5″ wide approx. Yale University Press, New Haven,
Connecticut.
Printed in blue and set in Standard.

HARVARD UNIVERSITY
CAMBRIDGE 38, MASSACHUSETTS

OFFICE OF THE PRESIDENT

505. 1958 UNIVERSITY LETTERHEAD
1″ × 5″. Anon. Harvard University, Cambridge,
Massachusetts.
Printed in black and set in Linotype Granjon.

Communications on printing should be addressed
to Charles Batey, Printer to the University, at the
University Press, Oxford.
Telegrams: Oxunipress, Oxford
Telephone: 57565/6/7 Oxford

AC. OX.

University Press
Oxford

506. 1958 UNIVERSITY PRESS LETTERHEAD
¾″ × 7″. University Press, Oxford.
Printed in blue and set in Caslon Old Face.

YALE UNIVERSITY PRESS
At the Earl Trumbull Williams Memorial
NEW HAVEN CONNECTICUT

507. 1958 UNIVERSITY PRESS LETTERHEAD
6¼″ wide. Yale University Press, New Haven, Conn.
Printed in blue and set in Linotype Oxford and
Cloister Black.

ILLIAM MORRIS SOCIETY
President Sir Sydney Cockerell
Honorary Secretary R. C. H. Briggs
260 Sandycombe Road, Kew, Surrey

508. 1958 LETTERHEAD
¾″ × 4″. R. C. H. Briggs des. University Press,
Cambridge.
Printed in black and red and set in William Morris's
Golden type. The initial is from a design by Morris.

Hans Schleger 148 Sloane Street London SW1 · Telephone Sloane 3730

509. 1958 DESIGNER'S LETTERHEADING
4¼″ wide. Hans Schleger typ. London.
Printed in black and set in Walbaum
and Walbaum Medium.

Philip Johnson Associates 375 Park Avenue New York 22 N Y PLaza 1 7440

510. 1958 ARCHITECT'S LETTERHEAD
5¾″ wide. Elaine Lustig typ, New York.
Printed in black and red and set in A.T.F.'s Craw
Clarendon.

 HANS KLEEFELD GRAPHIC DESIGN, 61 CHARLES STREET EAST, APARTMENT 306, TORONTO 5, CANADA, TELEPHONE WALNUT 2-7093

511. 1958 DESIGNER'S LETTERHEADING
6½″ wide. Hans Kleefeld typ. Toronto.
Printed in black and blue and set in grotesque
capitals.

Letterpress billheads

512. 1958 FESTIVAL LETTERHEADING
4½" × 1½". Anon. San Juan, Puerto Rico.
Printed in black and red and set in a variety of
revived nineteenth century typefaces.

513. 1959 BOOKSELLER'S LETTERHEAD
2" × 2½". John Sewell typ. London.
Printed in black and green and set in Stevens
Shanks's Antique No. 6 and Times New Roman.

514. 1958 BUSINESS LETTERHEADING
1½" × 6½". I.B.M. Art Dept. New York.
Printed in black and khaki and set in City Medium
'For release' and linotype Bodoni italic. The letters
I.B.M. are drawn.

515. 1958 LEATHER MANUFACTURER'S LETTERHEAD
1⅝" × 6¾". Brownjohn, Chermayeff & Geismar typ.
New York.
Printed in black, red and brown and set in a grotesque; the letter 'R' is drawn.

Part 2 LABELS AND WRAPPERS

Labels and Wrapping Papers

If labels had not been a very real part of ephemeral printing, I would have been tempted to have left them out of this book, for of all the subjects that I have tried to deal with, this is by far the most difficult to cover adequately. After some reflection, I have limited myself to five representative groups, where early examples were available. The five groups are: tobacco; foodstuffs; beers, wines and spirits; pharmaceutical; and hardware labels. Any one of these headings could provide material to fill a book of this size, and as for the subjects that I have neglected – they are unlimited. For example, match box labels, which provide a most rewarding study. I have regretfully left them out because, on the whole, their interest is more pictorial than typographic.

The two main threads that stem from the engraved letter and from type itself are fairly evenly represented in labels, even up to today, though the foodstuffs and beers seem to follow the letterpress tradition, whereas wines and spirits are usually based on the work of the engraver, as are cosmetic and hardware labels.

Over the last thirty years there has been an energetic move to improve the appearance of packaging. Some beautiful work has come from Dr Hadank in Germany and Mr Milner Gray in England. Most modern labels, however, do not compare very favourably with either the delicacy of the eighteenth century engraved labels or the direct vitality of the early typographic and woodcut labels.

The continuity of certain themes is of interest. The sailing ship and blackamoor's head constantly occur in tobacco labels, as do the royal coat of arms on pin packets, and Chinamen and their pagodas on tea labels. The tradition of showing pictures of warehouses, works or shops on letterheads was by the beginning of the nineteenth century extended to a similar use on wrapping papers and labels. By the 1830's the copper engraving was being replaced either by wood engraving or by lithography, not always with happy results. In the Henry B. Gleason wrapper in Fig. 697, however, restraint and delicacy are in evidence; the drawn letters are based on contemporary typefaces and the illustration of the crockery and glass warehouse is lithographed with much skill. By the latter half of the century, the freedom of the lithograph was to produce results of appalling depravity. The horrors perpetrated by the German chromo-lithographers were soon equalled if not surpassed by printers in the United States and with perhaps rather less verve by their opposite numbers in Britain.

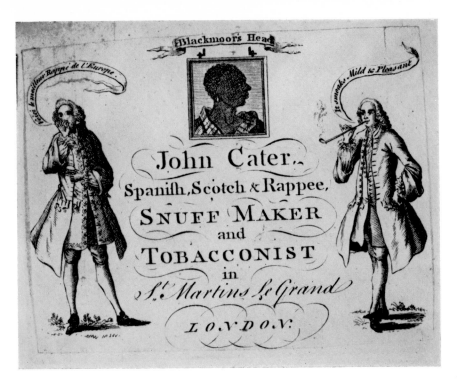

516. *c.* 1750 SNUFF AND TOBACCO LABEL
3⅝″ × 4¾″. Anon. London.
Copper engraved label for John Cater.

517. *c.* 1750 TOBACCO LABEL
4⅝″ × 3¼″. Anon. London.
Copper engraved label for 'Burdon's Virginia'.

Labels: Tobacco

This is no place to describe the origins of tobacco and particularly the growth of the Virginian tobacco plantations. However, certain characteristics of the early labels are worth noting, such as the engraver's idea of what the Virginian planter and his African slaves looked like. In these early labels there is little sign of the redskin who, long before Columbus had made his first contacts with cigar-smoking Cuban Indians, was smoking his pipe of peace. It was not until the end of the sixteenth century that tobacco smoking had become a widespread habit in England. In the seventeenth century, tobacco and snuff were wrapped in engraved tobacco papers such as those shown here. The engravings on these wrappers, as well as showing views of the plantations, followed the lead of the trade card engravers and had for their designs the signs that used to hang over the doors of the tobacconists' shops.

518. *c.* 1730 TOBACCO LABEL
2″ × 3″. Anon. London.
Copper engraved label showing a still.

519. *c.* 1730 TOBACCO LABEL
2⅝″ × 2″. Anon. London.
Copper engraved label showing a tobacco roll.

Petum optimum fubter Solem.
Le meilleur Tabac desous le Soliel.
The Best Tobacco under the Sun.

520. *c.* 1730 TOBACCO LABEL
4″ × 3⅜″. Anon. England.
Copper engraved label with a somewhat unlikely
view of a Virginian Harbour, with a slogan printed in
Latin, French and English.

Imperial Tobacco Company

ESCOURT'S
At the Ship Fronting
Hungerford Market
in the Strand -LONDON

521. *c.* 1700 TOBACCO LABEL
3¼″ × 2⅜″. Anon. London.
Copper engraved label for Escourt's tobacco.

Imperial Tobacco Company

Hurt & Charlton's Best Virginia
Crown & Dolphin LONDON.

522. *c.* 1730 TOBACCO LABEL
3½″ × 2½″. Anon. London.
Copper engraved label for 'Hurt and Charlton's Best
Virginia', with two *putti*.

Imperial Tobacco Company

John Bowden's
Mild-Tobacco
Threadneedle Street LONDON.
With all Sorts of Snuffs

523. *c.* 1745 TOBACCO LABEL
3″ × 2⅜″. Anon. London.
Copper engraved label for 'John Bowden's Mild
Tobacco', with Highlander and blackamoor, in a
rococo frame.

Imperial Tobacco Company

524. *c.* 1675 TOBACCO LABEL
$2\frac{5}{8}'' \times 3\frac{1}{8}''$. Anon. London.
Copper engraved label for 'Jones his Virginia'.

Pepysian Library, Cambridge

Tobacco labels: copper engraved

The Imperial Tobacco Company (of Great Britain and Ireland) Ltd has loaned an album to W. D. & H. O. Wills at Bristol, containing a most interesting collection of eighteenth century tobacco labels and wrappers. This album was compiled by a certain Ingham Foster, and was purchased after his death in 1786, at the sale of his effects, by Atkinson Bush. His descendant James Bush gave it to a tobacco manufacturer called Patterson just one hundred years after the compiler had died. From Patterson it finally came into the hands of the Imperial Tobacco Company. In this album there are a great number of copper and wood engraved labels though certainly more intaglio than relief engraved, unlike the album in the Bagford Collection in the British Museum. Figs. 516 to 523 and 536 to 543 give some idea of the quality of these engraved wrappers ranging, in the intaglio labels, from the elegant beaux in the label belonging to John Cater, 'Spanish, Scotch and Rapee, Snuff Maker and Tobacconist', or the prancing highlander and the little blackamoor set in John Bowdon's delicate rococo frame, or to the archaic highlander advertising Buchan's 'Best Virginia'. The crudity of the woodcut blackamoor for William Ridout clearly shows how confused the artists of these labels were, for here is the little negro boy dressed up as a redskin, in a feathered head-dress and a feathered skirt (Fig. 537).

525. *c.* 1675 TOBACCO LABEL
$3\frac{1}{4}'' \times 2\frac{1}{4}''$ approx. Anon. Wapping.
Copper engraved label for 'Thomas Marshall at ye Blackamoors-head'.

Pepysian Library, Cambridge

526. *c.* 1675 TOBACCO LABEL
$3\frac{3}{4}'' \times 2\frac{7}{8}''$. Anon. London.
Copper engraved label for 'Wood's Best Virginia'.

Pepysian Library, Cambridge

S*

219

Tobacco labels: wood engraved

These wood engraved labels come from the Bagford Collection in the British Museum. The artists and the engravers are unknown to me but in nearly every case they make excellent use of the space at their disposal. The early fashion for blackamoors and sailing ships for tobacco labels has endured to this day. These chapbook-style labels are about contemporary with the copper engraved labels and make an interesting comparison.

A label for a chewing tobacco (Fig. 559) produced in Holland in 1960 could well be put with the Bagford labels of the seventeenth century and would not, with the engraving of the be-feathered redskins, seem out of context.

The pirating of designs was for a long time a common fashion in the tobacco industry. The negro's head in an oval was used by several firms who tried to copy the package of W. D. and H. O. Wills. An example of one of these that was sold in the year 1880 was made by a firm which styled themselves W. D. and H. O. Wilis. On the back of the Wills Birdseye tobacco label, shown on page 226, is a warning against 'Many close imitations of an original and well-known Birdseye tobacco, both in colour and the wording on the label'. The Webb label (Fig. 555) is clearly one of the imitations referred to.

527. *c*. 1700 TOBACCO LABEL
$3\frac{1}{4}'' \times 2\frac{1}{2}''$. Anon. London.
Wood engraved label for 'London's Virginia.'

British Museum

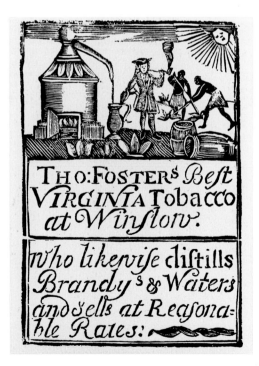

528. *c*. 1700 TOBACCO LABEL
$3\frac{3}{8}'' \times 2\frac{1}{4}''$. Anon. Winslow.
Wood engraved label for 'Tho: Foster's Virginia'.

British Museum

529. *c*. 1675 TOBACCO LABEL
$3\frac{1}{4}'' \times 2\frac{1}{2}''$. Anon. Sandwich.
Wood engraved label for 'Ketcherell's Virginia'. The oval frame with the product name has been in constant use since the seventeenth century.

British Museum

530. *c.* 1700 TOBACCO LABEL
$3\frac{1}{4}'' \times 2\frac{3}{8}''$. Anon. Ashford, Kent.
Wood engraved label showing blackamoors packing
tobacco leaves into barrels.

British Museum

531. *c.* 1700 TOBACCO LABEL
$4'' \times 2\frac{7}{8}''$. Anon. London.
Wood engraved label, showing the Royal Exchange.

British Museum

532. *c.* 1700 TOBACCO LABEL
$2\frac{1}{4}'' \times 3\frac{1}{4}''$. Anon. London.
Wood engraved label showing blackamoors and a
still.

British Museum

533. *c.* 1700 TOBACCO LABEL
$3'' \times 2\frac{1}{4}''$. Anon. Reighly.
Engraved label (probably on copper) for 'E. English'.

British Museum

534. *c.* 1675 TOBACCO LABEL
$3\frac{3}{8}'' \times 2\frac{1}{4}''$. Anon. London.
Wood engraved label, for 'T. Maulden's Virginia'.

British Museum

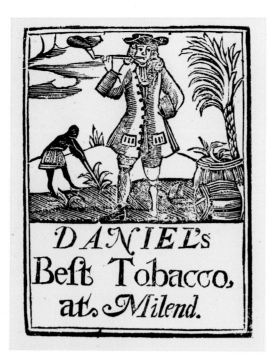

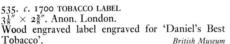

535. *c.* 1700 TOBACCO LABEL
$3\frac{1}{8}'' \times 2\frac{3}{8}''$. Anon. London.
Wood engraved label engraved for 'Daniel's Best
Tobacco'. *British Museum*

536. *c.* 1720 TOBACCO LABEL
$2\frac{1}{2}'' \times 3''$. Anon. London.
Wood engraved label for 'Cook's Virginia'.
Imperial Tobacco Company

Tobacco labels: wood engraved

Tobacconists in the seventeenth and eighteenth centuries advertised their presence by carved and painted figures of black boys, Red Indians, Virginia planters and Highlanders. These gaily painted figures (just such a figure as the Little Midshipman outside Solomon Gill's shop, described in such loving detail by Charles Dickens in *Dombey and Son*) were reproduced on tobacco and snuff papers. The reasons for using the blackamoor and planter on the tobacco labels are obvious enough, but the Highlander

has a more romantic origin. A tobacconist called David Wishart had a shop in Coventry Street, London. Outside Wishart's shop stood a tall painted wooden statue of a Highlander in doublet and trews and armed with a targe and claymore. In 1720 Jacobite conspirators used to meet under Wishart's roof. After the collapse of the 1745 Rebellion, the supporters of Bonnie Prince Charlie had to flee the city. The Highlander remained and became the traditional sign of the snuff merchant.*

* W. D. and H. O. Wills: *Tobacco: its history, culture and manufacture.*

537. *c.* 1720 TOBACCO LABEL
$3\frac{3}{4}'' \times 2\frac{1}{2}''$. Anon. London.
Wood engraved label for 'William Ridout's Best Virginia'. This very crude cut shows the figure of the blackamoor-redskin in its simplest form.
Imperial Tobacco Company

538. *c.* 1720 SNUFF LABEL
$3\frac{1}{8}'' \times 2\frac{5}{8}''$. Anon. London.
Wood engraved label for J. Cater, showing in the centre a press worked by a pony. Compare the copper engraved label for the same firm in Fig. 516.
Imperial Tobacco Company

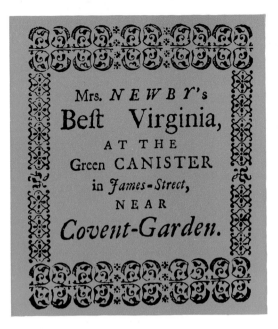

539. *c.* 1750 TOBACCO LABEL
3″ × 3⅛″. Anon. London.
Wood engraved and typeset label for 'Kippax's Best
Virginia'.
Imperial Tobacco Company

540. *c.* 1750 TOBACCO LABEL
3″ × 2½″. Anon. London.
Typeset label with fleurons.
Imperial Tobacco Company

Tobacco labels: letterpress and copper engraved

541. *c.* 1770 SNUFF LABEL
2⅛″ × 2⅜″. Anon. London.
Typeset label set in Caslon types and borders.
Imperial Tobacco Company

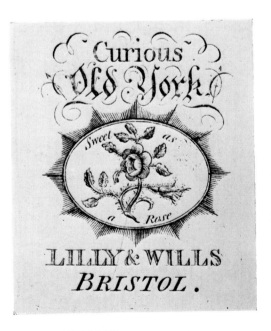

542. *c.* 1815 TOBACCO LABEL
2½″ × 3″. Anon. Bristol.
Copper engraved label.
Imperial Tobacco Company

543. *c.* 1795 SNUFF LABEL
2¾″ × 2″. Anon. Bristol.
Copper engraved label for one of the forerunners of
W. D. & H. O. Wills.
Imperial Tobacco Company

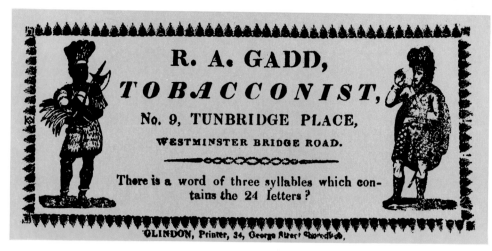

544. *c.* 1750 TOBACCO LABEL
2⅞″ × 2½″. Anon. London.
Wood engraved label for 'Buchan's Best Virginia'
showing a Highlander with targe, claymore and gun.

Imperial Tobacco Company

545. *c.* 1830 TOBACCO LABEL
2½″ × 5¾″. Glindon. London.
The tradition of the blackamoor is here continued
and coupled with the Highlander. The much worn
fat face italic loses some of its punch by this wide
letterspacing.

Oxford University Press

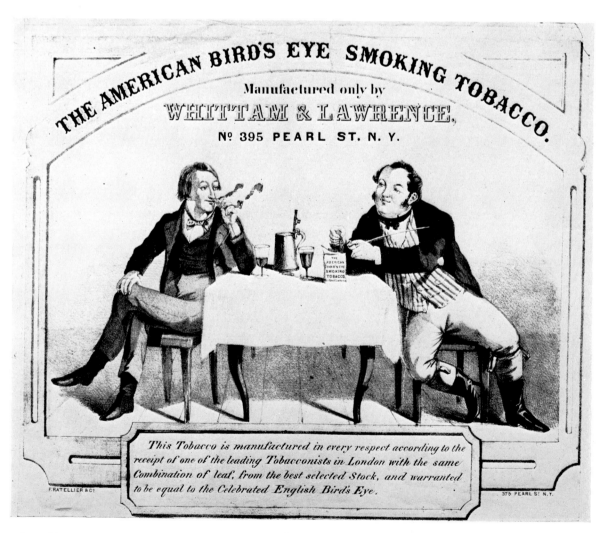

546. *c.* 1860 TOBACCO LABEL
10½″ × 12″. F. Ratellier, New York.
This large label is lithographed and printed in black.
The Tuscan letter used for the title, and the decorated
shadow letter used for 'WHITTAM & LAWRENCE' are
both based on contemporary typefaces.

Bella C. Landauer Collection, New-York Historical Society

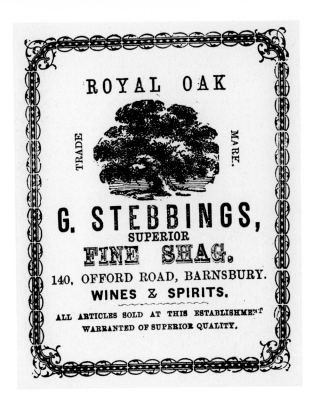

ROYAL OAK

G. STEBBINGS,
SUPERIOR
FINE SHAG.
140, OFFORD ROAD, BARNSBURY.
WINES & SPIRITS.
ALL ARTICLES SOLD AT THIS ESTABLISHMENT
WARRANTED OF SUPERIOR QUALITY.

547. *c.* 1860 TOBACCO LABEL
$3\frac{1}{2}'' \times 2\frac{7}{8}''$. Anon. Barnsbury.
'FINE SHAG' is set in Argentine, a shaded ornamental
type produced by Robert Besley, the successor to
William Thorowgood at the Fann Street Foundry.

Oxford University Press

GENUINE
VIRGINIA CUT.
THE BRITON'S DELIGHT.
Sole Manufacturers,
S. CAVANDER & Co.,
SHOREDITCH, N.E.

550. *c.* 1860 TOBACCO LABEL
$3'' \times 2\frac{3}{4}''$. Anon. Shoreditch, London.
An Ionic typeface is used for 'Virginia Cut'. The wood
engraving which is much worn may have originated
in Bewick's workshop.

Oxford University Press

551. *c.* 1860 TOBACCO LABEL
$3\frac{3}{8}'' \times 3\frac{3}{4}''$. Anon. England.
A revived use of a wood engraving of a much earlier
time. The decorated letters have lost much of the
verve of earlier ones, though they still have some
charm.

Oxford University Press

R. & J. HILL Limited.
Fine Shag
176 & 177,
SHOREDITCH.
Quarter Pound 1s. 1d.
Quarter Pound of Tobacco, Weighed without the Paper, and
packed at the Manufactory.

548. *c.* 1860 TOBACCO LABEL
$3\frac{1}{4}'' \times 5\frac{3}{4}''$. Anon. London.
Typographic label combining fat face and condensed
Egyptian.

Oxford University Press

L. WELLS,
TOBACCONIST,
44,
KENNINGTON PARK ROAD.

549. *c.* 1880 TOBACCO LABEL
$2\frac{1}{4}'' \times 3\frac{3}{4}''$. Anon. London.
Decay in type design is only too obvious here. The
cigar is wood engraved.

Oxford University Press

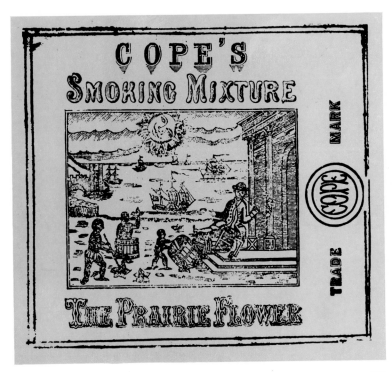

COPE'S
SMOKING MIXTURE
THE PRAIRIE FLOWER

225

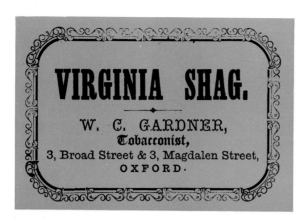

552. *c.* 1880 TOBACCO LABEL
$2\frac{1}{4}'' \times 3\frac{3}{8}''$. Anon. Oxford.
The somewhat debased border cannot certainly detract from the pleasant typefaces used here, particularly the pretty little Tuscan type used for 'W. C. GARDNER'. A different fount is used in each line.

Oxford University Press

553. *c.* 1880 TOBACCO LABEL
$1\frac{3}{4}'' \times 2\frac{5}{8}''$. Anon. London.
The boxed border here degenerates into this Gothic Revival border, which serves only as a head and tail decoration.

554. *c.* 1880 TOBACCO LABEL
$2\frac{3}{4}'' \times 2''$. Anon. Bristol.
Blackamoor's head printed in black for W. D. & H. O. Wills. This blackamoor looks more like Uncle Tom than most of the other negro heads, which were usually shown in eighteenth century costume.

Oxford University Press

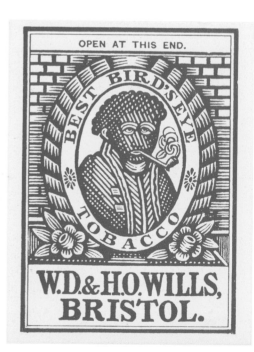

555. *c.* 1880 TOBACCO LABEL
$3\frac{1}{8}'' \times 2\frac{1}{2}''$. Anon. Bristol.
Blackamoor's head printed in red for W. M. & R. H. Webb & Co., who probably plagiarized the Wills label. The Wills trade mark was an eight-pointed star, as can be seen in Fig. 554.

556. 1893 TOBACCO LABEL
$3\frac{1}{8}'' \times 2\frac{1}{4}''$. Anon. Bristol.
Blackamoor's head printed in red for W. D. & H. O. Wills. This label continued in use until 1940.

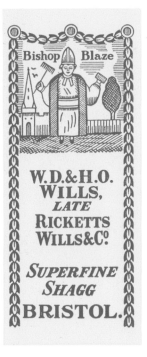

557. 1960 TOBACCO LABELS
3¼″ × 1¼″ each. Anon. Bristol.
Three blackamoor labels still in use by W. D. & H. O. Wills;
printed in red and black.

558. 1960 TOBACCO LABEL
1¼″ × 3⅜″. Anon. Bristol.
Printed in red from a line block.
Bishop Blaze was the patron saint
of the wool-combers.

Tobacco labels: letterpress

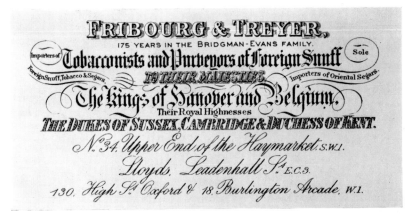

560. 1960 SNUFF LABEL
1⅞″ × 4″. Anon. London.
This handsome copper engraved label for Fribourg
& Treyer has been in use for well over a hundred
years. The shaded, decorated and gothic letters
combine most happily.

Tobacco label: copper engraved

559. 1960 TOBACCO LABEL
3¼″ × 2⅛″. Anon. Holland.
Label for chewing tobacco, printed from a wood
engraving and type in black on a yellow ground.

561. 1960 CIGARETTE PACKET
2¾″ × 3½″. Anon. Winston-Salem, North Carolina.
Printed in several colours. The lettering has a pseudo near-Eastern flavour and would appear to belong in character to the first decade of this century.

562. 1960 CIGARETTE PACKET
2¾″ × 3⅛″. Imperial Tobacco Company (of Great Britain and Ireland) Ltd, Nottingham.
Printed in several colours from a design that has been very slightly modified during the last half century. The outlined letter is based on an engraver's sans serif. This packet has at last been superseded (1962).

Cigarette packets

The packs for Camel and Chesterfield cigarettes are as well known in the U.S.A. as is the one for Players Navy Cut in Britain. The sailor's head and the two battleships H.M.S. *Hero* and H.M.S. *Britannia* were first registered as a trade mark by Players in 1891. The sailor should have had H.M.S. on his cap and three stripes on his collar – but the artist got it wrong. Registered as he drew it, it has remained unaltered ever since. As pieces of typography or design there is nothing to recommend any of these packs. Yet no doubt their ubiquitous familiarity after so many years use must endear them to a very wide smoking public.

Dr Hadank has contributed much to modern label design. These two packs (Figs. 567–8),

traditional in feeling, derive from their engraved predecessors. The superb precision of Hadank's work gives a unique quality to these designs. The yellow pack for Laurens, a Belgian cigarette, owes something to the Hadank style. It is effective, partly because the checkerboard pattern looks a little like shredded Virginia tobacco, and partly by the restraint of the typography.

The design for Wills Three Castles has been in use for many years. In spite of the feebleness of the lettering, it is a distinctive and charming package. Engravings of sailing ships and scenes of old quaysides and warehouses, like this one, seem to evoke the right atmosphere for tobacco and cigarettes.

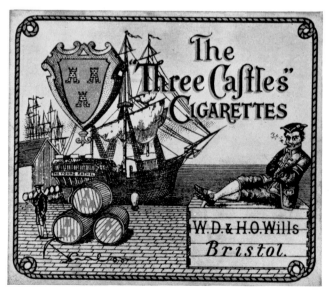

563. 1960 CIGARETTE PACKET
2¾″ × 2″. Anon. Richmond, Virginia.
Printed in several colours with the sloping title and swash tail to certain letters.

564. 1960 CIGARETTE PACKAGE
2¾″ × 3¼″. Anon. Bristol.
Printed in black and gold on a green card. The design is based on an old engraving.

565. 1937 CIGARETTE PACKET
3″ × 3¼″. Anon. London.
Printed in black, red, yellow and blue. The riverside
scene is taken from an old print of Bristol, the
traditional tobacco entry port for England. A handsome decorated Tuscan is used for the word
'Carreras' and the word 'Virginia', in a 'copperplate'
script, is in keeping with the engraved character of
this very beautiful pack.

566. 1960 CIGARETTE PACKET
3″ × 3″. Alan Ball des. London.
Printed in gold, red and black with a blind blocking
of a guardsman on the red panel. Set in Gothic 150
and Consort.

568. 1960 CIGARETTE PACKET
2¾″ × 4″. O. Hadank des. Cologne.
Printed in black, red and gold.

567. 1960 CIGARETTE PACKET
2¾″ × 2″. O. Hadank des. Baden-Baden.
Printed in green, red, yellow and gold.

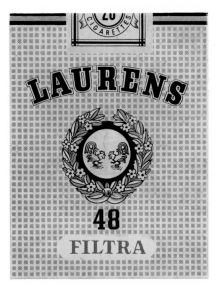

569. 1960 CIGARETTE PACKET
2¾″ × 2¼″. Laurens Studio, Brussels.
Printed in black, yellow and green, with
lettering based on an outline Egyptian.

The design for the pack for 'Carreras Guards
Filter Tipped Cigarettes' (Fig. 566) is in marked
contrast to all the previous tobacco labels,
which rely so much on evocative illustration, or
in rich and intricate decoration. There is, even
here, an illustration, blind blocked on the red
panel of a guardsman but so slight and vestigial
an illustration that the process camera missed it
altogether. Carreras have pioneered many handsome packs, none prettier than their riverside
scene on the 'Virginia' carton which appeared
in the late 1930's (Fig. 565). This pack had a very
short life. Cigarette selling has always been a
highly competitive trade, and it takes a lot to
wean smokers away from their favourite brand.
Why the Guards pack should have achieved this
in the 1960's whilst in the 1930's the Virginia
did not is a mystery. Both are splendid examples
of tobacco packaging.

570. *c.* 1775 TEA LABEL
4″ × 3½″. Anon. London.
Engraved label or wrapping paper for 'Samuel Doughty, Druggist.'

British Museum

Tea, Coffee and Grocery labels

Tea, coffee and sauces have a long tradition of fine labels and wrapping papers. The earliest wrapper shown here is the one above, for Samuel Doughty, Druggist. This fine free woodcut with its *putti* and vaguely baroque decoration would grace any tea pack today. The nineteenth century jobbing printer made excellent use of borders in many early labels. These varied from simple typographic rules to heavily decorated borders. Throughout the history of food labels and wrappers, there seems to have been a fairly well balanced use of engravings, both intaglio and relief, and type-setting. The sauce labels on pages 232 and 233 show a variety of engravings with, on the Mogul and Oyster Sauce labels, some beautifully arranged lettering.

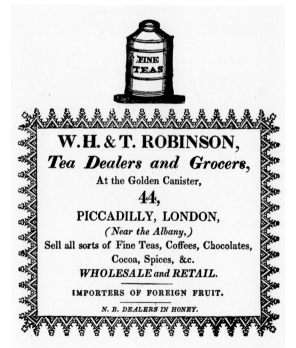

571. *c.* 1780 TEA LABEL
3⅞″ × 3½″. Anon. London.
Letterpress label set in typefaces that have a close affinity to those cut for John Baskerville.

Oxford University Press

572. 1810 TEA LABEL
4¼″ × 3⅝″. Anon. London.
Letterpress label with woodcut illustrations set within a Gothic Revival border.

Oxford University Press

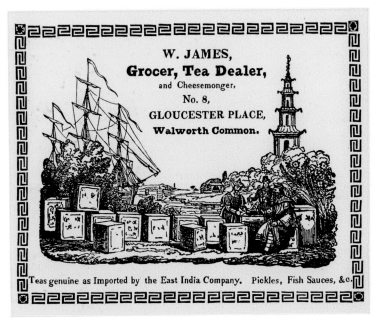

573. *c.* 1800 GROCER'S LABEL
2⅛" × 3¼". T. Bewick, Newcastle-upon-Tyne.
Wood engraved label for 'Davidson, Grocer & Tea-dealer'.

574. *c.* 1820 GROCER'S LABEL
4⅜" × 5⅝". Anon. London.
Letterpress label with wood engraving; for W. James
of Walworth Common, using a Greek key border.

Oxford University Press

Tea, Coffee and Grocery labels

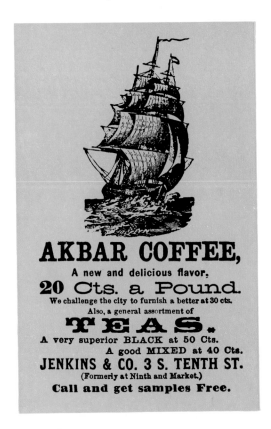

575. *c.* 1840. COFFEE LABEL
3¾" × 2¼". Anon. New York.
Printed in black and set in at least eight different
typefaces.

New-York Historical Society

576. *c.* 1839 TEA LABEL
4" × 4". Anon. London.
Wood engraved label, illustrating Temple Bar.

Oxford University Press

Sauce labels

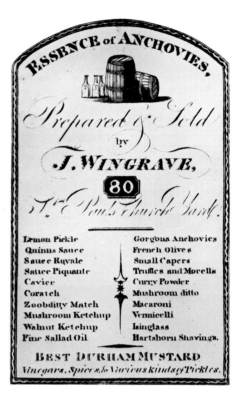

577. *c.* 1830 SAUCE LABEL
$3\frac{1}{2}'' \times 2\frac{1}{2}''$. Anon. London.
Engraved label showing a variety of shadow letters.

Oxford University Press

578. *c.* 1840 SAUCE LABEL
$3\frac{3}{8}'' \times 2\frac{1}{2}''$. Anon.
Engraved label.

Oxford University Press

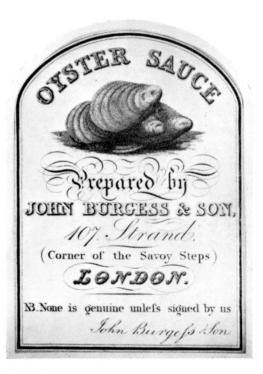

579. *c.* 1845 ESSENCE OF ANCHOVIES LABEL
$3\frac{3}{4}'' \times 2\frac{1}{4}''$. Anon. London.
Engraved label, printed in black.

Oxford University Press

580. *c.* 1830 SAUCE LABEL
$3\frac{3}{8}'' \times 2\frac{1}{2}''$. Anon. London.
Engraved label; the words 'Oyster Sauce' are in a letter very like the typeface Etruria which Stephenson Blake issued some thirty years later.

Oxford University Press

581. *c.* 1845 SAUCE LABEL
$3\frac{7}{8}'' \times 6\frac{3}{4}''$. Anon. London.
Engraved label on blue paper.

Oxford University Press

Sauce labels

The 'Piccalili' label in Fig. 582 is a simple, satisfying arrangement of type and engraving, not very well printed, on a brown paper. The Soho sauce label next to it is copper engraved, to which has been added the rather crude wood-cut words at the top and bottom. The intricate Royal Victoria label (Fig. 581) must surely be the culmination of the Bickham school of engravers, but made so much richer by the use of open and decorated capital letters. As the nineteenth century progressed, the letterforms deteriorated (see Figs. 590–3), but often, in spite of this the labels remained effective by their arrangement and colour.

582. *c.* 1820 SAUCE LABEL
$3\frac{5}{8}'' \times 2\frac{3}{4}''$. Anon. London.
Wood engraved label printed on brown paper with royal coat of arms.

Oxford University Press

583. *c.* 1820 SAUCE LABEL
$4\frac{1}{2}'' \times 3\frac{1}{2}''$. Anon. London.
Engraved label which is a combination of copper engraving for the centre panel and woodcuts for the top and bottom.

Oxford University Press

Grocers' labels

584. *c.* 1840 TEA AND COFFEE LABEL
3¼″ × 4½″. Anon. London.
Letterpress label with wood engraving. 'TEA' and
'COFFEE' set in Thorowgood's Fat Face.

Oxford University Press

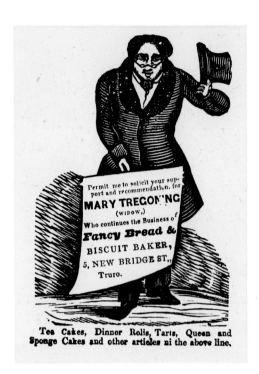

Permit me to solicit your sup-
port and recommendation, for
MARY TREGONING
(WIDOW,)
Who continues the Business of
Fancy Bread &
BISCUIT BAKER,
5, NEW BRIDGE ST.,
Truro.

Tea Cakes, Dinner Rolls, Tarts, Queen and
Sponge Cakes and other articles ni the above line.

Permit me to solicit your sup-
port and recommendation, for
MARY TREGONING
(WIDOW,)
Who continues the business of
FANCY BREAD &
BISCUIT BAKER,
5, NEW BRIDGE ST.,
TRURO.

Tea Cakes, Dinner Rolls, Tarts, Queen and
Sponge Cakes and other articles in the above
line.

585. *c.* 1840 BAKER'S LABELS
4″ × 2¾″ each. Anon. Truro, Cornwall.
Two labels with engraved figures holding typeset
banners.

Oxford University Press

FIELD & Co.

TEA DEALERS,

☞ No. 9,

WALWORTH ROAD,

Nearly Opposite the Elephant and Castle.

586. *c.* 1840 TEA LABEL
4½″ × 6¼″. Anon. Walworth.
Letterpress label, set in Thorowgood's Fat Face and
Antique (Egyptian) and sans serif.

Oxford University Press

587. 1857 GROCER'S BAG
7" × 6". S. D. & S. London.
Letterpress printed with elaborate wood engraving.
The open Tuscan used for 'P. H. Benn' comes from
Caslon, who first showed it in this year.

Oxford University Press

Grocers' bags

Grocers' bags and labels

Early paper bags were often decorated with
the most elaborate woodcuts with such illustrations as 'Tea Gardens and Temples, Shanghai'
on P. H. Benn's bag, or the portrait of the
Tichborne Claimant in Fig. 596. The final de-
basement of grocers' labels can be seen in Fig.
601 with a lithographed label whose typographic
ineptitude is only exceeded by its hideousness
of colour. In contrast, Derek Barson makes
effective use of a white line engraving technique
for Batger's 'Chinese Figs' (Fig. 604).

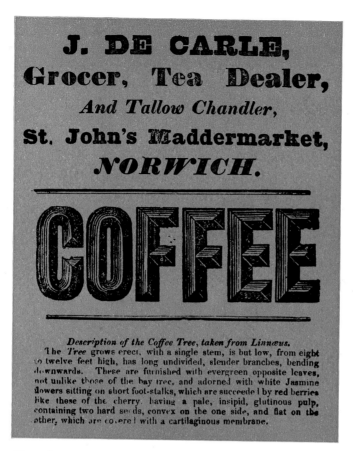

588. *c.* 1840 GROCER'S LABEL
$5\frac{1}{2}'' \times 4\frac{1}{4}''$. Anon. Norwich.
Letterpress label with word 'COFFEE' set in Stephenson
Blake's '10-line Sans Serifs Ornamented'.

Oxford University Press

589. *c.* 1840 SAUCE LABEL
$3\frac{1}{2}'' \times 2\frac{7}{8}''$. Anon. Reading.
Engraved label, printed in black on burnt orange
coloured paper.

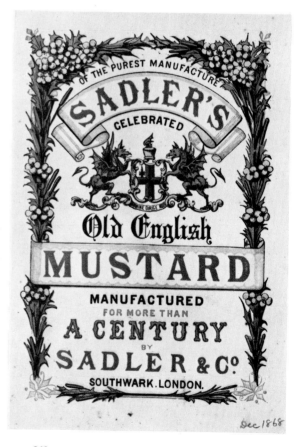

590. *c.* 1860 SAUCE LABEL
$4'' \times 2\frac{3}{4}''$. Anon. Worcester.
Letterpress printed in black on white paper.

Oxford University Press

591. 1868 MUSTARD LABEL
$6\frac{1}{4}'' \times 4\frac{1}{4}''$. Anon. London.
Lithographed in several colours and dated by hand.

Oxford University Press

592. 1878 SAUCE LABEL
4″ × 3½″. Anon. Maidstone.
Lithographed in several colours and showing a
fourpenny bit of 1878.

Oxford University Press

593. *c.* 1890 PICKLED ONION LABEL
4⅛″ × 2¾″. Anon. London.
Lithographed in dark blue, from a transfer engraving.

Oxford University Press

594. 1894 SAUCE LABEL
3½″ × 3½″. Anon. Worcester.
Engraved label, printed in black on burnt orange-
coloured paper.

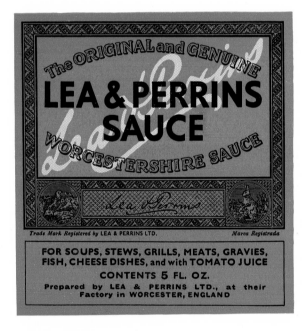

595. 1960 SAUCE LABEL
3¼″ × 3¼″. Anon. Worcester.
Lithographed label, printed in black and burnt
orange.

Grocery and Sauce labels

The continuity in design of sauce labels is shown admirably by the Lea and Perrins 'Worcestershire Sauce' label. Designed originally in 1840, it has been only slightly modified through the years, but still retains the same characteristics and style of lettering. These two labels for what must be the most famous sauce in the English speaking world, certainly show a marked continuity. Worcestershire sauce was first made in 1820 and Lea and Perrins still have, hanging in their board-room, the rather mutilated label used in 1840. In all these labels the border is made up of a repeat pattern of the names Lea and Perrins.

PORTRAIT OF ROGER CHARLES DOUGHTY TICHBORNE.

HE Portrait we give above represents the real MR. ROGER TICHBORNE, as he appeared eighteen years ago, previous to leaving England for a wild and wandering life abroad. He was born on the 5th of January, 1829; attended no regular school until 1845, when he was sent to the Roman Catholic Seminary, at Stonyhurst. Some time after that he was admitted into the army; and in October, 1849, joined the Carbineers, stationed at Portobello, in Dublin. In 1850, he paid a visit to Tichborne, and there formed an acquaintance with his cousin, Miss Kate Doughty. An attachment sprang up between the young couple, but the intercourse being objected to by the father of the young lady, Roger left the house, did not enter it again. In consequence of this, it is said and not being happy at home, he made a will and sold out of the army. After doing so, he went to Paris, and from thence to Havre; and in March, 1853, he embarked on board a sailing vessel called the "Pauline," bound for Valparaiso. After leading a questionable life in South America, this eccentric heir to vast estates ultimately found his way to Rio de Janeiro, and sailed in April, 1854, from thence in the "Bella," for New York. Shortly afterwards the news arrived in England that the vessel and all hands were lost.

FROM

WILLIAM WRIGHT,

GROCER, TEA AND PROVISION DEALER,

CORN & CHEESE FACTOR,

King Street, KNUTSFORD.

Dealer in Home-cured Hams and Bacon.
Flour according to Market Prices.

Fred. Jones, Printer and Grocers' Factor, 4, Temple Lane, Liverpool.

596. 1871 GROCER'S BAG
8″ × 6½″. F. Jones, Liverpool.
Letterpress printed bag, with engraving of Roger Tichborne, and a variety of decorative display typefaces, including a shadow rustic (or twig letter) for 'CORN AND CHEESE FACTOR'. The outline Tuscan used for 'William Wright' comes from the Caslon Foundry.

Oxford University Press

Grocers' bags and labels

597. *c.* 1880 GROCER'S BAG
6″ × 5¾″. W. S. Cowell Ltd, Ipswich.
Engraved design printed by offset in black and still
in use in 1960.

598. *c.* 1900 RENNET LABEL
3″ × 3½″. Anon. London.
Printed by offset in black on green paper.

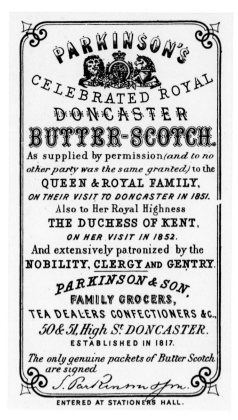

599. *c.* 1905 PICKLE LABEL
$4\frac{1}{4}'' \times 2\frac{5}{8}''$. Anon. London.
Lithographed in red and black.

Oxford University Press

600. *c.* 1910 BUTTERSCOTCH LABEL
$4'' \times 2\frac{1}{8}''$. Anon. Doncaster.
Lithographed label printed in black in the tradition of engraved labels but using drawn letters which are based on typeforms. Still in use today.

Grocers' labels

601. *c.* 1910 SUGAR LABEL
$7\frac{1}{8}'' \times 13\frac{1}{2}''$. W. S. Cowell Ltd, Ipswich.
Lithographed label, printed in red and blue with drawn lettering. This label was still in use after the last war. It shows every defect of the worst period of chromo-lithography.

602. 1948 COFFEE LABEL
$3\frac{3}{4}'' \times 10''$. John Brinkley des. W. S. Cowell Ltd,
Ipswich.
Printed by letterpress in black on a second colour.
This was one of a series of labels with the same
design, printed in different colours. The lettering is
hand drawn.

603. c. 1954 TEA LABEL
$2'' \times 7\frac{3}{4}''$. E. Hughes des. London.
Printed by letterpress in black on yellow paper.

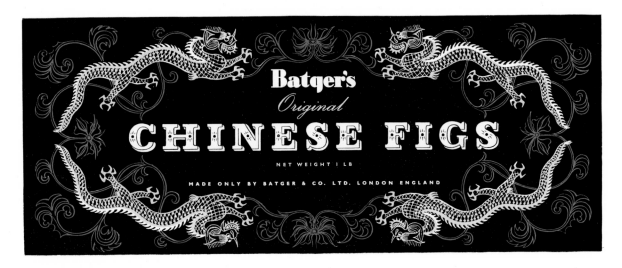

604. c. 1957. CHINESE FIG BOX
$3\frac{3}{4}'' \times 9\frac{1}{4}''$. Derek Barson and R. W. Talmadge des.
E. S. & A. Robinson, Bristol.
Printed by offset in black, red and yellow. The
lettering is hand drawn.

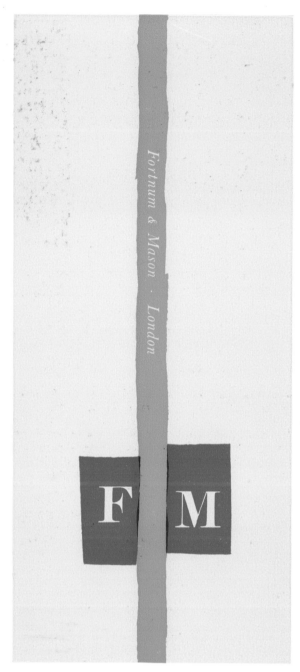

605. 1960 GROCER'S BAG
$13\frac{1}{2}'' \times 3\frac{1}{2}''$. Ruth Gill des. London.
Printed in green and red for Fortnum and Mason, from Baskerville and a modern type in reverse.

606. 1955 SUGAR CARTON
$4\frac{1}{8}'' \times 3\frac{5}{8}''$. Milner Gray des. London.
Letterpress pack printed in blue and gold from a drawn design.

Grocers' labels

Fortnum and Mason's famous establishment in Piccadilly has a pleasant range of bags and wrapping papers, which make use of the simplest typographic means. Milner Gray's blue and gold packet for Tate and Lyle sugar likewise extracts the maximum richness from a two-colour printing.

The last label in this section is from a $2\frac{1}{2}$-in. high spice jar, and is typographically as successful as any shown here. The band of green on which the word 'Dill' appears, combined with decorative engraved initial letters 'C' and 'H', which are based on printers' flowers, gives great richness to this little label. Its success is clearly due to the fact that the designer conceived this label, which is one of a series, purely in typographic terms.

607. 1960 SPICE LABEL
$1\frac{7}{8}'' \times 2\frac{1}{2}''$. Ashley Havinden des. Shenval Press, Hertford.
Printed in black and red grotesque typefaces. The initials 'C' and 'H' are based on printers' flowers.

608. *c.* 1840 STOUT LABEL
1¾″ dia. Anon. London.
Printed in black from relief engraved
letters.

Oxford University Press

609. *c.* 1860 BEER LABEL
2⅛″ dia. S. H. Cowell, Ipswich.
Roundel printed in black by letterpress, from
relief engraved letters.

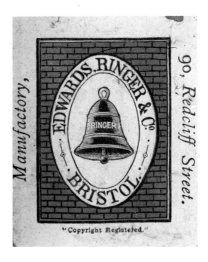

610. *c.* 1900 BEER LABEL
2½″ × 2⅜″. Anon. Bristol.
Oval printed by lithography in black and red.

Beers, Wines and Spirit labels

The labels for alcoholic drinks seem to reflect in
their design something of the markets for which
they were intended.

The main traditions in the design of wine and
spirit labels seem to be divided between the
engraved and typographic techniques but with a
strong bias in favour of the engraver. The
precise engraved effects of Dr Hadank's Hock
labels evoke the work of the engine-turned
engraving.

Soft-drink labels tend to follow the style of
beer labels. The 'Vals' label (Fig. 619) makes
good use of heavy shadow sans serif and Egyptian
letters.

Beer labels are firmly typographic in origin
and roundels and ovals seem to have been used
for a very long time. In the Courage labels
(Fig. 614) the designer has solved the problem of
combining two labels in one most ingeniously.

He has surrounded the I.P.A. label with a flat
black printing on which he has placed an oval
printed in red to indicate the shoulder label. The
rather less sophisticated Star Brewery labels on
the same page have the shoulder label incorporated in the actual design of the main label.
Illustrations appear on beer labels, either in the
form of a house sign, such as the Courage cock,
or as actual illustrations which have some
connection with different kinds of bottled beer.
For instance in the Star Brewery labels (Fig.
614), the reason for the three-masted sailing ship
on the India Pale Ale label is not just for
decoration but because, originally, India Pale
Ale was a beer strong enough to stand up to a
voyage to the East Indies. The ship on this
label is an East Indiaman. The reason for the
race horse on the Brown Ale label is lost in decent
obscurity.

611. *c.* 1890 CYDER LABEL
2⅓″ dia. Anon. Totnes, Devon.
Oval, printed by lithography in black, red
and blue.

612. *c.* 1890. BEER LABEL
3¼″ × 2½″. Anon. London.
Oval printed in black and red on yellow paper.

Oxford University Press

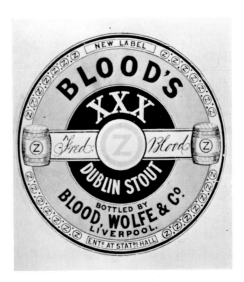

613. *c.* 1890 STOUT LABEL
3⅜″ dia. Anon. Liverpool.
Roundel printed in black and red.

Oxford University Press

Beer and Stout labels

614. 1956 BEER AND STOUT LABELS (*at the top*)
2″ wide approx. Milner Gray des. London.
Three labels for Courage, with an incorporated
shoulder label in the I.P.A. label, and a separate
shoulder label for Guinness, printed in two and three
colours by offset. The lettering is hand drawn.

1958 BEER LABELS (*at the bottom*)
2″ wide. John Lewis des. Woodbridge.
Three labels from a series for the Star Brewery,
Eastbourne, each printed by offset in black and one
colour, letters drawn by hand, based on a fat Egyptian.
A different illustration appeared on each label.

615. *c.* 1950 BEER LABEL
$2\frac{3}{4}'' \times 2\frac{1}{8}''$. Anon. London.
Label printed in three colours by offset.

616. *c.* 1950 BEER LABEL
$2\frac{3}{4}'' \times 2\frac{3}{4}''$. Anon. London.
Label printed in three colours by offset.

Beers and Soft Drink labels

617. *c.* 1900 SOFT DRINK LABEL
$2\frac{1}{4}'' \times 3\frac{3}{4}''$. Anon. Dresden.
Lithographed in mauve and gold, blue and buff.

Oxford University Press

618. *c.* 1950 BEER LABEL
$3\frac{1}{4}'' \times 4\frac{1}{2}''$. Anon. Newark N.J.
The value of condensed typefaces and an oval border
gives dignity even to so simple a label as this. Printed
by offset.

Bella C. Landauer Collection, New-York Historical Society

619. 1936 MINERAL WATER LABEL
$2\frac{1}{2}'' \times 4''$. Allier, Grenoble.
Printed in black and pale blue, using a heavy
Egyptian for 'Vals Saint-Jean' and a shadow
Egyptian and shadow sans serif for the blue printing.

U

621. *c.* 1890 RUM LABEL
2⅛″ × 3⅞″. Anon. England.
Printed in black by lithography. This simple design
is based on a silver decanter label.

Oxford University Press

620. *c.* WHISKY LABEL
7⅞″ × 2½″. T. Bewick, Newcastle-upon-
Tyne.
'Blank' whisky label, taken from a block
found in Bewick's effects.

622. *c.* 1880 GIN LABEL
1½″ × 4¾″. Anon. England.
Printed by lithography in gold.

Oxford University Press

623. *c.* 1880 WHISKY LABEL
5¼″ × 3¼″. Anon. London.
Engraved and printed in black by lithography.

Oxford University Press

624. *c.* 1890 RUM LABEL
4⅞″ × 3½″. Anon. London.
Printed by lithography in several colours.

Oxford University Press

625. *c*. 1900 GIN LABEL
4″ × 3″. Anon. London.
Printed in gold and black by letterpress.

626. *c*. 1900 GIN LABEL
5¼″ × 3¼″. Sir Joseph Causton and Sons, London.
Printed by lithography in seven colours.

627. 1961 GIN LABEL
4½″ × 3½″. Anon. London.
Printed by offset in black on white. This label with
but slight modifications has been in use for over
fifty years and is based on the original hand-written
labels.

Spirit labels

Spirit labels vary greatly. Rums tend to a pictorial treatment; gins, whiskies and brandies to simple lettered labels.

The origin of the Gordon's Dry Gin label is interesting. The copperplate label, shown in Fig. 627, was introduced about fifty years ago. Up to that time proprietary gins were practically non-existent, as this spirit was sold in bulk through bars and retail bottle departments. This particular dry gin label came into use because Tanqueray Gordon and Co. Ltd produced this gin for certain exclusive customers and first of all labelled their bottles with hand-written labels. When the demand increased, the hand-written labels were replaced by the nearest thing to the clerkly hand in which they were written, the copper engraved 'English hand' which is in use today. The term Dry Gin means a complete absence of sweetening matter, whereas 'Old Tom' (Fig. 625) is the traditional name for a sweetened gin. This name came into use in the early years of the eighteenth century, when gin was dispensed by inserting a penny into an effigy of a cat, which then poured out the quantity purchased.

628. *c.* 1880 LIQUOR LABEL
2″ × 3¼″. Mackellar, Smiths & Jordan Co.,
Philadelphia.
Wood engraved stock block from the Sanson Street
Typefoundry, Philadelphia, with type inset.

629. 1947 RUM LABEL
1¾″ × 2¼″. Reynolds Stone sc. Curwen Press,
London.
Wood engraved label printed in one colour.

Spirit labels

630. *c.* 1895 CRÊME DE CACAO LABEL
2⅞″ × 4″. Anon. London.
Printed by letterpress in pink and black.

Oxford University Press

631. 1947 RUM LABEL
2½″ dia. Reynolds Stone sc. Curwen Press, London.
Wood engraved and printed in one colour.

632. *c.* 1930 TOKAY LABEL
3⅜″ × 4¾″. Anon. London.
Printed by letterpress in black and two colours.

633. *c.* 1890 RUM LABEL
2⅛″ × 3⅞″. S. H. Cowell, England.
Printed in black by lithography.

634. 1948 RUM LABEL
3½″ × 2¾″. Lewis and Brinkley des. W. S. Cowell
Ltd, Ipswich.
Printed by letterpress in black and mushroom colour
from drawn lettering.

Wines, spirits and printing made a particularly felicitous combination, which in this case dated back to 1818, when the seventeen year old Samuel Harrison Cowell was launched by his father on his career as a printer, tea, coffee and spice warehouseman and wine and spirit merchant. Though Figs. 634–6 were not typeset but drawn, the intention of the designers was towards a typographic or formal engraved solution in reaction against the kind of coloured picture label that had been in general use since the beginning of the century.

These two labels for rum and the Irish whiskey and the cognac labels below are for the same firm of wine merchants, who happened to be a part of the company that printed them.

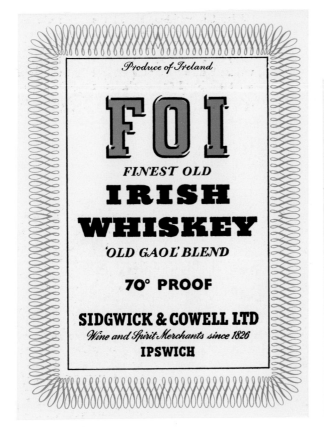

635. 1949 WHISKY LABEL
4⅝″ × 3¾″. John Brinkley des. W. S. Cowell Ltd,
Ipswich.
Printed by letterpress in black and yellow from
drawn lettering.

636. 1948 BRANDY LABEL
4½″ × 3¾″. Lewis and Brinkley des. W. S. Cowell
Ltd, Ipswich.
Printed by offset in black and red with lettering based
on engraved characters.

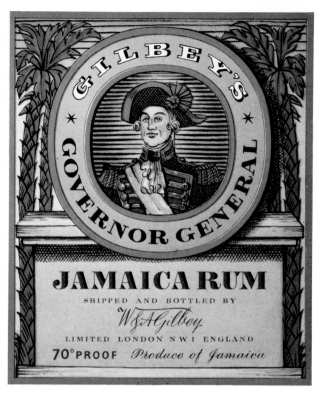

637. *c.* 1955 RUM LABEL
5″ × 4¼″. Milner Gray des. London.
Printed by offset in four colours. The letterforms, though drawn, are based on early nineteenth century typefaces.

638. *c.* 1955 RUM LABEL
5″ × 4¼″. Milner Gray des. London.
Printed by offset in four colours.

Spirit labels

The two Gilbey's rum labels revert to the pictorial tradition of the chromo-lithographer but the designer has formalized the designs, and has contained his picture in the ever effective oval frame, just as Ketcherell did for his Virginia tobacco label in 1675 (Fig. 529).

The 'Vat 69' label is undated, for all the documents relating to its origin have been lost in a flood. This Scotch Whisky is so named because at a whisky tasting, at Leith, over half a century ago, various blends were sampled and the one from a vat numbered 69 was chosen as

the best of those tasted. In view of this, the use of white stencilled letters for 'Vat 69' on this whisky label would seem to be singularly appropriate, and placed on a handsome, red-sealed Benedictine-shaped bottle, it looks very effective.

The Schenley label, designed by Paul Rand, makes an interesting use of the arbitrary arrangement of its typographic elements, yet the label is saved from too austere a look by the use of the marbled paper for the background. It is sad that an artist of this calibre has so rarely been used for problems of this kind.

639. 1961 GIN LABEL
5″ × 5″ approx. Paul Rand des. Lawrenceberg, Indiana.
Printed in five colours by offset, from typographic units placed on a background of marbled paper.

Bella C. Landauer Collection, New-York Historical Society

640. 1961. WHISKY LABEL
3½″ × 5″. Anon. Leith, Scotland.
Printed in black and gold. 'VAT 69' is most appropriately based on stencil letters. This label has been in use for some years.

Wine labels

641. *c.* 1870 LABEL FOR SAMPLE BOTTLE
2⅜″ × 5″. Anon. London.
Printed in blue and brown, lithographed from an
engraved design.
Oxford University Press

642. 1961 WINE LABEL
5½″ × 5″ approx. Anon. California.
The label is set in a combination of bold Egyptians
and script types.
Bella C. Landauer Collection, New-York Historical Society

643. *c.* 1900 MONTRACHET LABEL
3″ × 4½″. Anon. England.
Printed in mauve, green and black.
Oxford University Press

644. *c.* 1900 WINE LABEL
2½″ × 4½″. Anon. Germany.
Lithographed in full colour.
Oxford University Press

Wine labels are of fairly recent origin, as until
towards the end of the nineteenth century few
bottled wines had printed labels, though no
doubt some wine merchants from as early as the
eighteenth century had their own engraved
labels. The term 'Wine Label' is usually given
to the silver labels that were hung from the
necks of decanters, and had engraved on them
the words Claret, Port, Sherry, etc.

French château-bottled wines usually show
on their printed label an engraving of the
château. German estate-bottled wines have
labels of more typographic and design interest
and show a coat of arms or a view of a vineyard
and usually free use is made of black letter. And
there is no doubt that a rich black letter is a
much more decorative thing than a roman letter.

645. *c.* 1920 MADEIRA LABEL
$1\frac{3}{4}'' \times 3\frac{1}{4}''$. Anon. London.
Wood engraved label.

646. *c.* 1950 SHERRY LABEL
$5\frac{1}{8}'' \times 3\frac{1}{2}''$. Reynolds Stone sc. Curwen Press, London.
Project for sherry labels engraved on the wood and printed in one colour.

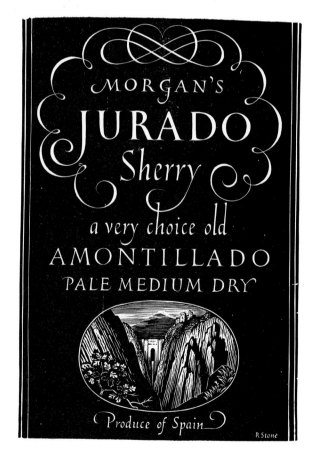

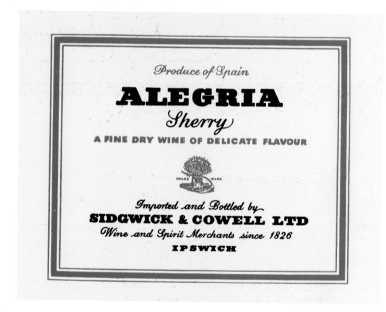

648. 1949 SHERRY LABEL
$3'' \times 3\frac{3}{4}''$. Lewis and Brinkley des. W. S. Cowell Ltd, Ipswich.
Label printed by letterpress in black and brown from drawn lettering.

647. *c.* 1950 SHERRY LABEL
$5\frac{1}{8}'' \times 3\frac{1}{2}''$. Reynolds Stone sc. Curwen Press, London.
Project for sherry labels engraved on the wood and printed in one colour.

649. *c.* 1900 WINE LABEL
3″ × 4½″. Anon. France.
Lithographed in gold, mauve and black.
Oxford University Press

Wine labels

650. *c.* 1955. PORT LABEL
4½″ × 4½″. Milner Gray des. London.
Printed by letterpress in black and gold.

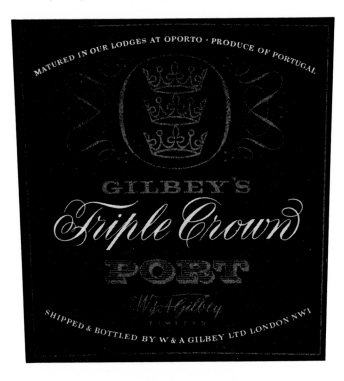

651. *c.* 1955 PORT LABEL
4½″ × 4½″. Milner Gray des. London.
Printed by letterpress in black and two colours.
'Fine Old Tawny' is embossed.

652. 1961 WINE LABEL
5″ × 4½″ approx. Anon. New York.
Label lithographed, and using a variety of nineteenth century open and decorated letterforms. The word 'Mourestel' is in a shadow Tuscan.

Bella C. Landauer Collection, New-York Historical Society

The two labels for Morgan's sherry were both engraved by Reynolds Stone, sc., R.D.I. The superb precision of this artist's work and his ability to handle letterforms with effortless skill would seem to make him an obvious choice for labels that call for dignity and clarity, and white line engraving would seem to have a quality that is ideally suited for packaging. These handsome labels were, I believe, never actually used, which must show a very blind spot somewhere in the wine trade.

This short section of wine labels is limited mainly to those printed in England or America, though there are a few exceptions. The Langenbach labels (Figs. 655, 657, 659 and 660) by O. Hadank are shown here for their superb precision. The Gilbey labels are of interest, as they are designed to reach a wide and perhaps previously non-wine-drinking public.

653. *c.* 1920 WINE LABEL
$3\frac{1}{2}'' \times 4\frac{7}{8}''$. Anon. London.
Printed by lithography in five colours, with the name
of the wine overprinted by letterpress.

654. *c.* 1925 WINE LABEL
$3\frac{5}{8}'' \times 5''$. Anon. London.
Printed by lithography in three colours.

655. 1952 WINE LABEL
$2\frac{3}{8}''$ wide. O. Hadank des. Germany.
Shoulder label printed in offset in gold, black and
pink.

656. *c.* 1945 WINE LABEL
$3\frac{3}{8}'' \times 4\frac{1}{4}''$. Anon. London.
Printed in black and two colours.

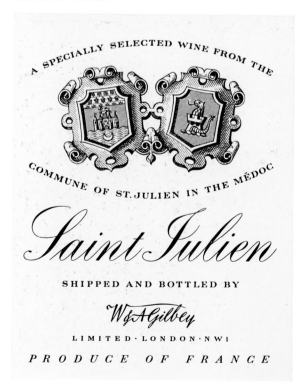

657. 1952 WINE LABEL
$4\frac{1}{2}''$ wide. O. Hadank des. Germany.
Printed by offset in gold, red and black.

658. 1955 WINE LABEL
$4\frac{1}{4}'' \times 3\frac{1}{4}''$. Milner Gray des. London
Printed in black offset on white paper.

659. 1952 WINE LABEL
4½″ wide. O. Hadank des. Germany.
Printed in gold and black.

660. 1952 WINE LABEL
3″ × 4½″. O. Hadank des. Germany.
Printed by offset in gold, brown and green.

Wine labels

661. 1957 WINE LABELS
1⅜″ high. Milner Gray des. London.
Two shoulder labels printed in black and red and
black and yellow.

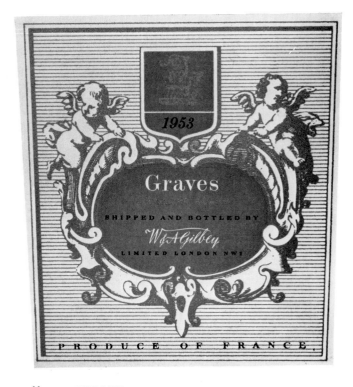

662. c. 1955 WINE LABEL
4½″ × 4½″. Milner Gray des. London.
Printed by letterpress in black and two colours.

663. 1955 WINE LABEL
3½″ high. Milner Gray des. London.
One of a series of labels using a baroque cartouche,
printed in gold, green and black.

664. *c.* 1800 CHEMIST'S LABELS
s/s T. Bewick, Newcastle-upon-Tyne.
Wood engraved labels from Bewick's workshop.

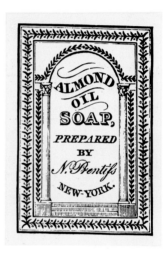

Pharmaceutical and Perfumery labels

Fine perfumes and scented soaps would seem to call for dainty wrappings and pretty labels. In the early years of the nineteenth century, the engravers were widely employed producing delicate little examples of their art for perfumers and soap manufacturers and hairdressers. Thomas Bewick and his associates engraved a number of blocks for chemists, as did his American follower Alexander Anderson (Figs. 677 and 679). Roundels were common, for so many pomades and medicines were made up in little round jars or pill boxes.

Late nineteenth century labels tended to be rather less attractive though Peter Maverick's lithographed label for Palm Soap has a certain charm, with its two simpering Misses in their splendid hats. Patent medicines have always tended to cram their typesetting to bursting point, and 'The Green Mountain Vegetable Ointment' is no exception to this, though the printer has filled the area within his Greek key border with some skill.

665. *c.* 1800 MEDICINE LABELS
s/s T. Bewick, Newcastle-upon-Tyne.
Wood engraved labels.

666. *c.* 1830 SOAP LABEL
$2\frac{1}{8}'' \times 1\frac{1}{2}''$. Anon. New York.
Copper engraved label printed in black and set within a copy of a typefounder's border.

New York Public Library

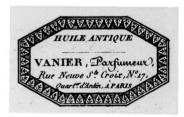

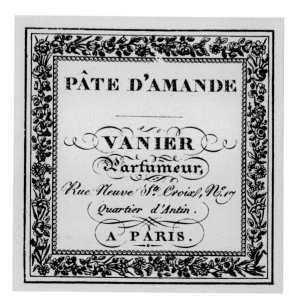

667. *c.* 1830 PERFUMER'S LABELS
$2\frac{5}{8}''$ wide (largest). Anon. Paris.
Group of four engraved labels making use of decorative borders.

Oxford University Press

668. *c.* 1830 CHEMIST'S LABEL
$2\frac{1}{8}'' \times 1\frac{3}{4}''$. Anon. Philadelphia.
Engraved 'blank' for an American pharmacist.
Oxford University Press

669. *c.* 1830 HAIRDRESSER'S LABEL
$1\frac{3}{4}''$ dia. Anon. England.
Engraved label.
Oxford University Press

670. *c.* 1820 PERFUME LABEL
$2\frac{1}{4}'' \times 1\frac{1}{2}''$. Anon. Derby.
Engraved label.
Oxford University Press

671. *c.* 1860 SOAP LABEL
$2\frac{1}{2}'' \times 1\frac{3}{4}''$. Anon. London.
Engraved label printed in black on green paper.
Oxford University Press

672. *c.* 1840 PERFUME LABEL
$2\frac{7}{8}'' \times 2\frac{1}{8}''$. Anon. Gloucester.
Letterpress label printed from type and ornaments.
Oxford University Press

673. *c.* 1860 CHEMIST'S LABEL
$2\frac{1}{2}''$ dia. Anon. Bishop's Stortford.
Letterpress label printed from type.
Oxford University Press

674. *c.* 1880 HAIRDRESSER'S LABEL
$2\frac{1}{2}''$ dia. Anon. Worcester.
Engraved label, with a repeat border
pattern struck from counter punches.
Oxford University Press

675. *c.* 1870. SOAP LABEL
4″ × 5½″. Peter Maverick lith. New York.
Lithographed label.

Bella C. Landauer Collection, New-York Historical Society

676. *c.* 1880 HAIRDRESSER'S LABEL
3⅛″ × 3¼″. Anon. London.
Engraved label, incorporating the signature of the
manufacturer.

Oxford University Press

677. *c.* 1850 DENTIFRICE LABEL
2″ × 2″. Alexander Anderson, New York.
Roundel and lettering engraved on wood.

New York Public Library

Pharmaceutical and Perfumery labels

The dire effects on ephemeral printing of the
chromo-lithographer, forerunner of the commercial artist, can be seen only too clearly in
the two corn-cure labels, one British, one
American (Figs. 682–3). There is little to choose
between them, for they are equally repellant.

The Jeyes labels (Figs. 684–5) date from the
1890's and are still in use. The labels shown on
page 262 are all relatively modern. The John
Evelyn label was one of a series of herbal labels,
printed in different colours. Herbal concoctions
were traditionally sold in a strawboard carton
with a typographic wrapper of archaic crudity.
This series of packs maintained a decent feeling
for tradition, yet they were thoroughly appetising
in appearance.

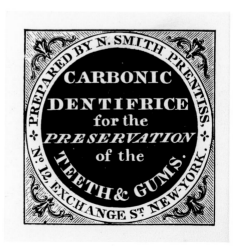

THE GREEN MOUNTAIN
VEGETABLE
OINTMENT,

IS A POSITIVE REMEDY FOR

AGUE IN FACE, SWELLED BREASTS,

SORE NIPPLES, BRONCHITIS, SORE THROATS, QUINSY, CROUP,

Felons, Ring-worms, Burns,

SCALDS, BURNS, SHINGLES, ERYSIPELAS, SALT RHEUM,

PILES,

INFLAMMATION OF THE EYES AND BOWELS, BRUISES,

Fresh Cut Wounds, Bilious Cholic, Scrofulous and

MILK-LEG SORES, INFLAMMATORY RHEUMATISM & GOUT.

No other **OINTMENT** in existence of equal power and
mildness for subduing inflammation and pain. Its
soothing influence is realised at once, and in most
instances permanent cures are effected. { See Circulars for Directions.

———————

PRINCIPAL DEPOT, NO. 38 COURTLANDT ST., NEW YORK.

ARMSTRONG & HURD, Proprietors.

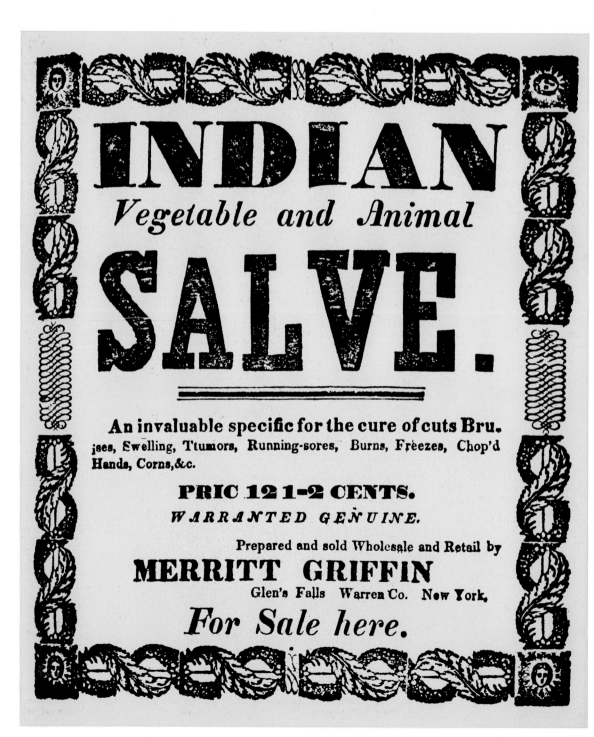

682. *c.* 1890 CORN CURE LABEL
$3\frac{3}{4}'' \times 2\frac{3}{8}''$. Mayer, Merkel & Ottman lith. New York.
Lithographed in four colours.

683. 1892 CORN CURE LABEL
$4\frac{1}{2}'' \times 2\frac{1}{2}''$. Anon. London.
Lithographed in four colours.

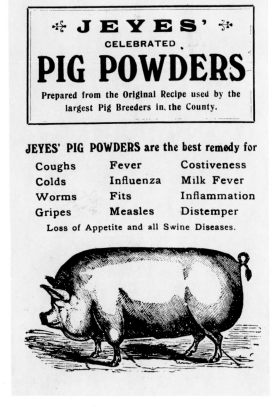

684. 1959 VETERINARY LABELS
$4'' \times 3''$. Anon. Northampton.
Printed by letterpress and set in a style of the 1890's.

685. 1959 VETERINARY LABEL
$4'' \times 3''$ Anon. Northampton.
Printed by letterpress from a singularly debased set
of typefaces.

686. 1950 CHEMIST'S CARTON
1¾″ × 5⅜″. Albert E. Smith des. London.
Printed by letterpress in orange and black, this was one of a series of cartons using the same design but printed in thirty different colour schemes.

Pharmaceutica and Perfumery labels

The wrapper for Pears Transparent Soap, the soap immortalized in the history of advertising by the use of Sir John Millais's painting 'Bubbles', is artlessly effective. Lastly the simplicity of the 'Draught for Cow,' which must have been in use for many years and the Chanel Gardenia label (which follow a house style of typography established in 1923) show how effective plain typographic statements can be.

687. 1960 VETERINARY LABEL
2″ × 3″. W. S. Cowell Ltd, Ipswich.
Letterpress label set in Grotesque No. 9 and Engravers Roman.

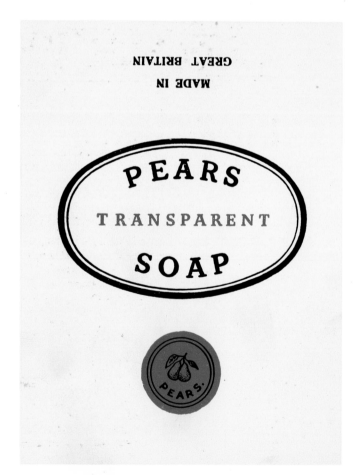

688. 1960 SOAP WRAPPER
3¾″ × 2¾″. Anon. London.
Printed in black and red, this artless wrapper makes effective use of the simplest typographic means.

689. 1961 SOAP PACK
3⅜″ × 2⅛″. Anon. Paris.
Printed in black on white board, from sans serif type and rules. This basic design has been in use since 1923.

690. *c.* 1700 PIN WRAPPER
$5\frac{1}{2}'' \times 3\frac{1}{2}''$. Anon. London.
Engraved wrapper printed from the wood block.
British Museum

691. *c.* 1820 PIN WRAPPER
$5\frac{3}{4}'' \times 2\frac{1}{4}''$. Anon. London.
Engraved wrapper probably transferred to the stone and printed by lithography. The Royal Arms include those of Hanover, which were abandoned at the accession of Queen Victoria.
Oxford University Press

Hardware labels

This survey of label and wrapping papers finishes with a number of what – for want of a better term – I call 'Hardware' labels. They range from pin packets and watch papers to labels for ice axes and ink powder. They all show a sturdy belief in traditional forms. Things obviously do not change very quickly in the pin and ice axe market. The first and last labels in this section, the pin packets shown here and the sailmakers' needle packets on page 272 are two and a half centuries apart, but they have much in common, including a belief in the mercantile value of coats of arms, and in the use of borders. The nice arabesque border of the 1700 pin wrapper becomes somewhat meaningless in the 1820 pin packet, but the latter is still a pleasant thing.

A point of interest is that all the labels in this section are engraved on wood, copper or steel, or drawn on lithographic stones. The only ones that have any typesetting are the 'Razors' label in Fig. 704 and the printers' stock stereo in Fig. 708.

692. *c.* 1820 WATCH PAPERS
2″ dia. approx. Anon. Great Britain.
A group of early nineteenth century engraved watch papers. The classical figure in two of these is Hope, leaning on an anchor.

Oxford University Press

Watch papers

Watch papers were used as dust excluders in pocket watches. They were placed between the works and the outer case, and from being mere slips of linen or paper they became vehicles for advertising, but usually in the most charming and elegant vein. Watch papers date from the latter half of the eighteenth century. The pretty engravings of classical figures such as Hope with her wooden stocked anchor, soon gave way to lettered designs, first engraved and later typographic, with a liberal use of copperplate script and black letter. They are a very charming and indeed somewhat neglected facet of printed ephemera.

Gunpowder labels

693. *c.* 1790 GUNPOWDER LABEL
4¼″ × 6¼″. Anon. England.
Engraved label in the best 'writing-book' tradition.

Oxford University Press

x

694. *c.* 1820 GUNPOWDER LABEL
4⅜″ dia. Anon. Hazardville, Connecticut.
Engraved label still on its original flask.

Bella C. Landauer Collection, New-York Historical Society

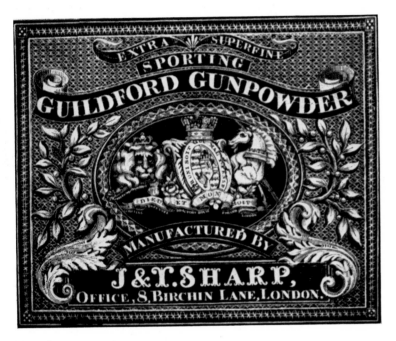

695. 1830 GUNPOWDER LABEL
3¼″ × 4″. Anon. London.
Engraved label with engine-turned decoration.

Gunpowder and Ink Powder labels

The three labels shown here reveal very different sides of the engraver's art. Fig. 693 is good English writing master stuff, with a discreetly decorated black letter for 'best' and appropriate flourishes. The 'Kentucky Rifle Gunpowder' is a pretty roundel illustrating a Davy Crockett-like hunter, still on its original flask in the Bella C. Landauer Collection. The 'Guildford Gunpowder' label would appear to have been executed by some kind of engine-turning engraving machine. Dr Alexander Anderson, the engraver of 'North & Warrin's Ink powder' label in Fig. 698, as well as copying a number of Bewick's works, produced a quantity of engravings for ephemeral printing. He was particularly strong on the American Eagle.

696. *c.* 1860 HARDWARE LABEL
2⅛″ × 5⅞″. Anon. Sheffield.
Engraved label with a shaded decorated letter, based on a contemporary display type, for the manufacturer's names.

Oxford University Press

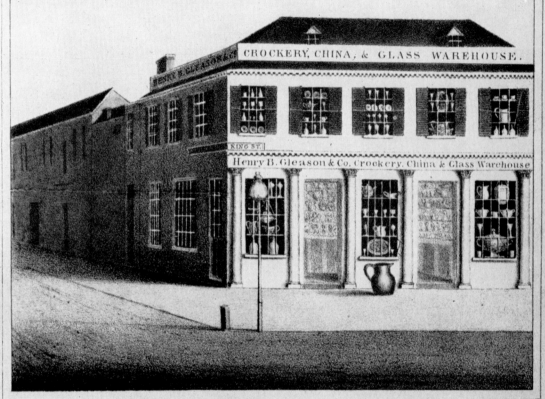

697. *c.* 1830 CROCKERY WRAPPER
8¼″ × 6⅜″. Pendletons lith. Boston; Mass.
Lithographed wrapping paper for crockery and glass warehouse.

Bella C. Landauer Collection, New-York Historical Society

Crockery and Glass label

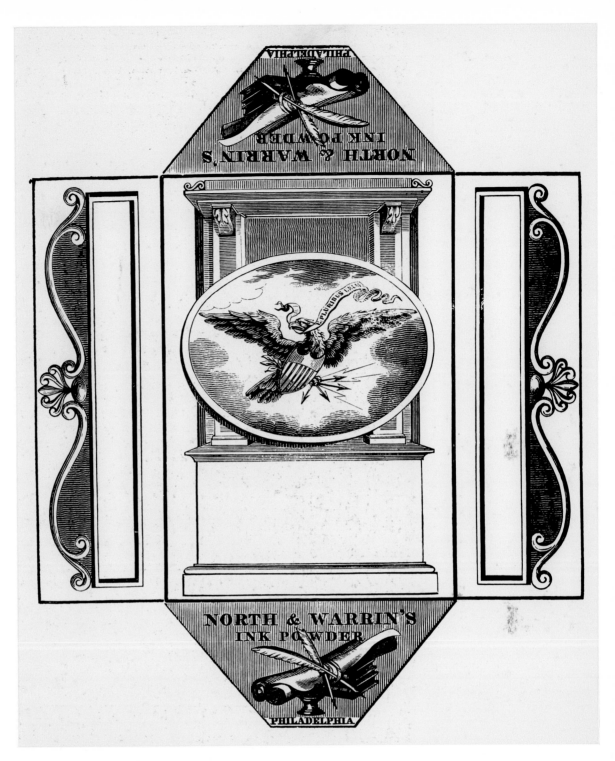

698. *c.* 1850 INK POWDER LABEL
7″ × 6″ approx. A. Anderson, New York.
Wood engraved label printed in black.

New York Public Library

699. *c.* 1850 COLOUR LABEL
1¾″ dia. A. Anderson, New York.
Wood engraved roundel printed in red.

New York Public Library

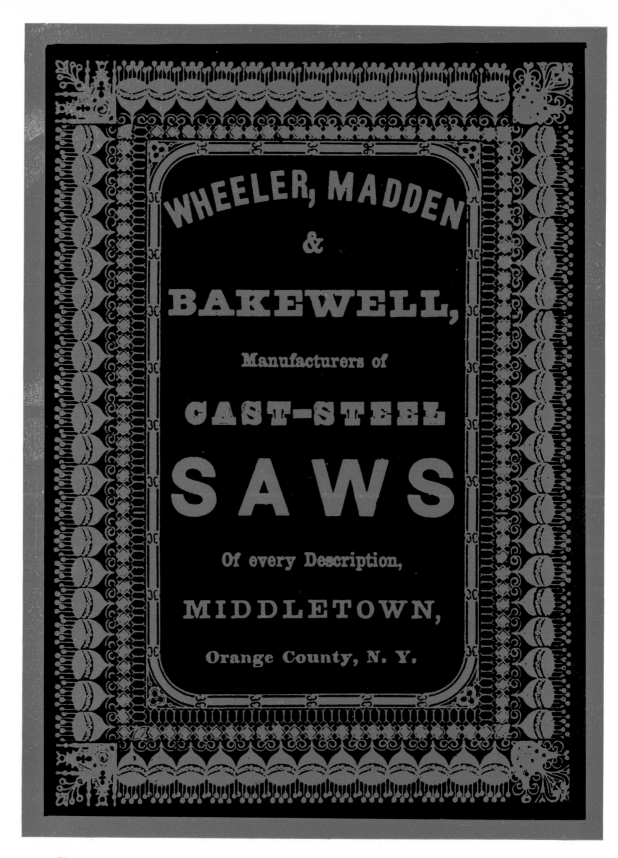

700. *c.* 1860 SAW LABEL
4″ × 2¾″ approx. Anon. Orange County, N.Y.
Typographic label with elaborate border of printers'
flowers printed in opaque ink on a dark paper. This
reproduction is considerably larger than the original.
Bella C. Landauer Collection, New-York Historical Society

Hardware labels and wrappers

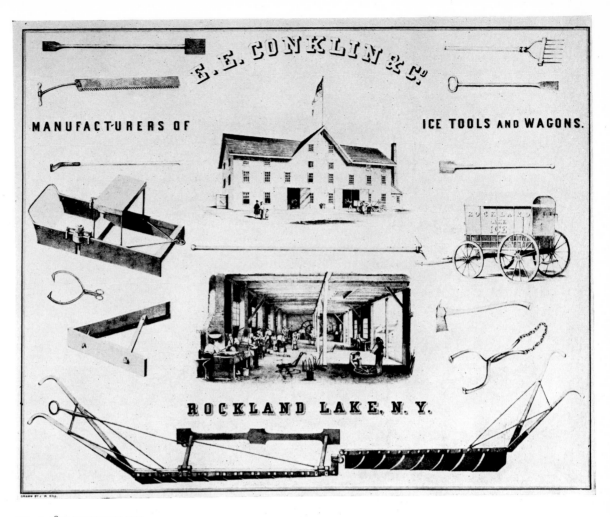

701. *c.* 1850 HARDWARE LABEL
8⅛″ × 10⅜″. J. W. Hill des. Rockland Lake, N.Y.
Lithographed label for manufacturer of tools and
wagons.

Bella C. Landauer Collection, New-York Historical Society

Hardware labels and wrappers

702. *c.* 1860 CUTLERY LABEL
2⅞″ × 1¾″. Anon. Sheffield.
Engraved label.

Oxford University Press

703. *c.* 1860 CUTLERY LABEL
2⅜″ × 2¼″. Anon. Sheffield.
Wood engraved label, printed in red.

Oxford University Press

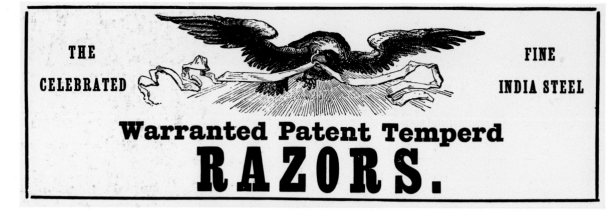

704. *c.* 1860 RAZOR LABEL
2″ × 6¼″. Anon. Sheffield.
Wood engraved design with type.

Oxford University Press

Hardware labels and wrappers

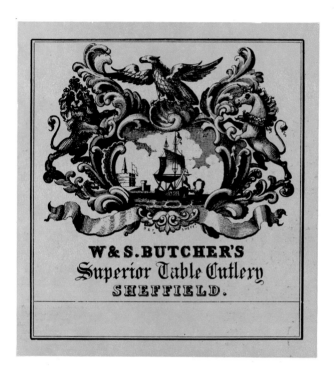

705. *c.* 1870 CUTLERY LABEL
3⅜″ × 3″. B. & T. Sheffield.
Engraved label with Egyptian shadow and black letters based on contemporary typefaces.

Oxford University Press

706. *c.* 1870 NEEDLE WRAPPER
2½″ × 1¾″. Anon. London.
Engraved wrapper.

Oxford University Press

707. *c.* 1870. FILES LABEL
2¾″ × 7⅛″. Anon. Sheffield.
Engraved label printed in two colours.

Oxford University Press

Cutlers' and Toolmakers' labels

Labels for these trades, on both sides of the Atlantic make a wide use of engraving. The 'Spear & Jackson' tools label (Fig. 696) is a finely balanced engraving, with a nice decorated Egyptian at the head. The italics used in this label for 'Ledger Blades & Cutters, etc.' are an interesting departure from the English hand, and are nearer to a sloped roman than to a script.

Engraving was used frequently, in a negative manner, that is with a white, coloured or gilt line on a black or very dark background. The Orange County N.Y. label (Fig. 700) for saws is typical of this style and produces a light and lacy effect with its decorative border. The two Tillotson labels (Figs. 707 and 709) are also in this style. When the engravings are in a positive black line, a use of coloured and shiny papers provides a richly decorative effect.

708. *c.* 1880 HARDWARE STORE LABEL
$3\frac{1}{4}'' \times 2''$. Mackellar, Smiths and Jordan Co.,
Philadelphia.
Printer's specimen stereo, which cost $1.50.

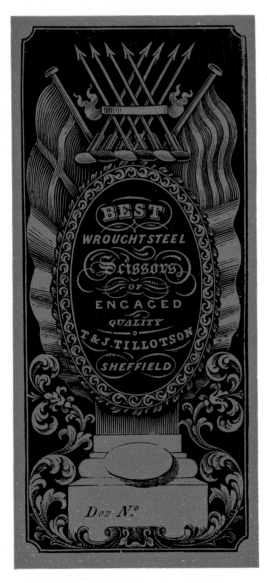

709. *c.* 1870 SCISSORS LABEL
$6\frac{3}{8}'' \times 2\frac{3}{4}''$. Anon. Sheffield.
Engraved label printed in red.

Oxford University Press

710. 1960 FILE LABEL
$6\frac{1}{8}'' \times 2\frac{3}{4}''$. Anon. Holland.
This English label was printed in Holland by offset in black and green from a transfer of an engraving.

271

Crockery and Glass label

711. *c.* 1930 CROCKERY LABEL
4⅝″ × 4⅜″. Eric Ravilious des. London.
Wood engraved label, printed in black and brown.

An interesting comparison with the 1830 crockery and glass wrapper (Fig. 697) is shown here in this label. This was engraved on wood by the late Eric Ravilious, an English artist and designer of great sensitivity who was killed flying over the Arctic in the 1939–45 war. Manufacturers have been slow to recognize the decorative value of engravings for labels and packs. Yet their value is only too clearly shown both by the wood engraved Ravilious label and by the two sailmakers' needle packets, which have been in use for over a hundred years and are still delightfully fresh today.

Sail Needle labels

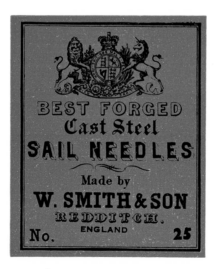

712. 1960 SAIL NEEDLE WRAPPER
2⅜″ × 2″. Anon. Redditch.
Engraved label, printed in black on sealing wax red paper. This was engraved over a hundred years ago.

713. 1960 SAIL NEEDLE WRAPPER
2⅛″ × 3″. Anon. Redditch.
Engraved label. Printed in black on green paper with letterforms based on contemporary typefaces.

Index

Artists, designers and typographers

Engravers and lithographers

Printers

Typefounders, type designers and typesetters

Typefaces

Chronological Index

The numbers are those of the illustrations, not of the pages.